MW00629561

EVERYDAY LAW IN RUSSIA

EVERYDAY LAW IN RUSSIA

Kathryn Hendley

CORNELL UNIVERSITY PRESS   ITHACA AND LONDON

First published 2017 by Cornell University Press

Printed in the United States of America

Library of Congress Cataloging-in-Publication Data

Names: Hendley, Kathryn, author.
Title: Everyday law in Russia / Kathryn Hendley.
Description: Ithaca ; London : Cornell University Press, 2017. | Includes
    bibliographical references and index.
Identifiers: LCCN 2016034698 (print) | LCCN 2016035243 (ebook) | ISBN
    9781501705243 (cloth : alk. paper) | ISBN 9781501708091 (epub/mobi) | ISBN
    9781501708107 (pdf)
Subjects: LCSH: Law—Russia (Federation) | Courts—Russia (Federation) | Russia
    (Federation)—Social conditions—1991–
Classification: LCC KLB68 .H46 2017 (print) | LCC KLB68 (ebook) | DDC
    349.47—dc23
LC record available at https://lccn.loc.gov/2016034698

Cornell University Press strives to use environmentally responsible suppliers and materials to the fullest extent possible in the publishing of its books. Such materials include vegetable-based, low-VOC inks and acid-free papers that are recycled, totally chlorine-free, or partly composed of nonwood fibers. For further information, visit our website at www.cornellpress.cornell.edu.

Contents

List of Figures   vii

List of Tables   ix

Acknowledgments   xi

Note on Transliteration, Translations, and Exchange Rates   xiv

List of Abbreviations and Commonly Used Russian Words   xv

Introduction: Lawlessness in Russia? Rethinking the
Narratives of Law   1

1. Legal Consciousness(es) in Russia   18

2. Dealing with Damage from Home Water Leaks   58

3. Dealing with Auto Accidents   90

4. The View from the Benches of the Justice-of-the-Peace
Courts   134

5. The View from the Trenches of the Justice-of-the-Peace
Courts   179

Conclusion: Rethinking the Role of Law in Russia   222

Appendix A: Empirical Analyses of Russian Legal
Consciousness   237

Appendix B: Background on Focus Group Participants   249

Appendix C: Results from the Analysis of the ABA Survey   251

Russian Legal Sources   255

References   257

Index   279

Figures

1.1 Responses to the statement: If a person considers the law unfair, he has the right to "go around it" 25

1.2 Responses to the statement: If government or political officials do not obey the law, then ordinary people can disobey the law 26

1.3 Responses to the statement: It is impossible to live in Russia without violating the law 27

4.1 An apartment building that also houses a JP court (Ekaterinburg) 139

4.2 A former kindergarten that houses a JP court (Moscow) 139

4.3 A typical office for a Justice of the Peace (Ekaterinburg) 140

5.1 Form documents posted in the corridor of a JP court (Pskov) 183

5.2 A courtroom with a cage (Velikie luki) 193

5.3 A courtroom without a cage (Moscow) 193

5.4 The corridor of a JP court, with an informational bulletin board and benches (Moscow) 194

Tables

1.1 Results of polls of Levada Center from 1990 to 2007
on "Is it possible to live in Russia without violating
the law?"   27

1.2 Reactions to two hypothetical situations from the
2008 INDEM survey   39

1.3 Comparison of respondents' reactions to two
hypothetical situations from the 2008 INDEM survey   43

2.1 Background information on focus group sites as of
the end of 2007   67

3.1 Information about cases involving traffic accidents
brought to the Russian courts, 2008–2011   97

4.1 Average monthly per judge caseload in the JP courts   149

4.2 Overview of the civil docket of the JP courts   150

5.1 Civil cases decided by JP courts broken down by
type of litigant   181

A.1 Regression results for legal compliant attitudes
in the 2006 round of the RLMS-HSE   238

A.2 Regression results for legal compliant attitudes
in the 2012 round of the RLMS-HSE   240

A.3 Regression results for change in attitude about
law from legal nihilism to law abiding between
the 2006 and 2012 rounds of the RLMS-HSE   242

A.4 Regression results for change in attitude about
law from law abiding to legal nihilism between
the 2006 and 2012 rounds of the RLMS-HSE   243

A.5 Regression results for responses to hypothetical 1
in 2008 INDEM Survey   243

A.6 Regression results for responses to hypothetical 2
in 2008 INDEM Survey   244

A.7 Regression results for use of courts in 2008
INDEM Survey 246

B.1 Background information on focus group
participants 249

C.1 Descriptive statistics from the ABA Survey 251

C.2 Logistic regression estimated odds ratios for
respondents' assessment of their experience
at the JP courts as successful in the ABA Survey 252

Acknowledgments

This book has been gestating for a very long time. Since the collapse of the Soviet Union, I have immersed myself in studying various aspects of Russian law with the goal of understanding how Russians experience law. What follows reflects my knowledge and insights about post-Soviet Russian law. The analysis is, of course, my own, but many people and institutions contributed to making the research and writing of the book possible.

The book is grounded in many years of field research that was funded by grants from a number of institutions, including the National Science Foundation, the National Council for Eurasian and East European Research, the Law School, and the Graduate School of the University of Wisconsin-Madison. I received a Fulbright Research Fellowship and an Ed A. Hewett Policy Fellowship that allowed me to spend the 2011–12 academic year in Russia. I was fortunate to be awarded a residential fellowship from the Law and Public Affairs Program at Princeton University for the 2012–13 academic year, which provided me with a quiet place to work through my voluminous field notes and begin to write the book.

Organizing research in Russia is never easy. I have been blessed with good friends and colleagues who helped at every step along the way. Polina Kozyreva and Mikhail Kosolapov of the Institute of Sociology of the Russian Academy of Sciences invited me to include a module of questions about law on the Russian Longitudinal Monitoring Survey–Higher School of Economics, which they manage. These questions, which were part of the 2004, 2006, and 2012 rounds of the RLMS-HSE, form the foundation for my analysis of Russian legal consciousness. Kozyreva and Kosolapov also worked with me to organize the focus groups that animate chapters 2 and 3, generously allowing me to call on their network of sociologists who helped me in the more far-flung locales. Elena Zobina, who facilitated the focus groups, seemed to channel my spirit as she poked and prodded the participants to get them to share their experiences. Ekaterina Mishina, who was a law professor at the Higher School of Economics in Moscow when my project began, generously shared the data from the survey she coordinated for the INDEM Foundation. These data provide the other piece of the puzzle for my analysis of Russian legal consciousness. She also put me in touch with researchers at the Judicial Department of the Russian Supreme Court, who provided me with detailed statistics drawn from the work of justice-of-the-peace courts (the "JP courts").

Gaining access to the JP courts was more complicated. In each location, I relied on different people, all of whom were remarkably supportive. In Moscow, Aleksey Scherbakov laid the groundwork for me. In Ekaterinburg, Sergei Belyaev, whom I have known since the early 1990s, facilitated my work. In Pskov and Velikie luki, Sergei Sherstobitov, the overall manager of the JP courts, took an interest in my work and arranged for me to spend time in several courts. In Petrozavodsk and Rostov-na-Donu, John Dooley and Karin Bourassa put their contacts at my disposal, which gave me access to JP courts. In Voronezh, Elena Nosyreva prevailed on her friends and colleagues to open doors for me.

Fieldwork in Russia has its ups and downs. Whenever my spirits waned, I was blessed to be able to reach out to a remarkable group of fellow legal scholars. They were always ready to debate the likely trajectory of Russian law. Most were more pessimistic than me, but they never lost enthusiasm for the project. Their skepticism kept me motivated. These colleagues included: Tatiana Borisova, Anton Burkov, Olga Ivanchenko, Ekaterina Mishina, Ella Paneyakh, Olga Schwartz, and Olga Sidorovich. Several members of the expat community, including Thomas Firestone (then the representative of the Department of Justice at the U.S. Embassy), Melissa Hooper (then the head of the ABA's Moscow office), and William Simons (then a law professor at the University of Tartu), were likewise stalwart colleagues, as were William Bianco and Regina Smyth, who were fellow Fulbrighters.

While writing the book, I have been able to call on a remarkable group of friends as sounding boards. In particular, Cynthia Buckley, Marina Kurkchiyan, and Kathleen Smith have read multiple drafts of chapters and acted as honest brokers as I worked to hone the arguments. My University of Wisconsin colleagues have been very supportive. Howard Erlanger helped me refine the presentation of the survey results. Stewart Macaulay and Peter Carstensen read early drafts of several chapters; their comments steered me in more productive directions. I am grateful for insights gained through conversations with colleagues such as Mark Beissinger, Jane Burbank, David Engel, Cathy Frierson, Jane Henderson, Eugene Huskey, Robert Kagan, Jeffrey Kahn, Stanley Katz, Herbert Kritzer, Peter Maggs, Inga Markovits, Lauren McCarthy, Stanislaw Pomorski, Kim Scheppele, Gordon Smith, Peter Solomon, Alexei Trochev, and David and Louise Trubek. I had the opportunity to present portions of the book and receive feedback at a wide variety of forums. These include the Harriman Institute, the Higher School of Economics (Moscow), Indiana University, Oxford University, University College, London, the University of Helsinki, the University of Illinois, the University of Michigan, the University of South Carolina, the Wissenschaftskolleg (Berlin), as well as annual meetings of the American Political Science Association, the Association for Slavic, East European, and Eurasian Studies, and the Law and

Society Association. The book also benefitted tremendously from the comments of the anonymous reviewers for Cornell University Press, as well as the gentle suggestions of my editor, Roger Haydon.

I owe a great debt to the graduate students who have worked with me as research assistants over the years, some of whom have gone on to distinguished academic careers of their own. These include Galina Belakurova, Evgeny Finkel, Pilar Gonalons-Pons, and Maayan Mor. I have also had the benefit of research assistance from talented undergraduates, including Anne Redmond and Yuliya Barsukova. The support staff at the University of Wisconsin Law School has more than made up for my technical shortcomings. The superb librarians at the law library were tireless in tracking down obscure sources. Thanks are due to Theresa Evans, Jennifer Hanrahan, Susan Sawatske, and Danielle Topp for assistance in formatting tables and other tasks, and to Darryl Berney and Eric Giefer for solving my many computer woes.

An earlier version of chapter 2 appeared as "Resolving Problems among Neighbors in Post-Soviet Russia: Uncovering the Norms of the *Pod"ezd*," *Law & Social Inquiry* 36, no. 2 (2011): 388–418.

As I wrote the book, I was sustained by the friendship of Cynthia Buckley, Carin Clauss, Stewart Macaulay, and Kathleen Smith. When in Moscow, Elena Shevelova and her family have offered me a home away from home for many years. My father, Samuel Hendley, who passed away while I was working on this book, was a constant source of support and encouragement. But my greatest debt of gratitude goes to my sister, Margaret Brown. I could not have undertaken the many trips to Russia that were required for the book without her unflagging practical and emotional support. She and her children, Jason Brown and Adam Brown, have always provided a welcome port in the storm.

Note on Transliteration, Translations, and Exchange Rates

For Russian names and titles in the references and notes and for Russian words in the text, I use the Library of Congress transliteration system (e.g., *iu* and *ia* rather than *yu* and *ya*). I have also used the familiar English form for place and personal names in the text (e.g., Khodorkovsky rather than Khodorkovskii) and omitted soft signs to enhance readability (e.g., oblast rather than oblast'). If a Russian author has published in English, I use her preferred transliteration (e.g., Kaminskaya rather than Kaminskaia).

Unless otherwise noted, all translations from original Russian texts are mine.

During 2007–8, when I conducted the focus groups that are analyzed in chapters 2 and 3, the exchange rate hovered around 30 rubles to the dollar. By 2011–12, when I conducted the observational research in the JP courts that is dissected in chapters 4 and 5, the exchange rate hovered around 50 rubles to the dollar.

The names of the focus group participants have been changed to preserve their anonymity.

Abbreviations and Commonly Used Russian Words

ABA Survey	Survey of JP court users in Leningrad oblast, Nizhni Novgorod oblast, and Rostov oblast, sponsored by the Moscow office of the American Bar Association in 2009, that asked about their use of the courts and levels of satisfaction.
Advokaty	Individuals with university degrees in law who have passed an exam. They hold a monopoly on the representation of criminal defendants.
Arbitrazh courts	Courts that handle disputes between legal entities.
Chastnoe obvinenie	Criminal case brought by an individual rather than a prosecutor. Typically involves minor altercations, often between family members.
INDEM	Information Science for Democracy, a Moscow independent policy institute that fielded a nationally representative survey in Russia about law in fall 2008.
ILPP Project	Project carried out by the Moscow-based Institute of Law and Public Policy in 2010 that monitored the activities of JP courts in Perm krai and Leningrad oblast.
Iuristy	Individuals with university degrees in law. They can represent clients in any setting other than criminal proceedings.
JP	Justice of the peace or *mirovoi sud'ia*. Judges who preside over the justice-of-the-peace courts.
JP courts	Justice-of-the-peace courts or *mirovye sudy*. These courts were authorized in Russia in 1998. They are part of the courts of general jurisdiction. They handle simple cases.
Opredelenie	Judicial order sent to litigants to notify them of the time and place of their hearing.
Pravo	One of two Russian words for "law." Captures broader idea of law that looks beyond written law to include fairness.
Po-chelovecheski	Phrase used to capture civilized or humanistic behavior. Sometimes used interchangeably with *po-sosedski* (neighborly) or *poriadochnyi* (upstanding).
RLMS-HSE	Russian Longitudinal Monitoring Survey–Higher School of Economics. Nationally representative panel survey of Russians that included law-related questions in 2004, 2006, and 2012.

Sudebnyi prikaz	Judicial order issued on the basis of pleadings without the need for a full-fledged hearing in simple civil cases.
Zakon	One of two Russian words for "law." Refers to written law.
ZhKU	*Zhilishchno-Kommunal'nye Uslugi* or Housing-Communal Services.

EVERYDAY LAW IN RUSSIA

Introduction

LAWLESSNESS IN RUSSIA?
RETHINKING THE NARRATIVES OF LAW

Almost without exception, when I meet someone for the first time and tell them that I study Russian law, I am greeted with a quizzical look and asked whether Russia has law. Sometimes there is a humorous tone to the question, sometimes it is asked in earnest. Perhaps the question is motivated by the deluge of press reports of politicized justice in Russia or is a remnant of Cold War thinking. This belief in the myth of Russia as a lawless state is not limited to foreigners. Russians of all walks of life are likewise quick to dismiss the relevance of law. Public polling data suggest that they are skeptical of the capacity of their courts to mete out justice. My countless conversations with Russians about law tend to begin with some variant of this attitude, often expressed in the pithy aphorism "the fish rots from the head," referring to the propensity of the powerful to ignore and manipulate law to serve their interests.

In many ways, this book is an effort to determine whether the fish truly does rot from the head when it comes to law in Russia. In other words, does the fact that the Kremlin is able to dictate the outcome of cases seemingly at will—a phenomenon popularly known as "telephone justice"[1]—deprive law of its fundamental value as a touchstone for society? This is certainly the popular

---

1. This term "telephone law" or "telephone justice" persists despite the fact that the wishes of the Kremlin and other powerful actors are often conveyed by other means or by informal signaling (e.g., Popova 2012; Sakwa 2010; Ledeneva 2008).

1

interpretation. Russia consistently languishes near the bottom of indexes that aim to measure the rule of law.[2] Given that the cornerstone of any definition of the rule of law is the equal treatment of all before the law, Russia's low stature within these indexes is almost certainly a result of its willingness to use the law as an instrument to punish its enemies.

Yet this common wisdom captures only part of the story. The politicized cases that have come to symbolize the irrelevance of law in Russia actually amount to a drop in the bucket. The Russian courts hear well over sixteen million cases per year—the vast majority of which are of little interest to anyone not directly involved. To date, neither the popular media nor scholars have paid much attention to them. Similarly little light has been shone on the willingness of Russians to invoke law when problems arise in their daily lives. Building on the literature on "everyday law" (e.g., Markovits 2010; Kushkova 2010; Ewick and Silbey 1998; Sarat and Kearns 1993), I argue that careful observation of the routine behavior of individuals, firms, and institutions reveals more about the role of law in Russian life than do sensationalized cases. Therefore, this book looks beyond the high-profile cases to focus on how ordinary Russians experience the law and the legal system. Rather than focusing on the "supply" of laws, it concentrates on the "demand" for law. It is grounded in over two decades of fieldwork, including countless days watching judicial proceedings of various stripes, a series of focus groups in which Russians talked about problem-solving strategies, and many hours of conversations with Russians.

I was moved to write the book because the reality I came to know is so remarkably different from the popular perception of Russia as a lawless state. Talking to Russians about how they cope with the sorts of disputes we all face, such as substandard work by a plumber or a neighbor with an incessantly barking dog, reveals that law matters to them. Like their counterparts elsewhere, their first reaction is to try to work out a solution informally that is colored by the dictates of the law. Moving out of the shadow of the law into the formal legal system is rarely the first choice, but going to court is generally viewed as a viable option. To that end, the past decade has witnessed a steady increase in the number of cases brought to the courts. How should we understand the role of law against the background of widespread expressions of disdain and mistrust?

---

2. Russia also scrapes the bottom of the barrel in companion indexes that measure other indicators of democracy, such as protection of civil liberties, regulatory quality, political stability, control of corruption, and government effectiveness. Analyses that make use of these data inevitably conclude that Russia lacks the rule of law (e.g., Melville and Mironyuk 2016).

Reconceptualizing the Russian Legal System as Dualistic

A more nuanced picture of the role of law in Russians' everyday life allows for a dialogue on how we should theorize legal systems like Russia's. We have long recognized that a gap exists between the law on the books and the law in practice in all countries. Russia forces us to grapple with how to think about legal systems that pay attention to the law most of the time but ignore or manipulate it in spectacular fashion in a small number of cases. And Russia is not alone. It is part of a surprisingly large group of authoritarian or quasi-authoritarian countries in which the courts mostly function within the law, but in which the political leadership feels entitled to use the courts to serve its goals and turns a blind eye to others with power or influence who are doing the same.

As a result of the relentless emphasis on high-profile cases in countries like Russia, a backhanded consensus has emerged that politicized justice is a cancer that, once present, will inevitably take over the organism. The belief lends credence to the popular image of Russia as lawless. Further buttressing this image is the sad reality that predicting outside intervention is impossible. Put differently, we can anticipate that political leaders will work to discredit prominent opponents by initiating criminal cases and ensuring convictions. But this is far from the full set of cases in which telephone justice is possible. It is not just political elites who manipulate the system; economic elites use their financial resources to influence the results in cases of interest to them. This gives rise to a netherworld that exists uneasily between politicized show trials and mundane claims. Examples of the cases that fall into this messy middle category include the thousands of prosecutions of obscure businessmen who have been railroaded into prison as a result of criminal charges typically orchestrated by their business rivals (e.g., Romanova 2011; Iakovleva 2008). Also troubling is the fact that judges who, with one breath, resolve mundane cases according to the law, can with their next breath bend to the political or financial winds. The arbitrariness brings the integrity of the entire legal system into question. Indeed, if adherence to the law is uncertain in thorny cases, some wonder whether law is illusory more generally. Pinning down every scenario in which the outcome will be extralegally predetermined is a fool's errand and is not the goal of this book.

Focusing on this view of Russia as lawless fails to capture the full richness of Russians' experience of law. It leaves no room for the everyday reality revealed by my research that Russians routinely negotiate resolutions to their problems with others in the shadow of the law or, when informal efforts prove futile, take their problems to the courts and have them resolved in accordance with the law. A more promising avenue is suggested by Ernst Fraenkel's work (1969) about Nazi Germany, which, he argued, should be seen as a dual state composed of a normative state and a prerogative state. In the former, law reigns, whereas in the latter, politics trumps law. Robert Sharlet incorporated this insight into his work on the role of law in Soviet Russia, arguing that "if modified, the 'dual state' has heuristic value as a theoretical framework within which to analyze the continual tension between legality (*zakonnost*) and party orientation (*partiinost*) in the administration of justice in the Soviet Union." Then as now, most cases had little political resonance, and hence, even during the worst of the Stalinist purges, law retained its relevance for mundane cases (1977, 155–156). Though no longer motivated by Communist Party ideology, the Kremlin's desire to dictate the outcomes of politically charged cases has not dissipated.

Fraenkel's argument contains a nugget that can be applied to legal systems like Russia's, namely, that courts do not necessarily have a single institutional identity.[3] The same court—even the same judge—can follow the law to the letter or openly disregard it, depending on the context. Though Fraenkel laid this out as a duality between law-abiding and extralegal behavior and Sharlet's use of it as a heuristic device retains that structure, it is not limited to two forms. Within both these behavioral patterns it is possible to observe a multiplicity of narratives. In my view, this is a more productive way to conceptualize how law works in all countries in which telephone law is a reality. By neither demonizing nor whitewashing, we are able to lend credence to the full range of experiences and understand why demand for law can flourish alongside politicized justice.

Logic dictates that, just as judicial behavior can vary, so too can popular attitudes about law and the courts. Context matters. An individual who is comfortable having a court resolve his divorce may feel more conflicted when he has a dispute with the tax authorities. Along similar lines, a firm that routinely turns to the courts for help with collecting from delinquent customers may be more nervous when facing off with a company that dominates the local economy. How then can we understand dualism in a context specific way in Russia?

---

3. Some scholars have applied the "dual-state" concept in a more whole-cloth fashion to Russia (e.g., Flikke 2016; Sakwa 2013; 2010; Smith 1996). For example, Sakwa (2013) draws a contrast between an administrative state, which is his substitute for Fraenkel's prerogative state, and a constitutional state, in which law matters. This approach has been taken with respect to other countries, e.g., Meierhenrich 2008 (South Africa); Jayasuriya 2001 (Singapore and Malaysia). My preference has long been to limit the application of Fraenkel's ideas to the legal arena (Hendley 2011; 1996). Markovits's (2010; 1992) studies of East Germany likewise draw a distinction between everyday and exceptional cases.

The Persistence of Dualism and the Reluctance to Embrace Multiple Narratives of Law in Russia

Hindsight allows us to see the dualism at the heart of Russians' attitudes toward law and legal institutions dating back to the Great Judicial Reforms of 1864 and perhaps further. But this dualism has rarely been openly acknowledged. Russians and Westerners alike have always seemed to want to believe the worst about the capacity for law to matter in Russia. And they have proven resistant to the existence of multiple narratives, preferring a simpler story grounded in the lawlessness of Russia. The rhetoric has played out differently as the political regime shifted from tsarism to communism to the hybrid form of authoritarianism and market democracy of Putin's Russia. The sources available and the methodologies employed play a critical role in the persistence of this simpler story. As researchers have had the opportunity and desire to probe into the realities of everyday life and the role of law, a richer set of stories has emerged. A look back at Russian law in the tsarist and Communist periods reveals the long-standing role of dualism, a syndrome that undergirds present-day attitudes.

Dualism in Late Tsarist Russia

The reputation of law among both elites and peasants had the same sort of one-note quality in the late tsarist period as in the present day. As the nineteenth-century critic of the tsarist system Alexander Herzen wrote: "Whatever his station, the Russian evades or violates the law wherever he can do so with impunity; the government does exactly the same thing."[4] Piling on, in a much-quoted essay from 1909, the legal philosopher Bogdan Kistiakovsky said: "The Russian intelligentsia never respected law and never saw any value in it. Of all the cultural values, law was the most suppressed. Given such circumstances, our intelligentsia could not have hoped to develop a sound legal consciousness, which, on the contrary, remains at the lowest possible level of development" (Kistyakovsky 1977, 113). Many scholars accepted these statements as reflective of empirical reality and took it as a given that nineteenth-century Russians saw law as peripheral.[5]

This attitude also extended to the courts, which had been reorganized as part of the modernizing reforms of 1864 (Wortman 1976, 243–268; Lincoln 1990,

---

4. Quoted by Huskey (1991, 68) and Tumanov (1989, 21).

5. Some even argued that Russians lacked legal consciousness at the time of the 1917 Revolution, a statement that suggests a conflation of legal consciousness and faith in the law (e.g., Engelstein 1993; Shelley 1992; Pipes 1986). The concept of "legal consciousness" is more commonly understood as encompassing societal attitudes and behavior regarding law and the legal system. Thus it could be argued that Russian legal consciousness was pejorative or skeptical, but not that it was nonexistent.

105–117; Kucherov 1953). In the wake of the end of serfdom, the state introduced a bifurcated court system that divided jurisdiction between urban and
rural. City dwellers went to justice-of-the-peace courts (*mirovye sudy*), whereas
peasants had access to the township or *volost* courts. On paper, the courts seemed
quite different because the former were governed by statutory law, whereas the
latter took local customs into account as well when resolving disputes. Both types
of courts put a premium on finding peaceful resolutions through mediation and
conciliation; judges used their formal powers sparingly.

Much as in the present day, high-profile criminal cases captured the public's
imagination and colored their views of law (McReynolds 2012). The subset of
these cases with political overtones, symbolized by the trial and acquittal of Vera
Zasulich, likewise influenced popular opinion (Engelstein 2009; Wortman 1976,
282–284; Kucherov 1952). Indeed, Richard Wortman argues that, as a result of
the Zasulich trial, the tsarist regime "gave up its pretense of legality in its struggle
against the revolutionaries. . . . The strained tolerance the autocracy had showed
toward its judiciary now turned into open animosity. . . . The result was a state at
war with its own court system" (1976, 283–284).

Wortman's analysis focuses primarily on the urban courts. The dualism argument extends to the *volost* courts, albeit in a different form that has surprising
resonance for present-day debates. In the decades following their creation, the
apparent reliance on custom by *volost* courts gave rise to lively debate about the
merits of these courts. As Cathy Frierson explains:

> Supporters of the court argued that customary law was a manifestation
> of rural legal consciousness and that this form of legal consciousness was
> legitimate. . . . Opponents of the court argued that legal consciousness, by
> definition, meant understanding of and respect for formal law as a system
> of consistent legal norms. They criticized the perpetuation of the isola-
> tion of rural society from the rule of formal law through the volost court,
> and called for its subordination to the general legal system. (1986, 530)

Put bluntly, many concluded that rural Russia was lawless (Lewin 1985). Jane
Burbank suspects that "most observers considered peasants too primitive to understand 'real' law and too uneducated to administer 'real' justice" (2004, 5). Illustrating her point is Sergei Witte's comment that "essentially, the court system
did not exist among the peasants, but took the crude form of justice in the shape
of the *volost* court" (Frierson 1986, 526). Critics assumed that customary law
was inherently capricious and unpredictable. To be sure, ascertaining the parameters of custom was often challenging. Yet for some of the most common claims
brought by peasants, namely, those involving questions of family relations and

inheritance, the norms were unchanging and well-known to all (Popkins 2000; Czap 1967).

In an eerie parallel to the contemporary debate, a consensus developed that the *volost* courts were inadequate and, consequently, irrelevant to peasants' daily lives. Presaging the rhetoric of the 1990s, some scholars of the tsarist era have argued that peasants were unable to rely on formal legal institutions such as the courts and the police to safeguard them and that various forms of self-help emerged as stopgap measures. Among these were arson and *samosud*,[6] an informal form of summary justice that often took the form of violence against alleged perpetrators that ranged from floggings to ostracism to hangings.

Whether these informal mechanisms supplanted or supplemented the courts is a matter of considerable dispute among scholars. At one end of the spectrum is Stephen Frank, whose work is consistent with those who argue that Putin's Russia is lawless. He views the *volost* courts as impotent when it came to dealing with criminal behavior. He quotes approvingly from a 1908 report of the governor of Riazan: "the peasantry's participation in incidents of *samosud* is evidence of the unquestionable collapse of their trust in the court . . ." (1999, 297). He sees the late nineteenth century as a time of increasing crime and instability in the Russian countryside, and contends that "violence and the ignoring of state law . . . were not features of *samosud* alone but characterized Russian justice far more broadly" (248). At the other end of the spectrum is Frierson (1997b), who recognizes the dualism within choices made by peasants. She argues that self-help remedies coexisted with formal legal remedies. Much as I argue that present-day Russians understand when going to court is feasible, Frierson and scholars such as Jane Burbank (2004), Peter Czap (1967), Beatrice Farnsworth (1986), Gareth Popkins (2000), and William Wagner (1997), who have delved into tsarist court archives, argue that prerevolutionary peasants intuitively knew which way of dealing with their problems was best under the circumstances.

Frierson contends that peasants went to court when the rules were uncertain and resorted to self-help when the communal norms were well-established.

> Peasants took petty, primarily financial, disputes to the cantonal [*volost*] court. . . . The large numbers of financial disputes signified that economic relations and agreements in the village no longer functioned according to rules that were 'tacit, informal, and intuitively perceived'. Instead, the rules themselves were contested; it was up to the court to

---

6. *Samosud* is a compound word. It combines the word for doing something oneself (*samo*) with the word for court (*sud*) to create a word that captures a do-it-yourself court.

decide them. . . . But there was little such uncertainty in community attitudes toward serious wrongdoing that violated community norms of morality. Community culture remained strong for offences which the peasants perceived as criminal. . . . For these infractions against community morality and well-being, the appropriate response often was not, in the peasants' view, a day in court following prescribed procedure, but swift and often, final punishment in the form of *samosud*. Self-help constituted justice, which, in turn, consisted of re-enforcing community norms. (1997a, 333)

The scholarship of other historians who have studied court archives buttresses Frierson's argument. In her book on the *volost* courts, Burbank makes a passionate case for studying their everyday practices. Much like I am arguing against reducing contemporary Russian law to what happens in show trials, Burbank rails against the tendency of some scholars to treat *samosud* and other exotic extralegal strategies as typical. Though not denying their persistence, she sees them as part of the story rather than as the whole story. Burbank documents the increasing use of the courts in the late tsarist era. Because the bulk of these cases were brought to the *volost* courts voluntarily, notwithstanding the existence of alternative venues, she believes the increasing foot traffic demonstrated peasants' trust in this institution. This trust may have been situational—present for disputes over inheritance but lacking when a much-needed horse was stolen or a barn was torched. Peasants can be as rational (or hopeful) as modern citizens in forum shopping.

This line of scholarship that focuses on peasants' use of courts as revealed through the archives treats the provocative statements by Herzen, Kistiakovsky, Witte, and others as polemics rather than as statements of empirical reality. Historians of everyday law have been able to find the balance between being overly pessimistic—dismissing post-Emancipation Russia as lawless—and being too optimistic about the prospects for law. Burbank's findings are measured: "A close reading of how rural people engaged township courts reveals a legal system at work as well as the values, practices, expectations, and social resources of individual users of the law" (2004, 16). The point here is that these courts were seen as legal arenas. Their embrace of custom did not cause peasants to see them as unreliable or arbitrary. In contradiction of the common wisdom about peasants' lack of legal consciousness, those who have dug into the archival records have found that peasants saw the *volost* courts as a viable alternative and understood how to use them. Slowly but surely, these courts were unearthing community norms and holding litigants accountable to them.

Farnsworth's (1986) study documents the propensity of less powerful family members—daughters-in-law—to invoke the law to protect themselves. Law became an equalizing force in an unequal society. In Burbank's words, "township courts enabled gradual changes in the patriarchal order of the countryside. The rules of evidence at court meant that a positive outcome for a local strongman was not a foregone conclusion" (2004, 113).

The story told by these historians who have mined the court archives is one of dualism that reveals multiple narratives. Going to court was only one option. The disgruntled might also turn to village elders, to informal tribunals, or take matters into their own hands. This is a familiar story the world over, but one that was absent from the contemporaneous narrative of tsarist law. Much like today, the unrelentingly negative assessments of the potential for law by the leading intellectuals and policymakers of the day held sway. This gave rise to the simple story of the irrelevance of law that persisted through the Soviet era and into the present day.

Dualism in Soviet Russia

Following the October 1917 Revolution, the Bolsheviks' negative rhetoric about law and their decision to displace career judges in favor of those with the requisite revolutionary fervor convinced many that law could not be meaningful under communism. Or, perhaps more accurately, that law was simply a means to an end. Richard Pipes (1986, 13) argues that "once Lenin came to power he promptly transformed justice into the handmaiden of politics." For support, he points to N. V. Krylenko, who served as commissar of justice under Stalin and who wrote that "expediency" (*tselesoobraznost*) was the defining feature of socialist law. Pipes presages Franks' position when he argues that this sort of instrumentalism was possible only because of the legal backwardness of the peasantry. "Russian *muzhiks*, who constituted approximately four-fifths of the population, had had little exposure to the law in its more abstract, philosophical form" (16).

The use of law by the political elite as a crude instrument for achieving their goals was certainly a key feature of socialist legality as it developed following the October Revolution. The use of highly scripted show trials to rid society of real and perceived enemies was only the most obvious example. This tactic reached a fevered pitch during the Great Terror of the 1930s, but never entirely disappeared. Peter Solomon's interviews with émigrés who had experience in the Soviet legal system revealed that "no Soviet leader ever questioned the role of the party in political trials. . . . In the Soviet political system the prerogatives of power included the use of agencies of justice against persons deemed enemies of the state" (1992, 5). The involvement of the KGB in a case rendered it political and subject to telephone law.

At the same time, these émigré interviews opened a window into how the Soviet legal system worked that confirmed Sharlet's (1977) earlier conceptualization of the Soviet legal system, even under Stalin, as dualistic. These former Soviet citizens, finally able to speak openly about their experiences with the legal system, revealed a more complicated reality than had been thought. Intervention by party officials in run-of-the-mill cases was not the norm, suggesting that such cases were decided pursuant to the law.

These hints of a different approach to mundane or nonpolitical cases were difficult to confirm on the ground in the Soviet Union. The positivism inherited from the tsarist past combined with the official lack of interest in how law really worked led Soviet legal scholars to focus primarily on the law on the books. The Soviet state's lack of openness meant that foreign legal scholars' efforts to dig deeper were met with resistance. George Feifer's ethnography of the Khrushchev-era courts is a notable exception. He set out to explore "the kinds of cases Americans never hear about (Soviet terror and political trials make so much better copy) but which most directly affect Ivan, that average fellow. I wanted to know what happens to *him* when he falls afoul of the law, his wife, or his boss" (Feifer 1964, 15). What he found lends credence to the dualism thesis. As he sat in the courts, he was struck by the "everydayness" of the proceedings (50). His work draws out a previously suppressed narrative of mundane cases in which judges resolve matters through a combination of law and common sense. His conclusion that telephone law or other outside interference recedes in the face of the ordinary is not limited to the Communist era. Thanks to the relaxation of scholarly oversight by the state in recent years, I have been able to probe more deeply into how present-day Russians experience law, and my research confirms Feifer's insight that official interference is very much the exception in ordinary cases.

As historical archives from the Soviet period have become more accessible, a more nuanced picture of the role of law in the earlier decades of Communist Party power that recognizes its dualistic character has come into focus that is remarkably consistent with Feifer's findings and with Sharlet's larger dualism thesis. Tracy McDonald (2011) makes superb use of these resources to explore village life in the Riazan region in the 1920s. Her work recognizes the multiple identities of Soviet-era peasants and pays particular attention to peasants as legal plaintiffs. She found that the courts "dealt with a massive caseload" (87). Though peasants sometimes had to walk 25 or 30 kilometers to the nearest court, they persisted. They also made active use of legal advice bureaus, belying the common wisdom that they were uninterested in law and incapable of understanding it. At the same time, self-help remedies, including *samosud*, continued to exist in the countryside in uneasy harmony with the courts.[7]

Much like Frierson, McDonald argues that the type of remedy pursued depended on the circumstances. "When peasants chose to go to court, they made the courts their own to some extent. They would use the courts if they could but they would also resort to vigilante justice in matters they believed the regime failed to resolve adequately, such as the punishment of horse thieves or arsonists" (2011, 92). The main criticism of the work of the courts at the time was not that it was politicized, but that peasants were too quick to go to court over "trifles" (91). Of course, whether cases are petty or not is in the eye of the beholder. For my purposes, the revelation is that Soviet-era peasants were not reluctant to use the courts.

Soviet courts were not receptive to complaints about state policies or officials' behavior. Far from being silenced, however, Soviet peasants and urban dwellers deluged various state and party bodies with their complaints. This is a practice that was carried over from the tsarist era (Fitzpatrick 1996, 91) and was encouraged by Soviet authorities as a way of identifying official malfeasance (Alexopoulos 1997, 168). McDonald writes that "peasants flooded local and central offices with letters of complaint or explanation and with letters asking for information and advice. Letters were often written on tiny scraps of paper with pencil stubs. Once deciphered, they provided a colorful and diverse portrait of the Russian countryside" (2011, 24, n. 79). The literature emphasizes the rote quality of these letters, suggesting a horizontal sharing and learning process. Sheila Fitzpatrick characterizes the complaints as "a form of two-way communication. Writers could reasonably hope for a response to their letters and had the right to complain if they received none. Officials were supposed to respond and could be reprimanded for failure to do so" (1996, 102). Responses sometimes brought relief, but not always. As Golfo Alexopoulos notes, "the outcome of a complaint could prove most unpleasant for the writer" because sometimes those targeted in the letters (who were inevitably more powerful or more well-connected than the letter writer) sought vengeance, with devastating results including being fired, deported, arrested, or worse (1997, 168). The only recourse was a new round of letter writing, which offered no guarantees.

During the Soviet era (much as under tsarism), these multiple narratives of law were muted in favor of a simpler story of law as an instrument to be used by

---

7. "Samosud was a radical solution to the problem of large-scale or repetitive theft, utilized by villagers in an under-governed countryside in which it was deemed that the powers-that-be did not sufficiently protect peasant interests. Significantly, those involved in samosud . . . were often older, well-respected, and well-established members of the village community" (McDonald 2011, 240).

the Soviet state to achieve its ends. To be fair, however, the political realities of the time made looking past the law on the books perilous.

Dualism in Contemporary Russia

Interest in how law actually works has been slow to develop in Russia. When I arrived in 1989 to study how courts and industrial enterprises were dealing with changes in the labor law, my supervisor at the law faculty of Moscow State University saw little value in going to courts and factories. He rewrote my official "scientific plan" to limit my activities to studying the law on the books in the safety of the library. Using a variety of back-door channels, I succeeded in doing the project I had planned (Hendley 1996). But for many years my interest in observing law in action, whether by watching court hearings, talking to lawyers, or organizing focus groups, has been treated as somewhat eccentric by established Russian legal scholars. From the start, however, my fieldwork has revealed a picture of law in Russia that was at odds with the official story and has connected me with the research of the intrepid scholars who have also traipsed to dreary courts in urban outskirts or mined the files of rural courts in provincial archives.

Though greater openness has allowed socio-legal scholars to fill in some of the gaps, the narrative of politicized justice and legal nihilism continues to dominate the nonspecialized social science literature. For instance, in a 1994 speech at the Kellstadt Graduate School of Business at DePaul University, the then-chairman of the Board of Governors of the Federal Reserve, Alan Greenspan, said that "there is no law of contracts" in Russia. The very fact that such a claim, which is preposterous on its face, could be made by someone of Greenspan's stature illustrates the almost hysterical attitude that prevailed toward the Russian business environment, which was echoed by the Western media (Uchitelle 1992).

As inter-enterprise arrears mounted in the 1990s as a negative consequence of the transition from state socialism to the market, a scholarly consensus emerged that managers were avoiding the *arbitrazh* courts (a hierarchy of courts created in 1991 to deal with commercial disputes) and had privatized the enforcement of contracts to security firms with mafia ties that were staffed by former KGB agents (e.g., Varese 2001; Black and Kraakman 1996; Hay and Shleifer 1998; Greif and Kandel 1995). A seemingly endless series of colorful anecdotes of the "Wild East" fueled this view (Volkov 2002; Satter 2004; Handelman 1995).

The ethnographic fieldwork I was doing in the early 1990s in industrial enterprises and *arbitrazh* courts left me skeptical (Hendley 1998). In an effort to get a better sense of the use (or nonuse) of law by economic actors, I collaborated with several economists to organize a survey of over three hundred industrial firms spread out across six regions in Russia to assess their attitudes toward, and use of, law and courts (Hendley, Murrell, and Ryterman 2000). Our Russian counterparts openly ridiculed our interest in the courts, telling us that everyone knew that Russian firms distrusted the courts and never used them. The survey results painted a different picture. Much like the findings of the pathbreaking U.S.-based Civil Litigation Research Project studies and their progeny (e.g., Merry 1990; Engel 1984; Trubek, Sarat, Felstiner, Kritzer, and Grossman 1983; Felstiner, Abel, and Sarat 1980–81), our survey confirmed that Russian firms exhausted all other options before turning to the courts. Even so, almost 80 percent of surveyed firms had been to the *arbitrazh* courts during the two years preceding the 1997 survey (Hendley, Murrell, and Ryterman 1999, 853). This would be a high incidence of use for a system perceived as functional. For one that had the reputation of being unusable, it was astonishing. Subsequent surveys of Russian firms likewise documented this demand for law among economic actors (Gans-Morse 2012; Johnson, McMillan, and Woodruff 2002).

In more recent years, Russian social scientists have begun to study law in action. This work tends not to come from law faculties but from interdisciplinary scholarship. As I detail in chapter 5, several mixed-methods projects aimed at documenting how justice-of-the-peace courts (JP courts) operate and the experiences of litigants who use them have shown that judges follow the procedural rules and that litigants were generally satisfied with their experiences. These results support the thesis (which has been substantiated in many different countries) that being respected is a more important predictor of satisfaction than winning or losing (e.g., Benesh and Howell 2001; Kritzer and Voelker 1998). Yet the researchers were repeatedly pilloried by their Russian colleagues when they presented their findings in roundtables in Russia. Because the results did not fit the common wisdom about Russian courts as incompetent and corrupt, the researchers were peppered with questions about their methodology with the goal of exposing how the research had gone wrong. The skepticism exhibited supports Marina Kurkchiyan's contention that contemporary Russia is dominated by the "negative myth of the rule of law" (2003, 30).

The multiple narratives reflected in current research are rarely reflected in public pronouncements on law. Dmitrii Medvedev's comments in 2008 on the eve of his entry into the presidential race are illustrative: "Without exaggeration, Russia is a country of legal nihilism. . . . No other European country can boast of such a level of disregard for law" (Polnyi tekst 2008). This statement is an uncanny, but presumably unintentional, echo of the assessments of law from the late nineteenth and early twentieth centuries by Herzen, Kistiakovsky, and Witte. Much like those statements, Medvedev's remarks, which are entirely consistent with Kurkchiyan's characterization of Russian legal culture, have been taken by many as factual. A comparative assessment of the actual data suggests that Russians are no more nihilistic when it comes to law than are others (Hendley 2012d).

This negative characterization helps explain why the public polling data reflect such profound antipathy for law and distrust of the courts. Indeed, when I talk to Russians, the conversation invariably begins with some variant of this "right" answer about law and the courts. Russians' tendency to censor themselves is nothing new, but is an unfortunate carryover from the Soviet era, during which people learned to censor their public speech and to share their true thoughts with a small circle of family and close friends (if at all). As Stephen Kotkin argues, people learned to "speak Bolshevik." In his view, "It was not necessary to believe. It was necessary, however, to participate as if one believed—a stricture that appears to have been well understood, since what could be construed as direct, openly disloyal behavior became rare" (1995, 220). This division between a private and public self is not a uniquely Russian phenomenon. The high cost of revealing one's private self at an inopportune moment led many to bury their true selves deeply. Jochem Hellbeck notes that the private self often remained obscure, even in personal diaries, giving rise to a kind of "split consciousness or a 'dual soul' (*dvoedushie*)" (Hellbeck 2000, 85, n. 28). Historians of the Stalinist period recognize that, despite the outward appearance of totalitarianism, "Soviet society was neither homogeneous nor unitary" (Viola 2002, 8). Individuals possessed multiple identities.

A version of this sort of political correctness lingers on in present-day Russia. Perhaps it could be redefined as a need to "speak Putinism," given that the current expectation is to appear to toe the line on Putin's policy. Many Russians, especially those socialized in the Soviet Union, are unwilling to speak openly except with trusted family members and friends. Svetlana Boym comments that "'saying what you mean' could be interpreted as being stupid, naïve, or not streetwise" (1995, 1). In his memoir of life in Putin-era Russia, Peter Pomerantsev (2014, 199) reflects that "all cultures have differences between 'public' and 'private' selves, but in Russia, the contradictions can be quite extreme."

This predilection for toeing the line has certainly complicated my field research. Many Russians—particularly outside the cosmopolitan centers of Moscow and St. Petersburg—are skittish of foreigners. The ups and mostly downs of U.S.-Russia relations in recent years have further muddied the waters. Getting my Russian counterparts to open up has not been easy. Only after we establish trust have they been comfortable sharing their feelings about law and the courts. These are not always laudatory, but they are invariably more nuanced in that they are shaped by the respondents' own experiences or the experiences of those close to them. By shifting attention away from high politics and toward the everyday, the existence of a dualistic legal system undergirded by multiple narratives of law comes into focus.

The Plan for the Book

My goal in writing the book is not to convince readers that what they think they know about law in Russia is wrong. Rather it is to convince them that it is not the whole story. Legal systems everywhere are flawed, even those seen as models to be exported. Perhaps the problems with the Russian legal system are more obvious. The brazenness with which high-profile cases are manipulated cries out for excoriation. But it blinds us to the larger reality. This book is intended to present a fuller picture of how law is experienced in Russia by recognizing the dualistic nature of the courts and of attitudes toward law. Doing so reveals that law is very much relevant to the everyday lives of Russians.

Chapter 1 explores Russian public opinion about law and courts. Once again, the reality is more complicated than the sound bites provided by the media. The Russian press is fond of splashing results from public opinion polls that would seem to document society's disdain for the legal system. To be sure, in the periodic polls conducted by the well-respected Levada Institute on Russians' trust in various institutions, courts consistently come out at the low end of the stick. Between 2001 and 2013, the percentage of Russians who completely trust the courts has inched up from 13 to 21. By comparison, trust in the presidency has consistently been over 50 percent during this period and trust in the Russian Orthodox Church has hovered between 40 and 50 percent. The validity of these data when it comes to the courts is unclear. Despite the fact that Russia has three distinct types of courts (courts of general jurisdiction, commercial or *arbitrazh* courts, and a constitutional court), the question simply asked about courts (*sudy*).[8] Unpacking what sorts of courts respondents were thinking of when responding is impossible. Moreover, the exercise assumes that, despite the myriad activities of

---

8. The boundaries between the courts of general jurisdiction and the *arbitrazh* courts were blurred in 2014 when the Higher *Arbitrazh* Court, which had been the court of last resort for *arbitrazh* claims, was merged into the Supreme Court. The Supreme Court was reorganized to create panels to handle *arbitrazh* appeals. At the trial and intermediate appellate levels, the *arbitrazh* court structure remained unchanged. Though legal professionals and others familiar with the *arbitrazh* courts protested against this institutional change, most Russians were unmoved (Levada Center 2013b). For background on these changes, see Zaikin 2015a; 2015b; 2015c; 2015d; Solomon 2014. For more on the postmerger Supreme Court, see Vereshchagin 2015; Maggs, Schwartz, and Burnham 2015; Henderson 2015.

courts, people have a single reaction to them. As I noted earlier in the chapter, context matters. These data are, unfortunately, free of context.

Despite their shortcomings, the results of these public opinion polls provide a starting point. My analysis is grounded in different data. I rely on two surveys. The first is a nationally representative panel household-based survey[9] on which I included questions dealing with the legal system in the 2006 and 2012 rounds. The second is a nationally representative survey fielded in 2008 that was narrowly tailored to assess Russians' attitudes and behaviors related to the legal system.[10] The richness of these datasets allows me to explore not only how Russians think and behave with respect to their law and legal system, but also the reasons for their views. More specifically, I identify what segments of Russians are most and least hostile toward law and courts.

The next section of the book—chapters 2 and 3—flows from the focus groups I conducted in Russia in the summers of 2007 and 2008. They explore how Russians handle problems that could, but need not be, solved using law. In chapter 2, I investigate how Russians respond when water leaks into their apartments, a problem that, owing to the aging housing stock of Russia, is remarkably common. In Chapter 3, I study how Russians react after automobile accidents. The comparison of water leaks and automobile accidents allows me to contrast behavior among people who know one another and strangers. Much like socio-legal scholars who have studied disputing behavior in the United States (e.g., Emerson 2008; Engel 1984; Ewick and Silbey 1998; Merry 1990; Yngvesson 1985), I find that the responses depend on the nature of the relationship among those involved. For friends and neighbors, seeking compensation for damage is awkward. Whenever possible, they seek reconciliation. As the relational distance between disputants grows greater, litigation grows more possible. Yet Russians, much like their counterparts elsewhere, are reluctant litigators, not because they fear being on the wrong end of telephone law, but primarily because they fear the time and emotional energy required to see a lawsuit through to the end.

The courts take center stage for the third section of the book. My interest in the experience of ordinary Russians propelled me to focus on the justice-of-the-peace courts (*mirovye sudy* or JP courts). Authorized in 1998 and rolled out across Russia beginning in 2001, the JP courts handle mundane cases of all varieties and

---

9. Since 1992, the Russian Longitudinal Monitoring Survey of the Higher School of Economics (RLMS-HSE) has been fielded on a regular basis by the National Research University Higher School of Economics and ZAO "Demoscope," together with the Carolina Population Center of the University of North Carolina at Chapel Hill and the Institute of Sociology of the Russian Academy of Sciences.

10. The survey was conducted in 2008 by the INDEM Foundation, a Moscow-based public policy center (http://www.indem.ru/en/index.shtml) (Gorbus, Krasnov, Mishina, and Satarov 2010).

thus serve as the portal of entry to the judicial system for most Russians. Chapter 4 examines the JP courts from the perspective of the judges, and chapter 5 reverses the lens to report on how litigants experience these courts. The observational research I did in JP courts across Russia between 2010 and 2012 serves as the raw material for these chapters. The picture that emerges is not one of judges mindlessly obeying commands from their political superiors, but rather judges struggling to keep up with the overwhelming crush of cases. Their primary goal is to manage their dockets efficiently and to avoid being reversed because these are the indicators of success within the judicial bureaucracy. Like their counterparts elsewhere, litigants at the JP courts are rarely happy to be there. They tend to be frustrated by what they perceive as the judges' endless demands for various documents that they have to chase down. Yet most tackle the JP courts on their own. I found the judges and their staff to be surprisingly gentle with these legal neophytes, guiding them through the technical procedural requirements with a sure hand. Most emerged from the experience satisfied that they had been treated fairly even if they were disappointed by the result.

In the Conclusion, I close the circle by returning to the theoretical dilemma of how we should conceptualize legal systems like Russia's in which law can, but does not always, matter. In other words, how should a dualistic legal system, in which politicized law exists side by side with law that is enforced and obeyed based on its written terms, be evaluated in terms of the rule of law? Perhaps a rethinking of the very concept of the "rule of law" is needed.

LEGAL CONSCIOUSNESS(ES) IN RUSSIA

The media tell a simple and straightforward story of law in Russia. It is a story in which law does not much matter and courts are mostly peripheral (e.g., Gessen 2015; Latynina 2012; Nemtsov 2009). The bulk of the mainstream scholarly literature on Russia does little to dispute this common wisdom (e.g., Hale 2015; Ledeneva 2013; Hedlund 2005). The much smaller body of scholarship by specialists on Russian law is more nuanced, but the "parade of horribles" school of thought remains well represented and the story it tells is remarkably coherent. It is supported by a combination of public-opinion polling and anecdotal evidence drawn primarily from high-profile cases. In this chapter, I look past the common wisdom and dig into the available empirical evidence on Russians' attitudes and behavior regarding law and courts in order to answer two basic questions. First, does law matter to Russians? And second, if it does, then for whom and under what circumstances?

The chapter begins with an overview of the methodology employed in my analysis and then turns to an analysis of available data on these two questions. My goal is to explain what factors tend to encourage or discourage trust in the capacity of Russian law to matter and then to explore Russians' willingness to use the law to solve their problems. In contrast to the somewhat simplistic prevailing view of law, a much more interesting and complicated picture of the role of law in Russia emerges from this analysis. Russians are moving away from legal nihilism. They are increasingly open to viewing law as a set of norms and expectations common to all, rather than as quasi-rules that are enforceable only when they serve the interests of the powerful. Put more bluntly, law matters to an increasing number of Russians, which undergirds the growing demand for law. This is not to say that Russians view law as a panacea or that their views are always consistent. But they see law as one of the viable options for solving problems. Like their counterparts elsewhere, they shy away from the courts, tending to use them only when no other options are available. When choosing between formal and informal avenues for solving their problems, they are influenced by the situational details, thus confirming that context matters.

Russian Legal Consciousness

The concept of "legal consciousness," alternatively referred to as "legal culture," is notoriously slippery. Lawrence Friedman's (1969a, 266) definition of legal culture as "the term we apply to those values and attitudes in society which determine what structures are used and why; which rules work and which do not, and why" is a good starting point. It reminds us that understanding the role of law requires attention to both societal attitudes and behavior. His use of the words "rules" and "structures" rather than "laws" and "courts" signals that informal norms and institutions can be just as important as their formal state-sponsored counterparts. Other socio-legal scholars have emphasized the need to move away from law- and court-centric analyses, noting that courts are invoked when needed, but are rarely the preferred mechanism for resolving problems. Sally Engle Merry's ruminations on legal consciousness offer a useful gloss. Her basic definition— "the ways people understand and use law"—tracks Friedman's. But she clarifies that a person's attitudes and behavior can shift based on circumstance. "Legal consciousness, as a part of culture, partakes of both the particularity of a situation and the overall context in which the situation is considered. Moreover, as in any facet of culture, understandings of law are not constant but develop through experience" (1990, 5).

In her study of Russian peasants' use of the courts in the late tsarist period, Jane Burbank (2004; 1997) embraces a definition of "legal culture" that is consistent with this U.S.-based socio-legal scholarship. She explores the extent to which peasants accepted, employed, and respected legal institutions. In doing so, she rejects a more formalistic approach that had held sway among historians and social scientists studying Russia that judged legal culture in terms of citizens' knowledge of statutory law. It is this technocratic view of the concept that led some scholars to argue that Russia lacked legal culture or that Russians had no legal consciousness, a position that persisted into the Soviet era (e.g., Frank 1999; Shelley 1992).

I agree with Burbank that framing legal consciousness as a function of one's familiarity with formal law misses the point. In the pre-Internet age, this sort of approach acted as a proxy for interest in law. Simply finding the law was difficult. If a person took the trouble, it could be taken as an indicator of his commitment to obeying the law. In the contemporary period, however, the easy availability of basic codes, both in paper form and on the Internet, renders a definition of legal culture linked exclusively to statutory knowledge patently absurd.

An exclusive emphasis on formal law when studying legal consciousness in Russia risks missing a critical part of the story. The Russian language has two words for "law": *zakon* and *pravo* (Livshits 1991; 1989). *Zakon* is used when referring to legislation (*zakonodatel'stvo*) and explanatory regulations (*podzakon-nye akty*). The meaning of *pravo* is more elusive. It captures what Fuller (1969) described as the morality of law; it asks whether the law in question is just and whether it represents the will of the people. It serves as the root for the Russian words for justice (*spravodlivost*) and human rights (*prava cheloveka*). Distinguishing between *zakon* and *pravo* is not a linguistic technicality. The choice of the Russian word for "law" can have profound political implications. When Gorbachev called for a "rule of law state" in the late 1980s, which was grounded in an assumption that law would be applied equally to all, he used the Russian phrase *pravovoe gosudarstvo*, which has *pravo* as its root. By contrast, when Putin refers to "rule of law," the phrase he typically uses is *gospodstvo zakona*. The more literal translation of this phrase would be "supremacy of statutory law," which is entirely consistent with his general "power vertical" scheme. Figuring out whether and when a Russian adheres more to a *zakon*-like or *pravo*-like view of law can be quite revealing. It is an important piece of the puzzle of how Russians think about law and courts and the extent to which their attitudes are reflected in their behavior.

Methodology

Russia is a relative newcomer to socio-legal scholarship. During the 1960s and 70s, when social scientists in the West were pushing past the "law on the books" to probe "law in action," such approaches were anathema in the USSR. The Communist Party leadership realized that allowing scholars to study what was really going on could be dangerous because it might expose shortcomings. As the socialist realist literature and art of the Soviet period shows, putting a positive spin on reality was much preferred. Soviet legal scholars rarely chafed at these restrictions (cf. Petrukhin 1970). Having been trained with a civil-law approach that treats statutes as the fundamental source of law, the interesting questions for them were doctrinal; whether law was effective in practice was less pressing. Other social science disciplines, such as sociology and political science, were underdeveloped. Few scholars took on law-related topics. This began to change in the 1980s as Andropov and Gorbachev pressed for more accurate information about the functioning of Soviet society. Even so, a thorough review of the scholarly literature from the 1960s through the collapse of the Soviet Union in 1991 reveals only one dissertation that explored societal attitudes toward law (Rimskii 2007). This dissertation, defended by A. S. Grechin in 1984, focused on the legal consciousness of workers. He fielded a survey that revealed some remarkably nonsocialist views, especially as to property rights. His worker-respondents did not find stealing from the state-owned enterprises where they worked to be morally unacceptable, but they were bothered by thefts of their private property. The dissertation was promptly classified. Though declassified in the 1990s, as of 2016 it remains accessible only at the library of the Institute of Sociology in Moscow.

Unlike their Soviet colleagues, many Western legal scholars yearned to explore how laws functioned in the USSR. But their access was severely constrained. For the most part, the Western scholarly literature mirrored the Soviet literature in its emphasis on statutory analysis, primarily because such sources were available (e.g., Maggs 1965). Some coped by focusing on historical, rather than contemporary, topics (e.g., Solomon 1996; Huskey 1986). But many key archives remained frustratingly out of reach. Others made use of the information that could be gleaned from Soviet émigrés to the West through structured interviews and memoirs (e.g., Solomon 1987; Shelley 1984). Some sought to stretch the limitations imposed by the Kremlin. John Hazard's (1962) reflection on what we can learn by comparing the arrangement of the furniture in Soviet courtrooms with that in courtrooms elsewhere in Europe and in the United States is a wonderfully inventive example. In his ethnography of the Soviet courts of the 1960s, George Feifer (1964) seemingly ignored the restrictions as he populated those courtrooms with vibrant portraits of how law was experienced by ordinary Russians. His is not a tale of politicized law or judges as strategic actors, but of judges trying to do their best to mete out justice. He concedes that these judges were engaged in trying to inculcate the values of the Communist Party, but his vignettes of judges berating workers who were drunk on the job or others engaged in antisocial behavior has a ring of familiarity to those familiar with Western court-based ethnographies (e.g., Bogira 2005; Merry 1990; Bedford 1961).

As I began my scholarly research in Russia in 1989, I took inspiration from Feifer's work. Encouraged by my U.S.-based mentors, I faced an uphill battle in the Soviet Union, though enough barriers had fallen to allow me to carry out fieldwork in courts and industrial enterprises (Hendley 1996). My access resulted from back-door connections, as friends convinced their friends to allow me to ask my questions even though I lacked formal permission. Few Soviet legal scholars saw value to my approach. Their training convinced them that asking the "why" questions and digging into how law worked in everyday life was not the job of a scholar. Over and over again, I was told that my research was not about law. Upon hearing of my desire to go to factories and to talk to workers about their experience of the law, one eminent Soviet scholar asked me whether my goal was to become a member of the proletariat.

With the collapse of the Soviet Union in December 1991, many of the formal restrictions on scholarship diminished. Opportunities for social scientists—Russian and foreign—flourished. Getting access to governmental institutions and private companies remained difficult, but that does not mark Russia as unique. Those who persevered were generally able to carry out their research. Yet a cursory glance at the top Russian legal journals, such as *Gosudarstvo i pravo* or *Zhurnal rossiiskogo prava*, confirms that Russian legal scholars remain more interested in doctrine than real life. Over the past decade, this trend has started to change as Russian scholarship on law has begun to incorporate empirical methods. Surveys querying Russians about law-related topics have become more common. Because few Russian legal scholars are trained in quantitative methods, sociologists have taken a leadership role in these projects. The presentation of findings has been mostly limited to descriptive statistics (e.g., Volkov et al. 2012; Gorbus et al. 2010; Gudkov, Dubin, and Zorkaia 2010; Kriuchkov 2010). These are fascinating, but often raise just as many questions as they answer. The researchers involved rarely have the luxury of digging into the data to test additional hypotheses; their grant-based funding model requires them to move quickly to the next project.

What emerges from these Russian studies is a familiar story of marginalized law and widespread societal distrust of courts. In this chapter, I test this common wisdom through an analysis of the available data. My goals are modest. I make no claim to have created a comprehensive predictive model for Russian legal consciousness. Rather, utilizing data from two national surveys, I identify key indicators of respect for law (as opposed to legal nihilism) and of a willingness to turn to the courts when problems arise.

The first survey utilized is the Russian Longitudinal Monitoring Survey-Higher School of Economics (RLMS-HSE). The RLMS-HSE is a nationally representative household-based panel survey of Russians that uses a stratified cluster sample. It includes a standard battery of questions designed to uncover the living standards and health of Russians. It also includes basic demographic questions, such as age, sex, marital status, economic activity, educational level, and ethnicity. Although primarily intended as a way to track demographic trends, the survey periodically incorporates questions aimed at assessing various types of political attitudes and behavior. I included a set of questions related to law in the 2004,

2006, and 2012 rounds.[1] The responses to these questions, which capture the essence of Russians' attitudes toward law, open a window into the legal consciousness of Russians. The fact that a core group of respondents participated in all rounds allows me not only to capture this at specific points in time but also to assess how and why it has changed over time.

In an effort to pry open the window into Russian legal consciousness even wider, I turned to a second source, a nationally representative survey of 2,845 Russians fielded in fall 2008 by INDEM (Information Science for Democracy), an independent Moscow policy institute. In contrast to the RLMS-HSE, the INDEM survey honed in on Russians' views of their legal system and their willingness to use courts to solve problems. Other than standard demographic queries, this one-time survey included relatively few questions that were unrelated to law. By drawing on these two datasets, which are complementary in their coverage of issues relating to legal consciousness, I can fully explore both attitudes and behavior.

The analysis is divided into three parts. In the first two parts, I focus on the results of the 2006 and 2012 rounds of the RLMS-HSE as to attitudes toward law, taking each as a snapshot of Russian reality. The hypotheses explored center on three basic themes: (1) personal control over one's fate, (2) prior use of the legal system, and (3) receptivity to democracy. With respect to each, I ask whether its relative presence or absence, as measured by variables drawn from the RLMS-HSE, tends to enhance or undermine respondents' confidence in law. In the second section of the chapter, I take advantage of the longitudinal facet of the data by teasing out what tends to push respondents to gain or lose respect for law.

In the third and final portion of the chapter, I turn to the INDEM dataset to explore the willingness of Russians to use the courts to solve their problems. The hypotheses driving these analyses look to respondents' attitudes toward law and the courts as possible explanations of their choices. They were asked about their likely responses to two hypothetical situations. The choices offered included going to court as well as a myriad of informal strategies. The analysis strongly suggests that their reactions are deeply contextual. Use of courts in one setting does not automatically translate into a willingness to litigate when the circumstances are different. And, most provocatively, their reported preferences in these hypothetical settings turn out to be poor predictors of their actual court use.

---

1. The number of respondents was 8,472, 12,490, and 19,687, in 2004, 2006, and 2012, respectively.

Does Law Matter? Assessing Russians' Attitudes toward Law

My working definition of legal consciousness encompasses not only behavior but also attitudes and values relating to law. Thus, a first step toward understanding Russians' legal consciousness is to investigate how they think about law. Three questions included in the 2004, 2006, and 2012 rounds of the RLMS-HSE provide different vantage points on their thinking. Respondents were asked to agree or disagree with the following three statements about the role of law in Russia.

(1) "If a person considers the law unfair, he has the right to 'go around it.'"[2]
(2) "If governmental or political officials do not obey the law, then ordinary people can disobey the law."
(3) "It is impossible to live in Russia without violating the law."

Each question focuses on the capacity of law to order behavior and to constrain power, albeit from different vantage points. Each endeavors to assess respondents' respect for law and their willingness to obey it. I begin by presenting the basic results for each question on its own. Taken together, however, they provide a window into Russian legal culture by showing how Russians think about law. Using this composite as a dependent variable in a series of OLS regression models allows for an analysis of what causes Russians to be more or less respectful of law. Put more bluntly, we can begin to get a handle on what factors tend to enhance (or diminish) respondents' level of legal consciousness.

The first question captures the essence of legal nihilism by asking whether a person can go around the law when he sees it as unfair. By doing so, the individual is substituting his judgment for that of lawmaking authorities. Although nihilism is presumed to dominate Russians' thinking about law, these data tell a remarkably different story. Respondents were given the option of agreeing or disagreeing with the statement, or of expressing their ambivalence. Figure 1.1, which lays out their responses in 2004, 2006, and 2012, shows that nihilism is present among an ever-decreasing minority of Russians.[3] It has fallen from 28 percent in 2004 to 20 percent in 2012. The level of ambivalence has likewise decreased, though by a slenderer margin. Those who disagreed with the nihilistic sentiment of the statement, who constituted a bare majority of 50.2 percent in

---

2. The Russian verb used for "going around it" combines the prefix for circumvention (*ob*) with the basic verb of motion (*idti*). Russians use this verb—*oboiti*—when talking about avoiding life's annoyances, including law.

3. For a more in-depth analysis of this variable with a focus on the 2006 round of the RLMS-HSE, see Hendley (2012d).

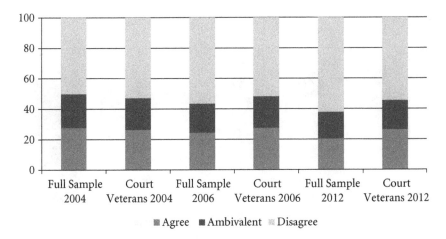

FIGURE 1.1 Responses to the statement: If a person considers the law unfair, he has the right to "go around it"

2004, had grown to over 62 percent by 2012. Moreover, earlier research by James Gibson (2003, 88) suggests that my results are not anomalous. He posed the same question to a nationally representative sample of Russians in surveys during the 1990s. Those who agreed with the statement decreased from about 30 percent in 1992 to 21 percent in 2000, while those who disagreed increased from 46 to 58 percent over the same period. Thus, law matters to a sizeable and growing percentage of the population.

The second question goes to the heart of the rule of law. This notoriously slippery concept is subject to a variety of definitions, yet at the heart of every effort at capturing its meaning is a recognition that the rule of law requires that everyone be governed by the same rules, irrespective of their power (Fuller 1964). A frequent criticism of Russian law dating back through the Soviet period to the tsarist era is its malleability. Many believe that those with power, whether economic or political, bend the law to suit their purposes (Dawisha 2014; Ledeneva 2013; Politkovskaya 2004). The RLMS-HSE question addresses this instrumentalism by asking whether respondents agree that, if officials disregard law, then they ought to be free to do the same. As compared with the first question, Figure 1.2 documents that fewer respondents were willing to commit to obeying the law if those in positions of authority did not than were willing to distance themselves from the practice of "going around" the law. No doubt the sense of being a patsy played a role. What is more interesting is the change in attitudes over time. The results are not as stark as for the first question, but the basic trend is the same. Those who hold with this anti-rule-of-law opinion have decreased; their

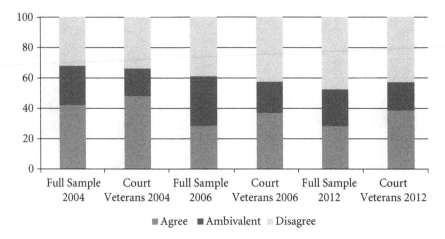

FIGURE 1.2   Responses to the statement: If government or political officials do not obey the law, then ordinary people can disobey the law

numbers dropped from 42 percent in 2004 to 28 percent in 2006. These numbers held constant through 2012. Those who embrace a rule-of-law mentality by disagreeing with the statement has increased steadily in each iteration of the survey, growing from 33 percent in 2004 to 40 percent in 2006 and to 49 percent in 2012.

The final question asks respondents to reflect on a frequently voiced sentiment about the impossibility of living within the law in Russia. Both Russians and foreigners point to inconsistencies and contradictions within the law and conclude that even those with the best intentions cannot possibly obey the law under such conditions (Browder 2015; Romanova 2011). Pollsters at the Levada Center asked this question periodically in nationally representative surveys between 1990 and 2010, though they did not give their respondents the option of expressing ambivalence. Their results are set forth in table 1.1. Their initial 1990 survey was, of course, conducted in the waning days of the Soviet Union. A third of those polled believed that one could be law abiding, whereas almost half felt this was impossible. In the post-Soviet period (regardless of the regime), frustration levels grew. In the surveys between 2007 and 2010, around 60 percent of those surveyed felt that living within the law in Russia was not feasible. The number who disagreed with this view stayed relatively consistent until 2007, when it began to creep upward, reaching a high of 41 percent in 2010 (Gorbus et al. 2010, 17).

These trends reflect a greater sense of cynicism about law than do the RLMS-HSE results, presented in figure 1.3. Both sources show an increase in the

TABLE 1.1   Results of polls of Levada Center from 1990 to 2007 on "Is it possible to live in Russia without violating the law?" (reported as percentages of the total unweighted sample)

	1990	1997	2000	2001	2007	2010
No (Nihilistic)	48	59	60	60	54	51
Yes (Law abiding)	33	26	33	30	36	41
Hard to say	19	15	7	10	10	8
Number in sample	1,600	1,600	1,000	1,000	1,600	2,300

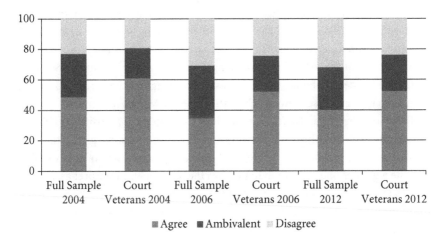

■ Agree ■ Ambivalent ▨ Disagree

FIGURE 1.3   Responses to the statement: It is impossible to live in Russia without violating the law

percentage of those who believed one can live in Russia and be law abiding. Both started at 33 percent, but the RLMS-HSE sample increased to almost 49 percent by 2012, whereas the Levada group grew to only 41 percent. The more troubling difference lies in the consistent majority of those in the Levada group who are convinced one cannot live in Russia and obey the law as compared with the RLMS-HSE sample who are less pessimistic. The results of the two studies are not directly comparable because RLMS-HSE respondents were able to opt for an ambivalent response whereas those surveyed by Levada were not.[4]

With respect to each of the questions from the RLMS-HSE, I recalculated the responses for the subset of respondents who had personal experience with the

---

4. See Carnaghan (1996) on whether saying that it was too difficult to respond is a rough equivalent to ambivalence.

courts (13 and 11 percent of the sample in 2006 and 2012, respectively). The results, which are a harbinger of what is to come in the regression analysis, show that
litigation veterans are more negative about the capacity of law to be meaningful
in Russia. As the Figures show, these respondents are much less likely than those
in the full sample to take the middle road.[5] Their views tend to be more negative.
They are especially skeptical of whether it is possible to live in Russia without
violating the law. Sadly, the RLMS-HSE data lack the detail necessary to tease out
what aspects of the court experience undermine confidence in the law.

The responses to these three RLMS-HSE questions over time suggest that law
matters and that its relevance has increased over time. The assumption that most
Russians have little respect for the law, which tends to be grounded in anecdotal
evidence, is simply erroneous. To be sure, a core of those surveyed expressed
skepticism about the feasibility of obeying the law, but their numbers are dwin-
dling. The incidence of ambivalence is also decreasing. Yet the percentage of respondents who expressed law-abiding attitudes is growing over time.

To explore this phenomenon in more depth, I created a composite variable for
each round that combined the responses to all three questions, giving the new
variable a range in values from 1 to 15.[6] Increases in the value of this variable
indicate a greater openness to living within the law, which I interpret as a proxy
for greater respect for the capacity of law to govern society. Lower scores reflect a
troubling moral flexibility as to whether one needs to obey the law. As the analysis
of the individual variables would predict, the mean value of this new variable
increases, albeit incrementally, over time. It grows from 8.76 in 2004 to 9.51 in
2006 and to 9.78 in 2012. Each cross-sectional change is statistically significant.

Although the trends revealed by these descriptive statistics are intriguing, the
next and more important step is to explore what socio-demographic factors are
most strongly associated with reporting law-abiding (or non-law-abiding) attitudes. This, in turn, will reveal the answers to our two organizing questions of
whether law matters and, if so, to whom and under what circumstances. I used
OLS regression analysis to explore the significance of these factors, taking the
composite variables generated from the 2006 and 2012 rounds of the RLMS-
HSE as my dependent variables. For each round, I start by examining the role of
the basic demographic characteristics of the respondents in explaining greater
respect for law (as opposed to legal nihilism). I then investigate the relationship between the willingness to treat the law as meaningful (as measured by the

---

5. The same relationship is observed if the court veterans are compared to respondents without
court experience (rather than to the full sample). It is also reflected in the results for a survey on attitudes about courts fielded by the Foundation for Public Opinion (Fond 2012).

6. Confirmatory factor analysis was performed on the resulting multivariate scale.

composite variables) and three sets of thematic variables: (1) personal control, (2) prior experience with the legal system, and (3) political attitudes. The additive model results are reported in tables A.1 (2006 round) and A.2 (2012 round) in Appendix A.

Demographic Factors

Gender emerges as statistically significant in both 2006 and 2012, with women being more likely to embrace law-abiding attitudes than men. Likewise, having a university degree is associated with such attitudes. The strong predictive power of these two variables is not unique to Russia. Comparative socio-legal research has confirmed that women tend to express more law-abiding attitudes, as do those with higher education (Tyler 2006, 42–43; Yagil 1998; Torney-Purta 1997). Recipients of these educational opportunities often emerge with a more sophisticated appreciation of the complexity of the legal system and are less willing to dismiss law out of hand.

Age matters and its role is more surprising. Those familiar with the blatantly instrumental use of law during the Soviet period by the Communist Party elite to achieve their goals might assume that the oldest generation who came of age under Stalin would be most resistant to the lure of law.[7] The fact that this generation was victimized yet again during the post-Soviet period owing to the ever-diminishing value of their pensions would only seem to lend credence to the expectation that they would be the most skeptical and cynical group as to law. Further buttressing this position is the literature that finds this older generation to be supportive of the ideals of the USSR and resistant to ideas associated with democracy and free markets (Colton and McFaul 2002, 112; Rose and Carnaghan 1995, 48; Bahry 1993). Yet the RLMS-HSE data tell a different story. The Stalin generation emerges as the least nihilistic. Each successive generation is less committed to living within the law than are these now-elderly veterans of the Soviet era.[8] (See Models 2 and 6 of tables A.1 and A.2.)

What explains these counterintuitive results? The commitment of the Stalin generation to the Soviet system is grounded in their belief that it is directly responsible for the triumphs of the USSR, including rapid industrialization and

---

7. In an effort to sharpen the analysis, I operationalized age into six generational cohorts, labeling them according to the leader in power when they came of age. Following the literature on generational effects in Russia, I assume that this period in their lives is when their attitudes toward the state and the legal system were crystallized (Rose and Carnaghan 1995, 34; Bahry 1987, 74–76).

8. The relationship is not linear, but curvilinear, suggesting that the oldest and youngest Russians share a commitment to law that is missing in middle-aged Russians. This is visible owing to the significance of the two age variables (Age and Age 2) and their opposite signs in Tables A.1 and A.2.

the victory over Nazism in World War II (Kiewiet and Myagkov 2002, 40; Gibson 1996, 397). Part of their nostalgic memories of the Soviet era is a commitment to law and order, which, for many, stands in contrast to the corruption and self-dealing of post-Soviet Russia. Though the scholarly and memoir literature is replete with examples of similar behavior by Communist Party elites (e.g., Clark 1993; Solomon 1992; Simis 1982; Smith 1976), this behavior was more discrete and may have escaped the notice of many survey respondents. Officially, Communist Party officials were supposed to be purer than ordinary citizens. Their misdeeds were often swept under the rug. Thus, what appears at first glance to be an incongruous commitment to rule-of-law ideals among older Russians may actually be a reflection of their childhood totalitarian socialization.

Those who came after the Stalin generation would have been put through an increasingly watered-down version of this totalitarian socialization. The memoir literature suggests that they began to question the viability of the system (Kaminskaya 1982). Few did so openly. Although the penalties for dissent had been scaled down from the Stalin period, wariness about sharing political views proved to be a difficult habit to break (Kotkin 1995; Young 1989).

But potentially more critical than their early socialization were their experiences during the 1990s. The 2006 survey asked respondents whether they had benefitted or suffered as a result of the economic upheavals following the collapse of the Soviet Union in 1991. Those who came of age under Brezhnev (born between 1951 and 1969) were the most likely to be negatively affected. Almost a third of them lost their job owing to layoffs or business failure between 1991 and 2006 (as compared with 27 percent for the full population of respondents). No doubt many were in the layer of midlevel managers that were sloughed off as the labor force was rationalized in light of market realities. By contrast, those who came of age under Gorbachev and Yeltsin (born between 1970 and 1976 and between 1977 and 1987, respectively) were more nimble. They were less entrenched in their workplaces and, consequently, were ready to jump ship for better opportunities before their enterprises foundered. Whereas only 22 percent of respondents reported having found a better-paying job since the collapse of the USSR, these percentages were much higher for the Gorbachev and Yeltsin generations—33 and 30 percent, respectively (Hendley 2012d, 176). Although the impact of the post-Soviet era on these now-middle-aged respondents appears to be different, what unites these generational cohorts is their common experience of instability. Few saw law as a way to protect themselves from the vagaries of economic change.

Logic would suggest a link between religiosity and attitudes toward law, given that religion and law share an affinity for rules and discipline. The RLMS-HSE data support this association. Self-identifying as a believer of any stripe

(37 percent of the 2012 sample) emerges as a strong predictor of pro-rule-of-law attitudes.[9] Adherents to Russian Orthodoxy make up most (89 percent) of this group. By separating them from Muslims (who make up 9 percent of the strong believers and are the only other confession to amount to more than a fractional percent), the extent to which Russian Orthodox believers are driving this result becomes clear. As compared with Muslims, they espouse more law-abiding attitudes.

Personal Control

The collapse of the Soviet Union ushered in an era of instability for most ordinary Russians. No longer could they be sure of having a job, a roof over their head, or enough money to support their family. A select few found a way to take advantage of this chaotic environment by feathering their own nests, often through quasi-legal or blatantly illegal tactics (Dawisha 2014; Politkovskaya 2004; Hoffman 2003). Most, however, soldiered on in obscurity, trying to find ways to cope in the new post-Soviet reality. Russians' expectations of law may be colored by their perceptions of personal control. This ought to reveal itself in both economic and personal relations. Thus, I hypothesize that those who feel a sense of desperation—either in the economic or personal realm—are more likely to embrace nihilistic attitudes. The analysis of the RLMS-HSE data tends to confirm this hypothesis.

I explore whether Russians who have experienced economic difficulties are more likely to resent law. They may come to question the universality of law, believing that it is simply another advantage enjoyed by the elite within society. Lending credence to this reasoning is the robust results for employment in the 2006 round. Those with a steady income are more likely to evince support for the importance of paying attention to law. It follows that those who are less secure about their economic future and who have taken on extra jobs to supplement their incomes[10] are less sanguine about law. As respondents' level of economic desperation rises, they become less accepting of law-abiding attitudes. The results are weaker for the 2012 round. Of the indicators that proved potent in 2006, only taking on supplemental work is significant in the full model in 2012. These results are consistent with the argument that Putin's economic recovery may be trickling down to ordinary Russians, leaving them less fraught. (See Models 3 and 6 in tables A.1 and A.2.)

---

9. Respondents were not queried about their religious beliefs in 2006.

10. Most respondents (78 percent in 2006 and 82 percent in 2012) had not taken on extra jobs. For those who had, I created a scale of economic desperation in which one point was given for each extra job.

Desperation is not limited to the financial arena. It often spills over into personal relations. As Shevchenko (2008) has argued, the disintegration of social supports taken for granted in the Soviet era has disrupted long-standing networks and has left many Russians feeling isolated and unable to exert control over their own lives. I wondered whether attitudes toward law might be a reflection of respondents' openness to others and their individual satisfaction with their lives. The support for this thesis is mixed; the argument holds more water in 2006 than in 2012. As a starting point, I focus on a question that asked respondents to assess the level of respect they command by placing themselves on a 9-step ladder, with low scores indicating a lack of respect and high scores indicating that one is well-respected. The results show a marked increase in perceived respect: the mean value for this variable in 2006 was 6, and rose to 6.4 by 2012.[11] Controlling for other variables in the model, individuals' reported levels of respect is significant in 2006, but not in 2012.

A good proxy for openness to new ideas and experiences is whether a person views others as basically trustworthy or whether they are viewed with suspicion or distrust. A willingness to trust others is positively associated with openness to the value of law.[12] As with the respect ladder, the significance of this variable is stronger in 2006 than in 2012.[13] On the other hand, when I turned to the darker side of respondents' emotional lives, I found that, for the 2012 round, those who describe themselves as completely unsatisfied with their current life are more likely to adhere to nihilistic views.[14] In the later period, pessimists seem to see law as yet another institution that has let them down.

Prior Exposure to Courts

Research outside of Russia has found that veterans of the judicial process are more likely to have a positive attitude regarding courts (Kritzer and Volker 1998; cf. Gallagher and Wang 2011). Whether this extends to law more generally is unclear, but is worth exploring. I test this hypothesis by introducing both attitudinal and behavioral variables to the OLS logistic regression models. The RLMS-HSE asked whether respondents had been to court within five years of the survey.

---

11. This difference between the mean score for this variable in the two rounds is statistically significant. The RLMS-HSE included two other "ladder" variables that assessed respondents' views of their own wealth and respect vis-à-vis others.

12. About 16 percent of respondents in both rounds believe that most people can be trusted.

13. In 2006, this variable is significant in both the model exploring the role of personal control and in the full model. In 2012, it is significant only in the preliminary model. See Models 3 and 5 of Tables A.1 and A.2.

14. This variable had no resonance for 2006 respondents.

As I noted earlier, this is a rather small group—13 percent of all respondents in 2006 and 11 percent in 2012. Echoing the trends visible in figures 1.2 and 1.3, court veterans are more likely to espouse legal nihilism than are those who have no experience with the courts.[15] (See Models 4 and 6 of tables A.1 and A.2). The effect is stronger in 2012 than in 2006.

On the other hand, when I shift from behavioral to attitudinal indicators for courts, a different story emerges. There is a positive and significant association between attitudes toward courts and law. Those who trust courts are more likely to see law as meaningful. As we will see when we delve into the more detailed results from the INDEM survey, this linkage may be tenuous. The RLMS-HSE data are not sufficiently detailed to distinguish between the various categories of court users, nor do they allow us to hone in on trust in particular courts.

Amenability to Ideals of Democracy

The relationship between general political beliefs and a willingness to obey the law has been documented in other settings (Tyler 2006). In his research on Russia, Gibson (2003, 89) found that "positive attitudes to the rule of law [were] moderately related to positive attitudes toward democratic institutions." My question is somewhat different. My composite dependent variable captures elements of the rule of law, but is not aimed at measuring that elusive concept. The context of my query is also different from prior studies that have focused on the United States (Tyler 2006) or Yeltsin-era Russia (Gibson 2003). By 2006, thanks to Putin's relentless drive to recentralize power, the fledgling effort at democracy under Yeltsin had been effectively neutered. The "power vertical" had drained democratic institutions of any real power (Dawisha 2014; Mendras 2012).

Both rounds of the RLMS-HSE inquired as to respondents' level of support for cornerstone principles of democracy, such as free elections, law and order, freedom of speech, an independent press, political opposition, and the protection of civil rights. Higher levels of support are a strong and consistent predictor

---

15. A similar trend is visible with regard to those who have gone through divorces. Avoiding the courts when getting divorced in Russia is almost impossible. Justice-of-the-peace courts handle simple divorces in which the spouses have agreed on the division of property and child custody (if relevant), whereas district courts handle more contentious divorces (art. 3, *O mirovykh* 1998; Hendley 2012a). In 2006, about 15 percent of respondents reported a divorce in their past. By 2012, this number had increased to almost 20 percent. As Model 1 in Tables A.1 and A.2 show, those who have had this unfortunate experience tend to be more nihilistic and less law abiding than those who have never been divorced. Because going to court is just one element of getting divorced, it is a somewhat crude proxy for the impact of prior court use and, consequently, its effect is less pronounced. See Hendley (2016) for a more detailed analysis of how attitudes toward courts vary among users and nonusers.

of respect for law. Shifting from the abstract, respondents were asked about their trust in key state institutions, including the legislature, the army, the police, political parties, and the government itself. Trust in these institutions reflects a democratic vision of the state with checks and balances. Thus, looking at these questions in an integrated way makes sense.[16] Higher levels of institutional trust also turned out to be a robust predictor of law-abiding attitudes in both rounds. (See Models 5 and 6 of tables A.1 and A.2.)

There is a risk that respondents were not thinking about these institutions in abstract terms, but that they personalized them. Given the heavy influence of Putin, some effort to tease out whether responses were tied to him is necessary. Fortunately, the 2006 questionnaire asked respondents about several of Putin's signature political policies. I isolate the supporters of term limits for elected officials as a proxy for support for Putin personally. Strong Putin supporters are more likely to embrace legal nihilism (see Models 5 and 6 of table A.1). This is intriguing on several levels. It confirms that we need to distinguish between support for democratic ideals and support for Putin's policies, even though the latter are often couched in the language of democracy. It also suggests that Putin's acolytes are able to see through this rhetoric to his real goal, which is usually raw power. Being on the lower end of the scale for the composite dependent variable reflects a comfort with instrumental uses of law that allow the interests of the elite to be prioritized. Put more bluntly, it facilitates telephone law.

Looking past the corridors of power in the Kremlin, the somewhat ambivalent relationship between the power of ordinary Russians and law is reflected in the findings for a variable that asks respondents to assess their own power. It poses a 9-step ladder where at one end are people with no rights and at the other end are people with a lot of power. Respondents tended to place themselves toward the lower end of this scale, with a mean score of 3.6 in 2006 and 3.95 in 2012.[17] When included in the analysis, it reveals those less confident of their rights to be more amenable to legal nihilism, at least in 2012 (the variable was not significant in 2006).

The analysis of the RLMS-HSE data confirms the salience of respondents' political attitudes and sense of personal control and well-being in explaining their levels of legal nihilism. It suggests a spillover between amenability to democratic

---

16. For each, I created a composite scale that aggregated respondents' views. "Belief in democratic principles" captures respondents' support of democratic ideals and "trust in governmental institutions" measures respondents' trust in key state institutions. See Models 5 and 6 in Tables A.1 and A.1.

17. This difference between the mean scores is statistically significant. It is not included in the full model because it is highly correlated with the "ladder" variable for respect, discussed earlier.

values and respect for the law. It also indicates that respect for law wanes when respondents feel that their lives are spinning out of their control. As their desperation rises, so too does their disdain for the law. Prior exposure to courts also emerges as a trigger for legal nihilism (as figures 1.1–1.3 predict).

Changes in Russians' Attitudes toward Law

One of the advantages of working with a longitudinal dataset is the opportunity to observe change over time. Thanks to the inclusion of questions relating to law in both the 2006 and 2012 rounds of the RLMS-HSE, I can trace a group of the 2006 respondents through to 2012, documenting the evolution in their attitudes toward law. These longitudinal analyses focus on the 5,849 respondents who participated in both rounds and answered the law-related questions. Sample assessments indicate that the basic demographic parameters of this smaller dataset are analogous to that of the full datasets.

Assessing the changes in legal attitudes requires a return to the two dependent variables for the earlier analysis of attitudes toward law. These are the composite variables representing respondents' answers to three basic questions in 2006 and 2012 that address their expectations of law in Russia (see figures 1.1–1.3). Those with high scores can fairly be regarded as more law abiding, whereas those with low scores harbor feelings of legal nihilism. Comparing the results of the two rounds reveals the resilience of law-abiding attitudes. Slightly over 58 percent of those who evinced such views in 2006 stuck to their guns in 2012. Of the remainder, 28 percent took an ambivalent stance and only 14 percent shifted to a position of nihilism. Those who voiced legal nihilism in 2006 were more likely to change their views. About a third shifted to a middle-of-the-road position and a slightly smaller number (31 percent) made a more significant shift to law-abiding views. Only 36 percent of the 2006 nihilists remained nihilistic in 2012.

Analysis of those who stuck to their guns—either as law compliant or as nihilistic—reveals that their defining qualities track those outlined in the previous section.[18] In other words, the odds of respecting law consistently are greater for women, those who have a university education, and older people, whereas those who remained nihilistic tend to be men, less well educated, and middle aged. Their experiences with the legal system likewise diverge. The negative effect of having been to court on overall trust for law visible in figures 1.1 and 1.2 persists. Nihilists are more likely to have been to court (often as part of a

---

18. For this reason, I have not included the results in Appendix A.

divorce) and to harbor distrust for the courts, whereas those at the other end of the spectrum have no litigation experience but express strong trust of the courts.

Change is inherently more interesting than stasis. To understand what qualities are associated with respondents whose views of the capacity of law changed decisively, I created dummy variables to capture two groups: (1) those who shifted from nihilistic to law-abiding attitudes (8 percent of the sample) and (2) those who embraced nihilistic views in 2012 after having been respectful of the value of law in 2006 (5.5 percent of the sample). I examine each in separate bivariate analyses. The results, which are reported in terms of odds ratios, are set forth in tables A.3 and A.4 in Appendix A.

The Shift from Legal Nihilism to Law-Abiding Attitudes

In contrast to the results for the individual rounds of the RLMS-HSE, respondents' demographic characteristics prove to be poor predictors of the change from legal nihilism to respect for law. The insignificance of gender and education may be explained by the fact that both university graduates and women are overrepresented in the group that consistently expressed strong law-abiding views in both rounds.

Once again, age is a potent factor. By breaking down the sample by generational cohort, it becomes clear that the chances of becoming more law abiding between 2006 and 2012 improves with age. Taking the youngest generation as the reference group, the analysis reveals that, controlling for other variables, these respondents' parents (the Yeltsin and Gorbachev generations) and grandparents (the Stalin, Khrushchev, and Brezhnev generations) are much more likely to have changed their views in favor of respect for law. For those in the oldest cohorts, the odds of such a shift are two times greater. This finding suggests that among this subset of those surveyed, the same sort of linear relationship between aging and greater conformity to law is present that has been observed in many Western countries. (See table A.3.) As I noted above, this goes against what those familiar with the historical trajectory of law in the Soviet era would expect. The older generations would have more firsthand experience with the blatantly instrumental use of law by the Communist elite. Yet it has not soured them on law more generally, as older generations appear more likely to support law, and moreover are more likely to shift from legal nihilism to law-abiding attitudes between 2006 and 2012, compared with all other potential shifts in legal attitude.

Given the overlap between law and government more generally, I anticipated that those who had become less nihilistic and evinced greater respect toward law as between 2006 and 2012 would be more likely to have softened their views toward state institutions and democratic ideals. To test this, I explore the extent to which respondents' attitudes toward democratic principles and trust in state institutions changed. More specifically, I was interested in whether their support had grown over time. The analysis reveals that, controlling for other variables, respondents reporting increased trust in state institutions were over 40 percent more likely to shift from legal nihilism to law-abiding attitudes, in comparison to any other change (or consistency) in legal attitudes (see Model 2 of table A.3). But an enhanced appreciation of democratic principles had no predictive power. This suggests that the link between respondents' underlying views of the state-society relationship and changing attitudes toward the importance of obeying the law is more tenuous than I expected.

I wondered whether having been to court might drive respondents' views of law. Interestingly, court-related attitudes emerge as more potent than respondents' actual behavior. Although being divorced (a crude proxy for litigation experience) initially appears to play a role, its effect dissipates as other explanatory variables are added to the mix.[19] On the other hand, respondents whose trust in courts was stronger in the 2012 round of the RLMS-HSE than in 2006 are significantly more likely to have rethought their attitude toward law more generally and to have become more law abiding. Once again, we see a disconnect between attitudes and behavior. The spillover effect between positive attitudes toward courts and law more generally is absent when it comes to experiential factors. Indeed, figures 1.2 and 1.3 remind us that respondents who have been to court tend to be more nihilistic than those who have never litigated. The positive relationship between trust in courts and a move toward greater respect for law is consistent with the larger trend revealed by the regression analyses for the individual rounds of the RLMS-HSE (see tables A.1 and A.2).

My thesis that positivity in respondents' lives tends to bleed into their attitudes toward law is confirmed. Put simply, variables that reflect a greater sense of personal control and hopefulness tend to be associated with the shift away from legal nihilism toward respect for law. For example, the relative odds of this shift are over 60 percent greater for those who feel themselves to be more respected by others in 2006 than in 2012. Along similar lines, being more satisfied with the economic conditions in one's life is a strong predictor of an attitudinal shift in the direction of being more law abiding.[20]

---

19. In Model 1 of Table A.3, being divorced increases the odds of greater respect for law by 20 percent. In Model 2, I used a variable that captured the 7 percent of the sample who had been to court in between the two rounds in lieu of being divorced. This sharper measure has no predictive power when it comes to this shift away from nihilistic toward compliant legal attitudes.

20. In an odd twist, the analogous variable that measures shifts in respondents' overall satisfaction with their lives was not significant.

The Shift from Law-Abiding Attitudes toward Legal Nihilism

An analogous trend can be seen for those who shifted away from respect for law in 2006 toward legal nihilism in 2012, who serve as the dependent variable. (See table A.4.) This time, however, the driving force is not hopefulness, but its polar opposite, declining perceived status, hopelessness, and despair. This is illustrated by both behavioral and attitudinal variables. As to the former, the odds of having transitioned from law abiding to nihilism are over 40 percent greater for respondents who reported having to take on an extra job in 2012 (but not 2006). The attitudinal predictors include feeling less valued by others. Even the finding that nonbelievers are more likely to have moved toward nihilism fits with this overall sense of pessimism about life.[21]

Given that court veterans tend to be more nihilistic (see figures 1.1–1.3), I anticipated that having been to court between the two rounds of the RLMS-HSE would be associated with an attitudinal shift away from respect for law in favor of nihilism. Along similar lines, I expected increased trust in courts to be negatively associated with this change. This seemed to be the case in my initial analysis. But it did not remain significant when institutional trust factors were added to the model.[22] Contradicting the predictions generated by figures 1.1 and 1.2, litigation experience is not significantly associated with the shift toward legal nihilism relative to other outcomes in changing legal attitudes between 2006 and 2012.

Although my prediction that enhanced confidence in public institutions and in democratic ideals would be associated with a greater respect for law fell short, it turns out that a decrease in these measures is a potent predictor of a shift toward legal nihilism. For this analysis, I included measures of decreased trust in public institutions and in democratic ideals. Both turned out to be robust predictors of a shift toward legal nihilism, which is consistent with the larger "race to the bottom" story. Much as the shift to law-abiding attitudes is a spillover of an optimistic worldview, the shift to legal nihilism reflects respondents' sense of pessimism and lack of control over their fate.

When Do Russians Rely on Law? The Use and Nonuse of Courts

Abstract attitudes are only one piece of the puzzle when it comes to legal consciousness. Equally important are the choices made when resolving concrete problems.

---

21. With the exception of religiosity and ethnicity, demographic indicators played little role in predicting the probability of a shift toward legal nihilism.

22. Model 2 in table A.4 tests this court-based hypothesis and yields the predicted results. When other explanatory variables are added to the mix in Model 3, the statistical significance of the court-related variables wanes.

TABLE 1.2 Reactions to two hypothetical situations from the 2008 INDEM survey (reported as percentages of the total unweighted sample)

	GO TO COURT	DO NOTHING	SELF-HELP	EXIT	OTHER
Hypothetical 1: Reprimand at work that seems illegal	20	15.5	29.9	10.1	25
Hypothetical 2: Child denied admission to neighborhood school	35.1	NA	18.45	24.3	22.55

Of particular interest is the extent to which legal institutions are viewed as a viable option for resolving problems. Teasing out the role of courts can be difficult. In chapters 2 and 3, I employ qualitative methods to unravel Russians' thinking by analyzing their discussions in focus groups. Here I explore the same question using survey data. The RLMS-HSE included only one question related to respondents' behavior, namely, whether they had any recent exposure to courts. To dig deeper into Russians' behavior, I turn to the 2008 INDEM survey, which focused more narrowly on legal issues. Respondents were asked how they would react to two hypothetical situations from a wide range of options, both formal and informal. The survey also gathered information about respondents' track record with the courts.

I begin by laying out respondents' preferred course of action with respect to the two fact patterns (see table 1.2). Because the situations are hypothetical, we cannot know what they would do if actually faced with these problems. Nor do we know whether they have ever faced the sorts of problems identified. Forcing them to pick only one path is also problematic. In reality, they might pursue several strategies, either simultaneously or sequentially, or they might abandon their chosen path when the going gets tough.[23] Yet forcing them to make a choice has the advantage of identifying their preferred path.

In an effort to understand what factors influenced respondents' choices, I explore four types of responses to the scenarios: (1) litigation, (2) self-help, (3) exit, and (4) doing nothing. Using multinomial logistic regression for each fact pattern, I examine individual-level factors that increase the probability of pursuing an option other than law (i.e., not going to court).[24] I use litigation as the reference category, while controlling for the other options. This allows me to

---

23. For example, when studying management's response to their customers' failure to pay in the 1990s, we found that managers often began by contacting recalcitrant customers and ratcheted up to litigation if those efforts proved unsuccessful (Hendley 2001; Hendley, Murrell, and Ryterman 2000).

24. In an effort to hone the results, I excluded respondents who refused to respond to the questions. This explains the variation in the number of respondents included in the various regressions.

compare the relative likelihoods of employing more informal problem-solving strategies (self-help, exit, and doing nothing) with seeking a remedy through the formal legal system.

As compared with the RLMS-HSE, the INDEM project focused more narrowly on law. Consequently, after working through the role of demographic factors, my analysis bores in on two sets of variables in explaining their problem-solving choices in both the hypothetical scenarios and real life: (1) their attitudes toward law, and (2) their attitudes and behaviors regarding the courts.

Responding to an Illegal Workplace Reprimand

The first hypothetical asked respondents how they would react to receiving what they regarded as an illegal reprimand (*nezakonnyi vygovor*) at work. No further details about the reprimand or the underlying circumstances were provided. Given that most participants had employment experience, this represents a familiar situation.[25] Inevitably their own life experiences as well as those of their friends and family colored their responses, as they would have in a real-life setting. Respondents were given fourteen possible courses of action, encompassing both formal and informal approaches. I divided these into five basic categories: litigation, self-help, exit, doing nothing, and a catch-all "other" category that encompassed consulting with third parties (including lawyers) as well as declining to respond. Seeking help from the trade union, which would have been the first step in any formal remedy in the Soviet era (Hendley 1996), was not offered as an option, which is a telling reminder of the sea change that has occurred in Russia since the collapse of state socialism. Table 1.2 lays out the distribution of responses. My analysis focuses on the first four categories, which comprise over three-fourths of the sample.

Thirty percent opted for self-help, making it the most common response. Among the different variants of self-help offered to respondents were negotiating with one's boss, appealing the reprimand to higher management, and using one's connections to influence higher management. The popularity makes sense. Pursuing these remedies would allow respondents to keep their job while still fighting the reprimand.

Twenty percent indicated they would be prepared to take management to court. This rather high rate reveals several truths about the Russian courts. It reflects the relative ease of going to court, especially the justice-of-the-peace courts

---

25. About 55 percent of the sample were employed at the time of the survey. An additional 2 percent were on parental leave and 20 percent were pensioners. Only 7 percent described themselves as unemployed. The survey did not ask respondents whether they had ever faced this sort of situation.

(JP courts), where this sort of case would be heard.[26] Not only are cases processed rather quickly and inexpensively, but the absence of the heightened emotions of the adversarial process also means that an employee can take an employer to court without making an enemy. In other words, regardless of the outcome, the respondent-employee would not become a pariah at the workplace. It also reminds us that the popular view of courts as dysfunctional does not typically apply to this sort of mundane dispute.

The remaining 26 percent of the sample is divided between the 10 percent who would exit the situation by looking for another job and the 16 percent who would simply endure. Doing nothing may appear to be the path of least resistance, but suffering in silence can come with high emotional costs.

Responding to a Child's Denial of Admission to School

The second hypothetical posited that the director of the neighborhood high school had denied admission to a respondent's child. It further assumed that the respondent had already appealed this action to the director's superiors in the department of education with no success. The survey asked what further action the respondent would take, offering ten options. In contrast to the first hypothetical, doing nothing was not an option. Even if the respondent-parent is resigned to the director's decision, she still has to find a place for her child. I treated this as exiting from the situation, though, like the option of doing nothing in the first hypothetical, seeking out a different school can be seen as the path of least resistance. Respondents were also offered several forms of self-help. Thus, the analysis focuses on three options: litigation, self-help, and exit. As table 1.2 shows, these account for 76 percent of the respondents. The remainder include those who would seek help from third parties (both lawyers and governmental officials), as well as those who declined to share their preference.[27] Though it might be assumed that the fact pattern resonated more deeply with those with children, it turns out that having children had no predictive power. No doubt childless respondents were nonetheless able to empathize, thanks to their own travails as students and the experiences of their friends and family.

The distribution of responses for the two hypothetical situations are quite different (see Table 1.2), revealing the contextual nature of respondents' preferences. Somewhat surprisingly, the most popular course of action in the face of having a

---

26. See chapters 4 and 5 for an analysis of JP courts.

27. Most (73 percent) of those in this catch-all "other" category did not respond. About half of those who refused to respond to the first hypothetical situation likewise refused to respond to the second hypothetical.

child denied a place in his neighborhood high school was to seek a remedy in court. Over 35 percent of those surveyed opted for litigation. The actions of school directors, as state employees, are subject to review by the courts. If a judge finds a director's decision to deny admission to be capricious, then the court has the authority to order the director to reverse his decision and admit the child. The stakes are higher for such a lawsuit than for a challenge to a workplace reprimand. Depending on the details, the involvement of the state and/or the connections of the school director may give it political overtones and raise the specter of telephone law. But this would be unusual. It would be more likely for it to be treated as a routine case and decided according to the written law. It would be heard by a district court (rather than a JP court). All of this would seem to militate in favor of avoiding the courts, but the data tell a different story. Perhaps the stipulation that an initial internal appeal had already failed pushed respondents toward the courts. In any event, the willingness to use the courts serves as powerful evidence of the relevance of courts to Russians when seeking solutions to problems they encounter in their everyday lives.

About a quarter of those surveyed chose exit, indicating they would give up on their neighborhood school and begin looking for another school for their child. Embedded in this choice is a grudging acceptance of the school director's edict and a decision to move on. It may also reflect a lack of informal connections that could be brought to bear on the director.

Almost 19 percent of the sample favored self-help strategies. They preferred to try to resolve the problem on their own, either by negotiating with the school director directly or by making use of existing connections to pressure the director to change his mind. As between these two, about two-thirds would take responsibility themselves, and the remainder would rely on third parties for help. Given the traditional preference for informal problem-solving methods, the lower-than-expected number likely results from the stipulation that the parent has already appealed internally, an approach that would be assumed to include behind-the-scenes lobbying. Some respondents may have presumed that these informal methods failed, and so opted for either litigation or finding another school.

Both of the self-help responses to the hypotheticals implicitly raise the specter of *blat* and corruption. *Blat* is a practice of plying those in positions of power with gifts or favors in an effort to encourage them to help (Ledeneva 1998). It was extremely common during Soviet period, when shortages of goods and services made these sorts of favors a more valuable currency than money itself. Though Russia is no longer plagued by shortages, *blat* persists, particularly in the service sector, which includes teachers.[28] Gifts of flowers and back-scratching favors tend

---

28. When talking to East German lawyers, Markovits was told that "under Socialism, there were five times as many strings that you could pull as today" (2010, 145).

TABLE 1.3 Comparison of respondents' reactions to two hypothetical situations from the 2008 INDEM survey (reported as raw numbers with percentage of total respondents in parentheses)

		HYPOTHETICAL 2				
		GO TO COURT	SELF-HELP	EXIT	OTHER[1]	TOTAL
HYPOTHETICAL 1	GO TO COURT	460 (20%)	21 (1%)	52 (2%)	10 (0.4%)	543 (24%)
	DO NOTHING	116 (5%)	89 (4%)	158 (7%)	44 (2%)	407 (18%)
	SELF-HELP	202 (9%)	298 (13%)	217 (10%)	74 (3%)	791 (35%)
	EXIT	40 (2%)	45 (2%)	156 (7%)	28 (1%)	269 (12%)
	OTHER[1]	72 (3%)	38 (2%)	56 (2%)	73 (3%)	239 (11%)
	TOTAL	890 (40%)	491 (22%)	639 (28%)	229 (10%)	2,249

[1] Includes respondents who refused to respond.

not to be regarded as bribes, but when the gifts are monetary, then most would view them as illegal bribes, though the lines are quite fuzzy (Ledeneva 2006). Not all Russians are comfortable with *blat* in any form, though most will concede that it is a sad reality of daily life.

Explaining Variation in Responses

A cursory glance at table 1.3 reveals that most respondents (57 percent) were not consistent in their responses to the two hypothetical situations.[29] This indicates that respondents cannot be neatly divided into those who always opt for court, self-help, or exit, but that their choices are driven by the situational details, supporting my argument for the existence of multiple narratives of law in Russia. Socio-legal research teaches us that individuals' responses to problems are influenced by a variety of intangible factors, such as the worldview they have developed through a lifetime of specific experiences (Felstiner, Abel, and Sarat 1980–81). Respondents' work history and their relationships with management over time (as well as the experiences of friends and relatives) surely colored their reactions to the imposition of an illegal reprimand. Along similar lines, respondents' prior interactions with school administration, both as students and as parents, certainly impacted their responses to the second hypothetical. Although surveys are helpful in sorting respondents by demographic categories and by basic attitudes, they are not sufficiently nimble to capture respondents' thought processes. These sorts of factors are best teased out through qualitative methods, as we will see in the subsequent chapters of the book.

---

29. For purposes of this analysis, I left out respondents who refused to make a choice.

Even with these limitations, Table 1.3 reveals several key trends. It confirms that most of the variation is among the different informal avenues for solving the problems. Relatively few respondents (about 20 percent) jump the fence between formal and informal. Thus, the fact that litigation is by far the stickiest behavioral pattern is to be expected.[30] Because the percentage of respondents opting for court was higher in the second hypothetical (41 percent) than in the first hypothetical (26 percent), the trend is more striking when comparing the results from the first hypothetical to the second than vice versa. Of those who opted for going to court in the face of an illegal reprimand at work, 84 percent would also challenge the decision to deny their child admission to their neighborhood school. By contrast, substantially fewer (53 percent) of those who chose court as a response to the second hypothetical had done so for the first. Of the remainder, the largest group (23 percent) indicated they would approach their managers or use other avenues of self-help. These are likely the people who would have opted for talking to the local school authorities in response to the second hypothetical if the question had not stipulated that this had already been tried to no avail. A significant number (13 percent) of those who opted for court as to the second hypothetical said that they would simply tolerate the situation put forward in the first hypothetical. Once again, they went for an option they were not offered in the second scenario.

The inconsistencies in the choices available raise a number of intriguing questions. How did those who took a wait-and-see approach to the imposition of an illegal reprimand respond to the school-based hypothetical, where doing nothing was not an option? Dismissing such respondents as fatalistic is tempting. The fact that a plurality (42 percent) said they would seek out another school for their child if denied admission to their neighborhood school—the most passive option offered—provides some support for this view. On the other hand, significant numbers indicated they would take a more activist path by either suing the school (31 percent) or mobilizing their connections (25 percent) to persuade the school director to change her mind. When these two are combined, we see that a majority of those who would do nothing when they experienced unfairness in the workplace would rise up against the authorities to protect their children's interests. This attests to the importance of both the context and the underlying stakes in determining behavior.

The two behaviors labeled as "exit" are far from mirror images of each other. As to the first hypothetical, it refers to a decision to quit an existing job in the face of unfair treatment and to seek a different job. As to the second hypothetical, it refers to a decision to forego extraordinary efforts to change the decision to deny admission to a neighborhood school and, instead, to find another school

---

30. The correlation between the two variables measuring court use is 0.48.

for the child. The relative voluntariness of these decisions varies. Whereas one could stick it out at a job, parents have no choice but to find schools for their children. Thus, it is not surprising that only a quarter of those who opted for exit in the second scenario did so in the first. Instead, these respondents divide themselves between those who opted for self-help in response to the illegal reprimand (35 percent) and those who did nothing under the same circumstances (25 percent). This reflects the schizophrenic quality of the choice of finding an alternative school. Some may regard it as the path of least resistance, much like tolerating unfairness at the workplace. Others may see it as a chance to find a better educational environment for their child, suggesting the need for the same sort of gumption required to lobby higher management to rethink a reprimand.

Explaining Patterns in Responses

What factors are associated with raising the probability of selecting a specific strategy in the two hypothetical situations? In an effort to sort through possible explanations, I ran a series of multinomial regressions. (See Tables A.5 and A.6.) In interpreting these findings, it is important to remember that we are comparing each of the subgroups who opted for informal strategies with the group who indicated a preference for going to court, while controlling for the selection of the other strategies. The results are reported as odds ratios.

I begin by exploring the role of basic demographic factors. Somewhat surprisingly, several characteristics—namely, gender, marital status, and economic well-being—that are consistently robust predictors of legal attitudes falter when it comes to explaining respondents' preferences in responding to the hypothetical situations.

Traditionally, educational levels are powerful predictors of legal attitudes and behavior. Both in Russia and elsewhere, those with higher education tend to hold more positive (less nihilistic) views about law and to be more prepared to use the courts to resolve disputes. I reason that higher education might make self-help options more appealing, given that the network of connections built with university classmates could be called on. These networks might also prove useful when searching for another job or an alternative school. The INDEM data provide no support for this line of thinking.

Another potentially rich source of connections for Russians is the workplace. Hence, I expected that being employed would be strongly associated with opting for informal solutions, but again, the data tell a different story. Although logic might suggest that respondents would call on coworkers when looking for another job or pressing contacts for help in sorting out a workplace reprimand or a child's school placement, respondents' job status is irrelevant. More surprising is the lack of predictive power of employment status when it comes to those who said they would do nothing if hit with an unfair reprimand at work. It would stand to reason that those with secure jobs would want to hold on to them, but apparently such fears did not motivate the INDEM respondents.

Because Russian courts are more accessible in urban settings, I reasoned that city dwellers would be more likely to opt for litigation over informal solutions. To the extent that location mattered, the explanation had little to do with proximity to courts. As to the first hypothetical, location mattered only for those who opted for exit. Their odds of living in a large metropolitan center were 60 percent greater than for those who opted for court. As a rule, job opportunities are greater in large population centers, enhancing the prospects for finding another job. As to the second hypothetical, those who responded to the slight to their child by looking for another school were significantly less likely to be from rural locales. Perhaps the inevitably richer assortment of alternatives to neighborhood schools in big cities as opposed to smaller towns and villages helps explain the appeal of self-help and exit strategies. If parents have no viable option to their neighborhood schools, this raises the stakes and makes litigation a more attractive choice.

Much as for attitudes toward law, age matters. But it plays out differently in each hypothetical, once again proving the importance of context. By using the youngest generational cohort—those born after 1977—the trends emerge most clearly. This effectively divides the sample into those who came of age during Soviet power and those who came of age in the post-Soviet era. When confronted with the possibility of an illegal reprimand at the workplace, the chances of electing self-help over litigation are significantly less for the Soviet cohort (those born before 1977). (See Table A.5.) The effect is strongest for the oldest cohort (the so-called Stalin generation, born before 1940), who is over 50 percent less likely to choose self-help over litigation. It weakens slightly with each successive cohort, but remains statistically significant. When it comes to those who opted to look for another job rather than appeal to the courts, the results are similar but less pronounced. The statistical significance is limited to the subset who came of age under Khrushchev (born between 1941 and 1950). Perhaps these results are being driven by the greater openness of older Russians to litigation (which is discussed below). But they also suggest that in the workplace setting, older Russians are more receptive to formal than informal strategies.

Any temptation to generalize from this finding is quickly halted by the results from the regression analysis for the second hypothetical. The effect of age is turned on its head. In the wake of having a child denied admission to the neighborhood high school, the chances of eschewing the courts and accepting the decision by seeking out an alternative school are much greater for the Soviet generations (born before 1977). (See Table A.6.) As compared with the first scenario, which asks about respondents' own interests, this scenario focuses on the interests of their children. Recognizing the importance of education for their children, these older Russians take the safer path of looking for an alternative school. Litigation would be a much higher-risk strategy that could stigmatize their child in the eyes of teachers and school administrators or even result in their child being denied a place in any school. A comparison of generational cohorts reveals an intriguing pattern. Looking from oldest to youngest, the chances of opting for this safer strategy over litigation initially increase for each successive generation, peaking with the generation who came of age under Brezhnev, who are more than two times more likely to choose this low-risk approach. The odds of pursuing this avenue then decrease somewhat for those who came of age under Gorbachev, thought they are still over 60 percent more likely to opt for seeking out another school over pursuing a court case. The same effect is visible among those who preferred to mobilize their connections rather than litigate, but is statistically significant only for those who came of age under Brezhnev (born between 1951 and 1969).

COURT EXPERIENCE—PAST AND FUTURE

What interested me more than these demographic indicators was the extent to which respondents' preferences would be colored by their openness to using courts, as measured by their past behavior and their forecast of future behavior. Whether prior litigation experience would push them toward informal or formal options when faced with these hypothetical situations was unclear, but I felt sure that it would play a role. The evidence is mixed. In preliminary models, I found that having brought a claim to court in the past significantly increased the likelihood of opting for court. But the statistical significance dissipated when variables that captured respondents' choices on the other hypothetical were added in. But the basic story remained the same. A preference for formal over informal (and vice versa) persisted from one hypothetical situation to the other. Those who opted for self-help over litigation in one situation are more than three times more likely to have done so in the other situation as well. Along similar lines, the chances of opting for informal solutions when faced with an illegal reprimand at work were over 80 percent less for those who opted for litigating in response to the school director's refusal to enroll their child. The story is the same for the second hypothetical. Litigation experience acts as a disincentive to using informal methods, at least in this hypothetical realm. (See Tables A.5 and A.6.)

The distaste for the courts exhibited by those who indicate a preference for informal methods of dispute resolution persists into the future. Respondents were asked about their willingness to go to court if a problem arose that could be solved by the court. Most were willing to entertain the possibility of litigation, though most indicated they would resort to the courts only after exhausting all other avenues. A few (11 percent) resisted the prospect of court under any scenario. Not surprisingly, the chances for members of this group to resort to informal solutions over formal institutions are generally two to three times greater. The socio-legal literature has repeatedly shown that experience in court—being a so-called repeat player—provides an advantage in subsequent court battles (Galanter 1974). These repeat players are not only better versed on the formal rules but, more important, they also understand how these formal rules work in practice as well as the informal norms of court practice. It stands to reason that those who lack this background would be hesitant to try their luck in court.

ATTITUDES TOWARD COURTS

The idea that attitudes and behavior mirror one another is appealing, but the evidence remains spotty. The INDEM respondents were asked to agree or disagree with the statement: "We have basically independent courts and a normal judicial system." Well over two-thirds of those who expressed an opinion took issue with this statement. We might logically expect this group to be less likely to go to court. The evidence was stronger for the second hypothetical than for the first. Those who opted for informal methods of dealing with their child being barred from their neighborhood school are about 30 percent less likely to have agreed with this statement as compared with their counterparts who opted for the courts. The fact that the same sort of relationship is not consistently present for those who preferred informal strategies to deal with the illegal workplace reprimand suggests that the link is probably highly contextual. The insignificance of variables that measure other aspects of judicial independence (e.g., even-handedness, dependence on political officials) further undermines any hope for a robust association between behavior and attitudes.

The inconsistency of the relationship between respondents' trust in the courts and their preferences with regard to the hypothetical situations provides additional evidence. A variable that measured general trust in Russian courts has no predictive power. A relationship emerges only when I refine the variable to focus only on the court in which the case would likely be heard, as specified by the question itself. A dispute about a workplace infraction would begin in the JP courts. For those who took a more activist approach by either calling on their connections to influence management or looking for a new job, trust in the JP courts matters. Having complete trust in these courts is positively associated with opting for courts; it is a disincentive to opting for more activist informal strategies. Trust is irrelevant as to the more passive route of simply tolerating the situation. As to the second hypothetical, I narrow the measure of trust to the courts of general jurisdiction where the challenge to the school director would be initiated. Here both informal options required gumption, albeit of different kinds. Although trust is a strong predictor of seeking out another school—again serving as a disincentive—it is irrelevant as to marshaling connections. The results suggest that trust can sometimes be a spur to using the courts; they are too uneven to support the sort of link between trust and behavior when it comes to courts that is often assumed. But they do remind us of the importance of refining the measure of trust.

Perhaps the most surprising finding in the INDEM analysis is the unimportance of bribery. Earlier I argued that the use of self-help remedies raised the specter of *blat* and/or corruption, particularly when it came to putting pressure on the director of the neighborhood school. I expected to find that those who were prepared to use connections were more tolerant of corruption. The INDEM survey did not include a question that raised this issue directly. But it did include several questions that asked respondents about their views on corruption in the courts. The question about whether they think the courts have a systematic bias toward the rich and powerful hints at the potential role of corruption. Respondents were asked a more pointed question, namely, to agree or disagree with the following statement: "Whoever pays more tends to prevail in our courts." With respect to each, initial analysis indicated that those who agreed were more likely to solve problems via connections than through the courts, but the statistical significance of this result dissipated as additional explanatory variables were added to the mix.[31] This suggests that views on corruption are, at best, weakly predictive of respondents' behavior.

ATTITUDES TOWARD LAW

In the preceding section of this chapter, the analysis of Russians' attitudes toward law suggests that those who are more law abiding are less likely to have used the courts. The INDEM data provide some support for this finding. Respondents were asked a series of questions about when it would be permissible to go around (*oboiti*) the written law. The reasons varied from a belief that the law is unfair or immoral to situations where everyone else seems to be ignoring the law. In an effort to tap into their level of legal nihilism, I created a scale that summed the number of times respondents endorsed violating the law. With respect to the second hypothetical, the chances of adhering to nihilism are significantly less for respondents who prefer informal methods over litigation. (See Table A.6.) Put differently, this group tends to be more law abiding, with those who would seek out another school being more resistant to legal nihilism than those who would

---

31. For this reason, it is not included in Table A.5 or A.6.

use their connections to remedy the problem. As to the first hypothetical, respondents' propensity for legal nihilism is relevant only for those whose reaction to the illegal reprimand is to use self-help to put pressure on management. (See Table A.5.) Mirroring the results for the school-based hypothetical, this group tended to be less nihilistic as compared with their colleagues who opted for court.

Respondents' views on the essential nature of law itself are not as determinative as I expected. They were asked to agree or disagree with the following statements:

(1) Every person has inalienable rights (*prava*) from birth that are more important than any statute (*zakon*).

(2) Any statute (*zakon*) or regulation (*normativnyi akt*) issued by the state is legal (*pravovoi*).[32]

These questions allow us to ascertain whether respondents' vision of law adheres more to *pravo* or *zakon*. The first statement divides the sample into those who regard human rights as inalienable (about 84 percent of the sample), a position that is consistent with a *pravo*-based view of law, and those who take the Sovietera position that such rights emanate from the state (about 16 percent of the sample), reflecting a *zakon*-based view of law. The second statement essentially asks whether *zakony* are always *pravovye*. In other words, respondents are asked to weigh in on whether it is possible for formal law to lack the fairness that characterizes *pravo*. About 73 percent of those who expressed an opinion agreed that statutes (*zakony*) are always legal (*pravovye*), putting them on the *zakon* side of the spectrum. The combination of the first and second statements allows us to distinguish between respondents who take a positivistic view of law as state generated, and those who seek a deeper meaning to law. The former group would disagree with the first statement and agree with the second statement. The results would be the opposite for the latter group.

Initial analysis suggested that respondents who shun the courts tend to embrace a more *pravo*-esque view of law. The strength of these results taper off when the responses to the other hypothetical are added into each regression. Nonetheless, some support remains. The first question dealing with support for human rights is a good but uneven predictor for those indicating a preference for informal over formal remedies. The strongest relationship emerges for those who said they would simply persevere in the same job in response to the illegal reprimand. The relationship is weaker for those who would seek out another job and weaker

---

32. The translation of *pravovoi* as "legal" fails to capture the nuanced meaning of the word. *Pravovoi* also integrates a core element of societal legitimacy, along the lines of Fuller's (1964) morality of law.

still for those who would call on connections to solve their dilemma. For all, the chances of endorsing the inalienability of human rights are substantially greater than for their court-prone counterparts. Turning to the second hypothetical, the group that would use their connections to persuade the school director to change her mind are more amenable to *pravo* than *zakon*. For them, the chances of disagreeing with the principle that all laws produced by the state are inherently legal are over 60 percent greater than for those who opted for court. Put more plainly, a distaste for a positivistic view of law is a strong predictor of a choice of self-help in the second hypothetical.

To restate this finding more simply, respondents who would go to court tend to hold a more rigid and positivistic view of law. As we will see in chapters 4 and 5, which explore the day-to-day reality of JP courts, they would find kindred spirits on the bench. Russian judges are sticklers about complying with the letter of the law. This follows from their training in the civil-law tradition, which emphasizes the centrality of written law. By contrast, those who opted for more informal problem-solving methods are more likely to be supportive of the inalienability of human rights and to believe that a written law (*zakon*) could be illegal (*nepravovoi*). Their approach to law leaves more room for individualized solutions to problems that may occasionally diverge from the prescriptions of written law.

Relationship between Hypothetical Responses and Actual Behavior regarding the Courts

The scenarios laid out in the INDEM questionnaire asked respondents to react to hypothetical situations. As I've already noted, many may never have confronted situations similar to those posed. Given that no one leads a completely charmed life, they have all surely had to deal with difficulties of some sort. As the hypotheticals suggest, lawsuits are just one option for dealing with problems. Reflecting the fact that turning to the courts is almost never the easy way out, only about 18 percent of the sample had taken some problem to court.[33]

The analysis reveals a remarkably different picture of those who actually brought lawsuits as opposed to those who said they would litigate in response to the hypothetical scenarios. This only further underscores the danger of assuming that Russians have a one-size-fits-all view when it comes to legal matters. When

---

33. I deliberately isolated those who initiated a claim, as opposed to those who had some sort of contact with the court. The latter is a larger group, making up about 35 percent of the sample. It includes not only those who brought lawsuits, but also the targets of lawsuits and those who served as witnesses or mere observers of court processes.

I explore what drives the voluntary use of the courts through logistic regression analysis, attitudes toward law and courts emerge as robust predictors, standing in contrast to the results for the hypothetical scenarios. (See Models 3 and 4 of Table A.7.) The most powerful factor is one that was not significant for the earlier analysis (and so was not included in Table A.5 or A.6). Respondents were asked how they were likely to respond to a violation of their rights, and were offered fifteen options. Those who indicate an openness to bringing a claim to court are almost six times more likely to have actually initiated a lawsuit. On the other hand, predictions of whether they would be willing to use the courts in the future—a factor that was consistently significant in the analysis of the hypothetical situations—is not helpful here.

Attitudes toward courts are relevant, but not entirely consistent. Trust matters, but as we saw for the analysis of the hypotheticals, only if measured in a meaningful way. When I include variables that assessed overall trust in the courts or limited it to the courts that the respondents were most likely to have used (the JP courts or the courts of general jurisdiction), trust seems unimportant. Only when I measure trust in a more individualistic manner does a relationship emerge. The survey divided the sample on the basis of trust in the courts. About 45 percent expressed trust, whereas almost 38 percent were less sanguine and the remaining 17 percent took no position. Respondents were then queried as to the basis for their opinions. I created dummy variables to capture those whose trust or distrust was grounded in personal experiences. Those whose views—whether positive or negative—were grounded in personal experience are significantly more likely to have initiated lawsuits. The effect is stronger for those who trust the courts. This group is more than twice as likely to have gone to court voluntarily. But any conclusion that good feelings about the courts lead to more use are quickly dispelled by the fact that those whose prior experiences have led them to distrust the courts are over 70 percent more likely to have initiated a lawsuit as compared with those whose distrust stems from institutional factors or rumors based on friends' experiences or media reports. Along similar lines, those who believe that the rich and influential receive better treatment in Russian courts are over 50 percent more likely to have gone to court than those who took a more sanguine view of the courts.

How can we make sense of this apparent cacophony? It makes sense only when we recognize that Russians use the courts when they believe they have no other choice (Hendley 2012c). Need rather than beliefs drives use. As a result, even when they are unconvinced of judges' evenhandedness, they will still bring their claims to the court. They do so with their eyes open to the realities of Russian courts, but still viewing the courts as a viable and worthwhile avenue to pursue.

This essential link between need and use is confirmed by the fact that resolving family disputes is the most commonly cited reason for using the courts. Such disputes, which include divorce, child support, and child custody, can only be definitively resolved in court. This also explains the robust results for marital status. Those who have gone through divorces are almost four times more likely to have initiated a lawsuit. The fact that divorces can, as a general rule, only be obtained through the courts might make this result seem a foregone conclusion. But that would assume that the respondent was always the instigator of the divorce. Logically this could not be the case. It may indicate that those who have survived a court process, even if it was not entirely satisfactory, are less reluctant than court neophytes to try their luck again.

Even more intriguing, their characterization of a problem as being appropriate for the courts or not tends to be fairly definitive, especially when they conclude that courts would not be helpful. When respondents were asked whether they had ever confronted a problem that could be resolved by a court, the very fact that only 28 percent responded in the affirmative suggests that they interpreted the question more literally than the text itself would seem to require.[34] Despite the wording of the question, which encouraged respondents to share any problems that could have been taken to court, regardless of whether they actually filed a lawsuit, the results suggest that respondents must have equated the possibility of being litigated with a requirement to resolve the problem through the courts. This explains why the absence of any problem that could be resolved in the courts turns out to be a perfect predictor of never having brought a claim to court. On the other hand, although the existence of such a problem drastically increases the likelihood of having gone to court—almost two-thirds of this group had brought a lawsuit as opposed to 18 percent for the sample as a whole—it did not ensure such an outcome.

If we expand the analysis to include those who have had any contact with the courts, the results are quite different. About 17 percent of those who claim never to have encountered a problem that could end up in court report having had some contact with the courts, presumably as a witness or defendant. The chances of contact with the court are also greater for those who acknowledge having had problems that could be solved in court (82 percent) than for the overall sample population (37 percent).

Attitudes toward law played out differently with regard to respondents' actual behavior as compared with their preferences for the hypothetical scenarios.

---

34. The text of the question: "Tell me, please, has a situation ever arisen in your life that could have been resolved in court? This situation could be connected with any sphere of your life. In this situation, you could have gone to court or could have opted not to go."

Legal nihilism, as measured by their receptivity to disregarding the law when convenient, proves to be a powerful driver of choices in the hypothetical settings, yet has no impact in predicting the likelihood of having filed a lawsuit.[35] On the other hand, respondents whose views of law are more grounded in *pravo* than *zakon* emerge as more likely litigators. Their skepticism as to whether it is possible to live in Russia without violating the law suggests that their *pravo*-centric views may reflect their aspirations rather than their reality. They are, nonetheless, intriguing, given the deep commitment to the written rules (*zakon*) reflected in the procedural rules and the day-to-day reality of Russian courts. As I document in chapters 4 and 5, Russian judges pay lip service to their dedication to fairness and justice, but in practice they assume that following the written law is the only path to achieving these goals. This sort of positivism can sometimes turn into a fetish for documentary evidence in which justice is sacrificed.

Two demographic factors—gender and employment—that were marginal in the explanation of respondents' choices in the hypothetical situations are more central when it comes to their actual behavior. (See Table A.7.) Women were almost 50 percent more likely to have initiated a claim in the courts than were men. This finding is consistent with my earlier work (as well as with the comparative literature more generally), where Russian women consistently emerged as more willing to turn to the courts (Hendley 2012c). Having a job was also a robust predictor. The chances of having initiated a lawsuit are 30 percent greater for those who have a job than for those who did not (this group included the perennially unemployed as well as pensioners and women on maternity leave). This strong association between being employed and going to court was somewhat unexpected. For those uninitiated in the Russian reality, having a job might seem essential because it would provide the resources necessary to pursue a claim. But the formal costs associated with litigating in Russia are surprisingly low. Russians tend to be more concerned about the time and emotional energy required. As we will see from the conversations in the focus groups described in chapters 2 and 3, many Russians fret over the need to collect the documents necessary to prove their claims, fearing that it will lead to long lines and unfeeling bureaucrats. The more informal resources needed to persevere would be in shorter supply for those holding down a full-time job. Moreover, as compared with the Soviet past, jobs have become scarcer and supervisors less sympathetic to workers taking time from their duties to chase down key documents or attend judicial hearings.

Age is a significant factor for the INDEM respondents. As with the RLMS-HSE respondents, the propensity to go to court is curvilinear, with the oldest and

---

35. For this reason, it was not included in Table A.7.

youngest being the most open to litigation. (See Model 1 of Table A.7.) When I break the sample into the now-familiar generational cohorts, older Russians emerge as most likely to turn to the courts. (See Models 2 and 4 of Table A.7.) By using those who came of age under Yeltsin—born between 1977 and 1987—as the reference group, we see that those in older generations are two to three times more likely to have brought a lawsuit as compared with their children and grand-children. The youngest generational cohort (born after 1988) is the least likely to have initiated a claim in the courts. Given the strong link between need and use, this result might be telling us that younger Russians have fewer problems. Or perhaps it reveals that younger Russians are less likely to view their problems as susceptible to resolution through the courts. A more prosaic explanation might be that Russians are now waiting until they are older to get married, which means that the inevitable divorces (which are often the entryway to the courts) come later as well.

Underscoring these differences between the factors that explain, on the one hand, the decision to bring an actual lawsuit and, on the other hand, the prefer-ence for litigation in response to the hypothetical scenarios, is the fact that those preferences have absolutely no explanatory power when it comes to initiating a lawsuit. Likewise, respondents' prior litigation experience was powerless in explaining their choices in the two scenarios. The reactions of the respondents provide a window into a usually impenetrable sector of the decision-making process. Their greater willingness to litigate, as reflected in the responses to the hypothetical situations, reveals a previously unknown amenability to courts that runs counter to the well-accepted assumption that Russians are hostile to for-mal institutions that runs through much of the social science literature (Hale 2015; Ledeneva 2013; Hedlund 2005). The disconnect between their responses to the hypotheticals and their actual behavior provides compelling evidence of the complexity of their thinking as to law and legal institutions. It leaves little doubt as to the presence of multiple narratives about law.

Summing Up

The goal of this chapter was to empirically examine the widely held view that law is irrelevant to Russians. The picture that emerges is strikingly different from the typical vision of law as marginal to the lives of ordinary Russians. The analysis of the RLMS-HSE data points to legal nihilism being on a downward trend. Today, for an increasing percentage of Russians, law matters.

The INDEM data confirms that Russians' confidence in law and legal insti-tutions is situational. Few are prepared to take every problem to court, but a significant number were willing to contemplate mobilizing the law to serve their interests in either the hypothetical scenarios or had used courts to solve real-life dilemmas. The subsequent chapters flesh out this reality, showing that their receptivity to using the law depends on the stakes as well as their sense of the odds of victory. Such calculations are hardly unique to Russians; they are commonplace around the world. Thus, belying the stereotype of Russians as exceptional in their contempt for law and the legal system, my analysis reveals Russians to be quite typical.

Exploring when and to whom law matters confirmed several of my starting hypotheses, but also revealed several surprises. Economic stability is a strong predictor of confidence in law. Support for the institutional infrastructure and principles underlying democracy is associated with respect for law. And an openness to trusting others tends to spill over onto trust in the legal arena. These trends are on clear display in the analysis of the change in attitudes between the 2006 and 2012 rounds of the RLMS-HSE. Respondents blessed by good fortune in their lives are more likely to have reoriented their thinking about law and courts. And vice versa.

On the other hand, the analysis exposed the negative relationship between court use and esteem for law. Rather than such experience opening the eyes of respondents to the difficulties of applying the law and building respect for law, litigation veterans from the RLMS-HSE sample seem to emerge embittered and more amenable to legal nihilism. Along similar lines, the INDEM respondents who chose litigation as their preferred method for resolving the hypothetical problems tended to be more nihilistic than those who opted for informal solutions. The fact that the court-bound INDEM respondents are more receptive to a view of law consistent with *zakon* rather than with *pravo* suggests that they expect the written law to hold the answers to their problems. If the written law disappoints them, they may write it off by turning to legal nihilism.

Trust in courts turns out to be mercurial when it comes to understanding legal attitudes and behavior. Although it proved to be a good predictor of respect for law, its role in explaining the willingness to mobilize law was more uneven. In the analysis of the INDEM data, a general indicator of trust in courts was insignificant for both hypothetical and actual use. As to the hypotheticals, it was only when respondents shared their views on the specific courts in which the case would be heard that trust emerged as a strong predictor of use. Even more telling are the results for actual use. When the view stems from personal experience—regardless of whether it reflects trust or distrust—it is a robust predictor of having filed a lawsuit.

The difference between generational cohorts in legal attitudes and behavior was unexpected. At the outset, I had assumed that the oldest cohort, who were born before 1940 and lived through the egregious abuses of the legal system under Stalin, would be the least receptive to law. Yet the RLMS-HSE data told a remarkably different story. This Stalin generation turned out to be the most open-minded as to the potential of law. The fact that the youngest cohort—the Putin generation born after 1988—is less nihilistic than their parents provides some hope for the future. Those generations in the middle—those born between 1941 and 1987—were the most devastated by the chaos of the 1990s. The inability to rely on law to protect them from arbitrary layoffs and other dislocations seems to have left them scarred. Whether this effect will diminish over time remains to be seen. The comparison of the 2006 and 2012 rounds of the RLMS-HSE provides some limited basis for optimism.

The trends as to the actual use of courts, as revealed by the INDEM data, exhibit the same trend. The Stalin generation emerges as the most likely to have gone to court, with each successively younger generation being increasingly less likely to have filed a lawsuit. Although it is tempting to imagine a link between respect for law and openness to the courts, the analysis does not support this. Instead, the driving force behind most litigation is need. Respect for law and/or trust in the courts may encourage litigation but is not necessary.

DEALING WITH DAMAGE FROM HOME WATER LEAKS

Life in post-Soviet Russia has been a bit of a roller coaster for ordinary citizens. The stability and stagnation (*zastoi*) of the Brezhnev era gave way to a seemingly never-ending series of crises that saw jobs and savings dissipate for many. Though studies of the impact of this pervasive instability have proliferated (Barnes 2006; Ledeneva 2006; Politkovskaya 2004), the question of how it has affected relations among Russians in their everyday lives has been less explored (Shevchenko 2009). In this chapter, I pursue this question by examining how Russians interact with those who are physically closest to them, namely, those who live in the same apartment building and who share the same entryway (*pod"ezd*).[1] Reasoning that the essence of relationships emerge through conflict, I focus on the problem-solving strategies employed when water leaks from one person's apartment into a neighbor's apartment. Such water leaks are remarkably commonplace in Russia. Listening to Russians in focus groups and follow-up interviews revealed three basic strategies: avoidance, self-help, and third-party intervention. Many employed a combination of strategies, especially those who resorted to third parties for assistance.

At first glance, law would seem to have little to do with how problems among neighbors are resolved in Russia. Russians are slow to invoke formal law. Litigation or even threats of litigation are the exception, not the rule. Some argue

---

1. Regardless of their size, Russian apartment buildings do not have a single entrance and long corridors as in the United States. Instead, each stairwell has its own entrance (*pod"ezd*), thereby creating a relatively small community of people who have to interact on a variety of household issues.

that this reticence is due to fears of corruption within the courts (Ledeneva 2008). Though Russians clearly recognize the inherently dualistic nature of the Russian legal system, my research suggests that, like potential litigants elsewhere, Russians who contemplate litigation with others like them are more troubled by the time, expense, and emotional energy required for litigation than by a fear of corrupt or politicized justice (Hendley 2010). Black's (1984, 3) observation, "the more we study law . . . , the more we realize how little people actually use it to handle their conflicts," reminds us that a distaste for resorting to formal law is not unique to Russians. Writing about personal-injury claims between residents in a small Midwestern town in the United States, Engel argued, "there are times when the invocation of formal law is viewed as an *anti*-social act and as a contravention of established cultural norms" (1984, 551–552). As this suggests, what is usually thought of as "law," namely, the statutes and regulations that emanate from the state, is only one source of legal consciousness. Unwritten norms or customs can be equally important, especially in a country like Russia where the legitimacy of the formal legal system has long been questionable.[2]

Focusing on this small corner of everyday life and practice provides insight into Russians' demand for law. One of the constant refrains in the focus groups and the interviews was the expectation that, when dealing with neighbors, one would conduct oneself in a civilized manner. Different phrases were used in Russian to convey this, such as *po-chelovecheski* (civilized) or *po-sosedski* (neighborly) or *poriadochnyi* (upstanding).[3] Although each has a slightly different meaning, they were used interchangeably by my respondents. At their essence, they share a commitment to fairness. This appears to contradict the common wisdom that Russians are legal nihilists. But perhaps the two images can be reconciled. Uncovering the informal norms of the *pod"ezd* provides a window into Russians' everyday experience; it represents an effort to understand Russians' internal metric of what is right and wrong, which is a critical element of legal consciousness (Ewick and Silbey 1998). It also reveals the messiness of their thinking, thereby confirming the existence of multiple narratives of law.

---

2. Gaps between unwritten customs and written rules exist everywhere. "The distinction of Soviet-type systems, perhaps, was that the former were followed, in fact, with fewer exemptions than were formal rules" (Ledeneva 1998, 160).

3. Many of the Russian phrases that I explore in this chapter are open to multiple translations, depending on the context. My rendering of them reflects their meaning in the context of the specific conversations.

The Role of Law in Problem Solving among Neighbors

U.S. Research

Interactions between neighbors has proven revelatory of deeper legal consciousness in a number of U.S.-based studies (Merry 1990; Yngvesson 1994; Ewick and Silbey 1998; Engel 1994). Building on the well-accepted precept that the propensity to litigate is inversely correlated to relational distance (Engel 1994; Black 1984), these studies have generally shown that neighbors who have a friendship or other valued relationship are unlikely to appeal to third parties (including the courts) for assistance. Merry's (1990, 39) study of an urban New England neighborhood showed that those whose problems degenerated into fights tended to involve "neighbors who knew each other by name and were superficially sociable, but rarely had a deep and personal friendship or a great deal of interest in reconciliation or restoration of a preexisting relationship." As she compares this urban neighborhood with a more affluent suburb, the importance of physical space becomes apparent. Unlike suburbanites, whose lawns and fences allow them to avoid troublesome neighbors,[4] urban apartment dwellers have more difficulty hiding from such neighbors. The economic realities of life for these two groups also played a role in shaping behavior. Her suburban respondents were more likely to have the necessary financial flexibility to move away if their problems with their neighbors grew unbearable. This was not a luxury shared by many of her urban respondents (Merry 1990, 39). Her work highlights how the inability to "exit" can exacerbate problems (Hirschman 1970). When unable to exit, her respondents exercised "voice" vociferously, both in their interpersonal relations and by dragging their neighbors through the courts.[5] Hirschman's cautionary note that "the *effectiveness* of the voice mechanism is strengthened by the possibility of exit" provides some insight into the frustration of Merry's subjects (ibid., 83).

Implicit in Merry's analysis is a familiar assumption that litigation constitutes a death knell for any relationship. Yngvesson disagrees. Her work shows that litigation can be used strategically by family members or neighbors to reframe their relationships. In her words: "In contrast to Black's well-known hypothesis, law is not only 'active' among intimates but shapes the terms in which intimate relations are

---

4. Baumgartner's ethnography of an affluent New York suburb confirms the tendency of suburbanites to shy away from direct confrontations with neighbors. Her work shows that the spaciousness of the houses facilitates avoidance for family problems as well. She contends that "it is even possible to speak of the suburb as a culture of avoidance" (1988, 11).

5. A study of U.S. college roommates showed that when exit is possible at a fixed point in the future, the likelihood of litigation dissipated (Emerson 2008).

played out. Beyond this, intimates repeatedly use law to continue or realign their relationship" (Yngvesson 1985, 641). She challenges researchers to extend their time frame for studying relationships, arguing that the twists and turns of relationships cannot be fully appreciated in studies that limit themselves to a short period of time. Her research focusing on a lower-class Massachusetts neighborhood is illustrative. She documents the role of the courts in molding relations among families and neighbors. Drawing on conflicts between neighbors, she shows how criminalizing their complaints about one another and bringing in the courts served to reshape the rights of the parties to engage in various activities. The result was not always a fissure between the parties. Sometimes their experiences with the legal system led to new alliances among neighbors. Yngvesson's findings were analogous with respect to problems among family members.[6] In her work, the courts are not merely a forum for dispute resolution, but become an active participant through their policies on what sorts of complaints to hear (ibid.; Yngvesson 1994).

Engel's study of a Midwestern community's reaction to litigation reminds us of the importance of context. His respondents resented those who pursued personal-injury claims, viewing them as taking advantage of an unfortunate situation. The insular nature of the community, that is, the fact that the parties to any lawsuit were likely to know one another and to have to interact in the future, tended to dampen litigation. Indeed, those who brought personal-injury claims were more likely to be outsiders. By contrast, far fewer reservations were voiced about contractual claims. Such claims were brought routinely by entrenched businesses against longtime residents. Engel (1984, 576) explains:

> The philosophy of individualism worked itself out quite differently in the areas of tort and contract. If personal injuries evoked values emphasizing self-sufficiency, contractual breaches evoked values emphasizing rights and remedies. Duties generated by contractual agreement were seen as sacrosanct and vital to the maintenance of the social order. Duties generated by socially imposed obligations to guard against injuring other people were seen as intrusions on existing relationships, as pretexts for forced exchanges, as inappropriate attempts to redistribute wealth, and as limitations on individual freedom.

This research clarifies that the extent to which the underlying relationship will be affected by litigation depends in part on the nature of the claim and how it is understood within the broader community.

---

6. Yngvesson (1985) found that domestic-abuse complaints were not brought with the goal of terminating spousal relationships, but rather to reset the terms of these relationships.

Neighbors and Their Problems in Russia

My work integrates the Russian experience into the literature on how neighbors resolve problems. My respondents consistently spoke of their neighborhood in terms
of their *pod"ezd* rather than the building or the region in which they lived. Leaks of
water from one apartment to another through the ceiling constitute a good prism
through which to explore the norms governing neighbors' relations in Russia and
how they play out through problem-solving strategies.[7] The aging nature of the
housing infrastructure makes them a relatively frequent occurrence (Prevost and
Dushkina 1999, 52, 56). Even in buildings where the plumbing is in good repair, the
local authorities' practice of cutting off the water supply periodically to buildings
and even to entire municipal sectors (Osadchuk 2008), both for planned maintenance and for unexpected problems, provides fertile ground for accidents. Not
infrequently, a resident will turn on the taps to no avail and will leave them open
on the off chance that the water will be turned back on. Forgetting they have done
so, they leave to run errands or for a business trip, only to find a sodden disaster in
their apartment and annoyed neighbors upon their return. Such carelessness can
also occur when the water supply has not been compromised.

The lack of any state-mandated procedure for resolving problems that arise
from ceiling leaks adds to its appeal as a focus for research. In contrast to disputes
between neighbors over property claims, which require the imprimatur of the
court in Russia, neighbors have complete freedom in deciding how to proceed
after a ceiling leak. Neighbors can resolve the problem on their own or can call
on the state for assistance. Thus, in contrast to the neighborhood-based studies of
Merry, Engel, and Yngvesson, which are focused on explaining litigation behavior,
I am more interested in understanding how Russian neighbors resolve problems.
Emerson's (2008) study of how college roommates in the United States respond to
problems, with its emphasis on informal mechanisms of social control, is helpful.
Like Emerson's college students, I found that my respondents preferred to resolve
their problems with neighbors without outside interference. Understandably,
given their extraordinarily close quarters, his undergraduates placed a greater premium on modifying behavior than did the Russian apartment dwellers I studied.

Though the ceiling leaks that plague Russians are less of an issue in the U.S.
context, where problems tend to center on noise,[8] dogs, children, and parking

---

7. In his monograph on Soviet housing, Harris (2013, 204) uses a water leak as a prototypical
example a problem between neighbors. A recent book on dealing with annoying neighbors devotes
an entire chapter to roof leaks (Puzakova, Zakharova, and Sycheva 2012) and a "how to" book on
housing disputes provides examples from court practice (Astakhov 2012).

8. Harris (2006, 179–184) reports that complaints about noise from neighbors became common
as Russians moved into private apartments in the 1960s.

spaces, the essence is the same. In both settings, neighbors have to figure out how to live in close proximity during and after conflicts. Like the New Englanders Merry and Yngvesson studied, Russians' living quarters tend to be quite cramped.[9] In addition, like these New Englanders, few Russians are able to move. During the Soviet period, most housing was allocated through the state or its proxies (Alexeev 1988). A shortage of urban housing relegated many families to shared or communal apartments (Harris 2013; Zavisca 2012; Boym 1995).[10] Getting a different apartment was a tortuous process, requiring either boundless patience (if you were awarded an apartment after waiting for years) or extraordinary craftiness (if you found a way to jump the queue or managed to arrange an exchange of apartments).[11] The privatization of housing in the 1990s gave rise to a real estate market in Russia for the first time in decades (Attwood 2012; Starodubrovskaya 2001).[12] Only a minority of Russians have been able to take advantage of this market. Participating requires a financial wherewithal that has eluded the average Russian (Attwood 2012; Zavisca 2012), as is documented by a national survey conducted in 2007 by the Foundation for Public Opinion in which 57 percent of respondents had been living in the same place for at least sixteen years. Indeed, more than a quarter of those surveyed had lived in the same place for their entire lives (Vasil'eva 2007). Thus, notwithstanding the existence of a housing market, most Russians are not terribly mobile.[13] This means that the population within *pod"ezdy* is not as stable as during the Soviet era. Whether these new residents buy into the existing behavioral norms of the *pod"ezd* or whether the existing residents treat their new neighbors differently remains to be seen.

Integrating my findings into the existing literature requires a brief reflection on the nature of the relationship among neighbors in Russia. In some ways,

---

9. According to Goskomstat data, the allocation of living space per person in Russia in 2007 was 21.5 square meters (231.42 square feet). This represents a substantial increase over the 16.5 square meters (177.6 square feet) allocated per person in 1991 when the Soviet Union collapsed (*Sem'ia* 2008, table 3.38; *Sem'ia* 1996, table VII-2). See Zavisca (2012, 89) for trends over time.

10. Gerasimova (2002, 208) reports that, in 1951, an average of 3.3 families lived in every Leningrad apartment.

11. For an account of the machinations, both familial and political, required to organize a housing exchange in the Soviet period, see Harris (2005); Trifonov (2002, 17–70); Voinovich (1977). On the politics of the waiting lists, see Harris (2013). On average, families spent about eight years waiting (Tumanov 2013, 26). Those who were too aggressive about trying to better their living conditions risked attracting the attention of the authorities and being dragged into court (Richards 1991, 194).

12. The housing privatization gave Russians a one-time right to assert ownership over their dwellings. Although about a third of the population benefitted (Yemtsov 2008, 323), as Zavisca (2008, 371) argues, it "exacerbated Soviet-era housing inequalities." Those who, thanks to their connections, had won the Soviet housing lottery were able to lock in these advantages (Attwood 2012).

13. The World Bank estimated Russia's residential mobility rate at 2 percent in 2005 (Yemtsov 2008, 323).

determining the place of the typical relationship with neighbors on the spectrum from stranger to acquaintance to friend is more important in Russia than in the United States (where the bulk of these studies are based). Most Americans could distinguish between their friends and acquaintances if pressed, but the dividing line would be somewhat murky. For Russians, the difference between an acquaintance (*priiatel* or *znakomyi*) and a friend (*drug*) is profound.[14] With friends, Russians reveal their "private" self, opening up an almost bottomless trust that stands in contrast to the guardedness exhibited with acquaintances (Shlapentokh 1989, 174–176). In the worst days of the Stalinist terror, people were understandably wary of entering into friendships and tended to show only their "public" selves by "speaking Bolshevik" (Kotkin 1995, 220). The memoirs of the period provide untold examples of neighbors betraying neighbors, often with an eye to expanding their living space (Figes 2007). In the post-Stalin era, people let down their guard a bit, but the danger that putative friends would betray your confidences to the state persisted (Harris 2013). Even so, friendship circles expanded and brought an expectation that your life would be intertwined with that of your friends (Fürst 2006). Few considered their neighbors to be friends.[15] Rather, friends tended to be drawn from among one's schoolmates and relatives (Trifonov 1983, 83; Raleigh 2006, 28, 225; Shlapentokh 1989, 178–180). In the post-Soviet era, as Russians have had to spend more time at work, the mark of friendship has become a willingness to devote time to one another and to share personal problems. A 2006 public opinion survey indicates that few Russians have brought their neighbors within this charmed circle of trust. When asked whether they share their problems with their neighbors, two-thirds of urban residents said they preferred not to. Rural residents were a bit more open to their neighbors; slightly less than half indicated they would do so (Shmerpina 2006b).[16] At the same time, most were acquainted with their neighbors and reported relatively few contentious incidents. All in all, this suggests that relations among neighbors in Russia typically fall into the "acquaintance" category. Whether this is due to the social alienation that is endemic to postindustrial societies or whether it is a remnant of the Soviet predilection for secrecy deserves further investigation.

---

14. The memoirs of foreigners who have spent time in Russia often comment on this distinction (Smith 1976, 137–142). Likewise, in rendering relationships in Soviet-era literary fiction, a distinction is typically drawn between friends and acquaintances (Trifonov 1983).

15. One of Smith's (1976, 142) respondents told him, "You know, we have lived next door to another couple all our lives practically. I have known the wife since childhood and yet I have never told her the honest truth. We have always been friendly. We have known them well. They have come to our apartment and we have been to theirs. But they are different people from us. We could sense that."

16. These findings were echoed in several interviews. In Shumerlia, Simon said, "in the countryside it is easier to rub shoulders with your neighbors. In the city, neighbors don't know each other."

Conceptual Framework for the Evolution of Disputes

When problems arose with their neighbors, including ceiling leaks, my respondents generally felt an obligation to behave *po-chelovecheski*. Exactly what this meant in practice varied, depending not only on the underlying relationship with the neighbor in question and the willingness to risk undermining it, but also on factors such as circumstances surrounding the incident, the damage caused, the familiarity of those victimized with their options (including their prior experience with the formal legal system), and the personalities of key players.

As I worked through the many examples of ceiling leaks provided by my respondents, three overarching categories emerged.[17] Some adopted an *avoidance* strategy, preferring to refrain from, or limit, any direct confrontation, even if this meant that they had to absorb the cost of damages themselves. Though the socio-legal literature tends to equate avoidance with conciliatory motives (Felstiner 1975, 695–698), my respondents' use of an avoidance strategy was laced with considerable resentment. Their anger over the denouement of their ceiling leaks was more palpable than those who had found themselves in extended litigation. A second strategy employed by my respondents was *self-help*. Like avoidance, self-help eschews the state. But in contrast to avoidance, self-help assumes the active involvement of the two parties to the ceiling leak in seeking a resolution (Emerson 2008). The bilateral negotiations can give rise to a variety of outcomes, ranging from simple forgiveness to having the party who caused the leak undertake the repairs personally or pay others to make the necessary repairs. But they tend to leave both sides relatively satisfied. The third strategy in evidence among my respondents was *third-party intervention*. As to ceiling leaks, the key third parties are the housing authorities[18] and the courts.[19] I use the word

---

17. Within the "pyramid of disputing" framework (see chapter 3), almost all of those flooded would be claiming (Felstiner, Abel, and Sarat 1980–81). A handful of the "avoiders" made no claim on their neighbors, but these were the exceptions. For an application of this framework to disputes arising from home repair projects in Moscow and Saratov, see Hendley (2010).

18. These authorities go by a number of different names depending on the ownership structure of the building. They are most commonly referred to as the *ZhKU* (*Zhilishchno-Kommunal'nye Uslugi* or Housing-Communal Services). They are a vestige of the Soviet past when almost all housing was owned by the state. Although much of the Russian housing stock has now been privatized, these *ZhKU* persist. Whether they act in the name of the state depends on whether the building has been privatized. They are expected to maintain the buildings and to ensure a steady supply of energy and water. They are often viewed as remote and uninterested in residents' problems.

19. Home insurance is relatively rare in Russia. A 2006 survey revealed that only 13 percent of the respondents had opted for homeowners insurance (Shmerpina 2006a). It is not regarded as essential. Among the respondents of the RLMS-HSE, about 7 percent reported having home insurance. By 2012, this percentage had dipped to below 5 percent.

"intervention" rather than "enforcement" deliberately because often the involvement of the third party was simply to provide a neutral assessment of damages that would allow the parties to resolve the problem themselves. But the category does encompass litigation, which brings with it the power of the state to enforce the court's decision. It is tempting to impute a linear directionality to these three categories. Though it is possible that as one's frustration grows, avoidance will lead to self-help, which, in turn, will lead to third-party intervention, there is no inexorable logic to the process (Emerson 2008). As will become apparent, many respondents' needs were satisfied by a single strategy.

Before delving into a more detailed discussion of these three strategies and the motivation for employing them, I provide some background on the research methodology and the respondents. I then lay out the informal norms that underlie the respondents' behavior, that is, what it means to behave *po-chelovecheski*. The discussion of the three strategies is followed by a reflection on what this case study of ceiling leaks reveals about contemporary Russian legal consciousness.

Methodology

In chapter 1, I analyzed the available survey data on legal consciousness. Although surveys provide a snapshot of societal attitudes and behavior, they are less capable of explaining the evolution of respondents' thinking. In order to get a deeper sense of Russian legal consciousness, I wanted to listen to how they talk about law when able to express themselves more freely than in closed-end survey questions. More important, I wanted to learn more about their problem-solving strategies and the extent to which they see law as relevant. To that end, I convened a series of twenty-nine focus groups during the summers of 2007 (Moscow and Saratov) and 2008 (Tomsk, Shumerlia, and Kushchevskaia). The selection of these locations for the research was designed to provide a contrast, as Table 2.1 documents. Each focus group included six to twelve individuals.[20] I worked with Polina Kozyreva and Mikhail Kosolapov of the Institute of Sociology in Moscow, which is part of the Russian Academy of Sciences, on the logistical side of the project. Since 1992, they have coordinated the RLMS-HSE (discussed in chapter 1). This work has given them a strong network of social scientists throughout

---

20. To accommodate the work schedules of the participants, the discussions took place on weekday evenings and weekends and lasted about two hours. They were recorded and were moderated by Elena K. Zobina, a research fellow at the Institute of Sociology, who is experienced in leading focus groups.

TABLE 2.1 Background information on focus group sites as of the end of 2007[1]

	POPULATION	AVERAGE MONTHLY WAGE[2]	UNEMPLOYMENT RATE	AVERAGE ANNUAL DIRECT FOREIGN INVESTMENT: 2005–7[3]	AVERAGE SQUARE METERS / SQUARE FEET AVAILABLE PER PERSON	POPULATION DENSITY (PEOPLE PER SQUARE KILOMETER / PER SQUARE MILE)
Moscow	10,470,300	23,623 rubles	0.8%	$7.4 billion	19.9 / 214.2	9,597 / 24,855
Saratov	836,100	10,601 rubles	1.17%		23.9 / 257.26	2,090 / 5,413
(Saratov oblast)	(2,583,800)	(9,103 rubles)	(8%)	($25 million)	(23.7 / 255.1)	(25.5 / 66)
Tomsk	496,500	16,091 rubles	0.66%		19.6 / 210.97	1,736 / 670
(Tomsk oblast)	(1,035,000)	(14,429 rubles)	(6.9%)	($219 million)	(20.3 / 218.51)	(3.3 / 8.5)
Shumerlia	34,100					
(Republic of Chuvashia)	(1,282,600)	(8,703 rubles)	(6.5%)	($30 million)	(21.5 / 231.42)	(69.6 / 180)
Kushchevskaia	28,362[4]					
(Krasnodarskii krai)	(5,121,800)	(10,260 rubles)	(8.8%)	($251 million)	(21.4 / 230.35)	(67.9 / 176)

Sources: Sem'ia (2008); *Regiony* (2008a); *Regiony* (2008b); *Regiony* (2008c).

[1] Data are generally available for the regional subunits of Russia. These have various names, e.g., oblast, republic, or krai, but are all equal members of the Russian Federation. Where possible, I have provided data for both the city and the surrounding region. Saratov and Tomsk are the capitals of their respective regions and therefore more information was available.

[2] At the end of 2007, the exchange rate was 24.55 rubles to the U.S. dollar.

[3] Because the amounts of investment can fluctuate wildly from year to year, I have taken the average of three years to provide a more accurate picture.

[4] The population data for Kushchevskaia is as of 2010 (Chislennost 2010).

Russia. We worked with their colleagues in each of the focus group sites to recruit participants.

In addition, I carried out follow-up interviews with seventy-nine of the focus group participants with the goal of probing more deeply into their attitudes toward law and their motivations for using or avoiding the legal system. The interviews took place within days of the original focus group meetings. The conversations ranged from one to two hours and were recorded. It was during these interviews that I was able to pursue the theme of dealing with ceiling leaks more systematically.

The twenty-nine focus groups and seventy-nine interviews serve as the source material for this chapter and the chapter that follows. (See Appendix B for background information on the respondents referenced in these chapters.) In recruiting the participants for both the focus groups and the interviews, the goal was to include a diverse set of Russians. Participants were given modest honoraria to compensate them for their time. We sought variation in age, gender, educational background, and work experience. Half of the focus groups included individuals who had recently completed home repair projects; the other half included those who had experience with personal injuries. This chapter draws on the discussion in the home repair focus groups; the next chapter is based on the personal injury focus groups.

The combination of focus groups and interviews permitted my respondents to speak at length on a variety of law-related topics (Morgan and Krueger 1993). Though these qualitative methods sacrifice the breadth of topics that a survey can cover, they allow for a depth that is not possible in a survey. More to the point, they facilitate greater spontaneity and flexibility in that the questioner can pursue topics that the respondent raises but were initially unanticipated by the questioner. Ceiling leaks was precisely such a topic. When it came up during the first round of focus groups and interviews in Moscow, I realized that it had the potential to elucidate fundamental norms of neighborhood relations, and so I raised it with subsequent respondents.

Dealing with Ceiling Leaks

Over the course of the interviews and focus groups, I gathered details of seventy cases of ceiling leaks in which neighbors were seen as culpable, spread across the five locations.[21] Of these, fifty-seven were actual events, of which forty-six

---

21. Of the seventy incidents, fourteen took place in Moscow, eighteen in Saratov, ten in Shumerlia, twenty-four in Tomsk, and four in Kushchevskaia.

were reports of events in which the respondent had been involved, either as the perpetrator of the leak (thirteen or 28 percent) or as the victim (thirty-three or 72 percent).[22] The remaining eleven events had happened to a close friend or relative of the respondent. Among the respondents who had had no personal or secondhand experience as victims of ceiling leaks, thirteen talked about what they would do if water leaked into their apartments from their upstairs neighbors.

Uncovering the Informal Norms That Govern Behavior

The discussions with the thirteen respondents who had had no direct experience of flooding, but who were willing to talk about hypothetical situations, provided the purest evidence of the informal norms among neighbors. When talking about how they would have behaved, the respondents had no need to defend their actual behavior. They were, instead, free to expound on the expectations that neighbors had for one another. The consistency of their responses lends credence to the norm's validity as a societal benchmark.

Boris, a security guard from Saratov, captured the sense of the group well, saying: "What should you do? Simply approach [the other person] in a neighborly fashion (*po-sosedski*) and talk about what happened." Everyone agreed that talking to one's upstairs neighbor to find out what happened was the appropriate first step. If it turned out that the neighbor was at fault, the consensus was that the neighbor ought to take responsibility. More specifically, as Rimma, a Tomsk factory worker who, like Boris, lived with her parents on the top floor of her building and so could not be a victim of this sort of leak, put it, "if I were flooded, I would say, excuse me, but you need to pay for the repairs." This shows that the norm of conciliation is laced with a strong dose of personal responsibility. At the same time, all saw the pursuit of elderly, poor, or incompetent neighbors as wrong. Some characterized such efforts as pointless owing to their lack of resources; others felt doing so would be morally wrong. No one was eager to come to blows with the *babushki* (older women)[23] in their buildings.

Emerging from these conversations centering on hypothetical ceiling leaks was an overwhelming preference for the self-help strategy. Irrespective of where they were from, the majority of respondents believed that any problem arising from a ceiling leak could be settled between neighbors without the need to look

---

22. When conveying the percentage of respondents who fit into various categories throughout the paper, the intent is to provide information about my sample, not to imply that these percentages are representative of the Russian population.

23. The literal translation of *babushka* is grandmother. The word is often used to refer to older women more generally. That is how I am using it.

outside the *pod"ezd* for help. Driving their optimism was their characterization of relations among the neighbors in their *pod"ezd* as generally friendly (*druzhnoe*). Most believed that these preexisting good relations would facilitate quick and easy resolutions. As Angelina, a hospital attendant from Shumerlia, told me, "I think it is possible to resolve things *po-chelovecheski*. Of course, this depends on what sort of neighbors you have. In our building, for example, the neighbors are friendly and so everything would be handled quietly and peacefully."

But even optimists like Angelina were willing to concede that there might be a few bad apples in any building. If a neighbor who was to blame for a ceiling leak refused to step up, she was prepared to take the matter to the *ZhKU* to establish fault definitively. But she, like the others who were open to bringing in the housing authorities, drew the line at going to court. If the determination of the housing authority failed to spur the neighbor into action, then she would not press her case further. Marina, a Moscow economist, spoke for many when she characterized suing a neighbor as "unacceptable" (*nepriniato*). Among the thirteen respondents who shared their views on hypothetical ceiling leaks, only one was open to litigation in the face of a recalcitrant neighbor. Viktor, a Saratov doctor, was resolute that going to court was "obligatory" if the neighbor refused to pay. He told me that this was a question "not of money, but of principle," but said that he would drop the claim if he learned that the neighbor was penniless.

Thanks to the respondents' reflections on how they would respond to a ceiling leak, the contours of what it means to behave *po-chelovecheski* came into focus. In such circumstances, the victim ought to approach the apparent culprit to find out what happened. Ideally, the two neighbors ought to be able to work out the problem on their own. If that proves impossible, then turning to the housing authority for help in establishing what really happened is acceptable, but going to court is not. The expectation that neighbors ought to compensate one another when damages result from a ceiling leak is tempered by a distaste for pressing neighbors who are down on their luck. The dedication to fairness is perhaps grounded in the recognition that a person who is the victim of a ceiling leak could easily be a perpetrator at some point in the future.

Avoidance

Embracing this norm sometimes led the respondents to employ an avoidance strategy. Felstiner (1975, 695) elaborates on its conceptual underpinnings:

> The notion of avoidance is that a party may change his behavior on account of the dispute in such a way that his relationship with the other

disputant is, at least temporarily, shrunk or terminated. The dispute, although not settled, is thus no longer a matter which the disputant believes he ought to do something about.

At its heart, avoidance is a nonoutcome. The victim takes no overt action. This makes it difficult to study. Much of the scholarship on avoidance is theoretical (Sandefur 2007). Emerson's (2008) research into problem solving between college roommates in the United States is an exception.[24] He shows that when the relationship is ongoing and immediate exit is not feasible, limiting contact with the other person can make life more tolerable. Though Emerson's respondents had the opportunity to shed their roommates at the end of the academic year, my respondents, like most Russians, were stuck in their apartments for the foreseeable future owing to financial considerations. My methodological approach of focus groups and in-depth interviews allowed me to probe not only into why Russians took action but also why they did nothing. For some, avoidance became a second-best alternative to exit.

The costs associated with avoidance vary depending on the circumstances under which it arises. In the handful of cases where the victim of the ceiling leak was stymied from taking any action whatsoever, the costs—both material and emotional—were high. Several respondents were unable to locate their upstairs neighbor and, therefore, were left on their own. For Karina, a Saratov doctor, the leak happened at the worst possible time, namely, during the New Year's holidays. Her neighbors had gone away but forgot to turn off their taps before leaving. She was unable to get into the empty apartment because her neighbors had installed an iron door for security. The easiest solution would have been to have the authorities turn off the water to the entire building, but she was unwilling to inconvenience her other neighbors. Eventually she was able to get the water turned off for the floor where the leak originated. When we spoke, three years had passed, but Karina was still seething over the fact that no one had ever apologized to her or even acknowledged their culpability. She felt she had no choice but to do the repairs herself, which involved replacing the wallpaper and repairing the ceiling. She said, in a facetious tone, "So what could I do? Go to court?" For her, the very idea of going to court was patently absurd. Interestingly, she contrasted her recent experience with a ceiling leak that occurred more than twenty years earlier when she was still in school.

---

24. Baumgartner's (1988) research into a New York suburb provides a wealth of examples of avoidance. Unfortunately the chasm between the lifestyles of New York suburbanites and urban Russians is too wide to permit useful comparisons.

> We forgot to turn off our tap—I don't remember the details—but in any event we flooded our neighbors—we were at fault. We went to see the neighbors and said, "Anna Mikhailovna, what can we do to make it right? Whatever you want." My father was a skilled workman. We offered that he would do the repairs himself—the wallpapering and whitewashing of the ceiling—whatever was needed. She agreed.

Karina insisted that what happened to her never would have occurred during the Soviet era. Her anger was driven more by the failure of her neighbors to live up to the informal norm than by the cost of the repairs.

A common thread among those who did nothing was the absence of any sort of meaningful relationship with the culpable neighbor. In Karina's case, she could recognize her upstairs neighbors by sight, but had never talked to them. In the other cases, the neighbor at fault was not a long-term resident, but had moved in recently. Their ability to relocate indicated a financial flexibility that was absent among most of my respondents. But the fact that the respondents lacked even a nodding acquaintance with their new neighbors suggests that these new residents had made little effort to learn about the informal norms. My sense was that they generally held themselves apart from the community. The best example of this was Vladimir, a Moscow mechanic, who was warned off trying to contact his upstairs neighbors after being flooded by others in the building, because they were believed to be tied into the mafia. Like Karina, he felt his hands to be tied, but remained angry about how the situation had played out.

Those who were rebuffed by their neighbors constituted a second variant of avoidance. Rather than the palpable anger that united those who had been unable to do anything, this group exhibited a sense of resignation. Zina, a Kushchevskaia doctor, shared the story of a friend. Her friend's upstairs neighbors had repaired some pipes, leaving a hole through which water flowed. When her friend asked the neighbors to fix this problem, they cursed at her. Zina told her friend, "forget about it, just get your husband off the sofa. It's a half hour of work; three bricks and that's it." Her friend tried to follow the norm and come to an accommodation with her neighbor, but her neighbors were having none of it. As Zina put it, "such neighbors, besides filthy language, you will get nothing from them." Her friend followed Zina's advice. A number of other respondents shared analogous incidents. Fixing the problem themselves was easier than pushing their neighbor to behave *po-chelovecheski*. Indeed, the very notion of forcing someone to behave *po-chelovecheski* runs counter to the norm.

Emerson's observation, made in the context of his study of U.S. college roommates, that "avoidance practices reflected a conviction that any relationship with the other, beyond incidental and perfunctory contact, was hopeless and impossible" applies equally to my respondents (Emerson 2008, 503). In all its forms, avoidance had the effect of reducing the salience of the dispute (Felstiner 1974; 1975). It cannot be said that my respondents embraced avoidance; they would have preferred to work the problem out with their neighbors. Hence the mix of anger and frustration that stuck with them resulted more from the emotional costs than from the actual financial outlays for repairs. But, as is characteristic for Russians, they made the best of a bad situation. They were living out Viktor Chernomyrdin's old saw, namely, "we hoped for things to get better, but they turned out the same as always."

Self-Help

In contrast to avoidance, where victims of ceiling leaks are left on their own to cope, neighbors working together to solve the problem in a mutually satisfactory fashion is the hallmark of self-help.[25] What some have described as the "radically decentralized" nature of self-help leads to wide variation in outcomes (Black and Baumgartner 1980, 206). The lack of procedural rigamarole allows for relatively speedy resolution. People figure out their own solutions, independent of state-sponsored rules and regulations, and their needs are far from uniform. Some have no interest in material assistance; they simply want an apology. Others are keen for help, whether financial or hands-on, in repairing their apartments. As this suggests, the goal is typically compensatory. The parties work to manage the problem and to avoid recurrences. Occasionally it can even be therapeutic or conciliatory, but rarely is it punitive or vengeful (Black 1984; Emerson 2008). Anger or resentment rarely follows in the wake of self-help.

Self-help is the strategy that hews most closely to the informal norms governing relations among Russian neighbors. Not surprisingly, it was the most commonly used approach among my respondents. It was the primary strategy used in thirty (53 percent) of the fifty-seven reported ceiling leaks.[26] In all of these cases the perpetrator of the leak acknowledged responsibility. Failure to do so led either to avoidance (if the victim decided not to pursue the problem) or to third-party intervention. These instances where the perpetrator conceded responsibility can be divided into two categories. In the first, the victim did not ask for any assistance. In the second, the parties agreed that the perpetrator would aid in repairing the damage caused by the leak, either through monetary relief or by renovating the apartment himself.[27]

---

25. As I conceptualize it, self-help is analogous to Emerson's (2008) dyadic complaint process.

26. In addition, the bulk of the cases involving third-party intervention began with an effort to resolve them through self-help.

27. The use of the male pronoun here is deliberate. I encountered no instance where the offer of hands-on help involved women doing the repairs.

Within this first category, there were a handful of cases in which the victims simply forgave their upstairs neighbors. For example, upon learning that the leak had been caused when Gloria's three children left their handkerchiefs in the sink after washing up, her downstairs neighbors told Gloria (a Tomsk tutor) that they would do the repairs themselves. No doubt the fact that the families had a long-standing good relationship facilitated this outcome. The almost-universal social norm of looking the other way when children's play leads to damage (assuming it is not too serious and does not recur too often) made the victims reluctant to press their claim.[28] Likewise, the grandparents of Arkadii (a psychologist from Kushchevskaia) declined to press their claim when their upstairs neighbors, who were mentally challenged, flooded them. In such cases, behaving *po-chelovecheski* required stepping back. Other times, those victimized by ceiling leaks chose to look the other way when the damage was minimal and the relations among those in the *pod"ezdy* were friendly.[29] The fact that the victims of these leaks chose to "lump it" rather than pursue damages might appear to constitute avoidance. But because the parties worked together to come to this resolution, it fits better into self-help, though it does illustrate that the dividing line between the two is rather porous.

A few of my respondents had to deal with repeated instances of water leaks from their upstairs neighbors due to their carelessness. Such negligence was typically the product of either old age or alcoholism. Tolerance tended to be greater for *babushki* than for alcoholics. Susanna, a Tomsk accountant, had been the victim of multiple leaks at the hands of her elderly upstairs neighbor. Each time, she went to see her neighbor and asked, "How many times are you going to flood us?" She explained that getting angry or yelling was pointless owing to her neighbor's advanced age. In her view, it was better to handle the problem *po-chelovecheski*.[30] Several others had similar experiences with elderly neighbors. At least one of them took money when it was offered, but did not demand it. This buttresses what I learned during the conversations about hypothetical ceiling leaks, namely, that pressing someone who was down on their luck, especially when such a

---

28. This mirrors what Engel (1984) found in his U.S.-based study, where community members tended to be inhibited from taking action that would contradict informal community norms.

29. For example, Feona, an accountant from Shumerlia, inadvertently flooded her neighbors when she took out some frozen fish, putting it in the sink with the water running. Forgetting she had done this, she went out. She discovered her mistake upon her return. She was mortified. She immediately ran downstairs and apologized profusely. She saw that her neighbors' wallpaper was soaked and offered to replace it. They told her, "Oh Feona, don't worry yourself. Everything will be fine. It will dry out."

30. In addition to her age, the fact that Susanna's neighbor had gotten her current apartment from the city after fire had destroyed her previous apartment left Susanna unwilling to ask for money to cover the damage caused by these leaks.

person was a pensioner, was unacceptable. Susanna and the others who were repeatedly victimized by negligent *babushki* were loath to violate this norm.

When the problem arose because of the repeated carelessness of alcoholic neighbors, however, my respondents were less forgiving. The experiences of two Shumerlia respondents allow for an interesting comparison. Marfa, a factory worker, grumbled about having been flooded more than one hundred times over the twenty-four years that her neighbor lived above her. Though now deceased, she and Marfa had had a stormy relationship. She was only two years older than Marfa, so could not assert age as a mitigating factor. Her carelessness was a direct result of excessive drinking. After every incident, Marfa went upstairs. She never asked for money, but concentrated on changing her neighbor's behavior. The neighbor would always promise to do better, but never did. Marfa would have liked to pursue the matter to court, but her husband was adamantly opposed. In her words, "my husband never wants to have any sort of connection to the court, not for any reason."[31] As a result, the two of them got used to the periodic leaks. Klavdia likewise had an upstairs neighbor who drank too much and frequently forgot to turn off the water before going to bed when inebriated. Like Marfa, Klavdia went upstairs and tried to reason with her neighbor each time, but to no avail. At her wit's end, she sued her neighbor. As Klavdia rationalized her decision to me, "she was such an unpleasant old biddy (*babul'ka*). . . . It was pointless to try to negotiate with her. Court was the only option." The others who lived in the *pod"ezd* applauded her decision. This alcoholic neighbor had caused trouble for everyone. Not surprisingly, the court decided in Klavdia's favor. Klavdia characterized the damages as mere "kopecks," but felt it was worth the effort because it caused her neighbor to change her behavior. "She finally learned that she needed to be civil (*dobrosovestno*). At first, she was nonchalant about flooding me. It was no big deal to her. But then [after the lawsuit], she began to behave more decently toward me. . . . I didn't have any further problems with her." Neither Marfa nor Klavdia was willing to forgive her drunk neighbor. Marfa's need for family harmony trumped her desire to teach her neighbor a lesson, so she did not sue her.

More often than not, however, the negotiations between neighbors that lie at the heart of the self-help strategy resulted in the perpetrator of the ceiling leak offering concrete assistance to his or her victim. This was the outcome in two-thirds (twenty of thirty) of the cases in which my respondents reported using self-help. Thirteen of these (65 percent) involved financial assistance. In the

---

31. Marfa's husband had no actual experience in the Russian courts. She explained that his distaste for litigation stemmed from his "nonconflictual" personality.

remainder, the neighbor at fault pitched in to fix the damage caused. In all cases, the parties emerged from the self-help process relatively satisfied.

Acknowledging responsibility and offering help is the essence of the informal norm underlying the desire to behave *po-chelovecheski*. As Veronika, who worked in the Shumerlia train station, reminded me, these same expectations were present during the Soviet era. She told of a leak that occurred in those days, and recalled that the party at fault paid for the repairs. The idea of bringing in third parties was unacceptable (*nepriniato*) among the families in her *pod"ezd*, where they all worked at the same place and raised their children together. She voiced a common refrain when she said "this could happen to any of us . . . today you are flooded, but maybe tomorrow you flood someone else. Life offers no guarantees to anyone." She conceded that her view of the past might be laced with nostalgia, and wondered out loud whether the dramatic increase in the cost of repairs in the post-Soviet era might make neighbors less willing to behave in a similar fashion. My respondents belie her doubts.

Over and over again, I was told that those responsible for ceiling leaks covered the cost of repairs. I heard this from respondents who were responsible for such leaks and from those who were their victims. For example, Sara, who is otherwise quite competent as the manager of a Saratov crisis center, sheepishly confessed that she has a bad habit of turning on the water and then getting distracted. As a result, she has repeatedly flooded her neighbors. Without fail, they have adopted a self-help strategy. In her words:

> We have never turned to the court for help in resolving such questions. I've always been able to come to an agreement with my neighbors about compensation for their damages . . . simply an oral contract. If the neighbor is capable of doing the repairs himself, then I need to provide money for materials. But if the person is not capable—if it is a *babushka* who cannot do the work—then I need to hire the workers to get it done.

When the tables were turned, the basic story remained much the same. In all locations, respondents told of how their neighbors had compensated them for damages caused by ceiling leaks. Their matter-of-fact recitations of what had happened convinced me of the power of the informal norm in favor of self-help when problems arose with neighbors.

Not all offers were accepted. Oleg, an entrepreneur from Tomsk, had to endure repeated ceiling leaks. His upstairs neighbor was an absent-minded *babushka* who frequently turned on the taps and then went out. Each time, she would come to his door and implore him to resolve the problem *po-sosedski*. At first, she tried to give him her entire salary to pay for repairs, but he felt that taking it would not be decent (*ne prilichno*). When a new young family moved in below him, he took it upon himself to warn them of his upstairs neighbor's proclivities and to explain that there was little to be done other than reminding her to shut off the water before leaving the apartment.

Some respondents were less charitable. Khristina and her parents were livid when their newly renovated Tomsk kitchen was flooded with scalding water. When the water had been turned off centrally for maintenance, their upstairs neighbors had left their taps on. When the water supply was restored, no one in this family was home and the water flowed freely into the apartment below. The wallpaper and linoleum that Khristina's mother had recently installed herself was destroyed. Their immediate reaction was to run upstairs and scream at their neighbors. These neighbors offered them an amount that was less than a third of the cost of the repairs. Ultimately, Khristina and her mother decided that pressing their claim further would be counterproductive. They were less affected by the poverty of their neighbors[32] than by the fear that they would be shunned within the *pod"ezd* if they took a hard line. They had lived in the *pod"ezd*, which she described as friendly (*druzhnyi*), for over eight years.[33] In her words, "if you litigate, it is as if you are going against your own. . . . It is not acceptable. All of your neighbors will be vexed with you. Situations vary, but resolving quietly and peacefully is better. Don't immediately run to the court or complain to the police." Not surprisingly, among those who used self-help, Khristina was one of the few who harbored some resentment long after the incident.

When those responsible for a ceiling leak have the necessary skills to make repairs, they often offer to do so. The older respondents indicated that this was more common in the Soviet era, probably because work-related demands on time were less. Arkadii confessed to having flooded his neighbors several times recently, but said that he always pitched in to help repair the damage. Sometimes the perpetrator offered either services or money. When Anastasia, a Saratov professor, and her downstairs neighbor were both flooded, her upstairs neighbor offered the services of her brother-in-law, who was a contractor. He showed up within an hour of the accident and sized up the damages. Anastasia accepted the offer of help and was pleased with the results. Her downstairs neighbor opted for a cash settlement.

---

32. Khristina characterized the family as poor (*maloobespechennaia*) and told of how the younger daughter had gone through three operations to improve her sight. The family included a son who had been a classmate of Khristina's. When they were younger, they had been part of the same crowd.

33. Confirming the close relations within the *pod"ezd*, Khristina related how all the residents had turned out for the funeral of a *babushka* who had lived in the *pod"ezd*.

Having the culpable neighbor do the repairs is most likely when the two families are close. The experience of Elena, a Moscow administrator, is instructive. Her family had a long-standing relationship with the pensioners who lived above them. They held spare keys to each others' apartments. Whenever one of them went to the dacha, they always brought something back for the other. When a ceiling leak developed in the wee hours, Elena called them. The neighbors found the problem, but not before enough water had accumulated to cause serious damage. They insisted on repairing the damage themselves. When Elena and her family were away for a few days, the neighbors came in and took care of the problem. As Elena said, "we returned and the apartment was already clean. They apologized a hundred times. They gave us a box of candy. . . . If neighbors are normal, this is how they behave." With her words, she captured the expectations embodied in the informal norm. Neighbors ought to work with each other and those responsible ought to offer either to do the repairs or to pay for the repairs. Both outcomes are clearly within the purview of the self-help strategy.

Third-Party Intervention

In Russia, as elsewhere, self-help does not always work. It requires both parties to be invested in solving the problem and, to that end, to be willing to contemplate compromise. If either side is obstreperous, then this self-help is likely doomed. Self-help also requires a modicum of trust between the parties. If either side is suspected of concocting a false claim, then self-help is futile.[34] Indeed, as Elena's case illustrates, the strategy works best when the parties have an ongoing relationship that they are eager to preserve. In other words, they are most likely to look to third parties for assistance when they do not know each other. This would seem to confirm the relational distance thesis (Merry 1990; Engel 1994; Black 1984).

The motivations for bringing in a third party vary. Sometimes the goal is simply to get a fresh pair of impartial eyes on the problem. Although such cases reflect a low level of trust between the parties, they can be seen as an extension of the self-help process. The goal remains compensatory. As the process ratchets up, however, less salutary motives can creep in. In its basest form, third-party

---

34. When the people who lived diagonally below Katia (a Saratov student) claimed she was responsible for flooding them, she resisted all efforts at negotiation. She told them: "the laws of physics haven't changed—water doesn't flow that way." Not being directly below Katia, the accusers were from a different *pod"ezd*. She stood firm, insisting that she would pay only if ordered to do so by the court. Yet when talking about what would happen if her upstairs neighbors flooded her, she was confident that the problem could be resolved through self-help, though she noted that she has a close friendship with these neighbors.

intervention evokes images of thugs imposing their will on others. Even when limited to state-sponsored third-party intervention, the desire for vengeance often spurs the process. It is rarely the sole motivating factor. Typically it is woven together with more socially acceptable goals, such as compensation.

Whether third-party intervention represents a failure of the informal norm favoring self-help depends on what form the third-party intervention takes. When resolving problems arising from ceiling leaks in Russia, there are two key third-party interveners: the housing authorities (or *ZhKU*) and the courts. Residents turn to the *ZhKU* to get a neutral assessment of who was responsible for the leak and an estimate of the cost of repairs. Sometimes this serves as the basis for renewed negotiations between the parties, leading to a settlement. In such cases, the housing authority acts to buttress and facilitate self-help. On the other hand, appeals to the *ZhKU* can sometimes serve as a precursor to litigation. This does not necessarily imply that the parties have given up on self-help. As Galanter reminds us, "invoking a court is not an abandonment of negotiation, but a shift in bargaining formats" (Galanter 1985, 653). Filing a lawsuit or threatening to do so often has the effect of reframing the discussion. Fear of the time, money, and emotional energy required to see a lawsuit through can jump-start negotiations (Albiston 1999, 877–879). For those seeking retribution, the courts serve a different function. Through their enforcement powers (which the *ZhKU* lack), punishing damages can be imposed on their neighbors.

Among my respondents, one-third (nineteen of fifty-seven) of those who had been involved with ceiling leaks sought help from their *ZhKU*. The *ZhKU* structure and the practice of using it to establish what happened in cases of ceiling leaks is a vestige of the Soviet past. Both then and now, the report (or *akt*) produced by the housing authorities can be used by the parties to set a limit on the amount of damages or it can serve as a first step toward litigation. The *akt* also includes the opinion of the *ZhKU* investigator as to the cause of the leak.

In only one of the post-Soviet cases was this *akt* dispositive on its own.[35] This is a reflection both of the low esteem that most Russians have for their local housing authorities and of their recognition that the *akt* cannot be directly

---

35. Oddly enough, the damage resulting from this ceiling leak was among the most serious reported to me. Aleksandra returned home from work to find several inches of standing water throughout her Tomsk apartment. She was without electricity for over three months. Not only was this a hardship for a family with two teenage children, but it was especially difficult for her son, who was dedicated to computer games. Aleksandra downplayed the family's difficulties. Even before talking to her upstairs neighbor, with whom she had only a nodding acquaintance, she contacted the *ZhKU* and got them to prepare an *akt*. With that in hand, she went to her neighbor, who told her to go ahead with the repairs. Reluctant to appear as if she were taking advantage of the situation, Aleksandra took a minimalist approach to the repairs. The neighbor still balked at paying her, but eventually did so.

enforced. Grumbling about *ZhKUs* was a theme throughout the focus groups and the interviews. The well-known tendency of housing authorities to play fast and loose with the facts whenever their workmen were implicated only further undermined their reputation.[36] A few respondents decided not to pursue their claim when their neighbors continued to balk at compensating them even after receiving the report from the housing authority. Faced with the prospect of a lengthy and messy fight, they opted for an avoidance strategy.

The *akt* was most effective when accompanied by a credible threat to file a lawsuit. The experience of Svetlana, a Saratov physician, captures this behavioral pattern well. She described what happened:

> It was an unpleasant situation. I was sleeping and had a clear feeling like in childhood when the rain was drumming. I opened my eyes and was in shock because . . . throughout the three rooms of my apartment, rain was falling from the ceiling. . . . Emergency services stopped the flow of water.

She knew her upstairs neighbors by sight, but had no relationship with them. She began with a self-help approach, trying to reach an accord with them, but found it to be impossible. Her comment about the reason why revealed her cynicism about human nature: "as a rule, people want to escape from responsibility." She turned to her housing authority. Armed with its *akt* and an estimate of the cost of repairs from a local construction company, she reopened the negotiations with her neighbors. She told them that if they continued to refuse to pay, she would file a lawsuit. Her neighbors understood that the *akt* and the estimate would give Svetlana the upper hand in court. They were sufficiently frightened by the prospect of litigation that they paid. She explained this change of heart by noting that Russians generally do not like to participate in judicial proceedings. More specifically, she believed that she benefitted from her neighbors' poor character (*ne poriadochnost*) and their reluctance to expose themselves to scrutiny. Svetlana was satisfied with the outcome. She had not been keen to initiate litigation, fearing that it would have taken too much of her time. Her consultations with a lawyer (*iurist*) friend left her with little confidence that the court would have

---

36. For example, Emilia flooded her neighbors in Tomsk. She agreed to pay for new wallpaper, but when the mother of her downstairs neighbor learned of this arrangement, she convinced her daughter to demand more. Emilia then brought in the *ZhKU* to evaluate the situation, which was complicated by the fact that the *ZhKU* had repaired the pipe that burst on the eve of the accident. Fearing that it would be held responsible, the *ZhKU* convinced Emilia to keep silent about the botched repair. As a result, the leak appeared to be a simple accident that was no one's fault. Emilia's neighbor agreed to return to their original deal, notwithstanding her mother's dissatisfaction.

awarded her as much as she ultimately got from her neighbors. Indeed, the lawyer warned her that the court would have denied her planned claim for punitive
damages (*moral'nyi ushcherb*), and would have cut the amount claimed for her
actual damages by as much as two-thirds. In her view, to get what she deserved,
she would have had to pursue the matter through multiple appeals.

Svetlana's passing acquaintance with her neighbor was typical for those who
turned to their *ZhKU*. Those who knew each other well found it easier to resolve problems on their own. Prior litigation experience turned out to be a good
predictor of how they purposed the *akt*. Those with such experience were more
likely to threaten and/or file lawsuits against their neighbors, whereas neophytes
tended to walk away.[37]

Filing a lawsuit against a neighbor would seem to contradict the informal
norm in favor of behaving *po-chelovecheski*. Yet lawsuits were more common
than I had expected, arising in nine (16 percent) of the fifty-seven ceiling leaks.[38]
Of these, only one was a clear violation of the norm. Most of the others involved
neighbors who were new to the *pod"ezd* or neighbors who barely knew one another. For example, Kira, a Tomsk accountant, told of how her new neighbors
refused to compensate their downstairs neighbors after flooding them. She was
surprised that the case ended up in court, particularly given that the victim of
the leak was a pensioner. She chalked it up to the fact that the perpetrator was
new to the *pod"ezd* and felt no sense of community. Following the prediction of
the socio-legal literature, Russians proved more willing to file lawsuits against
strangers than against friends. Lawsuits that did not involve strangers often were
brought against other kinds of outsiders, such as alcoholics, or involved genuine
disagreements over who was to blame.[39]

The norm-busting lawsuit arose after Berta, another Tomsk accountant,
flooded her downstairs neighbors when one of the hoses leading to her washing

---

37. Of the fourteen respondents who invoked litigation or ended up in court, thirteen had prior
experience. Of the seven who walked away or accepted the *akt*, only two had prior experience.

38. The nonrepresentative nature of my sample makes it difficult to know whether the penchant
for litigating is shared more broadly in Russian society. I am skeptical that it is. Earlier work on the
role of law in Russian business revealed that for every hundred transactions, twenty-four experience
potential disputes. Of these, sixteen are resolved through informal complaints, seven are resolved
through threats of litigation and/or penalties, and one is litigated (Hendley, Murrell, and Ryterman
2000, 633, n. 52). A U.S.-based study of disputing behavior found that "71.8 percent of individuals
with grievances complained to the offending party, and that a dispute arose in 63 percent of those
situations. Of these disputes, 11.2 percent resulted in a court filing." The authors concluded that "it
is clear that litigation . . . is by no means the most common response to disputes" (Trubek et al. 1983,
86–87).

39. For example, several respondents were involved in cases where the perpetrators of the leaks
alleged that their *ZhKU* bore some responsibility for what happened. Unwilling to shoulder the damages on their own, they left it to the court.

machine broke while she was at work. The water flowed uninterrupted for hours, damaging the apartments on the three floors below her. Her first instinct was to apologize to her neighbors and to offer to pay for the damages. She was able to reach an accord with those on the first and second floor. The woman who lived immediately below her was less accommodating. She was a lawyer (*advokat*) and was uninterested in a settlement from the outset. Though she was relatively new to the *pod"ezd*, she and Berta had become friends, sharing their problems with each other. Berta believed that the hose had exploded because of a sudden surge in water pressure, which meant that fault lay with the housing authority and not with her. Not surprisingly, her *ZhKU* was not interested in helping her prove this theory, preferring to point the finger of blame at her. Her downstairs neighbor took the easy way out by blaming her as well. She presented Berta with an estimate for repairs for 110,000 rubles, which Berta believed had been inflated by at least 70 percent. When their negotiations broke down, the neighbor filed a lawsuit. Having no prior experience with the formal legal system, Berta felt herself to be at a severe disadvantage.[40] She was cowed by the process, saying, "I was afraid to speak candidly, because any lawyer can take normal words and twist them against me. I remained quiet." She believed that the judge was biased in favor of her neighbor because of their preexisting relationship. Lacking faith in the evenhandedness of the judge, she settled the case for 40,000 rubles.

The case appears to reveal fissures in the informal norm. Ruminating on why her ostensible friend had pursued litigation, Berta said: "Every person treats others according to their own standards. When I was young, we didn't bother with contracts. I was raised at a time when it was possible to rely on someone's word, on their upstanding character. . . . But she took it to court. As a result, we had to have it out." Thus, Berta attributes her friend's behavior to her poor character, comparing her with the other neighbors who had also been flooded, who were more forgiving. Indeed, the person who lived on the first floor helped clean up the mess in Berta's apartment. Digging deeper, Berta's litigious neighbor can be seen as opting out of the societal norm in an effort to maximize her own interests. The contrast with the other neighbors is instructive. It suggests that there was a genuine community within the *pod"ezd* and that the *advokat* cared little about being ostracized from it. Perhaps this is because she had never fully integrated herself into it. Or perhaps, given her professional training, litigation had less emotional baggage for her. More puzzling is her willingness to forsake her

---

40. Often the advantages of those with extensive litigation experience can be blunted by hiring one's own lawyer. Berta tried to find a lawyer to help her, but ended up hiring someone who was not licensed to practice law. The judge unmasked him in open court, buttressing Berta's feelings that she was in over her head.

burgeoning friendship with Berta. It may have been that the friendship was more important to Berta than to her downstairs neighbor. Though Berta characterized her as a "friend" (*podruga*), her neighbor may have viewed Berta as a mere acquaintance. It is also possible that Berta's version of what happened glossed over some facts that would shed light on her neighbor's behavior. She may have said or done something to antagonize her neighbor. Or the damage may have been as extensive as the neighbor claimed.

Explaining Russians' Responses to Problems with Neighbors

Relationships

Though reading too much into any single case is perilous, Berta's case reminds us of the nested quality of informal norms. Between the focus groups and the interviews, I found no one who did not support the norm favoring self-help when problems arose between neighbors. Just the opposite: the respondents repeatedly emphasized that such problems should be worked out *po-chelovecheski*, that is, on an interpersonal level and without involving nonresidents of the *pod"ezd*. In fact, the consensus seemed to be that suing a neighbor could be grounds for ostracism. But it is possible for a person to adhere to such a norm as a general principle while, at the same time, viewing his or her situation as somehow exceptional. The review of the cases involving third-party intervention, especially those that gave rise to litigation, identify the tension points in the informal norm. As a rule, the respondents found it easier to sue someone they saw as an outsider. Using this rationalization, lawsuits were initiated against alcoholics and new residents (which sometimes slipped into a willingness to sue acquaintances).

The hypothesis that people are more likely to turn to the courts or other third parties when problems arise with strangers than with intimates held true for the Russians I studied. Echoing Engel's (1984) finding from his study of attitudes toward personal-injury lawsuits in a small Midwestern town, my respondents regarded litigation as being beyond the pale. Though conceding that it is sometimes unavoidable, the consensus was that it should be pursued only when no other alternatives remained. The strategic use of litigation reported by Yngvesson in her study of a Massachusetts urban neighborhood[41] was infrequent among my

---

41. Yngvesson's (1985) research also documented the potent role of the courts. The decisions of the court clerks to accept claims empowered the affected group and vice versa. This part of my research did not extend to the courthouse, but the more pedestrian nature of the claims being made

respondents. I found a slight hint of this sort of multilayered intent only in the lawsuits against alcoholics. Those who brought them were less interested in being compensated for the damages suffered than in changing the behavior of their alcoholic neighbors. Their goal was to deliver a wake-up call that would curb their neighbors' carelessness. As the experiences of Marfa and Klavdia showed, the results were mixed. But the bulk of my respondents who sued or threatened to sue had no agenda beyond paying for the repairs needed after the ceiling leak.

Institutional Infrastructure

Perhaps the claims did not give rise to recriminations because they were so straightforward. Among my respondents, lingering anger was typical only for those who avoided the problem. Those who engaged in self-help, even when it escalated into third-party intervention, were able to put the problem behind them once it had been resolved. This was not what those who studied U.S. neighbors found. In her study of New England neighbors who, like my respondents, shared close quarters and whose economic situation left them with little opportunity for exit, Merry found that

> when simple issues of shared space escalate into fights, there is usually something else involved. . . . Most of the parties were tied together only by proximity, by the fact that they could not easily avoid one another. The more they felt trapped together, the more intense and prolonged the battle. When avoidance was impossible or very costly—when there was no room to build a fence, for example, or when the victim of abuse could not afford to sell his house and move away—fights became more intense (1990, 39).

Unlike Merry, I heard no stories of drawn-out feuds. The nonrepresentative nature of my sample limits my ability to provide a definitive explanation, but I can suggest several possible reasons. It may be that ceiling leaks are not the sort of problem likely to give rise to simmering resentments. Unlike barking dogs or noisy children, a ceiling leak is a discrete problem that can be solved. On the other hand, Merry persuasively argues that the cause cited for instigating a feud is usually a pretext standing in for a series of lingering slights. A ceiling leak would seem capable of serving this function. Digging deeper, the differences between

---

by my respondents make it doubtful that Russian court clerks are playing a similarly influential role. Chapters 4 and 5, which focus on the courts, confirm this insight.

the two judicial systems may account for the variation in outcomes. Arguably, the U.S. judicial system eggs on feuds by treating the parties as adversaries and requiring them to battle it out, whereas the inquisitorial model found in Russia provides more fertile ground for compromise. These differences are, however, greater in theory than in practice (Kagan 2001). In both systems, engaging the legal process is seen as a hardship that most try desperately to avoid. This leaves us with cultural explanations. Though the stereotypes of Russians as resigned to their fate (Ries 1997, 83–102; Chekhov 1991) and Americans as combative (Kagan 2001; Friedman 1987) seem helpful, they are too superficial to serve as a convincing explanation. Indeed, my research provides little evidence to support the stereotype of Russians as passive. The informal norm militated in favor of activist problem solving, not grim suffering. As a rule, my respondents embraced this norm. Those who appeared to depart from it by avoiding the problem did so grudgingly and, long after the fact, remained angry about their inability to address the problem directly.

The commitment to self-help as a way to solve ceiling leaks may have a more mundane source. The aging nature of the plumbing infrastructure in the Russian housing stock, much of which has never undergone capital repairs of any sort, contributed to the equanimity with which most of my respondents dealt with ceiling leaks. Many had been both the victim and the perpetrator of such leaks. Yet it is important to remember that none of the fifty-seven instances of ceiling leaks on which this chapter focuses were the direct result of shoddy building maintenance. Such problems would be laid at the door of the housing authorities. Rather, my research is limited to leaks attributable to the negligence of neighbors and for which these neighbors are culpable. Both in the discussions of what they would do if flooded and what they actually did, many respondents commented on how the fact that tables could easily be turned had a calming effect on them.

Generational Effect

Those respondents who came of age in the Soviet system when moving was almost impossible learned the importance of establishing cordial relations with their neighbors in the *pod"ezd*. Realizing they were stuck together for the foreseeable future, they developed informal norms that minimized tensions. Encouraging self-help when faced with ceiling leaks made sense in that institutional context. Yet my conversations reveal that it is not entirely a vestige of the past, though it is beginning to show signs of wear and tear. When teasing out the norm by analyzing the "what if" conversations, I rely on respondents at both ends of the age spectrum. That those over thirty like Viktor (age thirty-three) and Marina (age fifty-eight) would adhere to the norm is not surprising. But the others—Boris, Rimma, and Angelina—were all in their twenties. They had no memory of life under state socialism. They grew up in a world where the existence of a viable real estate market made "exit" possible. For them, however, moving elsewhere to escape annoying neighbors was not realistic. Like the rest of my respondents, they lacked the financial resources needed to buy a different apartment. As Hirschman (1970) predicts, they reacted by utilizing "voice" through self-help.

Personal Beliefs

The obvious overlap between the commitment to fairness embedded in the norm favoring behaving *po-chelovecheski* and the basic tenets of most organized religions led me to explore whether those who broke with the norm by invoking litigation were more likely to be nonbelievers. I found no such correlation. Among the eight respondents who had threatened to, or filed, a lawsuit, there were no nonbelievers and only two agnostics.[42] The remainder self-identified as believers. This proportion of believers is roughly equivalent to that for the larger sample. As I noted above, a number of respondents expressed sentiments akin to the Golden Rule, but only Fatima, a twenty-five-year-old Moscow student who had recently converted from Islam to Christianity, openly invoked religion, telling me that she was prepared to submit herself to God's will in all matters.

Nature of Damages

Common sense pushed me to explore whether there was a link between the response to ceiling leaks and the damage caused. It is true that most of those who resorted to third-party intervention sustained serious damage. But the vast majority of the incidents reported involved serious damage, so the same could be said for those who opted for self-help and/or avoidance. Thus the extent of the damages was not the critical determinant of behavior. Instead, the key was the underlying relationship. More specifically, it was a combination of the attitude of the neighbor who caused the damage and the victim's perception of their circumstances. Almost without exception, being rebuffed by their upstairs neighbor after a ceiling leak caused my respondents to see red. Some ended up lumping it either because they realized their neighbor had no resources and/or because they

---

42. Although the dataset includes nine incidents that culminated in lawsuits, only three of these were filed by my respondents. In the others, the respondent telling me the story was either the defendant (as in Berta's case) or was relating what had happened to friends or family.

decided going after them would be too much trouble.[43] Others pursued their neighbors through the formal legal system.[44] Yet a number of my respondents who sustained devastating damage, including Sara and Elena, managed to work things out with their neighbors.

When both neighbors were invested in a self-help strategy, they might seek third-party intervention in the form of a neutral estimate of damages and fault from the *ZhKU*. Irrespective of the seriousness of the damages, none of these incidents devolved into litigation.

By the same token, minimal damages gave rise to a variety of responses. After being flooded multiple times, Klavdia sued her alcoholic neighbor, even though the cumulative damage was not serious. Her purpose was not to recover damages but to shame her neighbor into better behavior. At the other end of the spectrum, recall that Gloria was able to work things out with her neighbors after her children's carelessness led to a ceiling leak. Their response was prompted not just by an unwillingness to take advantage of an accident caused by children's play, but also by the minimal damage caused.

Attitudes toward Courts

At first glance, my respondents' distaste for litigation might seem to buttress the polling data that ostensibly documents Russians' lack of trust in the formal legal system. But the conversations told a different story. Though dissatisfaction with the courts was a recurring theme, being railroaded by a corrupt system was not the respondents' principle fear (cf. Ledeneva 2008). When pressed, most conceded that Russian courts can be "bought," but they felt themselves to be far removed from the high-stakes cases in which outcomes are settled by money-filled envelopes or by telephone calls from on high. Thus this sad reality about the Russian judicial system did not determine their attitudes about suing neighbors over ceiling leaks. Instead, my respondents' complaints about the courts were dominated by more prosaic concerns, such as the cost, time, and energy required (Hendley 2009). Vadim, a Saratov entrepreneur whose family, despite being

---

43. For example, when Galina, a fifty-six-year-old who teaches accounting at a Moscow college, was flooded by her upstairs neighbor, the damage sustained was the equivalent of three months of salary for her. Her neighbors pleaded poverty, but Galina was not convinced. Ultimately, however, she decided that pursuing them through the courts was not worth the emotional energy it would cost her.

44. When Rimma's in-laws in Vladivostok were flooded soon after completing an extensive renovation of their apartment, they ended up suing their neighbors. They sued as a matter of principle after their neighbors refused to acknowledge their fault. The seriousness of the damage, especially coming on the heels of their renovations, was relevant but not critical to their decision. Rimma herself expressed a strong commitment to behaving *po-chelovecheski*. See her remarks earlier under "Uncovering the Informal Norms that Govern Behavior."

flooded three times, chose not to pursue a claim against their poverty-stricken upstairs neighbors, reflected the views of many when he said: "Courts aren't necessarily good or bad. It's better not to have any connection with courts—it's a question of time, nerves, and money. Usually we try to resolve such problems in a friendlier way." These sentiments are not unique to Russians. Going to court can be a daunting prospect, even in societies considered to be litigious, like the United States (Merry 1990). Those who lack experience can come away feeling disadvantaged (Galanter 1974).

Prior experience with the courts seemed to embolden my respondents to go down that road again. All of the respondents who initiated lawsuits had been to court in the past. But this did not make them eager to return. Most saw litigation as a last resort, to be employed when self-help fell flat. The willingness of court veterans to return to the scene of battle provides a useful counternarrative to the findings from the RLMS data, which, as was discussed in chapter 1, suggested that court veterans were more nihilistic than those who had never been to court.

Summing Up

Theoretical Contributions

What does this Russia-based research add to our understanding of the role of law in disputes among neighbors? It confirms Engel's (1984) findings that members of relatively insular communities are less likely to sue one another. Much like his Midwestern small-town residents, my Russian respondents recoil from the prospect of suing one another. Though the details differ, they share a sense that going to court represents an abrogation of personal responsibility. Engel's respondents' distaste for litigation is driven by their sense that those who sued are trying to cash in on their misfortune. It never occurred to my respondents that they could recover anything more than compensatory damages. Even so, they view litigation as a personal failure, believing that neighbors ought to be able to resolve their problems on their own. Going to court ran the risk of social ostracism both for the Midwesterners whom Engel studied and the Russians I studied.

As the social-distance hypothesis that has been developed in the U.S. context by Black (1984), Engel (1984), Merry (1990), Yngvesson (1985; 1994), and others would predict, the willingness of my Russian respondents to pursue self-help solutions is strongly correlated with the potency of their relationships with their neighbors. Indeed, this hypothesis seems more robust in the Russian setting than in the United States. Merry's finding that neighbors who live in close proximity and lack exit opportunities are more likely to engage in bitter and lengthy battles is not born out by my research. Nor were my respondents open to engaging in the sort of strategic litigation that the Massachusetts residents studied by Yngvesson pursued. Instead, the Russians were more deeply committed to finding a solution through self-help. If that failed, then my respondents either avoided confrontation or escalated the dispute by turning to third parties for help. Interestingly, those who opted for avoidance were more likely to harbor resentment. This stands in contrast to the equanimity predicted by the literature (Felstiner 1975). In the Russian case, however, avoidance is often equated with the unwillingness of the culpable neighbor to live up to the norms of the *pod"ezd*.

My research departs from these classic studies in that I am not principally trying to explain litigation behavior. Much like Emerson's (2008) study of college roommates, my goal is to map the choices open to Russian neighbors who experience difficulties with their neighbors. Of course, the relative mobility of the two groups is different. The roommates are stuck for the academic year, whereas many of my respondents have been stuck in their *pod"ezd* for life. Yet the choices made during that year by the college students whom Emerson studied were remarkably similar to those of my respondents. Neither group was eager to rock the boat.

Insights on Russian Legal Consciousness

My respondents' strong commitment to the informal norm favoring self-help suggests that the communitarian ideals that successive Soviet regimes tried to inculcate took hold and continue to hold sway. But the tenacity of this norm has little to do with an attachment to Soviet ideals more generally. My respondents' continued adherence to it reflected its practical value in their lives. Having been thrown together with the neighbors in their *pod"ezd*, they recognized the need to get along. Hence, the general norm was adapted to create a quasi-law of the *pod"ezd*, which residents violated at their peril. Though the shadow of the law hangs over all of the reported incidents, the formal legal system was mostly an afterthought for my respondents. Their behavior was dictated more by their internal moral code and the code of the *pod"ezd* than by state-promulgated statutes or regulations. This reality reminds us that law flourishes best when it is in harmony with such codes.

My research suggests that the solidity of the informal norm is beginning to crack. No longer do the populations within *pod"ezdy* remain unchanged from one generation to the other. The privatization of the housing stock and the consequent emergence of a real estate market has brought with it the possibility for relatively rapid turnover. Few of my respondents had the financial flexibility to participate in this new reality, but they were impacted as those around them did so. It is surely no accident that the likelihood of third-party intervention increased dramatically when the neighbor was a newcomer. The informal norm to behave *po-chelovecheski* is grounded in interpersonal relationships. When neighbors did not know each other, they felt less of an obligation to live up to its ideals. This opens the door to using the courts and other formal institutions to resolve problems.

3

DEALING WITH AUTO ACCIDENTS

One of the most striking changes in Russia over the past two decades has been the drastic increase in car ownership. This process began in the latter decades of Soviet power, but accelerated after the Soviet Union broke apart.[1] In 1970, owning a car was extremely rare, with only 5.5 cars per 1,000 individuals. This number had increased to 30.2 by 1980 and to 58.5 by 1990. By the turn of the century, it had grown to 130.5. In 2010, there were 228.3 cars per 1,000 individuals (Table 6.36, Rossiiskii 2011). The rapid increase in auto ownership is unsurprising. Cars, like most big-ticket consumer goods, were in short supply during the Soviet era (Siegelbaum 2008). Obtaining one had less to do with scrimping and saving than with finding the right connection or simply waiting for one's turn, which took many years and was not always successful. With the collapse of state socialism, the Russian market was flung open, ending the deficit of cars. The only obstacle to acquisition was money. For those Russians fortunate enough to have good-paying jobs, cars quickly became indispensable. Although residents of Moscow and St. Petersburg continue to be more likely to be car owners than those who live in the hinterlands, the gap is narrowing. Russia still lags far behind Western countries in terms of the density of car ownership, but, like China, the pace of growth in ownership is much greater than in the West. The gender gap among drivers and owners of cars has decreased dramatically. Although

---

1. See Siegelbaum (2008) for a history of the role of cars in the Soviet Union dating back to the 1917 Revolution.

prejudice against women drivers persists, they are no longer an aberration on the Russian roads (Kuhr-Korolev 2011).

The increase in the number of cars in Russia has facilitated greater mobility for its population, but has also led to an increase in traffic accidents. Though there are fewer accidents per capita in Russia than in many Western countries, including the United States, Germany, and Japan, Russia has emerged as a world leader in fatal accidents. On a per capita basis, Russia has almost five times more fatalities than in Japan, about three times more than in Germany, and about 60 percent more than in the United States (Belova 2010). Recent years have witnessed a downward trend, but the sheer numbers of people injured and killed on the road is deeply troubling. In 2005, there were 23.7 deaths per 100,000 persons; by 2010, this number had dropped to 18.6 deaths. There has been much speculation in the popular and scholarly press as to the reasons for the high incidence of injuries and fatalities on Russian roads. Among those asserted are the increase in the number of cars on the road, which has contributed to paralyzing traffic jams in urban settings and makes it difficult for ambulances to reach the scene of accidents, the poor quality of many roads, and the relative lack of roads, which causes overcrowding on the available roads.[2] The human factor is inescapable, most notably the reckless disregard of many drivers for the basic rules of the road. Indeed, anecdotal evidence suggests that neophyte drivers often bypass the official exam, which is difficult even for experienced drivers, by bribing a traffic inspector to obtain a driver's license (Pomerantsev 2014). This sort of behavior fuels the general lack of respect for the traffic police (Belova 2010). The role of alcohol cannot be discounted, given that 9.4 percent of fatal accidents in 2011 involved drunk drivers.[3]

In this chapter, I explore the aftermath of Russian traffic accidents with an eye to what it reveals about Russian legal culture. Just as in the preceding chapter, the analysis is grounded in the twenty-nine focus groups and seventy-nine follow-up interviews I conducted in Kushchevskaia, Moscow, Saratov, Shumerlia, and Tomsk during the summers of 2007 and 2008. These conversations yielded seventy stories about various types of traffic accidents. In contrast to the incidents involving water leaks, which called on those victimized to find common ground with their neighbors, traffic accidents typically bring strangers together.

---

2. In terms of the density of roads per 1,000 square kilometers, Russia lags far behind others in the Group of 8. As of 2007, it had 43.7, compared with 68.8 for the United States, 3,169 for Japan, and 1,838 for France. There is considerable regional variation within Russia. The central okrug, where Moscow is located, has the greatest density of roads. The pace of road building is fairly even across Russia (Belova 2010).

3. In 2011, drunk drivers were involved in 7.8 percent of all traffic accidents, and 8.4 percent of accidents in which someone was injured (Table 2.84, *Transport* 2012).

I am interested in how they respond to the unexpected, in both personal and institutional terms, and in the role of law, if any.

I begin by sketching out the institutional support available for those who have the misfortune to be involved in auto accidents, with an emphasis on how this has changed over the years. I then turn to the data, examining how the focus group participants responded in the wake of accidents. As we saw in the preceding chapter, their behavior confirms the preference of Russians for working out solutions on their own. They are skeptical of the capacity of formal legal institutions to provide help. In the final section of the chapter, I reflect on the reasons for their behavioral choices.

Institutional Environment

In Russia, as elsewhere, traffic accidents can either be played by the book or can be handled privately. Going by the book generally means involving the traffic police and insurance companies. Both institutions suffer from a checkered reputation. The traffic police[4] are seen as deeply corrupt.[5] Russian websites publish city-specific price lists of the amounts that need to be paid based on the alleged offense.[6] As we will see, many of the focus group participants were convinced that the officers skewed the report on their accidents to favor whoever paid more,

---

4. Institutionally, the traffic police are part of the Ministry of Internal Affairs. Russians often refer to it as GAI, which is an acronym for the former name of the agency, the State Automobile Inspectorate (*Gosudarstvennaia avtomobil'naia inspektsiia*). Officers are usually *gai-shchniki*. The official name of the agency is now the State Inspectorate for Road Safety, or *Gosudarstvennaia inspektsiia bezopasnosti dorozhnogo dvizheniia*, or GIBDD (http://www.gibdd.ru/), an acronym that does not roll off the tongue as easily as GAI, which helps explain why the old name has stuck.

5. When asked about corruption within law enforcement agencies, Russians consistently identify the traffic police as highly problematic. In a December 2010 survey by the Levada Center, the traffic police came in first, with 56.8 percent of respondents listing it as the most corrupt. A similar survey fielded by the Foundation for Public Opinion in 2008 also put the traffic police in first place in terms of corruption (Rimskii 2012). Russians are skeptical about efforts to rein in the traffic police. When asked about the likely impact of the plan to increase oversight over the traffic police in a March 2007 poll by the Levada Center, only 30 percent felt it would decrease bribery. A solid majority (58 percent) was sure it would have no impact. About the same number believed that increasing fines for traffic violations would lead to bigger bribes for traffic policemen (Levada 2008, 72). The polling results on the police more generally paint a dismal picture. In surveys carried out regularly from 2004 through 2012, over 80 percent of respondents saw lawlessness and arbitrariness within the police as a serious problem (Zorkaia 2012, 104). The efforts to remake the police by renaming them as *politsia* rather than *militsia*, along with a series of deeper institutional changes, was dismissed by respondents as ineffective (ibid., 2012, 106). As part of this reform, salaries for policemen were tripled in an effort to deincentivize the practice of taking bribes (Robertson 2013, 170).

6. http://www.vashamashina.ru/bill.php#g1. See Khaliullina (2005) for a rational-choice analysis of bribe-taking based on interviews with traffic policemen.

irrespective of who was actually at fault. In an effort to curtail bribes, the rules about how traffic tickets were to be paid were changed. Violators no longer pay the traffic police directly, but are now given a ticket and asked to pay via bank transfer. This reform did little to stem the tide. A system has evolved where alleged violators are offered two prices. If they hand over cash to the officer, then the amount is reduced. But there is no documentary record of the transaction and, not surprisingly, this money goes directly into the officer's pocket.[7] Those who want to abide by the law can insist on getting tickets and paying the fines at their bank. Few bother. Not only do they see little value in upholding laws that the police themselves are openly flouting, but doing so also requires them to stand in line at their bank (Zernova 2012, 481).

Private insurance companies are a post-Soviet phenomenon. Indeed, Soviet officials were openly hostile to the very idea of liability insurance. Alice Erh-Soon Tay argues that they believed "it would be entirely destructive of the moral functions of civil liability and that a man who insured beforehand his carelessness was either half-intending it or, at least, not trying strenuously to avoid it" (1969, 15). The elaborate social safety net left the Soviet state as the primary insurer.[8] With the legalization of private property as part of the transition to the market, however, the role of the state has changed. It continues to provide basic medical insurance, but private insurance companies have stepped in to protect property interests. As to motorists, insurance became mandatory in 2003 (Ob obiazatel'nom 2002). Drivers are required to have a minimal policy for collisions, for which the rates are set by the state, but are free to buy supplemental insurance. Russians' concern about the high incidence of traffic accidents led them to be generally supportive of the move to mandatory insurance, but has not consistently prompted them to obtain this insurance.[9] Data collected by the National Agency for Financial Research show that the percentage of Russians who have the mandatory automobile insurance has risen from 20 in 2005 to 26 in 2012. Over the same period, the percent who opted for supplemental car insurance has

---

7. When surveyed in 2006 and 2007 by the Levada Center, only 20 percent of respondents said that the efforts of Russian police are mainly devoted to protecting citizens. Over 60 percent viewed police as being mostly interested in protecting their own interests. The remainder of the sample declined to respond (Levada 2008, 72).

8. For a thorough analysis of Soviet insurance law, see Rudden (1966). For a primer on contemporary Russian insurance law, see Belykh (2009); Moudrykh (2002).

9. In a survey conducted by the Independent Research Center ROMIR in the spring of 2004, 85 percent agreed that something needed to be done to protect victims of traffic accidents. Forty-eight percent of respondents viewed the law requiring insurance for drivers as necessary (Nuzhno n.d.). A survey carried out in the spring of 2005 by the All-Russian Center for the Study of Public Opinion documented the support of two-thirds of those polled for having the rates for mandatory insurance set by the state (VTsIOM 2005).

grown from 3 to 8 (Natsional'noe 2012a). Initially the fine for driving without insurance was 100 rubles (about $3). It was increased to 500 rubles (about $15) at the beginning of 2013 (art. 12.3, part 3, KoAP). Neither sum is likely to drive behavioral choices.

Despite their relatively short lives, Russian insurance companies have already managed to earn the disdain of their clients (Shmerpina 2006a). The focus group discussions are reflective of public opinion more generally in that people find insurance companies unresponsive at best, and manipulative at worst. Initially, victims of traffic accidents had to seek compensation from the insurance companies of the driver at fault. These companies had little interest in whether victims (who were not their customers) were satisfied with their services. In 2009, the rules were changed to allow those involved in accidents to work directly with their own insurance companies.[10] Tales of foot dragging by insurance companies persist in the Russian press and on web forums, on which people share their experiences and offer advice. More troubling are claims of systematic efforts to minimize claims by co-opting supposedly independent appraisers. When asked in 2012 by the National Agency for Financial Research why they had switched insurance companies, concerns with service were a close second behind increases in premiums.[11]

My interest is less in the twists and turns in the institutional evolution of the traffic police and insurance companies, but in how ordinary Russians understand and operate in this institutional environment. As with the water leaks, the choices available to those involved in traffic accidents fall into four basic categories: (1) doing nothing, (2) negotiating with the other driver, (3) calling on a trusted third party (other than a court) to assist in reaching a settlement, and (4) going to court. Informal mechanisms emerge as most popular. Only a handful of people resorted to the courts, and did so as a last resort after efforts to negotiate a settlement had failed.

By listening to the focus group participants, the factors that influence their behavioral choices become clear. Not surprisingly, practical considerations are at the forefront. The severity of the accident inevitably colors the choices available. Whereas the aggressor in a fender-bender can opt to pay off the victim on the

---

10. Russian insurance companies lobbied vigorously against the new rules and managed to delay their introduction for a year. Critics argue that insurance companies continue to exploit loopholes to avoid paying claims or to minimize them (Zinenko 2009). Industry spokesmen defend their record (Nikoforov 2009).

11. Respondents were allowed to check multiple reasons. The most common response was increase in premiums at 36 percent. The several responses related to service (dissatisfaction with the amount paid out for a claim, poor response to a claim) attracted a quarter of the respondents (Natsional'noe 2012b).

spot, someone who sustains life-threatening injuries is in no position to bargain for compensation with the other driver. The speed with which the traffic police arrive can make a difference. More interesting is the role of Russians' attitudes toward one another and their willingness to trust in the viability of state institutions in shaping their choices.

Before delving into the experiences of my respondents, a few words about the formal law governing traffic accidents is in order. Tort law was a mostly unwanted stepchild within the Soviet legal system. In the heady years following the October Revolution, Communist Party officials saw tort law as a vestige of the past (Hazard 1952). They believed that comprehensive social insurance would obviate the need for private causes of action.[12] By 1922, cooler heads prevailed and a chapter on tort law was included in the civil code (chap. 13, GK 1922). It was drawn from a never-enacted tsarist draft that, in turn, had been based on German law. The 1964 civil code made few changes in the area of tort law. Compensatory damages were available when a petitioner could demonstrate harm caused by another. Punitive damages were not allowed; they were seen as a "bourgeois legal institution" that amounted to unjust enrichment (Barry 1996, 183). Driving a car was deemed to be an inherently dangerous activity that triggered strict liability (art. 454, GK 1964). Liability attached to the driver of the car rather than the owner, which was a clever way for the state to avoid liability, given that most cars were the property of Soviet state-owned enterprises (Barry 1967, 76). But tort claims of any stripe were not numerous (Barry 1979, 237).

The post-Soviet civil code made few textual changes in tort law (chap. 59, GK RF part 2). One notable exception is the elimination of strict liability for auto accidents (art. 1079, GK RF part 2), which opened the door to liability insurance.[13] The obligation of insurance companies to pay is limited to those deemed to be victims. As a result, admissions of fault have profound legal consequences. Where neither or both sides acknowledge responsibility, insurance companies often refuse to pay (Arakcheev 2008). Situations where the traffic police are unwilling or unable to determine fault are particularly vexing.

---

12. Tay (1969, 8) quotes P. I. Stuchka from the 1922 meeting of the All-Union Central Executive Committee of the Bolsheviks: "It is undignified for the Worker-Peasant Government to initiate disputes in court to determine whether a man was injured on the railway track intentionally or by accident." Reflecting on this, she concludes that "a socialist government should be concerned with social harm, an objective social concept, and not with fault, a subjective individual one."

13. The list of inherently dangerous activities, set forth in article 1079, is not exhaustive (GK RF part 2). Means of transportation are explicitly included, but the last sentence of the article explains that liability for harm caused by the collision of two or more cars is not covered by strict liability. On the other hand, the Russian Supreme Court, in a 2010 decree, clarified that drivers who hit pedestrians can be held strictly liable (Postanovlenie 2010). See Iaroshenko (2015) for an overview of the present-day legislation governing auto accidents.

The Soviet-era ban on punitive damages has also disappeared. Though the chapter on torts is silent on this issue, the general provisions of the post-Soviet civil code are amenable to so-called moral damages (art. 151, GK RF part 1). Judges have considerable discretion in setting the amount. They are directed to take into account the nature of the suffering of the plaintiff and the nature of the defendant's actions. The amounts available are trivial compared with the huge sums awarded by U.S. juries in egregious torts claims.[14]

As I have argued in the preceding chapters, Russians' use of the courts has increased markedly in the post-Soviet era. Tort claims, especially those related to traffic accidents, are no exception. Table 3.1 lays out the data for 2008 through 2011. Though the raw numbers have almost doubled over this four-year period, they remain a relatively minor part of the civil docket, accounting for about 1 percent of all civil cases. The data do not speak to the question of how often victims of accidents bring claims against those at fault or their insurance companies. The comments of my respondents strongly suggest that suing is very much the exception rather than the rule. Much as Engel (2009, 260) found in his research on the propensity to litigate tort claims in the United States and Thailand, lawsuits tend to arise among Russians when efforts at settlement have broken down.

Table 3.1 highlights several notable features of cases dealing with traffic accidents. These cases tend to take longer than the prototypical case and petitioners are less likely to prevail. This reveals that these are cases that require full-fledged hearings on the merits; they do not lend themselves to expedited procedural mechanisms. Over the four-year period, only nine cases were resolved using judicial orders (*sudebnye prikazy*).[15] The higher-than-average delay rate along with the lower-than-average win rate makes it tempting to conclude that these cases are deeply contentious and that parties fight to the bitter end. No doubt this describes some cases. But conversations with Russian judges, buttressed by my observations in the courts, lead me to believe it is not the norm. Judges report that the results in most traffic-related cases are foregone conclusions. They grumble about the tendency of insurance companies to use every trick in the book to drag out the proceedings in order to avoid having to pay, a practice that is hardly unique to Russia.

The lower-than-average win rates are more of a puzzle. The focus group participants complain about the difficulty of assembling the requisite documents.[16]

---

14. For example, in a 2004 case decided by a Saratov district court, the victim of a car accident initially sought 155,000 rubles in moral damages, but was awarded only 18,000. By contrast, the court awarded the full amount requested for compensatory damages, which were grounded in documentary evidence (*Iliasov v. Lapin* 2004).

15. For more on judicial orders, see chapter 4.

16. The rules governing what documents must be presented to an insurance company are set forth in densely worded government regulations, which are difficult for laymen to parse (Ob utverzhdenii 2003).

TABLE 3.1 Information about cases involving traffic accidents brought to the Russian courts, 2008–2011

	ALL CASES RELATED TO TRAFFIC ACCIDENT	TRAFFIC ACCIDENT CASES AS % OF ALL CIVIL CASES	WIN RATE FOR TRAFFIC ACCIDENT CASES	WIN RATE FOR ALL CIVIL CASES	DELAY RATE FOR TRAFFIC ACCIDENT CASES	DELAY RATE FOR ALL CIVIL CASES
2008						
All courts	96,208	0.9	70.6	90.4	15.2	3.5
JP courts	52,065	0.6	72.4	91.5	14	2.8
2009						
All courts	126,525	0.95	76.3	88.8	10.4	1.9
JP courts	81,915	0.8	78.6	93.4	8.6	1.2
2010						
All courts	155,043	1.1	80.1	88.3	7.7	1.6
JP courts	84,221	0.8	83	94	6.9	0.8
2011						
All courts	190,340	1.7	82.6	86.1	6.2	1.6
JP courts	98,683	1.1	86	92.2	4.9	0.8

Sources: Otchet (2008, 2009, 2010, 2011); Otchet–JP Courts (2008, 2009, 2010, 2011).

Some are overwhelmed by the task and abandon any plans to pursue a claim. It may be that those who do go forward tend to fall short. The positivism reflected in the procedural codes leads judges to be unforgiving about missing documentary evidence. This may contribute to petitioners' losses. Unlike individual claimants, insurance companies are generally represented by legal professionals in court. Whether this gives them an edge is unclear. Judges complain about the poor quality of lawyering for insurance companies, attributing it to the low wages paid and the consequent high turnover rate within their legal departments. Unfortunately, the way the data have been collected do not allow me to determine whether individuals or insurance companies are more successful.[17]

Having sketched out the institutional landscape, I can now turn to the experiences of the focus group participants. In analyzing them, I make use of the conceptual framework of the "disputing pyramid" laid out by Felstiner, Abel, and Sarat (1980–81). It provides a language and structure for making sense of the process by which everyday disagreements evolve or fall by the wayside. The first hurdle is "naming," a process of determining whether to recognize an experience

---

17. As a general rule, plaintiffs tend to win their cases in the JP courts. Regardless of whether individuals are suing legal entities or vice versa, plaintiff win rates are well over 90 percent. Somewhat incongruously, the only group that has a poor track record is the state, which wins about two-thirds of the cases it initiates against individuals (Otchet JP Courts 2011).

as injurious.[18] The second hurdle is "blaming," a process of deciding whether there is a third party who is responsible. The final hurdle is "claiming," a process of deciding whether to seek a remedy from whoever is to blame. This final stage of claiming can be broken into a variety of types of claims. Injured parties may seek out recompense informally in lieu of, or as a prelude to, litigation. The pyramidal image is useful.

The working assumption is that a significant number of disagreements will fall away at each stage. The value of the model lies in its focus on the reasons why disagreements do or do not grow into full-fledged grievances. Though not losing sight of the role played by the nature of the disagreement and the relationship between the parties, Felstiner, Abel, and Sarat identify a number of factors that act as transformational agents by facilitating or discouraging the transition of disputes from one stage to another. Key among these is the worldview of the injured parties, which, in turn, is influenced by their religion, class, prior experiences with the legal system, and the underlying legal culture. From an institutional perspective, lawyers, who act as gatekeepers, emerge as especially important at the final stage of claiming.

The model of the disputing pyramid was developed with the United States in mind, and socio-legal scholarship on the United States has used it to good effect (e.g., Calavita and Jenness 2013; Albiston 2005; Engel and Munger 2003; Ewick and Silbey 1998; Merry 1990). The basic logic, however, transcends the U.S. experience, as is demonstrated by its use to elucidate disputing behavior in Canada (Kritzer, Bogart, and Vidmar 1991), China (Michelson 2007), Kyrgyzstan (Cormier 2007), and Thailand (Engel 2005). I have previously employed it in the Russian context to explore disputing behavior regarding overdue payments between industrial enterprises during the 1990s (Hendley 2001) and the decision-making process of homeowners who were left dissatisfied by home repair projects (Hendley 2010). Though the pyramidal structure of disputing is universal, the motivations for moving forward or abandoning a dispute are deeply contextual. Variation in the structure of legal institutions and in legal culture leads to differences in the identity and potency of transitional agents.

---

18. In their comparative study of the tendency to seek out compensation for various types of injuries in Canada and the United States, Kritzer, Bogart, and Vidmar (1991, 501) develop a slightly different vocabulary. They identify the barriers to moving from one stage to another. Initially, victims must overcome a recognition barrier. They argue that some view what happened as part of daily life and not as an injury. Victims then face an attribution barrier. Blaming someone else "requires a combination of information and a willingness to externalize the cause of an injury." Seeking out the person at fault requires them to triumph over a confrontation barrier. At the final stage, victims must confront a litigation barrier. Following the lead of Felstiner, Abel, and Sarat (1980–81), much of their analysis is devoted to the role of lawyers.

DEALING WITH AUTO ACCIDENTS

Responses to Involvement in Auto Accidents

Russians, like people everywhere, confront a variety of challenges over the course of their lives. Many (perhaps most) are dismissed as the annoyances of daily life (Kritzer, Bogart, and Vidmar 1991, 501). Traffic accidents are different. They are, by definition, jarring. It is not surprising that all of the focus group partici- pants who reported accidents recognized the experience as injurious. They have "named" the injury. This stands to reason, given that being in an auto accident is by its very nature upsetting and unpleasant at best and life threatening at worst. As we will see, this consensus quickly evaporates once we turn to the question of what to do about the injury.

Doing Nothing or "Lumping It"

In twenty-seven of the seventy accidents reported, the victims made no effort to seek a remedy. Doing nothing is a common, but understudied, response to problems. Even in the United States, with a populace that prides itself on defend- ing its rights, Sandefur (2007, 123–125) found that many opt for inaction when faced with problems that could be solved by mobilizing the law. She identifies three general reasons for opting out: (1) feelings of shame and embarrassment, (2) an unfavorable balance of power in the parties' relationships, and (3) frustrated resignation. These motivations turn out to be useful categories when analyzing the behavior of my Russian focus group participants.

One subset was stymied because they believed they were partially to blame for the accident, giving rise to a sense of embarrassment about the incident. As a result, they did not feel entitled to blame the driver. The basic fact pattern was the same for all these cases. The victim was hit while crossing the road in an unofficial crosswalk, sustaining serious injuries. A Saratov woman told of an elderly relative with failing eyesight who was killed after being struck by a car in St. Petersburg. Miroslava, a forty-year-old seamstress from Shumerlia, who had been struck when she was in the third grade, still walked with a limp. Neither the focus group members nor the victim-participants themselves felt much empathy. The fact that the victims were mostly children and the elderly, who are universally seen as among the most vulnerable in any society, made their lack of compassion striking. For the most part, the victim-participants took responsibility for their fates.

Intertwined with the shame felt by these victims at their foolishness was a belief that the law offered no remedy. As a result, they did not allow themselves to ponder who to blame or how to claim. The other members of the focus groups shared this understanding of the law. The most extreme example was provided by Regina, a cleaning woman from Shumerlia. Some years ago, her eight-year-old daughter had been hit while crossing the road by two soldiers driving a Moskv-ich.[19] The soldiers brought her home. They offered to take her to the hospital and to provide monetary compensation for the young girl's injuries. Regina declined, explaining that her daughter had probably not been paying sufficient attention. She understood that the soldiers felt badly, but did not believe they were respon-sible. As Regina told this story, others around the table nodded in agreement.

In reality, however, the situation was not as straightforward as they believed. Russian law embraces comparative negligence (art. 1083, GK RF part 2). In the-ory, this means that the liability of the driver could be reduced if the pedestrian is found to be at fault. Though the focus group participants were not conversant with the legal niceties, they saw the situation in stark black-and-white terms: the victims were to blame. In their view, the fact that the victims were not in crosswalks established them as grossly negligent and excused any negligence on the part of the drivers. In reality, however, the courts are generally unforgiving when dealing with drivers who hit pedestrians. In such situations, the law reverts back to the Soviet rule for strict liability. Though several of the focus groups included people with legal education, no one spoke up to correct this misimpres-sion. None of them had bothered to consult the law on this question. Yet their confidence in the unavailability of a legal remedy was complete, illustrating that sometimes what people believe the law to be takes on a life of its own (Hendley 2010; Ellickson 1991).

Others opted to do nothing because their accidents had been with people more powerful and well connected. These participants engaged in blaming, but saw the power differential as blocking any potential for claiming. For example, David, a security guard from Kushchevskaia, was the victim of a hit-and-run accident that sent him to the hospital. At the time, he was a soldier doing his mandatory service. Initially he hoped to get the other driver to cover the cost of his medicine. When it turned out that the culprit was the former police chief of a nearby town, the traffic police advised him to drop it. As he told the story, there was an implicit threat that the repercussions of pursuing a claim would be worse for him than for the driver at fault. He took the hint, saying that this sort of outcome was typical for Russia.

A power differential between drivers with no official government connections can play out in the same way. In the wake of the transition to the market, private firms and their leaders have gained great clout (Kryshtanovskaya and White 2005). Several focus group members shared their difficulties in this regard. Vladimir, a

---

19. The Moskvich was a compact passenger car manufactured during the Soviet era.

Moscow mechanic, sustained a concussion and was on bed rest for over a month after a 3 a.m. collision with a ZIL 130 truck that belonged to the powerful Mikoyan machine-building factory.[20] He admitted to speeding at the time of the accident. Unlike the pedestrian-victims who felt their negligence barred them from seeking a remedy, Vladimir's failure to take action was due to his belief that fighting the factory was "useless." The behavior of the traffic police at the scene only confirmed his sense of the political reality. Their report favored the truck driver. When the other focus group participants said that the driver from the Mikoyan factory had probably paid off the police, Vladimir did not disagree. Indeed, no one in the group faulted Vladimir for not pursuing the case. Several shared their own feelings of impotency. Ida, a Muscovite who worked as the chief accountant for a private firm, spoke for many when she said that Russians "have nowhere to go that guarantees a positive result." A few held out hope that the introduction of mandatory insurance would cure the sorts of difficulties faced by Vladimir, whose accident occurred before the law requiring all drivers to be insured had been passed.

Most accidents involve at least two drivers. A decision to do nothing does not necessarily act as a shield if the other driver decides to pursue the matter. When Elvira, a forty-four-year-old state bureaucrat, was hit while parked on a Saratov street to deal with engine trouble, she resolved to do nothing when she learned that the other driver was the general director of a local furniture factory. Though she saw herself as an innocent victim, she decided to let it go. She was convinced that he would be able to outgun her in court. To her surprise, he viewed himself as the victim, arguing that she opened her door with no warning. He demanded 15,000 rubles. When she ignored the claim because she thought it was absurd, she found herself the defendant in a court case. Much like Vladimir, she saw the bias of the traffic police as fueling the fire. Though all the witnesses said the other driver was at fault, the police report characterized it as mutual fault, thus opening the door to a lawsuit. We will return to this incident when discussing how courts deal with claims related to auto accidents. The point here is that doing nothing requires mutual assent.

In some ways, Sandefur's third category of frustrated resignation is a catch-all. These feelings animated those who talked themselves out of pursuing a claim out of fear of the possible backlash from more powerful counterparts. Though resignation can sometimes mask deeper anger, this was not the sense conveyed. Neither those directly affected nor others in the focus groups lashed out against the injustice of the system. Rather there was a collective shrug and a rhetorical "what can be done" question.

---

20. The Mikoyan factory assembled MIG fighter jets. A ZIL 130 is a large dump truck. For a history of ZIL (*Zavod imeni Likhacheva*), see Siegelbaum (2008, 10–35).

There were several categories of people who simply threw up their hands in resignation even though they had identified who was to blame. Some felt that the damage to their car or to themselves wasn't serious enough to warrant further action. In other words, the costs, typically measured in terms of wear and tear on their psyche, outweighed the potential benefits. Others were reluctant to go to war with adversaries that had greater resources, such as municipal authorities or insurance companies.[21] Even when they felt they had been swindled by their insurance companies, few relished the prospect of suing them. The most common refrain was that to do so would be "useless." Some felt stymied owing to the boilerplate language buried in their insurance policies. Anatolii, a midlevel manager from Tomsk, told of the aftermath of an accident involving a minivan owned by his wife. The van was used in her business; it was intended to be driven primarily by her employees, one of whom was driving it at the time of the accident. The traffic police found her employee to be at fault. Anatolii and his wife did not dispute this finding. Initially they thought the damage to the van would be covered by insurance. His wife had purchased comprehensive insurance with an eye to just this sort of situation, but learned to her chagrin that her policy did not include other drivers. When they purchased the insurance, no one pointed this out to them. Anatolii attributed this to the negligence of the insurance agent, but admitted that neither he nor his wife had read the policy carefully. They felt they had no recourse. The other members of the group commiserated. Some had gone through similar experiences. All agreed that they routinely signed contracts without reading them.[22] The bottom line was that the insurance company had no obligation to compensate them. Anatolii and his wife were left holding the bag. He was resigned to his fate, saying, "Such is life."

A general theme within the focus groups was the low level of legal literacy of Russians. Among those who decided to lump it, this attitude was particularly pronounced. Intertwined was the reality that many had sustained devastating injuries and preferred to focus on recovery rather than revenge. When Vavara, a graduate student, was eighteen, she broke her leg after being struck in a Saratov

---

21. Those who were injured by buses or other means of public transportation uniformly did nothing. Not only were they confused about what entity would bear responsibility, but they were also convinced they would be unable to gather the necessary evidence. These accidents often happened during rush hour when witnesses were hustling to and from work. Tracking them down to corroborate what had happened seemed overwhelming, especially given their injuries. Some thought about hiring a lawyer, but did not follow through because they assumed it would be prohibitively expensive. As a rule, those who fell into this category received medical care at no charge, which may have dimmed their ardor for seeking damages.

22. This was a common theme in all the focus groups (Hendley 2010). It mirrors what socio-legal scholars have observed about the United States (Macaulay 1963).

intersection while in a *zebra* (an official crosswalk). She and her parents did not follow up when the prosecutor declined to bring criminal charges against the driver. At the time, they were primarily concerned with getting her back on her feet, literally. She commented that "I understood little about my legal rights and the relevant laws, and so I failed [to take action]." It was noteworthy, however, that as she reflected on the incident, she said that she would not behave any differently if the same thing happened to her today. Her skepticism about the integrity of the system colored her thinking. She shared her suspicion that the driver had provided some "financial influence" to law enforcement organs.

An exception to the Sandefur typology is provided by two similar stories. Both incidents involved groups of people traveling from Shumerlia to the nearby republic capital of Cheboksary. In one case, the passengers were friends and coworkers. In the other, they were not previously acquainted but had been thrown together by happenstance. In both cases, the driver erred by trying to pass in a no-pass zone, and ended up crashing and causing serious injuries to the passengers. Both cars were totaled. Yet in neither case did the passengers make a claim against the driver, even though there was general agreement that he had been at fault. Much as in the examples of powerlessness and frustration, the injured parties were prepared to blame but not to claim. They were not motivated by fear or resignation, but by a sense of what was right. When telling their stories, both narrators stressed that Shumerlia was a small town. As a result, whether they had been friends or acquaintances before they set out did not matter. Even if they did not know each other personally, they still felt a sense of connection that was noticeably absent in larger urban centers. They did not want to be known as someone who had shafted other Shumerlia residents. Whether this somewhat romantic view of the interconnectedness of small towns is shared more widely is unclear. Other group members commended this behavior as *po-chelovecheski* or civilized,[23] but several expressed surprise that the passengers did not ask the drivers to help them with their out-of-pocket medical expenses. Along these lines, it is worth noting that the driver of the car with random passengers asked them to sign written releases, which is potent evidence that he was not willing to rely on small-town goodwill. The person driving his friends took their word.

Bilateral Negotiation with the Other Driver

A common response to accidents in Russia is to talk to the other driver to work out an informal accommodation. Doing so proved popular among the focus

---

23. See the preceding chapter for a discussion of this Russian phrase.

group participants. Over half of them took this route. Because the parties were almost always strangers, establishing trust was more difficult than with neighbors in the wake of water leaks, as discussed in the previous chapter. Indeed, it often proved elusive. What all those who sought to negotiate a settlement shared—regardless of whether their efforts were successful or not—was a firm internal recognition of who was to blame and a desire for a remedy. Put in terms of the Felstiner, Abel, and Sarat typology, they were "claiming." As we will see, the remedies were not always monetary. Sometimes victims simply wanted an apology or an acknowledgment of fault. When money was at issue, the amounts were not exorbitant, especially viewed in light of the massive punitive damages available in U.S. tort cases.

Negotiations suggest a willingness to forego punishment. A bilateral agreement could be limited to monetary damages, leaving open the possibility of pursuing criminal charges against the driver at fault. But the stories elicited from the focus group participants suggest that the purpose of releases—whether written or oral—is to settle all claims. This, of course, raises an ethical dilemma as to whether a driver should be able to escape criminal liability. When the injuries are minor, moral compunctions tend to be ignored. But when they are life threatening, some are troubled by allowing the driver to sidestep criminal responsibility.

The discussion in one of the Saratov focus groups is instructive. Filipp, a young salesman, told of a recent incident in which several of his friends were badly injured. In the revelry following their university graduation, several of his friends got into a car driven by a young man they did not know. All of them were drunk. The driver wrapped his car around a telephone pole. He was not injured, but his passengers were. One girl was in a coma for eight days. The other had a fractured hip and a variety of other internal injuries. According to Filipp, the driver approached the families of the victims with a generous settlement offer. Representatives from the prosecutor's office encouraged settlement, hinting that the girls' drunkenness could complicate any prosecution. Some focus group participants were pragmatic. They said that, were they in the unfortunate shoes of the families, they would take the money, noting that it could be helpful in paying for treatment. More generally, they argued that pursuing criminal sanctions should take a back seat to restoring those injured to full health and that they would prefer to spend their time and energy focused on their own recovery or advocating for loved ones rather than badgering the police to go after the other driver. Filipp reported that the parents of these young women were preoccupied with their medical care. On the other hand, despite criticizing his friends for getting into the car, Filipp was unforgiving when it came to the driver: "It seems to me that he's done something horrible—he's endangered the lives of others. One girl may be an invalid for her entire life, if she survives. He's a grown-up and needs to answer for his behavior."

SUCCESSFUL EFFORTS TO NEGOTIATE SETTLEMENT

Much as in the United States, many of those involved in auto accidents prefer to avoid involving their insurance companies. Unlike the United States, however, the rationale is not connected to fears over increased premiums. Most Russians have only the basic policy, for which the rates are set by the state. Instead, Russians settle privately to avoid having to go through the bureaucracy of their insurance companies.

A good illustration is provided by the aftermath of an accident involving Nikolai, a forty-two-year-old retail store manager. While sitting in a traffic jam in the city center of Saratov, he was hit by a jeep that did not notice him when turning into the street. In his words: "I started to dial the number to report the accident. Then [the other driver] says, 'What are you doing? Let's resolve this here and now.'" Even though the sum offered was less than the likely amount needed to repair his car, Nikolai went along because he understood that this was how things worked. He commented that pursuing the matter to court would inevitably have been more expensive for him. He was skittish about judicial procedure, describing it as "difficult and cumbersome." The other members of the focus group shared his distaste for the courts. When Nikolai said that he would go to court "only in an extreme situation—only if there is no other option," the group chimed in in support. They agreed that settling on the spot was the right choice.

In a Tomsk focus group, this same scenario was presented from the other side. Gennadii, who works as a department head in an industrial enterprise, was traveling in a Volga with several colleagues, one of whom was driving.[24] When they tried to overtake a Moskvich at high speed, the driver lost control and smashed into the other car. The Volga landed in a ditch. According to Gennadii, no one involved had any interest in going the official route owing to the inevitable paperwork involved. Neither side called the traffic police, though they showed up, as did a local TV news crew. In order to put a stop to any potential claims, one of Gennadii's colleagues simply bought the damaged Moskvich from the other driver. No receipts were exchanged. It was an oral agreement, but everyone left satisfied. The other driver was badly hurt; the payment for his car was presumably intended to cover any incidental medical expenses as well. Gennadii implied

24. See Siegelbaum (2008, 37–79) for a history of the Gor'kii Automobile Factory (GAZ), which produces Volgas, a sedan favored by top officials in the Soviet era.

that the traffic police and the camera crew were paid to hush up the accident. He stressed that the accident was never registered. Much like the Saratov focus group, the other members of this Tomsk group were entirely supportive of how the situation had been handled.

Money was the primary way of dealing with the aftermath of accidents. Few payoffs were as generous as Gennadii's. This led to grumbling among some focus group members who, upon reflection, felt they could have done better.[25] But most were relieved to have bypassed the bureaucracy of the traffic police, insurance companies, and courts.

Sometimes money was only part of the solution negotiated between the parties. Though there is no precise equivalent to the practice of one neighbor rolling up his sleeves and repairing the damage caused by a water leak that we saw in the preceding chapter, the experience of Vladislava, a Moscow economist, provides an intriguing counterpoint. After a late-night accident on her way home from her parents in the outskirts of Moscow, the other driver proposed that she take her car for repairs to the shop of his relative. He offered to cover any costs. She took him up on his offer and was pleased with the service received.[26] The other members of the focus group were surprised she had trusted a stranger. Vladislava said that her suspicions had been raised because the license plate on the other car indicated he was not from Moscow. The very fact that he had stuck around after the accident bolstered his credibility.[27] Even so, if she had been on her own, she might have rebuffed him, but her husband had arrived on the scene soon after the accident and he supported her decision. Also pushing her toward going along was her disinclination to go to court.

In situations where physical injuries were more profound, the assistance provided by the driver at fault sometimes took a more practical form. As with monetary payments, it is useful to look at the practices from both sides. Fatima, a university student who worked at a charitable organization, saw her life turned upside down when she accidently hit a teenager crossing a busy street in Moscow.

---

25. One Moscow woman described the 5,000 rubles she received as "laughable." She took it because she realized the other driver had no more money, and she had no taste for litigation. She was more annoyed by the fact that the culprit got off with a 100-ruble fine, despite admitting her responsibility.

26. After the car was repaired, Vladislava sold it. The service center helped her by turning back the odometer, which she described as a customary practice.

27. Vladislava's cynicism about human nature revealed itself when she said that perhaps the other driver had stuck around to wait for the traffic police because he assumed they would side with him over a woman. She too worried that the traffic police would blame her, which is why she called her husband immediately after the incident and asked him to come to the scene. Several times she noted that many Russian men harbor prejudice regarding female drivers. She admits that when the police arrived they "jumped all over him," probably because he was a bit tipsy.

She was stuck in traffic. Next to her was a large truck. As she was inching along in a crosswalk, she failed to see the teen darting through the maze of traffic. The girl sustained a compound fracture of her leg. During the months she spent in the hospital, Fatima was a constant presence, bringing food to sustain her and her mother (who was single with another child to support as well). She also provided over $3,000 to ensure that the girl received first-rate treatment and to cover her tuition for higher education, money that she raised by selling her car. At first, the family refused to talk to Fatima. As she put it, "the mother wanted to strangle me." After four months of apologies and material support, she wore the mother down, but the teenager never softened. During the frosty period, the family filed a civil suit against Fatima and supported the police in pursuing criminal charges. By the time these lawsuits were set for trial, relations had thawed and the family withdrew its civil claim and asked the court for lenience in the criminal case.

Viktoria, a Tomsk teacher, was hit while crossing a crowded street in 2001. The driver was immediately surrounded by witnesses. Much like Fatima, he said that he never saw her. She was not as badly hurt as the Moscow teen, but did sustain a concussion and later needed surgery to repair her leg. During the three months of her recovery, the driver was vigilant. When she was unable to walk, he carried her in his arms to his car and took her to her treatments. He paid for her treatment. In her words, "he did everything to ensure my recovery and to make amends." After three months when she was literally back on her feet, he offered her a final payment of 10,000 rubles and asked her to sign a release of liability. She went along. By that time, they had developed what she described as a "human relationship" (*chelovecheskoe otnoshenie*). She had no desire to ruin his life by going to the traffic police and bringing a criminal case that, at a minimum, would cause him to lose his license (which he needed for his job) for a sustained period.

In the discussion of cases like Viktoria's, the focus groups were openly suspicious of the motives of the do-gooders. The groups doubted their sincerity and believed that their help was cynically motivated to ensure that the victims forego legal action against them. The analysis of failed efforts at negotiation shows that Russia has its share of unscrupulous con men who promise the world only to disappear into thin air. Fatima provides some insight into how this happens. After her accident, she sought out a lawyer to help her sort through her options. He offered to help her create an alibi to avoid liability that would stand up in court. He counseled her against going to see the teenaged victim in the hospital and assured her that the girl would be helped with a generous "gift" in due course. The combination of the accident and her encounter with this lawyer gave rise to a road-to-Damascus conversion for Fatima. Raised as a secular Muslim, she converted to Christianity and thereafter devoted her life to charitable work.

She fired the lawyer and resolved to do right by the girl.[28] She explicitly linked her choices to her faith, saying that Christians do not bribe their way out of problems. "If a person has forgotten about God, he lives however he wants. If a person is a believer, then he does not budge; he is like stone. Of course, there can be exceptions. But I know of many people who will not betray their beliefs for any amount of money." She had the moral fiber to stand up to temptation, but not everyone does.

UNSUCCESSFUL EFFORTS TO NEGOTIATE SETTLEMENT

A number of participants in the focus groups told of unfulfilled promises. Most common were promises of money that never materialized. When this happened in the wake of a fender-bender, then the victim learns a lesson about human nature, but is not unduly harmed. More problematic are accidents that give rise to serious physical injuries, where the broken promises undermine the ability of victims to secure first-rate medical treatment. What happened to Anton, a Saratov geologist, is a tragic example. Some years ago when a student at the local university, he was waiting at a rail crossing when a car came barreling out of a nearby gas station and hit him. He lost consciousness. He awoke in the hospital with a shattered pelvis. The mother of the other driver, who was also a student, came to see him. She explained that her son had no money, but promised that her family would take care of everything for Anton if he signed a release. Once he signed, the mother and her son disappeared. Anton's initial treatment was botched. He was in and out of hospitals and on crutches for the next three years. In reflecting on what happened, Anton acknowledges that he probably could have pursued the other driver in court, but says that it would have been unlikely to produce a windfall, given that he was a student. His main concern at the time was not punishing the other driver or his mother, but getting better. Though as an agnostic he does not attribute his behavior to his religious beliefs, like Fatima, he is satisfied that he behaved *po-chelovecheski*.

Sometimes it is the victims themselves who are the scam artists. The Russian media is replete with stories of people who make a good living by jumping in front of cars and pretending to be more seriously injured than they are. Examples of ham-handed practitioners of this art can be found on the Internet. One goal of introducing mandatory insurance was to discourage this practice. Whether it has succeeded is difficult to know. The desire of many to avoid interacting with their insurance companies leaves them vulnerable. Liubov, who works as the chief accountant at a small Moscow factory, was with her husband when they

---

28. Fatima reported that when she refused the services of this lawyer, her tires were slashed.

hit an elderly man with their new car. He had been in his own car, but jumped out. He injured his head; blood was everywhere. They felt bad. When the old man and his daughter called to ask for money and help, they initially gave them money. Her husband also brought food to the man. But as the demands became more frequent and the amounts increased, they grew suspicious. They began to tape his calls. When he asked for $10,000, they played the tape for the police. The investigation was terminated and the requests stopped. No doubt many people lack the common sense and courage exhibited by Liubov and her husband, and so are held hostage to the demands of pseudo-victims. It is likely not coincidental that they were driving a new car when this happened. These con artists target the rich, assuming they have greater access to money and a strong desire to avoid the criminal courts.

Bribery can color the options available to the parties. When Ida's daughter was hit on New Year's Day in 2006, she sustained an open fracture of her right hip and leg. Ida spoke openly of how the doctors and nurses told her that they would provide aggressive treatment only if Ida paid them under the table. Not only did she have to navigate a corrupt medical system, but she also felt the consequences of corruption in her treatment by the legal system.[29] Her daughter had been in a *zebra* when she was hit. The driver, who was from Azerbaijan, was speeding and made little effort to brake for her. When Ida met him, his wife offered to pay her $1,000 to hush the incident up. It was Ida's understanding that the driver himself did not speak Russian. She did not take the money, not because she was squeamish about accepting a payoff, but because she was not yet sure how much her daughter's treatment would cost. In fairly quick order, the Azerbaijani couple vanished along with their offer. The indifferent attitude of the traffic police left Ida convinced that the money had gone to them. Some months later, she coincidentally got a job working for a prosecutor. He insisted that she hire an *advokat* to pursue the case.[30] Proving what happened was not easy. At the time of the focus group she was discouraged, saying that she had probably wasted her money on the lawyer. As this suggests, not all failed negotiations end with the victim doing nothing, like Anton. Sometimes such failures are merely a way station on the path to litigation.

---

29. Paying medical staff for ostensibly free treatment is not a post-Soviet phenomenon, but reflects a continuation of practices from the Soviet era. Heinzen (2016) draws on the Soviet interview project with émigrés to flesh out the choices, which ranged from bringing flowers or candy to large cash payments. Doctor-respondents justified them on the grounds that it was a long-standing custom and claimed that refusing such offerings would have insulted their patients. Whether either side viewed them as bribes or, rather, saw them as *blat* is unclear. See also Ledeneva (1998). Rivkin-Fish (2005) and (2014) document these practices in present-day Russia and Ukraine, respectively.

30. See chapter 5 for a discussion of the different variants of Russian lawyers.

Seeking Third-Party Assistance for Settlement

For those who are able to find a resolution short of litigation, but for whom bilateral negotiations proved ineffective, there are several third parties that have proven useful in resolving differences. Most notable among these are insurance companies and the traffic police. The former is to be expected. After all, one of the purposes of making insurance mandatory was to make it easier to deal with accidents. On the other hand, the low reputation enjoyed by the traffic police makes it surprising that anyone would turn to them in times of trouble. The analysis thus far has mostly documented their receptivity to bribery.

The incidents recounted during the focus groups spanned the time period before and after the imposition of compulsory insurance. There is no question that few Russians bothered to obtain insurance before they were required to do so. As I noted earlier, many drivers continue to flout the law. But most of those who had insurance were able to get paid. Not all came away satisfied by the experience, but only one of the focus group participants was sufficiently disgruntled to pursue her claim to the courts.

Not surprisingly, those who had purchased comprehensive insurance (rather than the minimal compulsory policy), were more likely to be content. They still complained about the endless red tape. Illustrating Felstiner, Abel, and Sarat's point about how the same event can be experienced differently, two twenty-something Muscovites who were paid within three months after gathering all the documents (*spravki*) came away with polar opposite impressions. Dmitrii, a student who worked part time at a travel agency, who sideswiped another car when he was unable to control his own car because of speeding, was satisfied. Polina, a social worker, was less sanguine. She grumbled about being forced to do the legwork for the insurance company, and was insulted when her agent left her with the impression that she was somehow to blame for the damage to her car, even though she had been hit by a drunk driver. She was also dissatisfied with the amount she received. In her words, "I tried to complain within the insurance company. . . . But it was to no avail—I was stuck with their procedures. They didn't help me. I came away disappointed in insurance companies generally." The idea of suing the insurance company was unappealing. "I understood that my health was more valuable and decided not to initiate a lawsuit." As a mother with several small children, Polina had less time than Dmitrii (who was single) to devote to pulling together the evidence her insurance company required before it would pay the claim.[31] No doubt the fact that she was the victim rather than the culprit also colored her view.

---

31. Many Russian banks require comprehensive insurance as a condition of providing a loan. This explains why both Dmitrii and Polina had this type of policy. Few opt for it voluntarily.

Those who had only compulsory insurance were uniformly dissatisfied, both with the way they were treated and with their payouts. They felt that their insurance companies had co-opted the so-called independent appraisers to underestimate the cost of repairs. Several told of how they got their estimates bumped up by bribing these appraisers. None of them thought it was worth the effort to litigate.

Traffic police proved even more unpopular among the focus group participants than insurance companies. Even so, several examples in which the traffic police acted as honest brokers show the danger of stereotypes. The most telling involves Oksana, a Kushchevskaia factory worker who was knocked off her bicycle by a hit-and-run driver. She had to stay home from work for two weeks to recover from her injuries. Two months later, she recognized the car at a farmer's market. The paint from her bicycle was still visible on the headlights. She called her husband and son, who alerted the traffic police. The officers confronted the driver, who admitted his involvement. They encouraged him to buy her a new bike. As Oksana explains: "The officer told him, if you don't want to lose your license, then pay this woman right now. If you don't, she will take you to court and, in that event, you'll both lose your license and you'll have to pay her." He agreed, but said he did not have that much money on him. The officers held his passport while he went home to fetch more money. Oksana was able to buy a new bike with the money.

This story is unusual in several ways. Not only does it put the traffic police in a good light, but it also shows that occasionally Russian officialdom is able to put aside its byzantine bureaucratic rules and do what is right for an individual who has been wronged. Oksana harbored no illusions about the traffic police. She had to be convinced to involve them, both at the time of the accident and when she came upon the car. She was not sophisticated—her formal education had ceased at the eighth grade—but against all odds her innate sense of what was right was rewarded.

Litigation

Going to court was no one's first choice. It represents a grudging response to an inability to resolve problems through negotiation. Russians' distaste for litigation lends potency to the threat to file a lawsuit and can stimulate parties to negotiate and to help their victims. Fatima's solicitude toward the teenager she hit may have initially been stimulated by her desire to avoid criminal liability, though she did not acknowledge as much. The wariness of the victim's family is demonstrated by its unwillingness to withdraw the complaint until the last minute. Anton's experience acts as a cautionary tale. He signed the release before receiving anything from the perpetrator's family and lacked the energy to pursue them when they vanished.

INITIATING LITIGATION

Taking on a lawsuit requires a strong commitment, regardless of whether the target is an individual or an entity. Some hired lawyers to help them. Even so, they took on much of the responsibility for assembling the bits and pieces of evidence needed to prevail. Proof problems were the most commonly cited obstacle to going to court—it was a much bigger concern than telephone justice.

Not surprisingly, stubbornness is a trait shared by those who took this route. They typically describe themselves as being driven by principle more than money,[32] which makes sense given that the amounts recoverable are rather modest, at least by the standards of U.S. awards of punitive damages. The targets of these lawsuits use every trick in the book to escape liability. After all, if the parties were open to amicable settlement, the case would not have gotten to court. A somewhat extreme example is the behavior of the driver who hit Katia, a Saratov university student. He plowed into her, sending her car flying across several lanes of traffic where it was stopped by a tree. He and his family walked away from the incident, but Katia was knocked unconscious and spent several months recovering in the hospital. The traffic police report declared him to be at fault, but he refused to acknowledge responsibility and made no effort to contact her. She tried to get criminal charges brought against him, but because he had not been drunk and she had survived the accident, the police were uninterested. She then resolved "to beat him up financially." For Katia, this was a matter of principle. In her words, "my parents told me to let it go . . . but I have such strong resentment and pain that I had to pursue it."

The lawsuit turned into a soap opera. Acting on the recommendation of friends, she located an *advokat* to whom she paid a 20,000-ruble retainer. They agreed that the lawyer would also get 15 percent of any amount recovered. The complaint sought 1 million rubles in moral damages. It is doubtful that she had any realistic expectations of recovering anything close to that amount. Not only are Russian courts disinclined to award such large amounts, but the driver was also a schoolteacher with a monthly salary of 4,000 rubles. In addition, anticipating a lawsuit, he had transferred all his assets (including his apartment) into his wife's name. When he received the complaint, he made an abortive suicide attempt and checked himself into a psychiatric facility, where he was beyond

---

32. This marks them as unusual. In a 2010 survey, only 8 percent of recent Russian litigants said they had sued out of principle. Most (60 percent) claim to have resorted to the courts only when they had no other options (Hendley 2016).

the reach of the courts. When we spoke, eighteen months had elapsed since the incident, but he was still there. Katia's lawyers had tried to convince the judge of his bad faith. The judge was sympathetic but told them that the case could not go forward until the defendant was declared legally competent. She ordered an independent psychiatric evaluation, but it was carried out by the same doctor who had been treating the defendant and he stuck to his guns. Over the months of waiting, Katia's ardor dimmed, but she was reluctant to abandon the case owing to sunk costs. Her belief in the ability of courts to right wrongs—which made her a bit of an outlier among the focus group participants—also kept her in the game.[33] But she did not view herself as an exception. As she said, "I think I am not the only person who believes in the law."

Sometimes litigation can be part of a grieving process. Anna, a Moscow real estate agent, was in a horrific accident in which she lost control of her car when a drunk driver darted into her lane of traffic. Her car flipped over several times. Her brother, who was a passenger in the car, had to be cut out of the car by emergency technicians. He died without regaining consciousness. Anna spent six months recovering in the hospital, and was unable to return to work for another several months. The other driver and his family received only minor injuries. They never contacted her to express their regret. Nor did they attend her brother's funeral. Though she had their contact information, she did not reach out. She felt that their behavior telegraphed their character.

No one questioned the responsibility of the other driver. He was prosecuted and received a three-year sentence for drunk driving. Seeing the other driver in jail was not enough for Anna. She brought a civil lawsuit against him, in an effort to recover her out-of-pocket expenses for medical care. She had been forced to pay under the table to get needed medications and to ensure she had the best surgeons.[34] Unlike Katia, she did not hire a lawyer. Though she had a law degree herself, she had no litigation experience. In reflecting on the court case, she speculated that she might have done better had she sought help from legal professionals, but noted the difficulty of finding reputable lawyers. The experience of her friends left her convinced that good lawyers were very expensive. She explained that any spare financial resources had gone to pay for her brother's funeral and her own medical expenses.

---

33. Skeptics might assume that she was new to the judicial system. In reality, however, she had been involved in a Dickensian case brought by her father's ex-wife to get title to an apartment that was owned by Katia and her father. Perhaps her faith was stoked by the fact that the court shared her view of her former stepmother's claims as bogus.

34. Rivkin-Fish's (2005) interviews with doctors suggest that they often regard such payments as superfluous. But Anna and the other respondents saw them as obligatory.

Though Anna won the lawsuit, she received no emotional closure from the experience. It only seemed to intensify her grief over her brother's death. She recovered 5,000 rubles, which was a small fraction of her actual medical expenses. The court took the formalistic position that medical care in Russia is free, thereby placing the burden on her to prove her financial outlays. She found the demands of the court for documentary evidence of her side payments to medical personnel to be unrealistic and humiliating. She felt pressured by the judge to drop the case and believed that the other side had bribed the judge. In contrast to Katia, Anna did not trust in the integrity of the legal system, arguing that "any judge can be bought." She concluded: "it is sad to live in a state where we are completely unprotected; where we have no hope."

Suing entities tend to be less driven by emotion. The one instance of a lawsuit brought against an insurance company is a good example. Kira and her husband resorted to litigation when their insurance company refused to pay their claim. Its stubbornness was driven by an odd glitch in the law, which it exploited fully. Kira was a passenger in the family car being driven to their dacha near Tomsk by her husband. When they were going through a green light at a traffic intersection, they were hit by a foreign-made car that came out of nowhere. Their car was totaled. There were four people in the other car, all of whom had been drinking. The other car sped off after the accident, but was quickly apprehended. In an odd twist, the traffic police were unable to determine who had been driving. Kira believes that this was a subterfuge designed to protect an influential local military official. Russian law requires a determination of who was driving before an insurance companies is required to pay.

The insurance company clung to the letter of the law and refused to pay. Kira and her husband found a *iurist* to represent them who was a coworker of their daughter's. The *iurist* explained what sort of evidence would be needed. Her husband then tracked it down, wooing witnesses to come forward with traditional Russian gifts of wine and candy (Rivkin-Fish 2005, 58). Thanks to the help of the lawyer, they prevailed at trial, only to face an appeal, which they also won. In the end, they had to resort to the bailiffs (*sudebnye pristavy*) to recover the judgment of 32,000 rubles. This amount was not sufficient to buy a new car outright. They used a third of it as a down payment on a loan. They used another third to pay the *iurist*.[35] She made no financial demands on them, but they were convinced that they never would have succeeded without her help, and so insisted that she take the money.

---

35. They put the remainder aside as a rainy-day fund. Both Kira and her husband had latent health issues that they worried could flare up at any time.

Though the experience was not pleasant—the litigation dragged on for eighteen months and required them to persist through "terrible red tape"—Kira felt the insurance company gave them no choice. She insisted they were motivated by justice and not by a desire to punish. In her words, they pressed forward because "we decided that the law was on our side. Plus we weren't to blame." In terms of her trust in the legal system, she falls somewhere between the extremes of Katia and Anna. She felt that they got justice from the courts and did not see their experience as an aberration.[36] The other members of her focus group were generally supportive of her choices. Several chimed in to say that the only way to get an insurance company to pay was to sue. Others said that they too would have sued in Kira's situation, but might have refrained if the amount at stake was less significant. Everyone—including Kira—was bothered by the fact that the identity of the driver was never established.

The distaste for paying may not be limited to insurance companies. When Irina, a Saratov doctor, was hit by a minivan owned by the Russian Pension Fund, her experience had some interesting parallels to that of Kira. The incident occurred in 2002, before insurance was made mandatory, so insurance was a nonissue. The traffic police established that the other driver's poor eyesight had caused the accident. Estimates of the cost to fix Irina's car hovered around 60,000 rubles. Realizing that they could not absorb this loss, her husband went to the offices of the Pension Fund to negotiate a settlement. The bureaucrats quickly showed him the door. They told him that he would have to sue to get anything from them.

Irina and her husband resolved to take a "completely legal approach." Neither they nor their friends had previously had occasion to go to court, so they got no advice as to how to proceed. They simply went to their local "legal consultation" office and hired an *advokat*.[37] He explained that they needed to arrange for an independent appraisal of the damages to the car and drafted a complaint, which was filed in the justice-of-the-peace courts. After several hearings, the parties reached a settlement (*mirovoe soglashenie*).[38] In contrast to the insurance company, the Pension Fund paid the amount of the judgment immediately. Irina had been concerned that the case would drag on forever, but it was over within two months. Her fears of corruption also turned out to be unfounded. In her words,

---

36. Kira had very different reactions to the trial and appellate courts. She felt validated by the trial court, where she and her husband were allowed to share their stories. By contrast, she found the appellate hearing off-putting because the three-judge panel had no interest in them but only wanted to query their lawyer about technical details.

37. They gave him a small retainer and agreed to pay him 5 percent of any amount recovered.

38. The Pension Fund did not lay down. They initiated a counterclaim that sought to place blame on Irina's husband. But neither the witnesses nor the report of the traffic police substantiated its position, leading to the settlement.

"I was very satisfied [with the court]. I was satisfied with our *advokat*. I was satisfied with the judicial process—how it was conducted—it was very competent (*gramotno*) with no red tape."

BEING THE TARGET OF LITIGATION

Getting sued is no fun. As I've discussed, those who were involved in accidents in which serious damage, whether material or physical, was sustained often took action to ensure they would not find themselves in court. Sometimes they did so right away, as with the driver from Shumerlia who had his passengers sign a release. Other times the request comes only after the culprit has proved himself by helping the victim with her recovery. The genuineness of the solicitude varies, as does human nature. Anton was left with only a piece of paper when the other driver disappeared after getting what he wanted. By contrast, the driver who hit Viktoria stuck around until she was back on her feet. Fatima never asked for a release. By the time the civil and criminal cases came to trial, she had won the trust of her victim's family (if not the victim herself) and they asked the court to spare her. No doubt behavior is driven largely by the internal moral compass of the individuals involved.

Of the participants in the focus groups, only Elvira ended up having to go through the full process as a defendant. As I noted earlier, she believed herself to have been the victim and had resolved not to pursue her claim. The status differential was a key factor in her decision. The other driver was the general director of a local furniture factory, whereas she saw herself as a lowly state bureaucrat. Unfortunately, the other driver saw himself as the aggrieved party and pursued her as a matter of principle. They met several times. She made him aware that her husband had connections to the local prosecutor's office in an effort to equalize their status, but he paid no attention.[39] When he would not budge from his initial demand, she said they would have to leave it to the court. Sure enough, he brought a lawsuit against her in the justice-of-the-peace courts.

Elvira felt out of her element in court. As the case proceeded, she believed that the judge consistently favored the other side, allowing him to go on at length, while cutting her off. She had the help of someone she described as an "assistant" (*pomoshchnik*), though he was a recent law graduate. She met with several more experienced lawyers who specialize in handling traffic cases, but their price was too steep for her. She did not bring a counterclaim to assert her version of what

---

39. This was an empty threat. Her husband had no legal training; he was not a prosecutor himself. He had previously worked as an assistant in the section of the prosecutor's office that handles environmental claims. He was unable to help her once the case ended up in court.

happened, explaining that she feared the expense of doing so. The decision went against her. Because she lacked the funds to pay it, a portion of her salary was garnished.

In reflecting on the experience, Elvira listed a series of strategic mistakes she had made. Even though she had few assets, her initial instinct had been to give the other driver what he wanted, but her assistant convinced her to stand firm. In her words: "I am sorry that I didn't just give him the money right away because the court hearings were unpleasant. If you go to court, you end up feeling guilty." She did not see the judicial process as being even-handed. She felt that the judge and the plaintiff were part of an insiders' circle to which she was not privy. In her view, "if I had been within this circle, then probably it would have been seen as mutual fault." If she had it to do over, she would make every effort to avoid the courts. If that proved impossible, then she would hire an *advokat*, who would "guarantee victory." Put more bluntly, she would find a lawyer who had the backdoor connections needed to bribe the judge. Though not convinced that the judge in her case was bribed, she believed that the law itself was a peripheral issue. In her opinion, the outcome was dictated by connections.

Explaining Russians' Responses to Auto Accidents

On the most prosaic level, the seriousness of the injuries sustained in an accident explains the responses. This is hardly unique to Russia. Regardless of the setting, people tend to have different reactions to minor fender-benders than to crashes in which cars are destroyed and life-threatening injuries are sustained. The evidence from the focus group confirms that Russians are more likely to "lump it" when the damages are insignificant. But there are many other factors at play, both institutional and individual. Many are carryovers from the Soviet past, whereas some are new to the post-Soviet era. Those inherited from the past rarely survive in their pure form.

Thinking more deeply about why some Russians do nothing and others pursue their causes with a Javert-like intensity requires us to return to the theoretical framework of Felstiner, Abel, and Sarat. They identify a series of possible transformational agents that, as the label suggests, have the effect of pushing the problem from one stage to another. Their analysis focuses on the United States, but many of the factors are universal. The genius of their approach is that it incorporates an interior perspective with societal factors. Each can be important on its own or they can be combined to make a kaleidoscope of patterns.

Respondents' Worldview(s)

Felstiner, Abel, and Sarat posit that how one looks at the world will have a profound effect on one's approach to problem solving. This insight plays out in an interesting way in the Russian case. As part of the transition away from state socialism, Russians have come to feel increasingly isolated. For many, the collapse of state services in the 1990s shattered their faith in the ability of the state to protect them. Their social support networks became frayed as people scrambled to support their families when the Soviet-era practice of featherbedding disappeared with the imposition of market incentives. Inflation made mincemeat of the pensions of the elderly, forcing many of them back onto the job market and leaving them unavailable for their traditional role of assisting with child care. The shattering of long-time norms into which they were socialized during the Soviet era has left many unsure of what is right or wrong. I suspect that this effect is more deeply felt among older generations, though the unrepresentative nature of my focus groups does not allow for the testing of this hypothesis.

The effect of this sense of social isolation is more evident in interactions among strangers. Thus, the analysis of the focus group participants' behavior in the wake of auto accidents provides a fascinating contrast to their responses to water leaks in their apartments. In the latter case, they were mostly dealing with people they had known for a long time, whereas their roadside difficulties uniformly forced them to interact with strangers. Even when they formed a bond with the other driver, as in the cases of Fatima and Viktoria, it was temporary and dissipated when the person injured was able to cope with daily life for herself. Thus, in their responses to these unexpected events, the focus group participants were guided not by the localized norms of their *pod"ezd* (or residential entryway) but by a combination of their internal moral compass and more general societal norms.

Whether post-Soviet Russian society has developed a clear set of norms that govern behavior in the aftermath of an auto accident is unclear. As I noted at the outset of the chapter, the proliferation of cars is a relatively recent phenomenon. In contrast to water leaks, those who are unfortunate enough to be in an accident cannot think back on how their parents or grandparents handled it. For most, it is an entirely new experience. Although there was an occasional nod to the need to behave in a civilized (*po-chelovecheski*) manner, the lack of concern with how one's behavior in the wake of an auto accident appeared to others was striking, especially when compared with the obsession with maintaining appearances that was exhibited in the preceding chapter. Instead, many respondents felt as though they were on their own. They relied on themselves and on immediate family members. Some were afraid to contact law enforcement organs, fearing that doing so would rebound to their detriment.

This sense of isolation, which may have been latent in the Soviet era, has become a powerful motivating force in present-day Russia, especially in large metropolises (Shevchenko 2009). Self-reliance can be a double-edged sword. It can express itself in a single-minded determination that makes all the difference in dealing with bureaucracies. After her brother was killed by a drunk driver, Anna said that "no one wanted to do anything." Many of the focus group participants felt similarly ignored and marginalized by officialdom. Kira knew no one else would help her get the money she was owed by her insurance company, and pressed forward to the court with her claim. As did Irina in her battle with the Pension Fund. But it can also express itself as selfishness, as in the case of Anton, whose desperate need for help in recovering was ignored in the eagerness of the driver at fault to escape responsibility. When the mother of the perpetrator was negotiating with Anton, she stressed her son's student status and his consequent lack of resources, conveniently ignoring that Anton was also a penniless student at the time. Such behavior reflects a hardness regarding the difficulties of others that may be a quasi-survivalist response to the economic chaos of the 1990s. Katia's case shows how self-reliance can sometimes result in a stalemate. Ignoring her parents' advice to move on, Katia pursued a scorched-earth strategy, filing a million-ruble lawsuit. The other driver responded in kind by transferring his assets to his wife and feigning mental illness.

Despite their complaints about being left to their own devices, many of the focus group participants drew on their membership in communities to help them through the experience. These ranged from the family at the microlevel to the community of believers at a more cosmic level. Turning again to Anton's experience, the other driver benefitted from being part of a family that was determined to preserve his options in life. Anton's family was no less concerned with his future, but his precarious physical condition took up all their energy. Along similar lines, Ida's identity as a mother led her to whatever was necessary, including bribing medical personnel, to ensure that her young daughter did not become an invalid. Her priority was her daughter's recovery rather than seeking out and punishing the Azerbaijani couple who were to blame. Some Russians have turned to religion as a way of making sense of their feelings of isolation.[40] In ordering their behavior, these believers are mindful of the Golden Rule of doing

---

40. According to periodic polling by the Levada Center, the segment of Russian society that identifies itself as Russian Orthodox grew from less than 20 percent in 1989 to about 80 percent in 2012. The percentage of nonbelievers took a precipitous nosedive during this period, dropping from over 70 percent to about 12 percent (Figure 16.1, Zorkaia 2012, 165). These same data suggest that, for some, declaring oneself as a believer was more a matter of fashion than a life-changing conversion. About three-fourths of those polled in September 2012 felt that many Russians are keen to show their involvement with the faith but are not true believers (Table 16.15, Zorkaia 2012, 163). Further

to others as you would have them do to you. Fatima, who grew up as a secular Muslim but embraced Christianity in the form of the Russian Orthodox Church after injuring a teenager with her car, is a good example of how genuine religiosity can lead to unselfish behavior.

Being an outsider also influenced behavior. For the focus group members, such feelings mostly served as a deterrent. A number of them did nothing in the wake of their accidents because they felt the other drivers were better connected and that pursuing them would come to naught. Elvira is a cautionary tale in this respect. Though she tried to keep her head down when she learned that the other driver was part of the local economic elite, he would not let it go. Once in court, she believed that her outsider status sealed her fate.

How a person sees herself as fitting in has a profound impact on her response. The Shumerlia respondents saw themselves as part of a relatively small and tight-knit community and worried about how an effort to recover damages after an accident would be viewed by friends and neighbors. They spoke of how everyone knew one another's business in Shumerlia. Recognizing that claiming was not a socially acceptable response, they signed away their rights. Such attitudes are reminiscent of the rural residents Engel studied in Sander County in the United States (1984), who saw injuries as a part of daily life on farms to be endured. He found that newcomers were more likely to pursue damages than longtime residents and to be ostracized for their behavior. Like their counterparts from Sander County, the Shumerlia respondents' concerns were individual, not collective. They feared that pursuing a claim would make them appear petty in the eyes of the community, but were not worried about rupturing its social cohesion. This stands in contrast to the more communitarian motivations of Thai villagers in the wake of accidents. Engel (2001) found that Thai villagers saw compensation, particularly in the form of elaborate and costly funeral ceremonies, as a way to return harmony to the community. His work reminds us of the ways in which different conceptions of "community" or "reality frames" can play out in terms of post-accident claiming (9).

Rather than worrying about how neighbors and others close will view their behavior, the common thread among the respondents from these larger cities was a concern over what sort of clout the other party to the accident might have. In this, we see the lingering effect of the web of personal connections that determined one's ability to survive and thrive in the Soviet era. As the scholarly, literary, and memoir literature remind us, the perennial shortages made coping

---

evidence comes from a November 2012 survey that reveals that over 60 percent of respondents had never read the Bible or any other fundamental religious text (Table 16.26, Zorkaia 2012, 167).

on one's own impossible (Baranskaya 1990; Ledeneva 1998; Young 1989; Smith 1976; Voinovich 1977). The abundance of consumer goods and the beginnings of a service economy has lessened the need to build and maintain personal networks. But all bets are off in the case of unexpected events like auto accidents. Many Russians still believe that law takes a back seat to connections when it comes to getting out of trouble. It is no surprise that the focus group participants preferred informal solutions to litigation. Nor is it unique to Russians. David Nelken (2009, 36–37) notes that in Sicily, "the key question after an accident . . . is not who is to blame but with whom you have to deal. It is important to find out as much as possible about the personal and social background of the person you have been in an accident with, getting information about the reputation of his or her insurance company, the lawyer, garage mechanic, medical expert available to him or her, and in general the person's larger network." Writing in 2012, Iuliia Latynina, a popular columnist, echoed these sentiments: "In Russia, the punishment varies depending on the status of the offender." She argued that prosecutors will throw the book at an ordinary drunk driver, but if the driver at fault is a vice president of a prominent company, then "the person killed by his car will naturally end up being found guilty" (2012b).

Corruption

The dividing line between connections and corruption is fuzzy at best. Corruption—both real and perceived—had a significant influence on the focus group participants' behavior at every stage of the post-accident process. There was literally no element of Russian institutional life that they did not view as being susceptible to corruption.

The frustrated resignation felt by those who did nothing was often prompted by a sense that any effort to engage the system would be futile owing to the willingness of officials to be swayed by bribes. For those who made claims, their efforts to settle reflect their lack of faith in the integrity of the state and private officials who were charged with protecting them. Over and over again, I was told that anyone could be bought. Some experienced this for themselves. Most acted preemptively based on common wisdom. Teasing out how much faith is placed in such rumors is an impossible task. For my purposes, what is more important is the extent to which my respondents were convinced of the futility of using the formal system and reacted by opting out, either by doing nothing or settling.

Much of the analysis thus far has focused on perceived corruption in the legal system. But corruption within both insurance companies (discussed below) and the medical establishment was also taken for granted. This explains why those close to victims with severe injuries were rarely able to focus on claiming and, instead, had to devote themselves to advocating for their loved ones within the medical system. Ordinary Russian hospitals provide few creature comforts to their patients. When Fatima brought food to the hospital for the teenager she had accidentally injured, she endeared herself to the teen's mother, who otherwise would have had to do this. Many respondents told of having to make side payments to get access to needed treatments and rehabilitation facilities. No one disagreed with these sad realities. Rather they chimed in with their own examples. Perhaps the most egregious example came from Ariadna, a Shumerlia insurance agent, who spent a month in the hospital after surviving a head-on collision. Her husband had been driving within the speed limit when a car came into his lane in an effort to pass a bus. He swerved to avoid the brunt of this car and they ended up in a ditch along with their three neighbors-passengers, all of whom were badly injured. Despite the obvious fault of this driver and the availability of the bus passengers as witnesses to what happened, no criminal case was ever brought. The medical records substantiating their injuries mysteriously disappeared. She believed that the doctors had been bribed to destroy them by the other driver. The other members of the focus group agreed. The traffic police told her that the fix was in; they had been pressured to go easy. In the end, Ariadna did nothing. She said that her friends and family convinced her that pursuing the case was not worth the effort.

Institutional Infrastructure

Felstiner, Abel, and Sarat point to a number of institutional factors that can encourage or discourage people to pursue their disagreements up the pyramid of disputing. Among these are the law itself and the receptivity of the courts to various types of disputes. They also identify lawyers as important gatekeepers. In the U.S. context, few contemplate litigation without consulting lawyers. A lawyer's willingness to take a case hinges less on his client's sense of injury than on whether he will be able to win. This is particularly true in tort claims, for which lawyers are compensated by contingent fees that depend on the damages paid by the other side. More often than not these damages are the result of settlement negotiations rather than court judgments, though threats of litigation can be potent weapons in stimulating such settlements.

An examination of the Russian context shows how these institutional factors can have a very different impact. It is a case study in the chasm that can exist between how institutions are supposed to work and how they actually perform in daily life. All too often, the goals of institutional design fall short in practice.

RUSSIAN LAW OF TORTS

As I noted at the outset of the chapter, Russia is a late developer as to torts. In the West, torts came into its own in the late nineteenth century as an antidote to the Industrial Revolution and the growth of the railroads (Baker 2009). As Friedman (1987, 53) cogently points out, "for efficiency in mangling people, en masse, there is nothing like the modern machine." Though industrialization was a signature accomplishment of the Stalin period, tort law did not grow apace, but was supplanted by the state as the insurer of last resort. Many were doubtless dissatisfied with the compensation provided, but political constraints (both formal and informal) prevented them from taking further legal action.

In light of the introduction of private property and the explosion of car ownership, the post-Soviet civil code largely abandons strict liability in favor of comparative negligence. The relevant article in the civil code provides that, in the presence of "gross negligence" (*grubaia neostorozhnost*) on the part of the victim, damages will be reduced to reflect the respective degrees of fault of the parties (art. 1083, GK RF part 2). Soviet judges took the requirement for "gross negligence" seriously, reflecting the preference for strict liability (Barry 1978, 322). Contemporary Russian judges, by contrast, have informally lowered their expectations. Any negligence on the part of the victim is likely to trigger an analysis of comparative negligence. It will not be presumed; the burden is on the defendant to prove the negligence of the plaintiff (art. 1081, GK RF part 2). The civil code gives judges the discretion to adjust damages in light of the economic wherewithal of the parties (art. 1083, GK RF part 2). Barry reports that Soviet judges made occasional use of an analogous provision. As a result, a defendant "might ... be compelled by a court to compensate, based on a consideration of the financial situation of the parties to the suit" (Barry 1978, 330). Post-Soviet Russian judges have ignored this provision, though it remains on the books.

Comparative negligence remains poorly understood by the Russian public, especially when it comes to accidents involving pedestrians. As I noted earlier, many who were injured while jaywalking assume that their malfeasance makes them ineligible for damages. Determinations of contributory negligence are made on a case-by-case basis. Whether the victim was in an official crosswalk or *zebra* would be relevant to the analysis. It is theoretically possible that a pedestrian-victim could be barred from recovering, though it is highly unlikely. As a general rule, drivers are held strictly liable when they hit pedestrians. A good example is the teenage victim of Fatima. She was darting through traffic at a busy Moscow intersection as cars were inching through. She must have known that she was not visible as she ran out of the shadow of a large truck into Fatima's path. Yet because she was in a *zebra*, her mother felt justified in pursuing legal remedies.

By contrast, those whose children were injured when crossing the road without the protection of an official crosswalk, such as Regina, felt they had no recourse. Worse, they blamed themselves and felt embarrassed by their children's foolishness. This confirms the role of law as a gatekeeper. A belief that the law is receptive to their situation is a necessary, but not sufficient, condition for Russians to make the leap from naming their injury to blaming and claiming.

LAWYERS

Confusion about the substance of the law is hardly unique to Russia. Lawyers might be expected to pick up some of the slack. But this assumes that people are comfortable bringing their problems to lawyers. Throughout the book I document the peripheral role of lawyers in Russian daily life. Dealing with auto accidents is no exception. Few bothered to consult with a lawyer to learn their rights before deciding how to proceed. The reasons why are by now familiar. The focus group participants assumed the cost of legal services would be beyond their means. Few had friends or acquaintances who were lawyers and so they did not know how to assess the qualifications or integrity of lawyers. Fatima initially ended up with a lawyer she described as a "bandit." She was horrified by his matter-of-fact advice to cover up her involvement and distanced herself from him. Others were less squeamish. In the aftermath of an accident on an icy road that injured an elderly woman, Zinaida, a Saratov doctor, did not hesitate to hire an *advokat* who had worked for many years as a *gaishchnik* (traffic police officer) to help her and her husband through the system. He gave them advice about how to minimize their potential liability and helped them recognize that the seemingly helpless elderly woman was a scam artist who supplemented her income by putting herself in harm's way and bilking unsuspecting drivers.

Lawyers mostly came into the picture for the focus group participants when they were seriously contemplating litigation. As chapters 4 and 5, which focus on the JP courts, demonstrate, consulting a lawyer in connection with a court case is not typical in Russia. But unlike the divorces, tax disputes, and traffic petitions, tort claims do not follow a standard text. They cannot be reduced to a fill-in-the-blank formula. Context matters. The greater willingness of those involved in auto accidents to seek legal counsel is understandable. Though my sample is small and unrepresentative, it is nonetheless interesting to note that those who had professional assistance did better than those who eschewed help.[41] Recall Anna who fought to recover damages from the driver who killed her brother and left her badly injured. Despite having a law degree and having previously worked in

---

41. Several (e.g., Katia, Kira, and Irina) even praised their lawyers.

the administrative structure of the courts, she was all thumbs when it came to assembling the requisite evidence. She ended up in the unenviable position of having devoted a great deal of time to the case but coming away with a pittance. Yet she had no regrets on this score. She told me of friends who had hired expensive lawyers and had come away empty-handed. By contrast, Elvira, who economized by hiring a recent law school graduate that she referred to as her "assistant," felt she would have stood a better chance had she retained one of the expensive *advokaty* she met with. Though she did not use Galanter's (1974) language, she was making his point about the advantages shared by courtroom veterans in terms of their understanding of the formal and informal rules of the litigation game. As a first-time litigant—Galanter's proverbial "one-shotter"—she felt out of her element against the general director, who was a "repeat player" who was at home in the courtroom and traveled in the same social circles as the judge.

COURTS

The messiness of tort claims arising from auto accidents make them an uneasy fit for Russian courts. As I argue in chapter 4, Russian judges prefer to decide cases on the basis of documentary evidence. Relying on witnesses to recount what happened makes them uncomfortable. Even worse are cases with two viable narratives of events that require them to assess witness credibility. On a more practical level, they dislike witnesses because hearing testimony takes more time than reviewing documents. Calling witnesses can lead to delays due to the vicissitudes of their schedules. The procedural codes validate the judicial preference for documentary evidence. When they want to call a witness, parties are required to submit a motion in which they justify the need for the witness. Merely requiring a motion is a way of discouraging the practice. Judges' openness to allowing witnesses varies. Their rulings are always grounded in assessments of potential relevance, but often this is a convenient subterfuge for a lack of patience with long-winded witnesses and a desire to comply with the statutory deadline.

This penchant for documentary evidence helps explain why the reports (*protokoly*) of the traffic police take on such importance. All understand that the determination of fault in the *protokol* usually dictates the outcome in any court case. At a minimum, it establishes a presumption of liability that must be overcome by the other side. It also casts a heavy shadow in any negotiations between the parties, whether conducted on the side of the road or when the dust has settled. Insurance companies rely on it, as Kira learned to her detriment. If the police report does not identify a culprit, then insurance companies generally refuse to pay absent a court decision. Those dissatisfied with the substance of a *protokol* rarely succeed in disproving the substantive account of what happened. Judges are predisposed to believe the police. Savvy courthouse players (whether lawyers or litigants) understand that the key to undermining a police report is to show that some element of procedure was violated in completing the report.

Protokoly and other documentary evidence may be sufficient to educate judges as to what happened in simple fender-benders, but do a poor job of capturing the details of the more serious accidents that tend to end up in court. Witnesses are needed to flesh out the story. Sadly, those involved in the accident are not always able to fill in the gaps. As the stories shared above indicate, concussions and loss of consciousness are not uncommon. This leaves bystanders. Tracking them down can prove arduous.[42] The skepticism of judges toward witnesses makes it unclear whether it is worth the trouble. A number of focus group participants abandoned the fight at the outset owing to fears of being unable to find eyewitnesses.

Putting aside police reports and witnesses to the actual accidents, Russian judges' expectations as to documentary evidence can be problematic. Requiring receipts for any payments for which compensatory damages are sought would seem to be uncontroversial. Yet in a society in which side payments are routine, demanding written evidence of such outlays is unrealistic. Anna's lawsuit is a good example. She was unable to recover the amounts that she paid to medical personnel to get access to newer medications recommended by her doctor that were otherwise unavailable to the public. The judge was not bothered by the bribelike character of the payments. Instead, Anna's efforts to recover were torpedoed by the lack of written substantiation.

This sort of formalism can lead judges to give a cold shoulder to claims for services from private clinics. Once again, Anna's experience is instructive. Like many Russians, she was skeptical of the quality of the medical care provided free of charge and opted to go to a private clinic for rehabilitation. The court refused to countenance these charges, telling Anna that she could have obtained treatment at no charge. Even though Anna had been educated as a lawyer and understood the inherent positivism of the system, she came away from the experience frustrated by the court's unwillingness to deal with the real-life challenges she faced. Others in the focus groups echoed her concerns. Demanding the impossible marks the courts as out of touch with reality. Judges take no responsibility; they point to the codes and say their hands are tied. In reality, however, the codes—both procedural and substantive—provide a considerable amount of wiggle room. The risk-averse nature of Russian judges makes them wary of exercising discretion.

---

42. A number of forums exist on the Internet in Russia in which people involved in accidents seek out eyewitnesses to their misfortune.

TRAFFIC POLICE

Russia is far from unique in treating police reports as determinative. In his study of the Japanese system, Tanase (1990, 673) notes that "the police report is accorded such weight that the facts as recorded are hardly ever challenged later in court." It is not just the authority and integrity of the police that give their reports such weight, it is also that the police work with those involved in the accident to "hammer out a consensual story as to what happened to which the parties agree and formally endorse by signing" (674). This approach limits their ability to come to court and put forward alternative narratives.

What makes the Russian courts' practice of giving credence to the reports of traffic police problematic is the low esteem in which this branch of law enforcement is held by the public. Despite its questionable integrity, the courts accept its reports at face value, much like in Japan. In essence, the *protokol* creates a rebuttable presumption of accuracy. In the JP court hearings I observed, though those who had been cited for traffic violations often quibbled with the version of events laid out, I witnessed no successful efforts to rewrite history. To do so would require a credible witness to buttress the self-serving claims of the driver. A personal friend of mine succeeded in challenging his ticket for reckless driving thanks to his wife's testimony, which the judge believed. It helped that the traffic officer who issued the ticket had only a vague recollection of the incident. An easier route to overturning a traffic violation (as I explain in chapter 5) is to harp on technical shortcomings in the report.

The experiences of the focus group participants with the traffic police help us understand why this institution is widely distrusted. Arkadii, a psychologist from Kushchevskaia, captured the feelings of many when he said: "I don't bother going to the police anymore. It is a waste of time. Forgive me for saying this, but they work as prostitutes. Whoever pays them more makes out." Concrete illustrations were plentiful. The involvement of those with political sway was routinely hushed up. Unlike the courts, where mundane cases are typically processed according to the law, the malfeasance of the traffic police spilled over into their everyday activities. Respondents readily admitted to making side payments to the traffic police when threatened with the loss of their license. As in the Japanese case, the Russian police negotiate the content of the report with those involved in the accident. But rather than working toward a narrative that reflects what happened, *gaishchniki* are thought to be willing to skew the *protokoly* to whoever pays them more. Such stories were told in every focus group. Some told of draft reports that were written to fudge fault in an effort to elicit a bribe. When the initial report downplayed the icy conditions that led her husband to lose control of their car on a Saratov street, Zinaida hired a second expert, who supported her position that her husband was not to blame. She was advised to do this by the former traffic policeman turned lawyer that she hired to help them. He knew how to beat his former colleagues at their own game. Respondents felt that their lack of respect for the *gaishchniki* was reciprocated. They reported waiting hours for someone to show up. When they did, victims described their attitude as "boorish" (*khamskoe*), and said that they were left feeling as if they were criminals rather than hapless victims.

Every once in a while the traffic police rose to the occasion. Recall the experience of Oksana who was able to replace the bike destroyed by a hit-and-run accident when the Kushchevskaia *gaishchniki* put pressure on the driver to do the right thing. Along similar lines, Timofei, a Moscow lawyer for the tax inspectorate, told of an incident from his adolescence when several drivers, including his father, were spooked by a horse and crashed into one another. The traffic police officer determined that all involved had been negligent and brokered an amicable settlement. Several others related similar stories, but these were the exception rather than the rule.

INSURANCE COMPANIES

In contrast to the traffic police, whose presence in Russians' lives dates back to the Soviet era, insurance companies are a new institutional player. Before liability insurance was mandated in 2002, few drivers bothered with it. Despite its now compulsory character, many Russian drivers remain uninsured. As I noted earlier, Russians are skeptical of the commitment of insurance companies to their clients' interests. These attitudes were reflected in the focus groups. In all locales, I heard complaints about the tendency of insurance companies to use loopholes to avoid paying claims. They were described as "greedy" (*zhadnye*). There was a general consensus that suing them was an uphill battle.

In Russia, as elsewhere, insurance companies are more experienced than most of their clients in dealing with auto accidents. To put it in the language of Galanter's (1974) seminal article, they are "repeat players" who understand how to maneuver through the system, whereas their clients are "one-shotters" who have no previous experience and tend to treat any accident as a one-time event rather than as a learning opportunity. They take advantage of the fact that those who were injured (or whose family members suffered injuries) are preoccupied with recuperation and the universal desire of those involved to put these mishaps behind them. They make it easy to get an estimate of property damage through appraisers of their choosing. Without exception, the focus group participants saw these mechanics as in the pocket of the insurance companies despite their claims to be independent. No doubt the mechanics understood that continued cooperation was contingent on lowballing their estimates. Though clients have the right to get their own estimate, this takes time and insurance companies drag their feet in reviewing such estimates. Indeed, some found that bribes were required to get mechanics to provide a realistic estimate. The reputation of mechanics has been sullied as a result of these practices. In my time at the JP courts, I saw countless cases in which an individual or her insurance company was seeking to recover the difference between the original estimate and the actual cost of repairing the car.

Some countries have introduced alternatives to court for resolving disputes with insurance companies. Japan, for example, has both private and state-sponsored alternatives (Tanase 1990). As to the latter, court-annexed mediation has proved to be a popular option. Though the amounts received through mediation tend to be lower than court awards, it is quicker. As to the former, a network of traffic accident dispute-resolution centers was established in the 1970s as a nonprofit corporation and was financed by profits from compulsory insurance. These centers offer private adjudication services. As to both, disputes that prove resistant to solution are forwarded to the courts. When writing in 1990 about the Japanese system, Tanase pointed to these managerial solutions as a key element of the reason why only 1 in 100 disputes arising from auto accidents ended up in court, as compared with 21.5 out of 100 in the United States. Russia has not followed this example, though the experiences of the focus group participants suggest that the Japanese solutions might be helpful. But these institutional innovations in Japan arose in an environment in which the traffic police are beyond reproach and public corruption is minimal. Lacking these starting conditions, any new tribunal might quickly "go native" and be driven by bribes rather than the law. Moreover, the tentative steps Russia has taken toward encouraging court-annexed mediation have been met with public indifference (Hendley 2015; 2013).

APOLOGIES

Much has been made of the role of apologies in the comparative literature on tort law. Often the United States, with its tendency to discourage apologies as an admission of liability (Cohen 1999), is compared with Japan, where a failure to apologize is seen as a lack of sincerity and can upend settlement negotiations (Wagatsuma and Rosett 1986). Comparing across geographic borders can be problematic (Haley 1986). Wagatsuma and Rosett (1986, 463) caution that "apology is an objective act that can be observed and measured, but its primary significance is in the social context. . . . Members of different societies attribute differences to social behavior because their assumptions about the world and themselves are different."

This debate has little resonance in Russia. Notwithstanding the critical role that admission of responsibility plays in the system, the narratives of the focus group participants put little emphasis on whether they had received an apology.

Rather, they spoke about whether the other side had "acknowledged its respon-sibility." The phrase used—*priznat otvetstvennost*—is bereft of emotion. It is legalistic. Indeed, it is the phrase used in criminal trials. Russian has other lin-guistic options that vividly convey regret and sorrow (e.g., *prosit proshchenie*). My respondents seemed to judge their injurers more by their actions than by their words. As the experiences of Fatima and Viktoria suggest, when a person's behavior conveys genuine regret, victims tend to lose their taste for vengeance. Vice versa, when the driver who caused the death of Anna's brother made no ef-fort to approach her, it fueled her desire to pursue her civil claim against him. For my purposes, what is more important is that apologizing carries no meaning in Russian judicial proceedings. It does not constitute an admission.

Russian Legal Culture

Much ink has been spilt in an effort to define legal culture. I agree with Fried-man's (1987, 31) definition of legal culture as "the ideas, attitudes, values, and opinions about law held by people in a society. The assumption is that these ideas and attitudes influence legal behavior, especially the level of demands placed on the legal system." Though originally intended to explicate legal culture in the United States, it is not geographically bounded and is entirely appropriate to the Russian context.

As I embarked on this study of Russians' behavior in the aftermath of auto accidents, I had expected it to be revelatory of legal culture more generally. Such claims are routinely made by socio-legal scholars of torts (Engel and McCann 2009; Nelken 2009). Mostly writing about the U.S. system, they argue that the "reasonable person" standard that is central to this body of law requires deci-sion makers—whether judges or juries—to incorporate societal norms into their calculations of liability. The acceptance of judicial precedent as a source of law makes every decision relevant as tort law is patched together. Just as informal norms influence the formal law, the incremental changes in the formal law also color informal norms. As Engel (2001, 17) notes: "The judge is a mythmaker. The court projects a version of reality back on the social setting from which the case emerges, and this refashioned version of local truths inevitably redefines them." Thus, tort law helps us understand larger societal attitudes toward risk and accountability.

Engel likewise highlights the symbiotic relationship between legal culture and tort law in his Thailand-based research (Engel 2009, 2005, 2001; Engel and Engel 2010). Like me, he studied how people react to accidents. His respondents were markedly less interested in identifying the proximate cases of their injuries than

were their American counterparts. Their Buddhism played a role; their willingness to take on all or part of the responsibility for accidents speaks to their preoccupation with karma (their own and that of those around them). "In the end,
they maintained, karma will ensure that justice prevails, although it may take
some time. If not in this lifetime, then in a future life, the consequence of the
injurer's actions will be apparent" (Engel and Engel 2010, 135). An overly aggressive claim could result in damage to the victim's karma, whereas failing to follow
through on social norms that mandate that the culprit cover certain expenses of
the victim could undermine social harmony (Engel 2009, 256–257). In the rare
instances where Thais took their grievances to court, judges were impatient with
these explanations centered on karma and required parties to stick to demon-
strable facts. Engel notes that his respondents were able to "shift easily from one
causal framework to another without any apparent sense of inconsistency" (255).
He argues that when faced with "a choice between legal action and adherence to
Buddhist principles of forgiveness and compassion," most opt for the latter over
the former. Rather than shaping the formal law, as in the United States, culture
stands apart from it in Thailand.

Russia presents yet another path. Much as in Thailand, the link between societal norms and tort law is tenuous. Unlike their Thai brethren, Russians do not
look beyond their present lives when constructing narratives of what happened.
They can be quick to blame themselves, but few believe in the concept of past
lives, so naturally they do not attribute accidents to bad behavior in prior lives.
Nor do they worry that their responses to accidents will lead to bad karma for
them or their children. The idea of luck, which might be seen as a very weak
corollary to karma, was rarely raised in the focus group discussions or in the one-
on-one interviews that followed. Concerns about restoring societal harmony in
the wake of an accident do not motivate Russians. Their explanations look more
like those offered by Americans. They tend to be linear and to hone in on a single
causal agent. Both settlement negotiations and litigation center on a determination of who caused the accident. Unlike the U.S. case, however, the Russian courts
take little notice of community norms when resolving cases. The civil code serves
as their touchstone. To some extent, the institutional structure of the Russian
legal system explains this approach. On a formal level, the law is less malleable.
The decisions of Russian trial courts lack precedential value, and juries are not
allowed in civil cases. As a result, each case is taken on its own merits. Little attention is paid to the larger implications, either in terms of the causes of the
accident or the repercussions of the decision. Judges do not see themselves as
responsible for identifying or solving society's problems. Moreover, their relentless positivism leaves little room for integrating informal customs and practices.
Though such evidence could be introduced through testimony, most Russian

judges would dismiss it as irrelevant if they allowed it at all. As I argue in chapters 4 and 5, judges shy away from witness testimony. In a move that is entirely consistent with their positivism, judges have taken full advantage of the statutory language that gives them discretion over whether to allow witnesses by keeping them out whenever possible.

Russian judges are not concerned with how their decisions might affect future cases or society at large. Instead, the judge burrows in on the question presented by the case before her, which is construed narrowly. In contrast to the rhetoric that is common in U.S. cases, Russian litigants do not seek to be made whole. Even when their lives have been shattered, their petitions tend to itemize outlays for car repairs not reimbursed by their insurance companies or for medical treatment. The idea that the court could restore them to their former selves is foreign to them. As a result, the link between identity and tort remedies for injuries posited by Engel in his comparative study of the United States and Thailand is not present in the Russian case.[43]

In an ironic twist, the basic behavioral patterns of accident victims is similar in the United States, Russia, and Thailand. Victims everywhere are reluctant to go to court, preferring to negotiate settlements informally. Socio-legal research allows us to unpack their motivations, which is where the diversity among these cases reveals itself. In Russia, victims' trepidation stems from their more general skittishness about officialdom, both private and public. Bilateral negotiations between those involved in accidents allows them to bypass the bureaucratic demands of insurance companies as well as the traffic police and the courts. This distaste for formal channels among Russians is well known. This study of behavior following auto accidents simply provides yet another illustration.

Yet law is far from irrelevant to these informal negotiations. Russians operate in the shadow of the law (Mnookin and Kornhauser 1979). Their bargaining positions are grounded in their understanding of the law and what they would likely receive through a formal claim (Ellickson 1991). As the focus group discussions demonstrate, those who believe they have no legal leg to stand on tend to do nothing.

But law is not the only factor that guides Russians. Those who have the misfortune to crash—literally—into people who they perceive as being more powerful are equally as likely to "lump it." Power is a fluid term. It extends to those who hold political office or have immense wealth as well as those who have strong

---

43. Engel (2001, 3) writes: "When we speak of remedies that will make the injured person 'whole,' we refer to a condition of 'wholeness,' an imagined self that can be restored through compensation or by other means. Concepts of injury and remedy, therefore, are inseparable from concepts of identity."

connections to such individuals. When they stumble into this world, many ordinary Russians view themselves as outsiders who cannot penetrate these networks of power and influence where a quiet word may be determinative. Others worry that decision makers will be bribed to look the other way. At the heart of these fears is a lack of power of law to trump connections and corruption.

Elsewhere it is often argued that formal legal systems favor the rich because they can hire better lawyers that allow them to maximize their chances. Once again, Russia confounds this common wisdom. Ordinary citizens are more likely to use the courts when dealing with people like them. The combination of the low cost of using Russian courts and the commitment of judges to a level playing field (even if this requires them to help less experienced litigants) leads to the unexpected result that ordinary citizens get a better shake in court. It is in their cases where judges are able to apply the law without fear of political repercussions.

This finding would likely come as a surprise to ordinary Russians themselves. Judging by the focus groups, few of them see the courts as inviting. Indeed, they mostly see the entire system as stacked against them, from the unresponsive and insolent attitudes of the traffic police in the immediate aftermath of accidents to the bureaucratic maze required to recover through insurance companies to the courts. They complain bitterly about the time required to assemble the evidence required to substantiate their claim and about the emotional energy needed. The outsiders' assessment of the several months needed to complete a case as speedy is not shared widely among Russians, who regularly vent on Internet websites and in the press about the slow pace of justice in the JP courts. As a result, their hesitancy to take their claims to the courts is entirely understandable.

THE VIEW FROM THE BENCHES OF THE JUSTICE-OF-THE-PEACE COURTS

How do judges at Russia's busiest set of courts see themselves and their role? In this chapter, I explore the justice-of-the-peace courts (JP courts or *mirovye sudy*). When ordinary Russians are unable to resolve simple problems on their own, the JP courts represent their port of entry into the legal system. For them, the justices of the peace (JPs or *mirovye sud'i*) are the face of the legal system. Many who come to the JP courts are legal neophytes who are feeling their way through the process on their own. JPs have to manage the expectations of unsophisticated parties with the demands of the law while coping with an ever-growing docket. They often find themselves in an awkward position as they seek to balance justice and efficiency. Their behavior provides an intriguing lens into the contemporary Russia judicial system, which is endeavoring to remake itself as an adversarial process guided by the law on the books, but which cannot entirely escape from its Soviet legacy.

My analysis is grounded in fieldwork carried out from 2010 through 2012 in JP courts in Ekaterinburg, Moscow, Petrozavodsk, Pskov, Rostov-na-Donu, St. Petersburg, Velikie luki, and Voronezh. As always, gaining access to courts was difficult. After an initial effort to gain official permission to carry out this research from the Supreme Court proved futile, I resorted to the tactics I have been using to open doors in Russia since the late 1980s, namely, working through my friends, acquaintances, and other connections. Sometimes this meant organizing the work through the agencies (*upravleniia*) set up to manage the JP courts in each region;[1] sometimes it meant working with regional appellate courts.[2] In the end, I had the opportunity to talk with sixty-five JPs as well as members of their staff, and to observe over one hundred cases of varying stripes. As a rule, I was the only spectator; Russia has no tradition of casual or scholarly observation of courts. I have supplemented this qualitative research with a critical review of published and unpublished caseload data for the JP courts and a thorough study of the Russian popular legal literature, with a particular emphasis on journals such as *Mirovoi sud'ia* that regularly interview and report on the activities of JPs.

I begin by explaining how the JP courts fit into the larger Russian judicial system, and how they have evolved over their relatively short life. I then turn to the question of how one becomes a JP and what sort of people tend to become JPs. The bulk of the chapter, however, is devoted to an exploration of the day-to-day reality of life for JPs. Through a series of sample cases, I illustrate the key challenges facing them and then explore the variation in responses. Both the similarities and differences between JPs and judges elsewhere will become evident.

The Justice-of-the-Peace Courts

The Russian judicial system has undergone significant reform in recent decades. Even before the collapse of the Soviet Union, efforts were underway to depoliticize the courts by eliminating the formal role of the Communist Party (Solomon 1990–91). The 1990s witnessed the creation of a stand-alone constitutional court (Sharlet 1992; Trochev 2008) and the transformation of the administrative mechanism used to handle disputes between state-owned enterprises, state *arbitrazh* (*gosudarstvennyi arbitrazh* or *gosarbitrazh*), into a full-fledged hierarchy of economic courts, known as *arbitrazh* courts (Hendley 1998). These courts have jurisdiction over most disputes involving legal entities. As in the Soviet era, all other disputes are handled by the courts of general jurisdiction (Solomon and Foglesong 2000). The basic structure of these courts remained unchanged until 1998 when the law authorizing the JP courts was passed (O mirovykh 1998). The impetus for the JP courts was twofold: to divert simple cases away from the district (or *raionnye*) courts, which were then the courts of first instance, and to make the legal system more accessible to ordinary Russians by creating

1. This was my strategy in Ekaterinburg, Pskov, and Velikie luki.
2. This was my strategy in Moscow, Petrozavodsk, and Rostov-na-Donu.

neighborhood courts.[3] They were consciously modeled on the JP courts of the tsarist era.[4]

Needless to say, creating an entirely new layer of courts was not accomplished overnight. V. M. Lebedev, the longtime chairman of the Russian Supreme Court, commented that "as with any radical reform, the creation of the JP courts in Russia is not proceeding easily or painlessly" (Butsevitskii 2007, 27). The Russian Federation was divided into judicial districts (*sudebnye uchastki*), each composed of fifteen to twenty-three thousand people. The JP court for each district has its own separate infrastructure, beginning with an intake bureau (*kontsilariia*) for complaints and ending with an archive for its case files.

Because the JP courts represent a collaborative effort between the federal and regional governments, laws authorizing the courts and detailing how JPs would be selected had to be passed by the legislatures of each region.[5] Then began the tedious work of staffing the courts and finding suitable premises. By 2003, 6,470 JP courts had been authorized, and JPs had been appointed for about 80 percent (or 5,248) of them (Potapov 2007, 4). By the end of 2011, the number of JP courts had been increased by 23 percent to 7,957, and JPs were in place in 92 percent (or 7,308) of them. Initially, the goal had been to situate each court in its district. The harsh reality of the Russian real estate market forced officials to adjust their plans. In all of the cities I visited, a majority of JP courts shared quarters. This allowed for certain economies of scale in terms of court services and facilitated the creation of a lively esprit de corps among the JPs, but at the expense of integrating the JP courts into local communities.

The geographic boundaries of judicial districts are not fixed in stone. For the most part, judicial officials started by dividing up the territory such that each district included the requisite number of people. This resulted in severe inequities in caseload among districts. Districts that include banks or shopping centers

---

3. The chairman of the Stavropol krai court, S. P. Korovinskikh, commented: "The introduction of the JP courts in 2001, which was aimed at maximizing access of the population to justice, was the most imported step in carrying out judicial reform in the Russian Federation and in Stavropol krai (Butsevitskii 2007, 26). For an overview of the politics behind the creation of these courts, see Solomon (2003). The desire for accessibility was also a key motivation behind the creation of JP courts in the nineteenth century. Neuberger (1994, 232) comments that "the mirovoi sud was considered an ideal classroom." Enhancing the accessibility of the judicial system to all strata of society was also a key motivation behind the introduction of small-claims courts in the United States (Best et al. 1994; Yngvesson and Hennessey 1975).

4. The JP courts were one of several courts established in the wake of the Great Reforms of 1864. See, generally, Burbank (2004) and Frierson (1986). On the tsarist JP courts, see Rodina (2007); Sharkova (1998); and Neuberger (1994).

5. For detailed information on the regional laws, see Kolokolov (2011, 380–399). The federal budget covers the salaries of JPs. All other costs, including the salaries of other courthouse staff and obtaining and maintaining the courthouses, are the responsibility of regional governments (arts. 9 and 10, O mirovykh 1998).

are flooded with cases, whereas districts that are primarily residential have many fewer cases.[6] Officials have responded by tinkering with district boundaries, to little effect. In Voronezh, officials took a more radical approach by abandoning the requirement that districts be contiguous. Instead, they doled out segments of the central business area to each district in an effort to even out the workload. When I mentioned this as a possible solution to court administrators elsewhere, I was met with puzzled stares. The Voronezh solution was too far out of the box for them.

The contours of the JP courts' substantive jurisdiction have been repeatedly adjusted in an effort to ensure that neither the JP courts nor the district courts have an unacceptable workload (Hendley 2012a). What remains unchanged is the commitment to having the JP courts resolve simpler cases. To that end, the JP courts hear criminal cases in which the punishment is less than three years' imprisonment (art. 3, part 1(1), O mirovykh 1998). In terms of civil cases, their jurisdiction encompasses divorces in which child custody is not contested, property disputes of amounts under 50,000 rubles,[7] and challenges over title to land (art. 3, part 1(2–8), O mirovykh 1998). Their jurisdiction over administrative cases is more open-ended (art. 3, part 9, O mirovykh 1998).[8] By 2011, when I carried out my research, the JP courts were handling almost three-fourths of all civil cases, about 45 percent of all criminal cases, and almost 95 percent of all administrative cases heard by the Russian courts (Statisticheskie svedeniia 2011). The caseload data confirm that the vast majority of cases brought to the Russian courts are relatively straightforward. As

6. For example, the busiest of the 211 JP courts in St. Petersburg is located in the heart of the tourist and business district. During the first three months of 2012, it decided 1,623 cases, comprising almost 3 percent of all cases resolved by the St. Petersburg JP courts. By contrast, the least busy JP court, located on the outskirts of the city, decided only 87 cases (http://mirsud.spb.ru/21/2201). The differences are less drastic in Pskov oblast, but the story is the same. The busiest court in the region is in the heart of Pskov. It resolved 375 cases during the first quarter of 2012, as compared with the 40 cases decided by the least busy JP court, which is located in the rural village of Usiat (http://mirsud.pskov.ru/copykvartal/).

7. Initially, the monetary cutoff was 100,000 rubles. Because JP courts were being swamped with civil cases, it was lowered to 50,000 in 2010. This change has had a disparate impact. It has had the desired effect in most of Russia, but has left many JP courts in Moscow and St. Petersburg twiddling their thumbs. JPs repeatedly pointed to this change in the law when I asked why their calendars were not busier. At the same time, they recognized that the change was necessary to assuage a crisis in the regions. No one was open to having different rules for busier jurisdictions. They found the very idea laughable.

8. From a comparative perspective, the cap of 50,000 rubles for civil cases, which, at the exchange rate at the time of my research of 50 rubles to the dollar translates into $1,000, is rather low. U.S. small-claims courts tend to hear civil claims ranging from $2,500 to $7,500 (Turner and McGee 2000). The English county small-claims courts have a cap of £15,000 (Kurkchiyan 2012, 223). The jurisdiction of Russian JP courts over mundane criminal cases also marks them as unusual, though it is consistent with the tsarist JP courts (Mikheev 2007).

I lay out below, many are able to be resolved through summary procedures because they lack any meaningful factual dispute. The more demanding cases are funneled to the district courts.

The JP courts are governed by the same procedural codes as all courts of general jurisdiction. As a rule, these codes place a premium on documentary evidence at the expense of testimonial evidence, which is a dual legacy of the Soviet and continental practices (Kurkchiyan 2013; Hendley 2007). The process is judge-centric. Judges begin by verifying the identity of the parties and their readiness to proceed. They then dive into the merits of the disputes. In all Russian courts, litigants are given fairly free rein to explain what happened. They are typically guided through their story by pointed questions from the bench. The atmosphere is not necessarily more informal at JP courts.

My fieldwork reveals that JPs' work conditions vary greatly. The cost of buying and maintaining facilities falls on regional governments. As a result, the relative luxury of the premises is highly correlated with the extent of regional resources and the willingness of regional authorities to devote them to the JP courts. Nowhere did I find a building that had been constructed specifically for the JP courts.[9] Often they were renovated office buildings. Occasionally they had a more colorful history as a kindergarten or toy store. Frequently they were nestled deep in residential neighborhoods, which sometimes made them difficult to find, though they were usually accessible via public transportation.[10] Once inside, the creature comforts varied. In Moscow and St. Petersburg, for example, the corridors were wide and were lined with benches for litigants. Each JP had a contiguous office suite that included her chambers, a courtroom, a separate room for judicial deliberations, and a reception area where her secretaries and her clerk[11]

---

9. This should not be taken to mean that Russia lacks buildings designed specifically for court use. The post-Soviet era has witnessed a massive construction campaign for courts. Pomorski's (2001) case study of the operation of a trial-level criminal court in Kranoyarsk notes that the court was housed in a building constructed for the courts. Many have been designed to limit opportunities for casual interaction between judges and litigants as a way of combating corruption (Hendley 2012b).

10. In her fieldwork in first-instance courts in Bulgaria, Poland, and Ukraine, Kurkchiyan (2012; 2013) found that they also occupied nondescript buildings.

11. By clerk, I am referring to the judge's *pomoshchnik*. The literal translation of this term is "assistant," but the word "clerk" better captures the position. In contrast to the typical judicial clerks in the United States, Russian clerks have permanent positions. They are very poorly paid. In a February 2012 group interview, several Moscow judges estimated that *pomoshchniki* earn about 12,000 rubles per month, hardly a living wage for Moscow (Ber 2012). Most people take this position with the hope of eventually becoming a judge. The turnover rate is very high, especially in the larger cities where the cost of living is high. In contrast to the influence of clerks documented by Rosen (2000, 88) in the qadi courts of Morocco or by Yngvesson (1994) in the United States, Russian clerks are peripheral figures for litigants.

FIGURE 4.1 An apartment building that also houses a JP court (Ekaterinburg)

FIGURE 4.2 A former kindergarten that houses a JP court (Moscow)

FIGURE 4.3   A typical office for a justice of the peace (Ekaterinburg)

had their desks. JPs also had designated space elsewhere in the building for an archive and for an office where pleadings were filed and processed. In some of the other sites I visited, the quarters were cramped, with no waiting areas for litigants, and JPs' chambers were not adjacent to their staff, complicating their working relationship. Outside of Moscow and St. Petersburg, the buildings for JP courts, many of which were home to five to ten JP districts, typically contained only one or two courtrooms that the JPs shared. Under these circumstances, JPs generally heard cases in their offices and resorted to the courtroom only for cases involving multiple parties or for criminal cases.[12]

The level of staffing also depends on the level of resources allocated by regional governments. Ideally, JPs have a support staff composed of a clerk and two secretaries. Clerks tend to be recent law school graduates who are interested in becoming judges and who assist in the preparation of opinions and other

---

12. Kurkchiyan (2012; 2013) reports that English and Ukrainian judges often heard cases in their offices, whereas hearings in the Polish and Bulgarian courts were mostly in courtrooms.

judicial acts.[13] Secretaries come in two varieties. One is a quasi-court reporter,[14] and the other takes care of the court's correspondence. In large cities, such as Moscow, St. Petersburg, and Ekaterinburg, JP courts were uniformly fully staffed. By contrast, in less prosperous areas of Russia, such as Pskov, Rostov-na-Donu, and Petrozavodsk, JPs sometimes had to make do without clerks or with only one secretary.

As of July 2010, all Russian courts have been required to maintain websites on which they post the court schedule and all opinions (Ob obespechenii 2009). The quality of websites varies widely. At their best, they have an easy-to-use search engine, an interactive map that helps litigants find the courthouse, a calculator that simplifies the task of computing filing fees, and an extensive database of form documents to be used for pleadings. At their worst, they do little more than provide the address of the court.[15] In talking to JPs and their staff, I encountered a broad range of opinions as to the usefulness of the websites. Some JPs take a curmudgeonly position, dismissing them as an annoyance. They complain that the obligation to keep the website current imposes additional work on their already overburdened staff, and doubt whether litigants pay much attention.[16] Other JPs

---

13. Until recently, law students could work as clerks (see generally Petrova 2012). Many JPs took this route, attending law school via correspondence (*zaochnoe obuchenie*). Though many observers criticize the quality of JPs on the grounds that relatively few of them attended the higher prestige law institutes, JPs themselves tout their educational background. They are openly contemptuous of those who took more traditional routes, saying that these people will have long forgotten the details of the law by the time they graduate. By contrast, by working as clerks, they were able to operationalize their lessons immediately.

14. Verbatim transcripts are not made for the JP courts, which marks them as different from their Soviet-bloc counterparts in Poland, Bulgaria, and Ukraine (Kurkchiyan 2012; 2013). The secretaries sit in the courtroom for civil and criminal (but not administrative) cases. Precisely what they do varies, depending on the preferences of the JP. Litigants are required to present their passports to identify themselves, and their representatives must present written authorization from their clients (generally known as a *doverennost*). Clerks often take down the details from these forms, though some JPs prefer to do it themselves. During the hearing, some secretaries take furious notes, whereas others stare into space. Some JPs will stop the hearing periodically to dictate material to their secretaries. The secretaries' notes are turned into an official record (*protokol*) of the hearing, which become part of the official case file. If the litigants object to the content of the *protokol*, they can petition the JP to change it. Audio recordings are now made at the *arbitrazh* courts, but this practice has not spread to the JP courts. In my travels, I encountered only one JP who regularly recorded her hearings. I asked her if she had sought authorization to do this. She shrugged and said that she had not; she said that the law did not forbid it, so she assumed it was permissible. She included a copy of the audio recording in the case file.

15. The websites for the JP courts of Moscow (http://www.mos-sud.ru/) illustrate the high end of this scale. The websites for the Voronezh JP courts (http://oblsud.vrn.sudrf.ru/modules. php?name=sud) reflect a more bare-bones approach.

16. At present, the staff is expected to maintain two sets of records, both the hard copies and the computerized records. When it comes time to compile caseload statistics, the staff relies solely on the paper records. As the web-based system was getting started, periodic glitches undermined confidence in it. Before posting opinions, the staff is charged with redacting any information deemed to be confidential.

are more enthusiastic, insisting that the websites have cut down on the number of potential litigants who drop by with questions. They point out that parties have begun looking at their prior decisions before their hearings. Occasionally, they even show up with copies of prior decisions in analogous cases, arguing that these cases ought to bind the judges' hands. The JPs are quick to tell such parties that prior decisions are not relevant to later cases, but they will often include a copy of the proffered decision in the case file.[17]

The JP courts represent the lowest rung on the hierarchy of the courts of general jurisdiction. If litigants are dissatisfied, decisions can be appealed to the district courts and on up the pyramid. Appeals are fairly rare. In 2011, less than 2 percent of the JP courts' decisions in civil cases were challenged (Otchet–JP Courts 2011). Like all Russian judges, JPs work hard to avoid being reversed. Without exception, every JP with whom I spoke regarded a reversal as a "mistake" for which there would be consequences.[18] At a minimum, a reversal would be the subject of a discussion among colleagues, at which the errant judge would be chastised and counseled as to how to mend her ways. At worst, it could lead to the loss of her year-end bonus or even termination. A JP from Velikie luki who has been with the JP courts since their inception bragged to me that he had never been reversed in a criminal case and that he had been reversed only fifteen times in civil cases.

The Justices of the Peace

When the JP courts were being conceptualized, some policymakers advocated opening the position of JP to all interested citizens. The possibility of following the tsarist practice and electing JPs was floated. In the end, however, it was decided that JPs should have legal training and should be chosen in the same way as

---

17. Traditionally, Russia has rejected judicial decisions as a source of law, but their role is in flux. Decisions of the constitutional court have been binding since its inception. More recently, the decisions of the Russian Supreme Court have likewise been given precedential value. Though decisions of intermediate appellate courts are not technically binding on the JP courts, JPs nonetheless scrutinize them carefully and heed them as they write their opinions. On the evolution in official attitudes toward precedent, see Henderson (2015); Pomeranz and Gutbrod (2012); Kartushev (2011); Zagainova (2009).

18. This conceptualization of reversals as "judicial mistakes" is routine within the Russian legal literature (Kazgerieva 2006; Petrukhin 1970). Several Moscow JPs complained that if their decisions are restored by the regional (*oblastnye*) courts, after having been reversed by the district (*raionnye*) courts, this still counts as a reversal or "mistake" for them.

judges for other Russian courts (O statuse 1992).[19] To be eligible, candidates must be at least twenty-five years old, hold a law degree, and have passed the qualifying exam.[20] Their merits are then assessed by the local judicial qualifications commission, who puts forward recommendations. At this point, the process for JPs takes a different track. Whereas the recommendations for judges at other courts go to the Russian president, who makes the formal appointments, the mechanism for JPs is dictated by regional legislation (Kolokolov 2011). Some regions followed the federal model and authorized their governors to appoint JPs. Others opted for having the regional legislature appoint their JPs.

Conversations with JPs suggest that getting through the appointment process can be harrowing.[21] Particularly daunting is the security clearance. Not only the potential judge, but all members of her family are investigated. A criminal conviction in the family immediately derails any candidacy.[22] Though the selection process has become less politicized and more objective since the Soviet era when the Communist Party handpicked judges, subjectivity has not been entirely eliminated. Nor has the quest for political loyalty disappeared, though its importance has receded. Qualification commissions want to be sure they know what they are getting with new judges.[23] As a result, they tend to recommend candidates who are known to them, such as judicial clerks or prosecutors. Lawyers in private practice are much less likely to end up on the bench. Although the process is

---

19. The JP courts' status as state organs and the choice to use professional judges distinguishes them from the comrades' courts of the Soviet era (Gorlizki 1998; Berman and Spindler 1963). Having read Feifer's (1964) ethnography of these courts, I was often struck by the parallel in the types of cases heard by the two courts and by the commonsense approach of the decision makers. When I asked JPs about this, they were quick to distance the JP courts from the earlier tribunals. They reminded me that the comrades' courts were social (*obshchestvennye*) organs that were not bound by law. In their use of professional judges, the JP courts also part company with the East German social courts (Sperlich 2007), the English magistrates' courts (Grove 2002), and many JP courts in the United States (Glaberson 2006; Conley and O'Barr 1990).

20. Whether there ought to be a special track in high schools and universities for those interested in becoming judges has been actively debated. In 2005, the qualification commission of Rostov oblast endorsed the development of a course designed to prepare candidates for the exam (Sachkov and Titukhov 2007, 44). Others point to the experience of European countries, such as France, as possible models for Russia (Ziabkin and Antonov 2008, 48).

21. See Ziabkin and Antonov (2008) for a list of the documents that candidates must assemble. When I spoke with JPs, they bemoaned the bureaucratic nature of the process and the time required to track down the necessary documents.

22. In Ekaterinburg, several JPs shared the story of a JP who had been forced to retire from the bench when a skeleton from her family closet came to light. It was presented as a cautionary tale.

23. Membership on these commissions tends to be dominated by court insiders. A 2011 report of the Moscow Helsinki Group criticized the resistance to inclusion of representatives from nongovernmental organizations (Tagankina 2011).

facially transparent and vacancies are publicly advertised, I was consistently told that the best predictor of who would be chosen was who had the endorsement of the chairman of the district court. At the courts I visited, the most common path to becoming a JP was to have previously served as a clerk.[24] Many had previously worked as court secretaries and had transitioned into being clerks. This has had a self-perpetuating effect. JPs who had traveled this career path repeatedly told me that it was the best possible preparation for the bench.[25] To be sure, this background provides a thorough education in the dos and don'ts—both formal and informal—of the Russian judicial system. It also helps ensure the political reliability of judicial cadres. But drawing JPs from the staff limits the ability to benefit from new ideas. Perhaps that is the point. Once their appointment is finalized, new JPs receive three months of formal training, organized by the Academy of Justice in Moscow or one of its many regional branches (Ershov 2016).

JPs are appointed for an initial three-year probationary term. Relatively few wash out. In contrast to other judges, who enjoy life tenure thereafter, JPs must be repeatedly reappointed. Their subsequent terms are set by regional legislation and range from five to ten years (Kolokolov 2011). Each time they are re-upped, JPs have to assemble a version of the packet of documents required for their initial appointment. When I was in Rostov-na-Donu, I spent time with a veteran JP who was busy tracking down these documents for her reappointment, and who complained bitterly about the process. As students of judicial tenure elsewhere are well aware, renewable terms make it relatively easy to get rid of ineffective or troublesome judges. They can also create informal incentives for judges to modify their decision making to endear themselves to those who hold their fate in their hands. This was certainly the experience with judges during the Soviet era.

In the courts I visited, JPs tended to be women. Other research confirms this gender bias within the Russian judicial corps more generally.[26] When I asked why,

---

24. Iuliia Sazonova is a typical example. She came to work at the courts after graduating from secondary school at eighteen. Over the next seven years, she rose in the ranks from intake clerk to secretary to clerk. She got a law degree by correspondence course and was successful in her application to become a JP at age twenty-five (Dziadko and Kraevskaia 2012).

25. Volkov et al. (2012, 20) document a similar dynamic in the analysis of their survey. Those who worked as clerks before going on the bench see that as the best preparation. Likewise those who came from the criminal justice system believe their preparation was ideal. Critics of the Russian courts condemn this practice because it effectively ensures the absence of fresh ideas (Ber 2012).

26. For example, in the 2011 survey of judges fielded by the Institute for the Rule of Law at European University, 75 percent of the 328 JPs in the sample were women. The dynamic was different for judges at higher courts. Of the 416 surveyed, 60 percent were women (Volkov et al. 2012). See also Pomorski (2001, 452). Data from the United Nations Economic Commission for Europe show that formerly socialist countries tend to have a higher percentage of women in the judiciary, which may be a historical artifact, reflecting the relatively low prestige of judges under state socialism. http://w3.unece.org/pxweb/quickstatistics/readtable.asp?qs_id=32.

I was told that the fast pace of the work was too demanding for men and that the detail-oriented nature of the work was more suited to a female temperament. One female JP in Rostov-na-Donu put it more bluntly, saying that the work was too boring for men. Some JPs reported that being a judge is a good job for working mothers. Though the hours are long, the judge is mostly able to control her schedule. Interestingly, these are essentially the same responses I got from Soviet judges in the late 1980s (Hendley 1996). At that time, I surmised that the low status of the judiciary played a substantial role in its feminization. In the intervening decades, considerable effort has been devoted to raising the status of judges, including increasing judicial salaries. Like judges in other countries with a civil-law heritage, Russian judges are seen as glorified civil servants (Merryman and Pérez-Perdomo 2007; Guarnieri and Pederzoli 2002, 66–67). Expecting them to have the sort of public respect enjoyed by their counterparts in the United States is unrealistic. Further confirmation of their relatively low status is the propensity for judges to obtain their legal education through correspondence (*zaochnoe*) courses. Often young women take jobs as court secretaries after high school and then obtain their law degrees in this way while maintaining their full-time jobs.[27] It is worth noting that people were generally surprised by my question about gender, almost as if the female domination of the profession was so accepted that no one gave it a second thought.

Unlike other Russian judges, JPs do not specialize. The jurisdiction of the JP courts is broad but shallow. JPs are expected to handle any cases that arise in their districts. A JP is a legal jack-of-all-trades, though she is expected to be a master of them all, which caused considerable grumbling among the JPs I encountered. They were particularly annoyed by the instability in substantive law, complaining about the difficulty of keeping up.

Almost all the JPs I met saw their position as a stepping-stone to bigger and better jobs. They hoped to move on to the district court and, eventually, to the regional court. These higher courts have separate divisions (*sostavy*) for civil, criminal, and administrative cases. Along with the increase in salary and prestige, the ability to specialize was seen as an appealing feature of being promoted. The uniformity of this desire to move on made my encounters with the handful of judges who were satisfied with being JPs especially interesting. Some of them no doubt preferred remaining a big fish in a small pond. One Voronezh JP phrased it slightly differently, saying that she enjoyed her independence. She hinted that

---

27. Legal education in Russia is an undergraduate enterprise. The Volkov survey data reveal that 55 percent of the JP-respondents had gone through a correspondence program, compared with 36 percent of judge-respondents from higher courts. Only a handful of JPs (5 out of 328) had earned a graduate degree in law, which makes sense given their heavy workload (Volkov et al. 2012).

if she moved to the district court, then she might be subject to greater pressure to toe the line.

The relative institutional independence of JPs is unusual within the Russian judicial system. At the higher courts, judges answer to the head of their division and to the chairman of the court. They worry about staying in the good graces of their chairman, who has the ability to make or break them (Volkov et al. 2012; Solomon 2007; Pomorski 2001). As I traveled around Russia, I saw considerable variation in the relationship between JPs and the chairmen of district courts.[28] At a minimum, JPs met as a group on a weekly or biweekly basis with the chairman of the district court to which their decisions would be appealed. These meetings were generally described as having an educational purpose. New developments in the law are discussed, as are any reversals of decisions of the JPs. JPs are also required to send their caseload statistics to the chairmen, which can reportedly result in public scoldings if JPs are unable to meet the statutory deadlines for deciding cases. My sense was that the personal character of the chairmen colored the relationship with JPs. The most extreme example was one Moscow JP court where the JP felt obligated to consult the chairman for trivial matters, such as my request to take a photo of an empty courtroom. She was also the only Moscow JP not to give me an open-ended invitation to return. Instead, she said that I would have to clear any return visit with her chairman.

Challenges Facing Justices of the Peace

Having sketched out the institutional environment in which the JP courts are situated and the type of individuals who tend to become JPs, I can now turn to the day-to-day reality of these courts. The task of a JP is relatively straightforward—she is charged with handling the cases that arise in her judicial district. JPs understand the key institutional indicators of success. They are expected to resolve cases within the statutory deadlines, to keep peace in their courtrooms even when the parties are at each other's throats, and to write decisions that will stand up to appeal. At the same time, they cannot lose sight of the loftier goal of achieving justice. By working through several cases I observed, the challenges facing JPs in achieving these seemingly simple goals can be illustrated.

---

28. In Moscow, I visited JP courts in six different districts with the permission of the regional (*oblastnoi*) court. The chairmen of the district courts were always aware of my activities. As a rule, they sent one of their clerks to facilitate my activities. All of these young women were puzzled by my interest in the JP courts. Sometimes they left me alone and sometimes they stuck to me like glue.

Managing the Caseload

Credit Card Debt. A middle-aged man on crutches arrives for a hearing in the office of a JP in Rostov-na-Donu. He is petitioning to reinstate the statute of limitations to allow him to challenge a "judicial order" (*sudebnye prikaz*) issued by the JP. This order ostensibly compelled him to immediately pay the balance of approximately 40,000 rubles owed on his credit card to his bank. The bank did not send a representative to the hearing. As usual, the JP begins by laying out his right and duties as a litigant. After reading aloud the petition from the bank, she turns to the man to hear his story. Although parties are required by law to stand when addressing the court, she takes account of his physical limitations and allows him to remain seated while speaking. He explains that about six months earlier he was involved in a serious automobile accident. When he went to the bank to sort out the payment he had received from his insurance company, he learned of the *prikaz*. Without waiting to hear his argument as to the merits of the assessed debt, the JP rules that she will reinstate the ten-day period for him to object to the *prikaz*.

Petty Theft. A group assembles in the office of an Ekaterinburg JP to deal with a case of petty theft. In addition to the judge, the participants include the defendant, his lawyer (*advokat*), the prosecutor (*prokuror*), and the victim. The case is being handled through a type of plea bargaining known as the "special process" (*osobyi poriadok*). The defendant, who is in his early twenties and looks younger, has acknowledged his guilt and agreed to make restitution to the victim for the value of the cell phone he stole from her. The JP begins the hearing by confirming that everyone is on board with this plea bargain. All present are given the right to question the defendant. The questions focus not on the crime, but on his plans for the future. During the course of the questioning, the defendant apologizes to the victim. He explains that the crime was motivated by poverty, but insists that he has learned his lesson. The JP gives the lawyers a chance to sum up. The prosecutor (who is a last-minute substitute for a vacationing colleague who had handled the earlier stages) reads from a prepared form document. The defense attorney asks the court to take the defendant's remorse into account. The defendant is given the opportunity for the final word, but he stays silent. The JP adjourns the hearing to write her decision. After about 40 minutes, she returns to sentence the defendant to the three months he has already served.

The official caseload data paint a dismal picture of daily life for JPs. As table 4.1 shows, JPs are expected to handle about two hundred cases per month.[29] Moreover, they are expected to move cases along expeditiously. When Stanislaw Pomorski spent time in the district courts in Kranoyarsk in the late 1990s, he found that the judges "seemed to be virtually obsessed with speed" (2001, 455). Little has changed. The procedural codes establish clear deadlines, which rarely give JPs more than a few months—sometimes substantially less time—to resolve disputes. As table 4.2 documents, JPs generally live within these constraints, ostensibly violating the deadline in less than 1 percent of cases in 2011. In reality, however, JPs (like all Russian judges) have developed a number of tricks that allow them to comply on paper while cases linger on. For example, the clock restarts on a case every time a new party is added. JPs confessed that they sometimes urge litigants to add a third party, even when he is clearly superfluous, simply to gain more time. Judicial authorities are well aware of these tactics and recently added several items to their regular battery of questions to suss them out. Rather than asking whether the case violated the statutory deadline, they asked how long the case had lasted. This revealed that, in 2011, 1.5 percent of cases lasted up to three months. An additional 0.5 percent took from three months to a year, and 0.01 percent took over a year to resolve (Obzor 2012, 54).

JPs are required to announce their decision immediately after the hearing(s) on the merits conclude. This can be a simple "thumbs up" or "thumbs down," though they were required to produce a fully reasoned decision within five days.[30] They complain about the workload bitterly, both in person and in print.[31] Many told tales of working late into the night and weekends simply to keep up. In an interview in *Mirovoi sud'ia*, a journal devoted to the JP courts, a Voronezh JP joked that the workload would be manageable if only there were forty-eight hours in a day (Raznikova 2004, 32). Without exception, they asked about the situation in the United States. When I told them that, for the most part, U.S. law did not prescribe deadlines for resolving cases, their eyes grew wide with wonder and disbelief. Their amazement at the lack of formal constraints on judges

---

29. This is a small fraction of the caseload that tsarist JPs managed. Rodina (2007, 3) reports that in 1895, JPs in St. Petersburg handled 3 to 5,000 cases per month. It also pales in comparison to the workload of some judges elsewhere. Bezdek (1992, 535) tells of a Baltimore judge who had as many as 2,500 landlord-tenant disputes on his daily docket.

30. In 2013, after my field research was completed, the civil procedure code was amended to eliminate the requirement for a full opinion by JPs in civil cases, unless specifically requested by the parties, with the goal of alleviating the burden on JPs (art. 199, GPK RF).

31. These sentiments are not unique to JPs. I have also spent a great deal of time in the *arbitrazh* courts, where judges also routinely sound off about the inequity of their workload (e.g., Shiniaeva 2012; Piskunova 2011; Bol'shova 2010).

TABLE 4.1 Average monthly per-judge caseload in the JP courts

	2009				2011				
	TOTAL JUDGES	TOTAL CASES PER JUDGE	TOTAL CIVIL CASES PER JUDGE	TOTAL ADMIN CASES PER JUDGE	TOTAL JUDGES	TOTAL CASES PER JUDGE	TOTAL FOR 2011 AS % OF 2009 TOTAL	TOTAL CIVIL CASES PER JUDGE	TOTAL ADMIN CASES PER JUDGE
Russian Federation	7,444	217.9	130.7	80.9	7,444	200.9	92.2	117.2	64.5
Central okrug	1,855	145.7	78.7	61.6	1,858	140.6	96.5	75.8	51.1
Northwest okrug	708	232.7	142	84.7	708	236.5	101.6	135.6	79.5
Southern and Northern Caucasus okrug	1,205	183.1	107.3	71.2	740	191.7		111.5	62.7
Northern Caucasus okrug[*]					466	113.4		57.8	49.1
Volga okrug	1,583	282.6	184.4	91.3	1,583	250.7	88.7	144.6	69.7
Siberian okrug	1,079	241.2	141.6	92.2	1,079	229.1	95	139.9	64.9
Urals okrug	621	234.5	126.8	99.3	621	232.2	99	131.3	74.8
Far East okrug	389	287.8	187.9	93.5	389	275.4	95.7	166.4	84.2

Sources: Nagruzka (2009–2010, 2010–2011).

[*] In January 2010, the Southern okrug was divided, thereby creating a separate okrug for the Northern Caucasus.

TABLE 4.2 Overview of the civil docket of the JP courts

TYPE OF CASE	TOTAL CIVIL CASES RESOLVED (2009)	TOTAL CIVIL CASES RESOLVED (2011)	AS % OF TOTAL CIVIL CASES	% OF CASES IN WHICH DECISION WAS ISSUED	% OF CASES RESOLVED THROUGH JUDICIAL ORDER	SUCCESS RATE FOR PLAINTIFFS[*]	% OF CASES THAT VIOLATE TIME DEADLINE
Total	10,220,011	9,165,323		94.4	71.2	92.2	0.85
Family disputes	981,464	944,203	10.3	88.3	29.9	98.6	1.0
Labor disputes	598,499	451,896	4.9	99.5	99.5	57.3	0.1
Disputes involving personal injury (including traffic accidents)	169,251	239,224	2.6	91.7	0.8	98.4	3.3
Housing disputes	1,873,025	1,912,387	20.9	92.6	57.4	97	0.9
Tax disputes:							
Initiated by state	4,566,383	3,838,734	41.9	98.5	93.5	50.7	2.3
Initiated by taxpayer	5,238	4,384	0.04	98.5	92.5	82.2	0.5
Disputes over credit contracts	590,243	495,315	5.4	96.8	77	97.2	0.8

[*] Denominator leaves out cases resolved via judicial order on the rationale that the plaintiff always prevails in such cases.

Sources: Otchet–JP Courts 2011; Otchet–JP Courts 2009.

was double-edged. They clearly longed for the freedom enjoyed by U.S. judges, but they were skeptical of how judges could possibly be accountable to the legal system and to society more generally absent such clear performance measures.

As I embarked on my field research, I wondered how JPs were able to manage such a large number of cases. I knew that the same judge handled the case from start to finish. How was it physically possible? I expected to find the JP courts to be a beehive of constant activity. My curiosity grew as I spent more time at the JP courts and witnessed the relatively small number of hearings. Sometimes I would show up at a building that housed many JP courts and be unable to find a single live hearing.

CIVIL CASES

Civil cases make up almost two-thirds of the docket of the average JP court. The vignette from Rostov-na-Donu helps explain the disconnect between the caseload data and the observed reality. The civil procedure code opens the door to the use of a procedural mechanism known as a "judicial order" (*sudebnyi prikaz*) to resolve simple cases in a summary fashion (chap. 11, GPK RF). Among the types of cases for which these orders are specifically authorized are many that are within the jurisdiction of the JP courts, such as child support, tax assessments, wage disputes, and debt cases (art. 3, O mirovykh 1998; art. 122, GPK RF). *Sudebnye prikazy* are issued without a full-fledged hearing solely on the basis of the pleadings.[32] Petitioners have an incentive to opt for *prikazy*, not only because it expedites the resolution of the case, but also because the filing fees are halved (art. 123, GPK RF). When a complaint requesting the use of this mechanism is received by a JP court, it must be resolved within ten days (art. 126, GPK RF). If a JP is uncertain as to whether a *prikaz* is appropriate, she can set it for a hearing on the merits, thereby allowing a full airing. The drafting of *prikazy* is largely mechanistic. In most JP courts I visited, clerks prepared them, subject to review by JPs.

The caseload data presented in table 4.2 document the popularity of judicial orders among both petitioners and JPs. Between 2008 and 2011, over 70 percent of all the JP courts' civil cases were disposed of via *sudebnye prikazy*. Not surprisingly, they predominated in certain categories of cases (Hendley 2013). In 2011, for example, virtually all wage disputes (99.5 percent) went this route, which makes sense, given that these cases present no real factual dispute. The factories do not question their obligation to pay their workers, they simply plead poverty. Over three-fourths of all petitions seeking child support payments opted

---

32. *Sudebnye prikazy* are somewhat akin to the process used in Germany for simple debt collection (Ruhlin 2000, 268; Blankenburg 1998, 21).

for *prikazy*. These are the petitions that make use of the statutory formula for child support. As with the factory owners, the delinquent parents have no legal defense to their behavior. In these cases, a hearing on the merits would add little. The data also show the widespread use of *prikazy* for tax disputes. Regardless of whether the initiator is the state or the taxpayer, *prikazy* are used in over 90 percent of cases. Though they respect the wishes of petitioners and issue *prikazy*, JPs are less sanguine about these tax cases. Especially as to petitions originating with the state, they reported to me that records are frequently out of date, leading to people being sent tax bills for apartments they have long since sold and cars they no longer own.

The first scenario provides a glimpse into the remedies available when the recipient of a judicial order believes it was issued in error. The text of the order itself explains how to challenge it. Recipients have ten days to put forward a challenge (art. 128, GPK RF). They need not make a substantive argument; they need only lodge a protest. Upon receipt of a challenge, a JP automatically cancels (*otmenit*) the order. This puts the onus on the original petitioner to decide whether to move forward with a request for a hearing on the merits. If the recipient fails to object within the mandated ten-day period, he is not forestalled from challenging the order, but must first move to reinstate the statute of limitations. As the scenario indicates, JPs tend to err on the side of the targets of *sudebnye prikazy* in such cases, recognizing that it is an inherently one-sided process. The Rostov debtor is typical in his claim to having never received the *prikaz*. Given the vagaries of the Russian postal service, JPs are predisposed to believe such claims.[33] The fact that the Rostov debtor was in the hospital when the *prikaz* was issued and unable to attend to business matters made this case easier.

Despite the apparent ease of challenging judicial orders, relatively few are. In 2011, recipients complained in less than 7 percent of cases. This enhances their appeal for the JP courts. After all, if *prikazy* routinely boomeranged back to the courts, then using them would end up being more work for JPs and their staff. For example, a somewhat analogous procedural tool languished unused by the *arbitrazh* courts because judges believed that the orders would be regularly challenged, which would require them to start over again with hearings on the merits (Hendley 2005). They did not mind holding these hearings. What worried them is that they would be unable to finish the case within the time allowed under the statute. Rather than risk violating the deadline, they preferred to go through the regular procedure. Only when the law was rewritten to clarify

---

33. Kurkchiyan (2013) found that judges in Ukraine, where the postal service is likewise unreliable, were also forgiving when it came to claims of mail gone missing.

when this tool could be safely used did *arbitrazh* judges fully embrace it (Hendley 2013). This line of thinking was less common among JPs, though I did hear something similar from a Moscow JP whose district included the headquarters of one of Russia's largest banks, Sberbank. She was inundated with cases brought by Sberbank against its depositors and credit card customers. She generally avoided using *sudebnye prikazy* owing to the same sort of fears voiced by *arbitrazh* judges.

The reasons why so few judicial orders are challenged is not entirely clear. A significant percentage (hopefully the vast majority) of them are accurate. Challenging them would only put off the inevitable. For the cash-strapped, such delays could be helpful.[34] It is always possible that when pushed, creditors will decide not to pursue their rights. If the recipient of a *sudebnyi prikaz* believes he does not owe the amount in question, then he has to decide whether the time and effort needed to challenge the *prikaz* is worth it. Often the amounts are small.[35] Some may decide it is less trouble to pay such amounts rather than going to court.[36] Others may be flummoxed by the process. JPs and their staff reported receiving a significant number of phone calls asking for clarification as to the meaning of *sudebnye prikazy*. Though their terms struck me as easy to understand, those unfamiliar with legalese may find them puzzling. Likewise my sense of the ease of the process may not be shared by many of the recipients. It may be that some categories of *prikazy* are more likely to be challenged. It stands to reason that the odds of a mistake in calculating a debt are greater for tax and credit card obligations than for child support payments (which are statutorily set as a percentage of the noncustodial parent's wages).[37] It may also be that certain categories of debtors are more legally sophisticated. Perhaps credit cardholders are more rights-conscious than the average taxpayer. Unfortunately, the available data do not allow for the testing of these or any hypotheses. The annual statistical

---

34. Russians invoke the courts even when the outcome of the dispute is clear to all at the outset. The low cost of going to court makes it an appealing delay strategy, which is regularly employed by insurance companies and other legal entities. See, generally, Hendley (2012c; 2004). The targets of *sudebnye prikazy* are mostly individuals, whose level of legal sophistication is generally lower.

35. In several of the challenges to *sudebnye prikazy* I observed, the amount at issue was less than 1,000 rubles, which translates into about $20.

36. Not challenging the court's action is the course of least resistance. The rationale for "lumping it" in Russia is discussed in chapters 2 and 3. See also Hendley (2010); Sandefur (2007); Felstiner (1975).

37. A clerk to an Ekaterinburg judge reviewed the files of *sudebnye prikazy* for 2011. They were used actively, especially to go after child support payments. She said that the petitioners tended to be women. They sought her out for help, but this clerk said that she was forbidden from giving legal advice. The best she could do was to point them to the sample form documents on the web and on the courthouse bulletin boards. For her district, about 10 percent of *prikazy* had been challenged. None of these protests involved petitions for child support. Rather, most came from bank-initiated cases to recover credit card debt.

forms provide only an aggregate number of challenges; they are not broken down by the type of case.

The willingness to believe claims of failing to receive *prikazy* in a timely fashion reflects a more general preference within the Russian judicial corps for limiting barriers to the courts. The formal prerequisites for petitions are relatively simple and straightforward. Sample complaints are posted on the courts' websites and on the bulletin boards throughout every court building. For most causes of action, petitioners simply need to fill in the blanks with the underlying facts. Even so, they often make mistakes. Whenever possible, JPs overlook problems, reasoning that they can sort through them at the hearing. They rarely reject petitions outright. In 2011, for example, of the 9.2 million cases that were filed, only 1,716 were returned to the petitioners.[38] This number would be smaller if the data allowed rejections based on jurisdictional problems to be pulled out.[39] When complaints are returned, the JP is obliged to send along a letter explaining the flaws and inviting the petitioner to resubmit after fixing the problems.

CRIMINAL CASES

In terms of sheer numbers, criminal cases make up the smallest part of the JP courts' docket. Some JPs told me that criminal cases almost never arose in their districts. Jurisdiction follows the defendant, so those whose districts include large shopping centers were plagued with a steady stream of shoplifting cases. In 2011, criminal cases accounted for about 3 percent of these courts' average monthly workload. But simply counting cases fails to capture the burden imposed by criminal claims. Because they have more moving parts, they tend to take more time than civil or administrative cases. Defendants are required to have representation by licensed lawyers (*advokaty*), the state's interests are represented by prosecutors (*prokurory*), and victims of crime have standing to seek restitution. Simply finding mutually convenient times for everyone involved to meet can be trying. In addition, the affirmative duties on both sides to prove (or disprove) the crime typically requires witnesses to be called, adding another layer of scheduling complexity.

---

38. A more cynical interpretation of these data was suggested by a conversation with a JP in Petrozavodsk. She pointed to the stack of about twenty complaints on her desk, saying that this was her intake from that day's mail. She said that she was likely to accept all of them, noting that it was more trouble to reject them. If it turned out that one or more of them failed to state a viable cause of action, she could find for the other side.

39. Jurisdictional problems can be either substantive or geographic. The websites of the JP courts list the streets within each district, but some petitioners still send their complaints to the wrong court. JPs cannot forward such a complaint to the appropriate court. They have to return it and hope the petitioner will follow up. The limited nature of the subject-matter jurisdiction of the JP courts can be confusing to laymen. If the JP court ends up with a case that belongs with the district court, the JP can send the complaint up the hierarchy.

A type of plea bargaining known as *osobyi poriadok* has evolved as a way to streamline criminal cases (Solomon 2011). As the second vignette illustrates, if a defendant opts for *osobyi poriadok*, then his guilt or innocence is not debated at the hearing, thereby eliminating the need to call witnesses. The job of the judge is simply to verify that the defendant has acted voluntarily, and to confirm that the victim has no objections. By going down this route, the defendant gives up his right to appeal his guilt, though he can appeal his sentence if dissatisfied. JPs like *osobyi poriadok* because it speeds up the processing of criminal cases. Defendants and their counsel appreciate the greater certainty as to sentencing that comes with it.

This form of plea bargaining has become quite popular at the JP courts. When talking to several JPs in Voronezh, they estimated that it was used in upward of 95 percent of all their criminal cases. Perhaps, but this would have been well above the average for JP courts. In 2011, about 60 percent of all criminal cases decided by the JP courts went through *osobyi poriadok*. For theft, the predicate crime for the second vignette, the likelihood of plea bargaining was higher. Over three-quarters of all such cases took this route.

The combination of *sudebnye prikazy* and *osobyi poriadok* helps explain how JPs are able to handle such a large caseload and why I had trouble locating live hearings. The data are misleading in that they create the impression that every case imposes an equal burden on the court. When the reality that a majority of these cases are disposed of through summary procedures is factored in, the workload of JPs begins to move into the realm of what is humanly possible.

Notifying the Parties

Voronezh Divorce. A couple in their forties show up for their hearing with a Voronezh JP in her office.[40] The wife is the plaintiff. The JP quickly moves through the formalities. She recites their rights and duties as parties and asks if they have any motions. They shake their heads, indicating that they are ready to move forward. The JP then elicits their personal details, learning that they have a six-year-old son. She asks whether there is any possibility of reconciliation. Both of them repeatedly assure the judge that they are ready for the divorce. The wife explains that she will have full custody of the son. The husband's silence is taken as assent. The hearing lasts less than ten minutes, after which the

---

40. Six JP courts were quartered together. The JPs had to share two courtrooms among them. They heard most cases in their offices, resorting to the courtrooms only when cases involved multiple parties.

JP kicks everyone out of her office to prepare her decision. The divorcing couple sit silently in the corridor. We are called back in fairly short order. The JP grants the divorce. She reads her decision aloud, during which the husband's eyes well up with tears. Afterward, she tells the couple how to get their divorce officially registered.

Velikie Luki Divorce. A woman seeking a divorce appears. The JP hears the case in one of the three courtrooms in the building. He explains the procedures for the hearing, telling the plaintiff that she should address him as "your honor" and stand when speaking. He runs through her rights and duties as a plaintiff. He asks her whether she thinks they can proceed without her husband. She is keen to move the process forward, telling the judge that her husband is trying to hold up the divorce by failing to appear. The JP is unmoved, noting that she picked her husband voluntarily. In his words, if the case file lacks written evidence that the defendant has been notified of the proceedings, then "I don't have the right to resolve this case." The wife grows frustrated. She reminds the judge that she has shown up twice before to no avail. She believes that her husband is deliberately refusing to accept the letter from the court. The JP puts the onus on her, saying that the court has sent several letters, all of which have been returned. He suggests that she find her husband and have him send the court a letter requesting that the case be heard without him.

In Russia, the courts are responsible for notifying the parties of the time and place of the hearing. When all parties are engaged, as they were in the Voronezh divorce referenced above, the court's job is easy. Though these spouses clearly had regrets about calling it quits, neither was trying to avoid divorce by hiding from the court. The Voronezh case is fairly typical of the nineteen divorce cases I observed. Often the spouses had been estranged for many years and the divorce held little emotional resonance for the parties. While waiting for the decision in this case, I struck up a conversation with one of her secretaries and commented on the speed of the process. She laughed and said that this case actually took a bit longer than usual. She said that they schedule divorces at ten minute intervals. As I visited other courts, I saw many divorces that were wrapped up in five minutes or less.[41]

---

41. Though five minutes is extreme, a 2010 project that monitored JP courts in Permskii krai and Leningradskaia oblast found that hearings in over half of the 1,800 observed cases took less than 30 minutes (Ivanova 2011, 76). This is consistent with Pomorski's findings, though he was not observing cases at the JP courts (which were not in existence at the time of his research in 1997–99), but at the district courts (2001, 461). Hearing cases in rapid succession is not unique to Russia. Conley and O'Barr (1990, 85) document that some U.S. small-claims courts schedule cases in 5-minute intervals.

Even when operating at breakneck speed, JPs are always careful to ask the couple whether there is any chance of working out the relationship. If they hold out hope for reconciliation, then the judge is obliged to delay the proceedings to give them time to work out their problems.[42] Judicial styles varied, reflecting their strategies for maintaining control over the process. Some JPs had a hair-trigger response and would terminate the hearing if either side hinted at doubt.[43] Others would query the parties as to whether they thought additional time would make any difference. If the judge sensed that it would not, then she would keep things moving.[44] Sometimes the JP repeated the questions if she got an unexpected result, dropping a heavy hint that the divorce would be delayed if they expressed ambivalence. Usually the parties got the message and reworded their answers to eliminate any uncertainty. It is worth noting that in deciding whether or not to grant a delay, JPs were not affected by their desire to avoid violating the statutory deadlines. Because these delays are contemplated by the law, the additional time is not counted when calculating the procedural deadlines.

---

42. This commitment to reconciliation is a carryover from socialist law. Markovits reports that East German judges were required to determine whether the marital relationship was salvageable (2010, 72). Present-day Russia JPs take a more pragmatic approach, driven by the desires of the parties rather than social policy.

43. For example, in a case I observed in St. Petersburg, the wife appeared on her own. Unlike the Velikie luki case, this hearing could go forward because the file contained a telegram from the husband, thereby confirming that he had received notice. When the JP asked the wife whether the marriage could be restored, she said no. But a few minutes later, when she asked the wife whether she had doubts, the wife said she did. Everything screeched to a halt. The case was delayed for a month. The wife was visibly upset by this turn of events. From the outset, when responding to the JPs questions, she kept saying that she did not understand what the judge wanted from her. She explained that it was her first time in court. Though she tried to engage the JP on why the hearing had gone off the rails and begged the JP to rethink the date for the next hearing because she would be out of town on that day, the JP refused to engage with her. The JP kept repeating that the hearing was over, and that the plaintiff would have to leave. This is reminiscent of the vignette from Philips (1998, 90–91) in which an Arizona judge ignores what a criminal defendant is actually saying in order to push forward with a sentencing hearing.

44. Along similar lines, JPs varied in terms of their reaction to questions from the parties about custody. The JP courts do not have jurisdiction over child custody. The district courts hear cases in which custody is contested. There is a delicate line. Almost all of the couples whose divorces I observed had children together. For the most part, they had worked out custody, with the wife taking responsibility. When the JP asked if there was a question, they either said no or explained their plans. So long as they were in agreement, the JP took no further interest. In a Petrozavodsk case, a disagreement over custody became apparent as the case proceeded. The JP explained to the couple that he would have to send the case to the district court. In St. Petersburg, I watched as a JP used this legal reality as a cudgel to discourage the husband from pushing for custody. To be fair, he simply said that he wanted to be sure that his time with his son was preserved. The JP told him that pressing for a formal decision would require her to turn the case over to the district court. She pointedly reminded him that he could always sue for custody in the future. He took the hint and did not pursue custody at that point.

Though the Velikie luki case is atypical for divorces, it is sadly typical for the docket of the JP courts more generally. Like judges throughout the system, JPs describe notice as a "sore point" (*bol'noi vopros*). Their reputation and remuneration depend heavily on their ability to manage their caseload efficiently. One key indicator of success is meeting the deadlines for resolving cases set out in the procedural codes. The clock starts running when the complaint is submitted. At most, JPs have a few months, often less. As soon as the JP has set the case for a hearing, her secretary will send a registered letter containing the decree (*opredelenie*) to all named parties. The mail service is Russia is notoriously slow and unreliable. JPs generally give themselves a cushion of at least two weeks for the letter to arrive, even when all the parties are located in the same part of town. But merely sending the *opredelenie* is not sufficient. To proceed, the court must receive the return postcard evidencing receipt of the letter. Though the JPs I met were clearly frustrated by the inadequacies of the postal service, they also pointed the finger of blame at the parties themselves. Many defendants simply refused to accept delivery of registered letters, resulting in their return to the court.

The tools available for Russian judges have improved. When I first started doing court-based research in the late 1980s and early 1990s, I would watch as secretaries spent hours addressing envelopes by hand and sorting through the mail to get the return postcards in the appropriate file. Often hearings would grind to a halt as judges dug through mountains of postcards, hoping to find the one that would allow things to move forward. At long last, this process has been automated.[45] The addresses are generated by computer. The envelopes and return postcards have bar codes that are scanned, thereby allowing JPs and their staff to have quick access to information. JPs are also able to check parties' addresses with the tax authorities.

But the courts of general jurisdiction remain stubbornly resistant to modernizing further. The *arbitrazh* courts have begun experimenting with electronic filing and sending notices via electronic mail (Avakian 2011). The JPs and their staff see little hope of moving in that direction. They point out that, in contrast to the *arbitrazh* courts, which serve legal entities that have considerable resources at their disposal, many people who use the JP courts have fewer options. Most of the JPs themselves, even those in their twenties, use e-mail only occasionally and are skeptical that others use it more regularly. They were more intrigued by the possibility of sending notice through text messages, which is a universal method

---

45. Not all aspects of case management have been modernized. Case files are still sewn together with needle and thread, which is then sealed with wax. Those who carry out this work cannot imagine any other way to ensure the integrity of the case file.

of communication in Russia. In February 2012, the Russian Supreme Court authorized using instant messaging for official court notices, but only if the parties had previously agreed to it (Postanovlenie 2012). JPs were openly frustrated by this limitation, telling me that it essentially makes texting a nonstarter for them. As to all these electronic tools, judges were unsure as to how receipt of notice would be proven, that is, what would be the functional equivalent of the return postcard. This same concern explains their reticence in using telephone notification and instant messaging services. Over and over again, JPs shared their fears of being reversed on the grounds of ineffective notice. They worried that defendants who had been contact by phone would later deny it. Though none of these JPs had the misfortune of having been reversed in this way, all were determined not to let down their guard.

The Velikie luki case provides an example of how some JPs cope with the problem of ensuring notice to defendants. The JP simply passed the buck to the plaintiff, reasoning that her desperation to get divorced would provide the incentive needed to unearth the defendant. In my experience, this tactic is not uncommon, especially in cases involving family members who are likely to be better able to track down one another than the court. But it is not always feasible. When the party who has shown up is poorly educated or inexperienced in the legal system, shifting this burden to her is futile. Likewise, when JPs are faced with cases in which the parties operated at arms' length, plaintiffs are unlikely to have inside information as to how to locate defendants. If the judge believes the address is genuine, then after several mailed notices have been returned, she may opt for sending a telegram. I spent the day with a JP in St. Petersburg who had twenty-six cases on her schedule. All were cases brought by a housing management firm against residents who were delinquent in paying maintenance fees. Registered letters with *opredeleniia* had been sent to the defendants, but none of the case files contained the postcard verifying receipt. The JP was sure that she had the right address, but was equally confident that none of the defendants would ever pick up a registered letter from the court. She explained that she would set the cases for another hearing, and would send telegrams to all the defendants. She did not expect this to provoke any defendant to show up. In fact, the JP characterized them as "nonappearance" cases (*neiavochnye dela*), indicating that she had no reasonable expectation that either side would ever show up. But the record of having sent the telegrams satisfied the requirement of notice, allowing her to decide the cases within the statutory deadline.

Notwithstanding the uniform rules governing notice, I noticed that local norms had evolved. Moscow JPs were more reluctant than their St. Petersburg counterparts to send telegrams because they were required to get permission from their regional managers first.[46] There was also a small-town effect. In smaller cities, such as Pskov and Velikie luki, judges' secretaries routinely called parties to remind them of upcoming cases. They were nonplused by my surprise at this practice. In larger jurisdictions, such as Moscow, St. Petersburg, and Ekaterinburg, this sort of hand-holding was frowned on. Sometimes JPs would delay the start of a hearing if a litigant called to let them know they had been held up by traffic, but not always. More often people who were out of breath from having run in the hope of arriving for a hearing were turned away without a second thought if the hearing had been formally closed. They were informed of the date to which their hearing had been postponed and sent on their way.

Conciliating among Litigants

Private Criminal Claim—Petrozavodsk. I squeeze into a small court-room to hear a dispute brought by a woman against her ex-husband. The room has a desk for the judge and for the court secretary and four chairs. The chairs are taken up by the parties and their counsel, so the secretary grabs an extra chair from another courtroom for me. The wife claims that her ex-husband became verbally abusive when she went to the apartment that she used to share with him to get some of her belongings. He counters that, as she was no longer registered (*propisana*) at the apartment, she had no right to be there. He refused to allow her to take any of her things.

As the proceedings begin, it is immediately apparent that this is far from the first meeting of the group. The purpose of the hearing is to take testimony from a police officer who was summoned pursuant to a motion of the ex-husband at the last hearing. The policeman had been present for part of the fracas. Once the JP calls the session to order, her secretary calls him into the already-crowded room. He is not in uniform and stands while giving evidence. The JP asks a series of open-ended questions that are aimed at discerning what he knows about the events. Both parties are given an opportunity to question him. The plaintiff goes first. Her representative, who is not an *advokat*, asks pointed questions. The defendant does his own questioning despite being represented by an *advokat*. The witness's memory falls short on a number of issues. Because he saw the incident as a "family problem" (*semennyi*

---

46. Each region of Russia has an agency (*upravlenie*) that is charged with managing the budget of the JP courts. Though JPs are employees of the federal government, their staff members are recruited and employed by these *upravleniia*.

skandal), he made no official report. The JP asks some final clarification questions, then releases the witness.

The parties then turn to a motion by the defendant to postpone the case indefinitely on the basis of his poor health. He claims that he has dangerously high blood pressure and was released from the hospital to attend this hearing. He says that he will not be ready to resume participating in the case for a month. The JP's face betrays her annoyance at this turn of events. She sets the next hearing for two weeks in the future. He expresses doubt that he will be recovered by that time. She tells him that he must provide the court with written evidence of his inability to participate. Without such documentation, she will move forward.

Private Criminal Claim—Pskov. A taxi driver has brought a claim against a passenger who physically assaulted him and skipped out on the fare. Both men are present. Neither is represented. The case has been scheduled twice before, but the plaintiff failed to show up for the first hearing and neither of them came to the second hearing. The JP begins by asking the taxi driver about his age, address, family status, and employment history. He peppers the driver with questions about his failure to show up for the earlier hearings. The plaintiff explains that he was ill for the first hearing and failed to receive the notice of the second. He corrects the court's record as to his address. The JP repeats the same questions for the defendant, without quizzing him about his nonappearance.

In an unusual twist, before asking the parties to tell their stories, the JP asks whether they might be willing to settle. The plaintiff says he is willing, but that the defendant has made no such proposal. The JP keeps things on an even keel by saying that he is simply trying to understand whether they are open to the idea. The taxi driver says he would walk away if the defendant paid him 3,000 rubles. The defendant says that the amount is acceptable to him, but that he has only 2,000 rubles with him. The JP asks how long he needs to raise the additional funds. The defendant estimates that he can have it within an hour. The JP declares a recess for 90 minutes. When the case reconvenes, the defendant hands over the money and the plaintiff withdraws his complaint.

These two vignettes provide a glimpse into criminal cases initiated by individuals (*chastnoe obvinenie*) rather than the state. JPs uniformly describe these cases as the bane of their existence. They arise when the police decline to pursue an individual's claim arising from a physical or verbal altercation. As a rule, the primary injuries are emotional rather than physical, which explains the unwillingness of the police to open a case. But when the victim has been struck, the Russian law allows him to bring a claim against the perpetrator.[47] In addition to criminal sanctions, the victim can simultaneously pursue civil damages.

Several factors drive the JPs' distaste for cases of *chastnoe obvinenie*. Primary among them is their perception that they take an inordinate amount of time. Judges' obligations are ratcheted up. All pretense of adversarialism is abandoned, as they are expected to take responsibility for investigating the underlying charges. In other words, they take on the roles usually fulfilled by the police and prosecutors in criminal cases. Because the parties are rarely represented, JPs also find themselves in the awkward position of having to explain the law and its implications. In particular, petitioners rarely appreciate the profound consequences of a criminal conviction on defendants' lives. They are driven by anger and a desire for revenge. Indeed, judges find it difficult to cope with the heightened emotions that usually characterize cases of *chastnoe obvinenie*. As with the first scenario, the prototypical case arises among family members (or former family members) at home.[48] This complicates the task of getting to the bottom of what really happened. Often the event has no witnesses other than the parties themselves. This forces the judge to rely heavily on her assessment of their relative credibility. Russian judges are more comfortable grounding their decisions in documentary rather than testimonial evidence.

Even when there are witnesses, as in the first scenario, they rarely add much. The testimony of the police officer did little more than confirm what the judge already knew, namely, that an altercation took place. He was unable to shed light on the appropriateness of the parties' conduct, which stood at the heart of culpability. Had she been hearing the case with unrepresented parties, she

---

47. Article 318 of the Criminal Procedure Code (UPK RF) authorizes private prosecution for minor offenses akin to battery that are covered by articles 115, part 1, and 116, part 1 of the Criminal Code (UK RF). In late 2011, the law was changed to eliminate criminal liability for slander or other verbal injuries as part of a larger effort to "humanize" Russian criminal law. Although pleased at any reduction of the scope of *chastnoe obvinenie*, JPs reported that this legislative change had made little difference to them because the bulk of these cases are predicated on physical injuries. During the summer of 2012, criminal liability for slander was restored.

48. The high cost of housing in Russia has resulted in multiple generations residing together and in divorced couples continuing to share the same apartment. The close quarters, combined with the well-known tendency of Russians to relax with alcohol, create hospitable conditions for fights involving physical injuries. See generally Zavisca (2012). A number of cases I observed involved tense relations between women and their mothers-in-law that erupted into physical violence. Farnsworth (1986) shows that such problems are nothing new, though her research indicates that daughters-in-law tended to be the victims in the tsarist era, whereas my fieldwork suggests that mothers-in-law are more likely to be the victims in contemporary Russia. Both share the sad fate of being the most unwanted person in the family unit.

probably would not have granted the motion to call him. Whether to allow witnesses is within the JP's discretion. In cases of *chastnoe obvinenie*, judges are barraged by motions to call witnesses. One Moscow JP told me of a case where one side wanted to call fifteen witnesses to testify as to his stellar character. She allowed only one of these witnesses, seeing little value to having the same points made repeatedly. But the subtlety of her argument escaped the litigant. JPs have to be careful to avoid having the parties redirect their anger at one another toward the bench when judges repeatedly reject their motions.[49] A JP's reaction to a request to call witnesses depends on how it is framed. Those with courtroom experience, such as the ex-husband's *advokat* in the first vignette, are better able to make a compelling argument as to the potential value-added of a witness. As a result, represented parties are more likely to prevail in such motions.

The first scenario illustrates the challenge of working with parties who have a shared history. Both were clearly dug into their positions. The petitioner was unwilling to back down. The defendant was using every trick in the procedural book to delay the case. There was a sense that they were replaying battles from their marriage. Except now they had brought in champions to defend them and an umpire to rule on who was right. This sort of case is a JP's worst nightmare. It resists the usual strategy adopted by JPs, which is to assume the role of mediator and to push the parties to see the larger picture and to settle. When family members are battling one another, JPs find it useful to remind them of the consequences of a criminal conviction, not just for the defendant but for the entire family as well. Such a stain on the record effectively disqualifies immediate family members from many civil service jobs. JPs report that petitioners often withdraw their complaints when they have time to reflect on this harsh reality. The JP had encouraged the couple involved in the first scenario to find a less lethal way to resolve their differences. The failsafe tactic of tugging at their heartstrings by stressing the devastating impact of a criminal conviction was ineffective because they shared no children. The wife clearly reveled in the opportunity to exact

---

49. Not only would this disrupt the proceedings, but many JPs also worry that disgruntled litigants will file petitions with the judicial qualification commission. In addition to managing the selection process, this commission also handles complaints about judicial behavior. JPs are sufficiently self-confident not to be concerned about punishment or removal from the bench. But answering complaints consumes valuable time and puts their ability to meet the statutory deadlines for resolving cases in jeopardy. For an example of a complaint filed against a Novosibirsk JP that cited her rejection of over twenty motions from the defendant, see https://gorskayann.pravorub.ru/personal/22731.html. A search of the website of the Novosibirsk qualification commission reveals no response to this complaint, but does document the promotion of the JP in question to the district court, suggesting that the complaint was viewed as lacking merit. http://nvs.vkks.ru/publication/31515/.

revenge on her former husband and had no interest in settling. The involvement of lawyers may also have decreased the likelihood of settlement. Lawyers are compensated by the number of hearings they attend, creating an incentive to keep cases going.

The second vignette is atypical in that it involves strangers, but is typical in that the parties were unrepresented and were open to settling the case. The official caseload data confirm that the odds of settlement are higher for cases of *chastnoe obvinenie* than for any other category of case.[50] In 2011, settlements were reported in over 70 percent of such cases, as compared with 36 percent of criminal cases more generally.[51] As the second scenario reveals, the impetus for settlement is more likely to come from the JP than from the parties. JPs often cloak their behavior in terms of what is best for the parties, but privately confess that settlement is best for them as well. It gets the case off their docket, thereby eliminating the risk that it will drag on beyond the statutory deadline. It also frees them from the emotional burden of having to decide who is telling the truth.

The JP's strategy in the second sample case is to raise the option of settling before either side is able to tell his story. He believes that doing so increases the chance for settlement because neither side will have to back down. It is certainly unorthodox. The usual pattern in all cases, including *chastnoe obvinenie*, is to give the litigants an opportunity to present their versions of the facts. Had the defendant not jumped at the chance to put the case behind him, the JP would have gone back on script. He is able to get away with this deviation because neither side will appeal.

JPs see their task in these cases as more of a social worker or conciliator than an objective evaluator of the legal merits (Kapitaniuk 2010). Indeed, the "he said—she said" nature of these cases makes law somewhat beside the point. They have to approach the parties with patience and take an active role in shaping how the case proceeds. Most parties have no prior court experience and do not hire lawyers. As a result, they look to the judge for guidance. JPs always hope that the parties will settle quickly, as did the taxi driver and his fare. Few fold so easily, however. Often it takes several hearings before the parties can grasp the folly of pursuing their dispute in a legal forum. It takes time for the anger that provoked the lawsuit to abate.

---

50. In this context, settlement connotes a withdrawal of the criminal complaint and, if there is an accompanying civil suit, a voluntary side agreement between the parties (*mirovoe soglashenie*) as to the amount to be paid by the defendant to the plaintiff.

51. Less than 1 percent of civil cases are settled. Elsewhere I have analyzed the reasons why Russians eschew settlement (Hendley 2012c).

The Parameters of Judicial Discretion

Drunk Driving—Rostov-na-Donu. A young man wearing a tank top and shorts shows up in the office of the JP to contest a traffic ticket. As always, the JP begins by reciting the defendant's rights and duties. She has him sign a form document acknowledging that he has been so informed. She then summarizes the facts of the case, drawing from the report (*protokol*) prepared by the traffic police. The defendant was stopped on suspicion of driving while intoxicated. He denied the charge and refused to take a field sobriety test. A citation was issued. The defendant remains defiant. He tells the JP that he did nothing wrong. The JP sets him straight, explaining that merely refusing to take a sobriety test violates the law. She cuts him off as he tries to argue the merits of the case. She asks him to leave while she makes her decision, but allows me to stay in the room. She tells me that this fact pattern is so common that a form document has been developed for the decision. She just has to fill in the particulars of this case. The defendant loses his driving privileges for several months.

Petty Theft—Petrozavodsk. A forty-eight-year-old woman, who carries herself as if she were two or three decades older, arrives at the office of the JP to answer the charge of having shoplifted food at a local grocery store. She is loaded down with plastic bags; her glasses are held together around her head by a piece of heavy string. As the JP goes through the standard recitation of the rights and duties of litigants, the defendant's befuddlement is obvious. The JP walks her through the various provisions. The defendant breaks down and starts to cry. The judge maintains her composure. She does not offer the defendant a tissue, nor does she bend the rules to allow her to remain seated while addressing the court. The JP summarizes the basic facts. The store alleges that the defendant stole cucumbers and chocolate worth 84 rubles (less than $2). She gives the older woman a chance to tell her side of the story. The defendant provides a rambling explanation. She explains that she finds the store relaxing and enjoys spending time there. Her purpose that day was to buy butter. She digs through her plastic bags and produces a receipt for the butter. She cannot explain how the cucumbers and chocolate ended up in her pocket rather than in her shopping basket. She says that the checkout girl rushed her. As she talks, she continues to paw through the documents in her bags, pulling out receipts and other documents and placing them in piles on the table in front of her. Periodically the JP urges the defendant to calm down. After about a half hour of this, the JP tells the defendant that she is free to go. The defendant's gratitude is palpable. Yet she does not stop talking. It takes the JP another twenty minutes to get her out of her office.

Child Support—Ekaterinburg. A woman in her thirties comes to the office of the JP to petition for increased child support payments from her ex-husband. The hearing I observe caught the case in midstream. The JP previously sent a request to the tax authorities for a certified copy of the ex-husband's tax declaration and her secretary called to hurry the process along and was promised that it would be faxed that morning. Unfortunately, the document did not show up in time for the hearing. The JP and the plaintiff discuss whether to proceed or reschedule. The plaintiff is keen to have the hearing. Her ex-husband is not present, but has sent an answer (*otzyv*) in which (among other things) he asks the court to proceed in his absence. The plaintiff has studied this document. She is an accountant by training and brings that methodical approach to the problem at hand. She argues that her former spouse is hiding income to avoid his obligation to his daughter. Before the divorce, he worked as a fireman and made enough money to support the family. He quit that job and now works for a private company, where he makes 6,000 rubles (about $120) per month according to the official records. Relying on evidence that the defendant submitted himself as well as credit card records she uncovered, the plaintiff attempts to convince the judge that the defendant's current lifestyle could not possibly be sustained on the salary he claims. She shows that he spent 25,000 rubles on a four-day period while on vacation. The JP listens attentively, occasionally asking questions of clarification. Ultimately, however, the case is stalled until they receive the tax document.

THE ROLE OF THE CODES

Like judges in other countries with civil law legal traditions, Russian judges do not see themselves as policymakers. Their task is not to make law or even to tweak the law, but to apply the codes to the facts presented.[52] Experience has shown that, despite the best intentions of legislators, codes are rarely comprehensive (Fuller

---

52. Assessed in terms of the typology presented by Conley and O'Barr (1990), JPs tend to be a mixture of strict adherents to the law and proceduralists. I encountered no JP who would fit into their category of lawmaker. Although I did observe JPs occasionally acting as mediators, they did so grudgingly as a way to get potentially time-consuming cases off their dockets.

1964). In Russia, the top courts within the judicial hierarchies are frequently called on to fill gaps and to resolve differences of opinion among lower courts about the appropriate interpretation of the codes. They do this through case decisions and guidelines issued periodically, which are considered to be binding (Maggs, Schwartz, and Burnham 2015; Barry and Barner-Barry 1974). Keeping up with changes in legislation and the pronouncements of the top courts used to be laborious. When spending time in the Soviet courts in the late 1980s, I would often see well-worn copies of the codes and the commentaries to them to which judges had paper clipped amendments and excerpts from court decisions and guidelines (Hendley 1996). Locating these materials was not easy. Fortunately, present-day Russian judges have easy access to a comprehensive computerized database of Russian law. Now the problem is different. The breakneck pace of change makes staying current difficult. Court leadership helps by holding regular meetings to discuss new laws. The broad jurisdiction of JP courts and the expectation that JPs will handle any case that arises in their district puts them at a comparative disadvantage within the Russian judicial system.

On the other hand, many of the issues that JPs confront on a daily basis are remarkably straightforward. Traffic cases are a good example. Judges have a bit of wiggle room when it comes to sanctions, but are hamstrung by the code when it comes to culpability. On paper, these make up about a third of the administrative cases decided by the JP courts. In terms of time, however, they are much less demanding. JPs are able to power through them rapidly. Few defendants bother to show up for their hearings. When they do, the hearings tend to go quickly, primarily because the underlying law provides little judicial discretion.

The law governing drunk driving is quite unforgiving. The loss of driving privileges is mandated for any trace of alcohol in the blood (art. 27.12, KoAP). When the driver refuses to participate in a field sobriety test, he is generally taken to a hospital for a blood draw. For some reason, this did not happen for the driver in the first vignette. But his refusal nonetheless sealed his fate. In such cases, the law essentially presumes inebriation. The JP was uninterested in the defendant's testimony. The documents told the story. Similar sentiments were expressed by JPs and their staff elsewhere. One clerk in Petrozavodsk reiterated the general disaffection for witness testimony, especially when it came to cases of drunk driving. She emphasized the inherently imperfect nature of memory.

Defendants are more likely to hire lawyers and/or show up for their scheduled hearings when the penalty is a loss of driving privileges. Especially for those whose jobs depend on being able to drive, the stakes are very high. With or without a lawyer, the only sure way for a defendant to win a traffic case is to challenge the official documents on technical grounds. Examples include failing to sign a report or neglecting to complete a required section. When faced with a colorable

claim along these lines, a JP will postpone the hearing and summon the traffic policeman who wrote the report to attend the next hearing. As a rule, the
questioning centers not on the details of the incident, but on the report itself.
For example, a lawyer in Velikie luki was able to get his client's case tossed by
documenting that the police report contained multiple violations of procedure,
most notably that the reason stated for giving his client a sobriety test was not
among those permitted by the code. This was confirmed by the policeman himself, though it was not clear that he realized he was shooting himself in the foot
with this testimony. The positivism of the JP courts cuts both ways.

THE ROLE OF EMPATHY AND COMMON SENSE

JPs occasionally toss caution to the wind and allow empathy to color their decisions. When talking to me after the defendant in the second vignette left, the
Petrozavodsk JP said that she struggled with how to handle cases of minor theft
of food by poor people. She faced a lot of these cases because her district includes
a large shopping center with a big grocery store. This particular defendant, who
was a disabled pensioner, represented a tough case. Her defense of having forgotten to pay would have been laughable had it come from a well-functioning person.[53] The judge conceded that the defendant's mental challenges, which became
increasingly apparent as the hearing proceeded, convinced her that punishment
would serve no useful purpose. She also expressed doubt about the wisdom of
imposing a fine (which would have been the sanction in this case)[54] on a person
who had been reduced to stealing cucumbers.

The limited number of cases that I observed make it impossible to know how
often empathy leads JPs to resolve cases on equitable rather than legal grounds.
I did not often witness it. More typical in my experience was a case brought
by a Pskov pensioner in his eighties to challenge a 1,000-ruble fine imposed by
the Pension Fund when he failed to pay an annual assessment of 10,000 rubles
required of those registered as independent entrepreneurs. His registration
dated back to the 1990s when he had operated a kiosk selling *pirozhki* for several
years. He had shuttered the kiosk long ago. The JP explained that, according to
the records of the Pension Fund, he was still registered as an entrepreneur and,
therefore, was liable for the annual assessment. They had a lively exchange on
this question. His commonsense argument that he was not functioning as an

---

53. For example, a young man who stole a can of Red Bull as well as several bottles of expensive
alcohol from a grocery store in Ekaterinburg earned no sympathy from the judge. The defendant was
gainfully employed at the time of the crime. To be fair, he did not try to excuse his behavior.

54. Because of the small amount at issue, this case was treated as an administrative case rather
than a criminal case.

entrepreneur and so should not be liable for the obligations of an entrepreneur
fell on deaf ears. He told her that he had visited the Pension Fund on several occasions, but had been unable to find anyone who would help him. The JP was
clearly sympathetic to his plight. She admonished the young woman who had
come to court to represent the Fund, telling her that the Fund ought to be more
responsive to citizens' needs. She asked him why he was still working at his age.
But she told him that her hands were tied by the code. Even though her heart was
with him, she could not let him off the hook.

THE ROLE OF APPEALS

Likewise, in the third scenario, the Ekaterinburg JP's options are constrained by
the code. Or, more accurately, by her fear of how the appellate court would interpret the code. In observing her interactions with the plaintiff, it seemed to me
that she was keen to rule in her favor. This was confirmed in remarks she made
to me afterward. She said that the plaintiff's evidence convinced her that the ex-
husband was engaging in subterfuge to avoid having to pay child support for the
daughter they shared. Yet she was skittish about ruling in favor of the plaintiff.
The Family Code lays out a default rule requiring that noncustodial parents pay
one-quarter of their salary in child support (art. 81, SK RF). That amount can be
increased if needed, but requires a hearing to justify the change. On paper, the
Code appears to give judges a fair amount of discretion in setting the amount
(art. 83, SK RF). Indeed, one of the commentaries to the Code stresses the expansion of judicial discretion as compared with the previous version of the law.[55] In
practice, however, JPs are uncomfortable with such wide discretion. They look to
the noncustodial parent to sustain the burden of proving the need for an amount
in excess of what is provided for by statute. On paper, the welfare of the child is
given top priority. The Code directs that every effort be made to allow the child
to maintain the lifestyle she had before the divorce. In this case, the plaintiff has
to prove that 25 percent of her ex-husband's salary is insufficient to cover his half
of their daughter's cost of living. Given his claim of a monthly income of 6,000
rubles, this translates into 1,500 rubles. This figure, which amounts to roughly
$30, is patently inadequate. Proving that he is capable of paying more—that he
is receiving additional remuneration under the table—is a tougher task. In the
hearing I observed, she presented circumstantial evidence. She asked how someone who is earning 6,000 rubles per month could spend over four times that
amount over a long holiday weekend. The JP clearly empathized, but told her

55. The commentary notes that the judge has the right to raise the idea of opting out of the statutory default rule on her own, illustrating the breadth of her discretion (Kuznetsova 1996).

that she would need to back up her allegations with convincing documentary evidence. Her word was not good enough.

This fact pattern was sadly familiar to the JP. In the past, she had found in favor of mothers who had sought increases in child support payments on the basis of the sort of circumstantial evidence put forward by this plaintiff. She had been reversed by the appellate court on the grounds that the documentary evidence of the noncustodial parent's ability to pay more was insufficient. She pulled a binder off her bookshelf where she kept all her reversed cases. She shook her head as she reread the appellate opinion, saying that they were unrealistic in their demands for evidence. But she was unwilling to risk another reversal. The earlier case had created a chilling effect, making her second-guess herself, and upping the ante for future plaintiffs.

This desire to avoid reversals is a major motivating force in the lives of Russian JPs. It informs almost every aspect of their daily lives. The Petrozavodsk JP who let the pitiful shoplifter off would not have done so had she thought the case might be appealed. Given that the grocery store, the ostensible victim, did not bother to send a representative to the hearing, the JP could be fairly sure they would not appeal her decision. On the other hand, many state agencies, such as the Pension Fund and the Tax Police, have firm internal policies requiring staff attorneys to appeal any decision that goes against them, even when the amounts are trivial. As a result, the Pskov JP had less freedom of movement. She knew that any momentary pleasure the pensioner-defendant might take in a victory in her court would be shattered when the Pension Fund appealed the decision to the district court. I suspect that the JP was less worried about his feelings and more about her track record, especially given that she was waiting for her appointment to the district court to be finalized.

A concern with being reversed is not unique to Russian judges. Nowhere do judges enjoy being told that they got it wrong. Moreover, the use of reversal rates as a mechanism to assess the quality of judges' work is fairly common in countries with civil law legal traditions, though elsewhere greater efforts are made to employ qualitative indicators as well (Solomon 1997, 243). Encouraging judges to do their best would seem to be uncontroversial. In practice, however, the quest to avoid reversals has had a number of perverse results in Russia. It has led judges to focus on procedural details at the expense of substantive justice. They want to build a case file that is invulnerable to criticism from appellate judges. This helps explain the obsession with having written documentation of notice to the parties and the strong preference for documentary over testimonial evidence in civil cases. It also helps account for JPs' reluctance to dismiss cases when parties show up empty-handed. The procedural codes clearly impose an obligation on parties to present evidence to substantiate their claims, thereby opening the door to dismissing cases when parties fail to do so, especially when it happens repeatedly. But JPs almost never take the first opportunity to dismiss a case (or even the second or third). They take such action only when up against the wall of the statutory time deadlines. All the time, they are complaining vociferously about their heavy caseload. When I raise the obvious option of being more aggressive about dismissing cases for nonresponsive parties, they recoil in horror. They tell me that doing so would be pointless because the cases would simply show up again after the appellate court reverses them. JPs are firmly convinced that parties will win the sympathy of appellate judges by telling them that they never got an opportunity to tell their story. Few had had one of their own cases reversed on these grounds, but every JP with whom I spoke claimed to know someone who had. Whether this is an urban legend or not is almost irrelevant. The mere belief in such reversals drives judicial behavior.[56]

Whether this concern with being reversed leads JPs to insist on a thorough examination of the issues raised in order to ferret out the truth or, rather, to be focused on creating a case file that gives that appearance to outsiders is unclear. Along these lines, Kurkchiyan (2012) contrasts Polish and Bulgarian judges. She sees the former as being genuinely dedicated to finding the truth, whereas she views the latter as ticket punchers. In my conversations with them, Russian JPs invariably stressed their obligation to get to the bottom of what had happened. Their behavior sometimes belied that commitment as they rushed to tie up loose ends before the proverbial clock struck midnight.

ROLE OF LAWYERS

JPs frequently encounter litigants whose low level of education and lack of legal experience render them incapable of framing a viable legal argument. The Petrozavodsk shoplifter is a poignant illustration of this phenomenon. Almost as common, however, are litigants who are operating under a skewed understanding of the law and who believe themselves to have been wronged.[57] This behavioral pattern is exemplified by the young man from Rostov who challenges his drunk-driving charge. Less common are litigants like the Ekaterinburg accountant who is trying to hold her husband accountable, who know the legal rules but struggle to understand and meet the burden of proof.

From the JPs' point of view, these disparate problems would almost certainly be ameliorated if the parties had legal counsel. Although criminal defendants are required by law to have licensed lawyers (*advokaty*), relatively few noncriminal

---

56. I have observed similar behavior among *arbitrazh* judges (Hendley 2007).

57. As Ellickson's (1991) seminal study reminds us, this tendency of laymen to believe they know the law and to order their behavior accordingly is not limited to Russians.

litigants are represented in JP courts.[58] I will return to the reasons why in the next chapter. At present, I am more interested in how JPs cope with neophyte parties. Given their commitment to giving everyone a chance to tell their story, this puts them in a quandary. Is it their obligation to help these clueless parties find their way through the legal maze? Or should they sit back and do nothing as they flail? What I observed was a disconnect between words and action. JPs' insistence that they were prohibited from offering legal advice to litigants was a common refrain. JPs told me that they routinely advised struggling parties to hire lawyers. I witnessed these conversations on numerous occasions. Yet they typically had the feel of an obligatory exchange that neither side really believed would lead to anything.

In reality, JPs often found themselves explaining the substance of the law in order to clarify what sort of evidence was needed to prove the claim. This is evident in all three scenarios, even though the sort of information conveyed was tailored to the case and to the capacities of the litigants. JPs were uniformly horrified by the idea that parties who were more knowledgeable about the law or who were more experienced litigators would prevail. Most saw it as their job to level the playing field to allow the facts to speak for themselves. They explained that the case would be reversed if they allowed it to proceed in a one-sided fashion. The enthusiasm with which they took up the causes of beleaguered parties varied tremendously.

In addition to rationalizing this helping hand as a way of avoiding reversals, JPs also justified it as part of their pedagogical role. This idea that judges are charged with improving society by teaching litigants about the importance of obeying the law is a carryover from the Soviet days (Berman 1963). Though JPs have ostensibly left behind the goal of creating the new Soviet man, I occasionally felt like I had time traveled back to the 1960s, as described by Feifer, as I listened to a JP harangue a young person about how he needed to straighten up his act. Of course, lecturing litigants about their behavior is not limited to socialist judges. I could just as easily have stumbled into a Russian-language version of *Judge Judy* or *The People's Court*.[59]

---

58. The available comparative data show variation on this question. Litigants in small-stakes cases in Bulgaria and Poland are generally represented (Kurkchiyan 2012). By contrast, lawyers are in short supply in mundane cases in Ukraine (Kurkchiyan 2013). Baldwin (1997, 9) reports that about a quarter of the participants in cases in the county courts in England and Wales were represented. A study of small-claims courts in Iowa reveals that around 40 percent of litigants were represented (Elwell and Carlson 1990, 471–472), though attorneys are barred in nine other states (Turner and McGee 2000, 180–182).

59. There are, in fact, several Russian-language imitators of these venerable American shows. One in particular, *Chas suda* (The Court Hour), focuses on the sorts of mundane disputes that often end up in JP courts. In contrast to its U.S. counterparts, the parties are portrayed by actors.

Images of JPs

In my travels around Russia, I found a remarkable consistency to the self-images of JPs. Though not a terribly self-reflective group, they presented themselves as highly competent managers of teams of professionals charged with resolving disputes between mostly unsophisticated parties (Floyd 1994; Resnik 1982). Their public face was confident, both in terms of their legal knowledge and their ability to command respect in the courtroom. As I met JPs who were at different career points, I came to see this confidence as a veneer that was honed through experience. I could almost see them put it on along with their robes as they transitioned from talking informally with me to hearing a case. Younger JPs spoke openly of the difficulty of making the psychological transition from clerk to judge. All had worked their way up from secretary to clerk, so they knew court procedure inside out. They told me that, although they had been prepared for the workload, what had surprised them was the emotional toll of being in charge. All eyes were on them. Litigants looked to them to be omniscient as to the substantive law, while their staff looked to them to take responsibility for the ebb and flow of cases.

Precisely how this competence manifests itself in judicial hearings varies. In her research on first-instance judges in Poland, where the judicial corps is also composed primarily of women, Kurkchiyan (2012, 237) argues that they gain control over their courtrooms through fetishizing the procedural rules. She contrasts this with English county court judges who are able to establish their control over the process more subtly and who take full advantage of the flexibility in the procedural rules to introduce informality into the proceedings to make fledgling litigants more comfortable (230). Like both the Polish and English courts studied by Kurkchiyan, the Russian JP courts employ a judge-centered process, but Russian JPs cannot be so easily categorized. As a rule, they wear robes and have the trappings of state power nearby, such as the flag and state seal. As the vignettes illustrate, some JPs are sticklers for procedural niceties and insist that litigants address them as "your honor" and stand when speaking to them, and some are not. In terms of managing hearings, JPs generally insist on sticking with the basic format of ruling on motions that might preclude going forward with the case before turning to the merits. Within those general parameters, however, they exhibit a great deal of flexibility and willingness to tolerate informality in the presentation style of the litigants. When parties become overly rambunctious and begin talking over one another, JPs rein them in, reminding them that they are at court and that they must bow to the judges' authority. Some JPs are more heavy-handed than others, reflecting both their personal style and their level of annoyance. Their willingness to take an activist role as conciliators depends on the circumstances. My sense was that their heavy caseload constrained their natural tendencies to work with parties to find a compromise.

The cluelessness of those who come to the JP courts, combined with the highly emotional content of many of the cases, requires JPs to take on a more expansive managerial role as quasi-mediators.[60] Some reported that they often feel more like social workers than judges. They did not take any particular pride in this. Just the opposite. They would often cite cases of *chastnoe obvinenie* as prime examples of how their time was wasted getting to the bottom of petty personal disputes. They saw the value to the parties of avoiding the stain of a criminal conviction that could reverberate throughout the extended family, but invariably begrudged the time necessary to get the parties to settle. Whether JPs were motivated more by these altruistic goals or by their selfish desire to get these time-consuming cases off their docket so as not to risk having the case linger on beyond the statutory deadline was unclear to me. Indeed, it seemed to me that JPs themselves had trouble untangling their motives.

Russian JPs are always searching for an equilibrium between justice and efficiency. These two goals reflect their two audiences: litigants and officialdom. Litigants are mostly worried about whether judges get it right in their case and whether they are treated fairly.[61] Any interest in efficiency is limited to their case; they care little about larger trends. Officials within the Russian judiciary, by contrast, tend to dwell more on efficiency, as measured by their ability to manage their docket and avoid reversals. In the interest of self-preservation, JPs' concern with efficiency probably trumps their desire to do justice. Or more accurately, their patience wanes as the deadline for resolving the case approaches. To their credit, they worry that the need for speed compromises the quality of justice rendered. JPs frequently likened the process to a conveyor belt. But this does not translate into a lack of respect for litigants.[62] Though some litigants probably feel bulldozed by the brisk pace, it is worth remembering the vignettes with the disabled pensioner in Petrozavodsk or the pensioner-entrepreneur in Pskov where judges took the time to listen to their woes and explain the process to them. As a general matter, the introduction of websites and the expansion of the hours

---

60. JPs in the tsarist era also acted as mediators and conciliators, but were frustrated by the avalanche of cases, which often forced them to rely on statutory law (Neuberger 1994, 236).

61. Socio-legal research suggests that litigants are generally satisfied by their treatment in the JP courts (Hendley 2016). This issue is addressed in more detail in the next chapter.

62. Kurchiyan (2013) argues that Ukrainian courts are consumed by their bureaucratic functions. Despite sharing a Soviet heritage with their Ukrainian counterparts, Russian JPs manage to balance their preoccupation with pleasing their bureaucratic masters with a devotion to serving the needs of litigants.

during which petitioners can submit their documents reflects an increased concern with providing better service on the part of the JP courts.

As this implies, JPs take pride in their work, but it is a pride laced with a healthy dose of victimhood. Without exception, every JP I met made a point of emphasizing the number of cases she was handling. Over and over again I was shown stacks of case files and told of the nights and weekends given over to writing opinions. Never did they bring up the procedural tools that allowed them to accelerate cases. When asked about *sudebnye prikazy*, they conceded that these were helpful and that their staff did most of the work, but always reminded me that they took ultimate responsibility for these orders, just as they did for all work coming out of their chambers. Often this conversation took place in the presence of their staff, who seemed to take no offense at being put in their place.[63]

Several common attributes of JPs stood out to me, but were not part of most JPs' self-image. As Markovits (1992, 57) notes in her study of the collapse of the East German judicial system, "even people trying to give an honest account of their work are unlikely to dwell on its most negative aspects." The profound divide between public and private identities inherited from state socialism also contributed to their reticence (ibid., 121; Ledeneva 1998; Kotkin 1995, 220). As a group, Russian JPs are decidedly risk-averse. This quality is reflected in many aspects of their work. Most obvious is their fear of reversals and of violating the statutory deadlines for resolving cases. Less apparent is the ripple effect of this concern. The obsession with keeping on schedule combined with the vicissitudes of the Russian postal service have led judges, including JPs, to list the evidence each side should bring to the hearing rather than trusting the parties to figure this out for themselves. When asked why, JPs tell me that if they leave it to the parties, they will likely show up empty-handed. To resend the notice of the hearing will take another two weeks, leaving them with little time to deal with the merits of the case. They openly acknowledge that they are ignoring the procedural rule that places the burden of proof on the parties. To do otherwise is too risky.[64]

JPs' behavior has the short-term benefit of ensuring their job security. In the long run, however, it has facilitated the continuation of the paternalism that

---

63. In private conversations with clerks and secretaries, they acknowledged that their judges would be punished for any mistake on their part. Some gave this as the reason why they preferred to remain in the trenches rather than trying to get on the bench.

64. Conley and O'Barr (1990, 22) begin their study of small-claims courts in the United States with a composite case in which the judge is frustrated by the petitioner's failure to present all the relevant evidence at the first hearing. They note that the typical response is for the judge to write out a list of the necessary documents and to delay the case by a week. This shows that the sorts of problems faced are universal. Russian judges simply do not feel that they have the luxury of delaying for this reason.

characterized the Soviet legal system. Markovits (1992, 57) argues that the transition away from state socialism required people who had been "coddled by their legal system" to cope with a system that "expect[s] them to look out for themselves." This transition has been solidified in the law on the books but, thanks to the enabling behavior of JPs (and other judges), it has been slow to be reflected in the law in action (Hendley 2007). Judges routinely list the documents each side is expected to produce at the hearing on the merits. Their purpose is not to derail the shift toward adversarialism. Rather their behavior is driven by their professional survival instinct. My efforts to engage JPs on this subject came to naught. When I asked about the sections of the procedural codes that shifted responsibility to litigants and that opened the door to dismissing poorly framed complaints, pointing out that these provisions would enhance efficiency, they mostly shrugged away my arguments. They agreed with me on paper, but were firmly convinced any efforts to move in that direction would be met by reversals at the appellate level. Again, their resistance to risk carried the day.

The paternalism evident in the relationship between JPs and litigants is replicated in the relationship between JPs and their bureaucratic superiors. JPs are enveloped by an atmosphere of quiet resignation. No doubt many of them have creative ideas for solving the problems plaguing their courts, but no one has asked for their input. They do not chafe at their institutional isolation. They understand and accept their role as cogs in a judicial machine. They are too busy coping with their mountainous caseload to worry about larger policy questions. Whether they believe they would be punished if they took a more activist role is hard to say.

What I found in the JPs was a judicial corps that was characterized by patience and efficiency, but where political courage was nowhere to be found. This raises the question of the independence of the JP courts. As I noted in the Introduction, the track record of political authorities—from the Kremlin downward—of dictating outcomes to the courts in politically resonant cases renders moot any argument as to full judicial independence in Russia. With that in mind, what marks the JP courts as unique is their relative independence. The source of their independence is rooted in the lack of political importance of the cases they handle and their odd place in the institutional structure. Scholars of the Russian judiciary contend that it is the chairmen of the courts who act as the enforcers of political will (Volkov et al. 2012; Solomon 2007). This does not always require arm twisting. Clever chairmen exert control through case assignments. More pliable judges are assigned the politically tricky cases. Along similar lines, judges who hear criminal cases understand that acquittals are anathema (Volkov et al. 2012; Pomorski 2001, 457; Solomon 1987). Rarely do they need to be explicitly told what to do. But from an institutional point of view, JPs live in a different world from other Russian judges. Each judicial district is its own universe; all cases that arise within its boundaries are heard by the JP. There is no chairman to whom JPs must kowtow on a daily basis. Relative few criminal cases come to the JP courts and most that do are resolved through plea bargaining.

On the other hand, precisely what constitutes political resonance in a case is fuzzy at best. When Markovits was exploring this issue with East German judges who insisted that they had not been subjected to political interference, one judge told her of her experience handling the divorce of a "second-rank functionary at the Central Committee." The official called her chairman to share his thoughts on how the case should be resolved. The chairman took the call, promising to pass along the message to the judge handling the case. He did not, which, in the view of the judge telling the story to Markovits, proved the independence of system (1992, 66–67). She could not see that the very fact that the official felt comfortable making the call brought the integrity of the system into question. The larger point is that any case—even the mundane disputes brought to the JP courts—has the potential to become a politically charged case.

An interview with Iuliia Sazanova, a former JP, illustrates this point. Her judicial district overlapped with the site of an unauthorized protest led by the opposition leader Gary Kasparov in November 2007. After a four-hour hearing, during which she did her best to follow the law, she sentenced him to five days in jail. Kasparov described the hearing as "a choreographed farce from beginning to end" (Levy 2007). Sazanova disputes this, saying that she had received no "orders" from above as to how to decide the case. By 2012, she had come to rethink her decision, but she continues to insist that, at the time, she truly believed he deserved the sentence. She explains:

> When you are inside the system, you take on its way of thinking. You truly believe that . . . you are doing justice. This is my subjective opinion. Maybe there are hypocrites who consciously make unjust decisions, but this was my experience—I really believed that these people [the protestors] were trying to shirk responsibility and that the police and the prosecutors were with me—that I could believe in them (Dziadko and Kraevskaia 2012).

Though she was pilloried by opposition activists on the Internet, the only repercussions she faced afterward from her bureaucratic superiors were about her failure to deal with the others arrested in a timely fashion. Nine other protestors were brought in with Kasparov. It was midnight by the time she finished with his hearing. Her superiors were unimpressed with her time-management skills. She said that this case had effectively ended any chance she might have had for career advancement. Soon after, she left the bench to become an in-house lawyer for the Russian railways (ibid.). Much like the judges Markovits interviewed in the waning days of the East German judicial system, no one needed to tell Sazanova what to do. She had been socialized into the system. She reflects the "go along to get along" attitude that prevails among the JPs I observed. They are not prepared to stand up to political pressure. Thus, any independence of the JP courts is shallow and unstable.

In terms of the institutional contribution of the JP courts, the caseload data make a persuasive case that they have fulfilled the goal of relieving pressure on the district courts. Whether they have insinuated themselves into the fabric of communities is less clear. The decision to have each JP take responsibility for a specific geographic region is part of a larger long-standing effort to maximize societal access to the courts. In theory it could have led to the bubbling up from below of community norms as JPs got to know residents and became sensitive to local practices. In reality, the cost of real estate and the desire of management officials to save money on court guards has meant that the community-building element of the JP courts has come to naught. Yet this has not stemmed the ever-increasing demand of ordinary Russians for help from the JP courts.

THE VIEW FROM THE TRENCHES OF THE JUSTICE-OF-THE-PEACE COURTS

Courts can look remarkably different depending on one's vantage point. The views of judges are unlikely to mirror those of litigants. For judges, the judicial process represents routine behavior, whereas for most litigants, it opens a Pandora's box of formal rules and informal norms that are unfamiliar and mysterious. This is particularly true for the JP courts, which handle the simplest cases. The participants in these cases run the gamut from companies who send their representatives to the court on a daily basis to individuals and entities who are encountering the legal process for the first (and perhaps only) time in their lives. In this chapter, I focus primarily on the latter class of litigant. I explore how they experience the JP courts. Taking a leaf from Friedman's (1969b, 34) definition of legal culture as a "network of values and attitudes . . . which determines when and why and where people turn to law or government or turn away," I argue that their willingness to turn to the courts provides a window into the demand for law and, more generally, Russian legal culture.

I begin by focusing on access to justice in Russia. As I noted in the preceding chapter, the creation of the JP courts was part of an effort to bring the courts closer to the people. Even before this initiative, however, the courts in Russia were remarkably accessible, at least on paper. Whether this impression of openness is shared by Russians themselves is less clear. Going to court to resolve a dispute is never the easy way out, regardless of the simplicity of the procedural rules. This is true in Russia as elsewhere. Using a variety of sources, I dig into the attitudes of ordinary Russians toward the JP courts and assess the extent to which this translates into behavior. As with the previous chapter, I illustrate my arguments with cases drawn from my fieldwork in the JP courts.

It follows that much of the analysis in this chapter is grounded in my fieldwork in the JP courts from 2010 to 2012. Given that my access to litigants was more limited than my access to judges, I draw on several additional sources. These include focus groups that I conducted from 2007 to 2009 in Moscow, Kushevskaia, Saratov, Shumerlia, and Tomsk, in which I investigated attitudes and behavior vis-à-vis law in Russia. These were supplemented by in-depth follow-up interviews I conducted with members of the focus group that allowed me to probe more deeply into their motivations for using or avoiding the courts when problems arose. In addition, I make use of data on the JP courts gathered by Russian research groups. The first is a project that the Moscow-based Institute of Law and Public Policy carried out in 2010 with funding from the World Bank, which monitored the activities of JP courts in Perm krai and Leningrad oblast (Ivanova 2011; Voronkov and Ezhova 2010). Trained monitors observed over nine hundred civil cases in each locale, where they documented the compliance of JPs with various procedural niceties, including wearing robes, as well as the extent to which litigants relied on others to represent their interests. They also conducted structured interviews with litigants about their level of satisfaction with the courts (hereafter the "ILPP Project"). The second data source is a 2009 survey of individuals in three regions of Russia (Leningrad oblast, Nizhni Novgorod oblast, and Rostov oblast) that asked about their use of the JP courts and levels of satisfaction with that experience (hereafter the "ABA Survey").[1] It was conducted under the auspices of the Moscow representative office of the American Bar Association with funding from the U.S. Agency for International Development.

One reality of Russian JP courts that cannot help but color litigants' experiences is that plaintiffs tend to win most of the time in civil cases.[2] In 2011, for example, they prevailed in 92 percent of cases that were resolved through a full-fledged judicial process.[3] (See table 4.2.) The data collected by the ILPP Project show the same trend, though defendants' track record was better than the national average. These results are not driven by state-initiated cases. Though cases brought by the state constitute a plurality of the total civil docket, as table 5.1 shows, the state wins only about two-thirds of its fully contested cases. By contrast, the success rates for individuals, regardless of whether their opponent is another individual, a legal entity, or a state organ, is over 90 percent. A more

---

1. The ABA published a monograph laying out the results (Kriuchkov 2010). References to the ABA Survey are based on my own analysis of these data rather than on the monograph.

2. Such results are not unique to Russia. A study of the Denver Small Claims Court found that plaintiffs had a success rate of over 80 percent (Best et al. 1994, 358).

3. In other words, my calculation excludes cases resolved through the summary judicial orders (*sudebnye prikazy*) discussed in the previous chapter, on the rationale that the victory in such cases is a foregone conclusion.

TABLE 5.1 Civil cases decided by JP courts broken down by type of litigant

NATURE OF THE PARTIES	TOTAL CIVIL CASES RESOLVED (2009)	TOTAL CIVIL CASES RESOLVED (2011)	AS % OF TOTAL CIVIL CASES	% OF CASES IN WHICH DECISION WAS ISSUED	% OF CASES RESOLVED THROUGH JUDICIAL ORDER	SUCCESS RATE FOR PLAINTIFFS	% OF CASES THAT VIOLATE TIME DEADLINE
Individual vs. individual	1,297,958	1,160,999	12.7	87.1	30.8	97.3	1.6
Individual vs. legal entity	915,991	991,481	10.8	90.9	50.8	92.9	2.1
Individual vs. state institution	107,326	82,346	0.9	89.7	32.2	95.5	1.0
Legal entity vs. individual	3,668,975	3,138,855	34.2	94	67.9	95.7	1.0
State institution vs. individual	4,288,630	3,776,822	41.2	98	90.7	68.1	0.2
Legal entity vs. legal entity	1,131	14,760	0.16	93.2	85.8	94.6	0.5

Source: Otchet–JP Courts 2011; Otchet–JP Courts 2009.

compelling, albeit partial, explanation for the lopsided nature of the results is the tendency of Russians to bring cases to court that are disputes in name only. Sometimes this is unavoidable, as in divorce.[4] Other times it is more puzzling. For example, in 2011, plaintiffs in personal injury and housing cases won more than 97 percent of the time (Otchet–JP Courts 2011). The precise reasons are likely numerous, but a key factor is that, in most of these disputes there was no real disagreement over the basic facts. Even so, the case goes forward, often with an absent defendant. Elsewhere, I have argued that the relatively low cost and quick turnaround times of the Russian courts encourages their use in cases that would be settled in less efficient judicial systems (Hendley 2013, 2012c, 2004).

Access to Justice

Like most legal concepts, access to justice has taken on a wide variety of meanings in the scholarly literature. The U.S.-based scholarship focuses almost exclusively

---

4. Russian law requires most divorcing couples to go through the courts. Divorces always go into the win column for the petitioner. If the couple decides to reconcile, this would be coded as a withdrawal of the petition, not as a victory for the defendant.

on the ease of retaining legal counsel (Sandefur and Smyth 2011; Rhode 2004; cf. MacDowell 2015). Of course, the complexity of the procedural rules governing the U.S. system makes representation critical. Elsewhere, a broader understanding of the concept has taken hold. The availability of legal expertise remains part of the story, but is supplemented by inquiries into the various costs of using the legal system. These include the fee required to initiate a lawsuit, the time required to see it through, and the emotional costs of litigating. The complexity of the procedural rules, the transparency of the law, and the overall efficiency of the court system are also factored in. My analysis embraces this more pragmatic approach.

Somewhat surprisingly, Russia has a fairly good track record on most elements of access to civil justice. The procedural rules are straightforward. Judges' expectations for civil complaints are low. If the petitioner puts forward a colorable claim, they will set it for a hearing. In 2011, for example, of the cases dismissed by the JP courts, only 1.1 percent resulted from procedural deficiencies in the complaint.[5] As I argued in the preceding chapter, institutional incentives push JPs to err on the side of accepting complaints rather than clearing their docket by being overly fastidious. If they do find an insurmountable problem, they are obligated to return it to the petitioner with a detailed explanation of how to remedy the flaws.

Petitioners are not left twisting in the wind. The websites of most JP courts contain a plethora of forms that litigants can use as a starting point. Additional forms are available on other law-related websites, together with advice about how to fill them in. For the web-phobic, hard copies of the forms are posted on bulletin boards throughout the buildings that house the JP courts. These bulletin boards are a carryover from the Soviet past. For many of the most common types of claims, such as suits to recover child support and collect on overdue debts, litigants need only fill in the blanks. Because judicial precedent is generally not a source of law in Russia, litigants do not have to familiarize themselves with case law. The only citation needed is to the controlling statutory code section and, for most causes of action, the forms supply this detail. If litigants are interested in learning how similar cases have been resolved, they can find prior decisions on the court's website. Though not formally binding on the JP, reviewing them can provide insight into the mind-set of the judge.

---

5. The vast majority of cases concluded prematurely were dismissed at the behest of the parties. In almost 80 percent of these cases, plaintiffs withdraw their complaints. Settlements account for another 18 percent. Indeed, more cases (1.7 percent) are terminated because of the unexpected death of one of the parties than because of failure to comply with the procedural rules (Razdel 4, Otchet–JP Courts 2011). Nor was 2011 an outlier. The 2009 data tell a similar story (Razdel 4, Otchet–JP Courts 2009).

FIGURE 5.1   Form documents posted in the corridor of a JP court (Pskov)

Potential litigants have the text of the laws themselves, both procedural and substantive, at their fingertips. Basic statutory law is freely available through several sources. Computerized commercial databases, such as *Garant* and *Konsul'tant plus*, offer access to the main codes at no charge, though supplementary materials require a paid subscription. New laws are regularly published in the national newspaper, *Rossiiskaia gazeta*, and back issues are available at no charge online. For those without ready access to the Internet, bookstores throughout Russia stock copies of the major codes as well as a variety of "how to" books that are pitched at different levels of legal sophistication. Those interested need not hunt down a specialized legal bookstore; these volumes are on sale at mainstream bookstores.

The resources available on the Internet has made finding the law much easier in the post-Soviet era. Previously law was largely the province of specialists. As it was enacted, Soviet legislation was published chronologically in an official reporter (*Sobranie zakonodatel'stva*). Though technically satisfying the obligation to make the law public, the fact that these reporters were housed in law libraries not open to the general public and the absence of a comprehensive index combined to made it difficult for laymen to find the law and/or to know whether the version they found contained was up to date. Finding administration regulations was even more laborious (Huskey 1990). Publication was somewhat arbitrary, with some, but not all, regulations published in an assortment of official journals that were generally beyond the reach of nonspecialists. Many so-called sublegal regulations (*podzakonnye akty*) were classified and not made publicly available, but were nonetheless binding, leaving ordinary Soviets in a quandary and undoubtedly undermining their respect for law.

The computerized databases, which were developed in response to market demand driven by business lawyers, make it possible to locate relevant laws quickly. The explosion of publications—both online and in paper form—that offer advice to laymen has proven helpful. Even so, ordinary Russians sometimes struggle to make sense of how to frame their complaints. As I heard from some focus group participants, living with problems often seems more palatable than going to court. One fifty-nine-year-old Moscow pensioner, spoke for others: "The very idea of court strikes terror in me. I don't need it. For me, court is akin to death. Maybe some people love litigating—it's like going to the theater for them and they get pleasure from it. Not me. Just hearing the word 'court' saps all of my energy." This fear of the institutional unknown is not unique to Russia (Baldwin 1997, 105; Merry 1990).

The courts have taken steps to make litigating easier, such as posting form pleadings on their bulletin boards and websites. In addition, judges and their staff make themselves available to the public during weekly "office hours" (*priemnye chasy*).[6] During the Soviet era, this was just one of many outreach activities that were seen as fulfilling judges' pedagogical function. Some have questioned the wisdom of having judges continue to hold office hours (Popova 2012; Ivanova 2011). Militating in their favor is the opportunity they provide for newcomers to be schooled as to how to put together a case. Yet perhaps this is exactly the problem. Judges are not supposed to be giving advice, especially on an ex parte basis. In conversations with me, JPs consistently paid lip service to the rule prohibiting them from counseling litigants on legal questions. Yet my observations reveal a more complicated picture. When sitting in on office hours, I noticed that JPs would frequently veer over the line.[7] In their defense, however, the advice was never overtly partisan, but was aimed

---

6. Whether JPs held their scheduled office hours was explored as part of the monitoring project of the Institute for Law and Public Policy. Their data show that JP courts do not shirk their obligation. They monitored over 70 sessions in both Perm krai and Leningrad oblast and documented that office hours were held 78 percent of the time in Perm and 90 percent of the time in Leningrad oblast.

7. Other small-claims courts struggle with this issue. A study of the Iowa small-claims court comments that "where dissemination of information ends and legal advice begins ... is often cloudy" (Elwell and Carlson 1990, 468).

at helping the litigant put together a viable cause of action.[8] It almost always came with a recommendation to seek out advice from a lawyer, though JPs conceded that few litigants followed through. Not surprisingly, the staff was less reticent about helping litigants, even though they too are barred from giving legal advice. Sometimes this would take the form of directing women seeking child support to the bulletin boards. More often, secretaries would find themselves proofreading complaints and pointing out potential problems to inexperienced litigants.[9]

As I noted in the preceding chapter, after accepting a case, the JP sends out a decree (*opredelenie*) by mail that notifies parties of the time and place of the hearing. This information is also posted on the court's website. The two-page *opredelenie* is thick with boilerplate language about the rights of litigants, often rendered in small type. At the end of the document, the JP lists the documents that the parties are expected to present at the hearing. These are, of course, specifically tailored to each case. Even so, many litigants remain bewildered by the expectations placed on them.

Legal Literacy: Negotiating the JP Courts without a Lawyer

The very fact that litigants flock to the office hours of JPs and their staff indicates that my assessment of the ease of the process is not shared by all court users. Notwithstanding the efforts of legislators and judicial officials to make going to court less scary for ordinary Russians, it can still be a daunting process. Many litigants have no prior experience with the courts, leaving them unfamiliar with the norms. Legalese has gradually crept into the liturgy of the court, which leaves some legal neophytes bewildered.

> *Debt Collection.* Two older Muscovite women are quarreling over an overdue debt. The plaintiff is a pensioner, and the defendant is a year

---

8. The results of the ILPP Project confirm my observations. Though the most common reason for stopping by was to drop off a complaint, which does not compromise judicial neutrality, a significant percentage of petitioners wanted the JP to weigh in on whether their complaint was ready to be submitted (Ivanova 2011, 54–55).

9. The monitors found that petitioners' primary purpose in visiting court secretaries was clerical, for example, to drop off complaints and supporting documents or to check on whether the final text of the decision was available. As with JPs, many solicited the secretaries' opinion as to whether their complaint was ready to go (Ivanova 2011, 53–54).

away from pension eligibility.[10] Neither is represented. The case is heard in a small courtroom. As always, the JP begins with a recitation of the statutory language that lays out the parties' rights and duties. Both sides sign an affidavit acknowledging that they've been informed. The ritualistic nature of this document quickly becomes apparent. The defendant peppers the JP with questions about attaching the document certifying that she is registered as unemployed to the case file. The JP is visibly annoyed as she tells the defendant that this request is premature. She has to repeatedly remind the defendant to stand when addressing the court. When the JP asks whether either side has any motions (*khodataistva*) that might preclude hearing the case—a standard question—the defendant is unfamiliar with the term and is unsure of how to respond.

The basic facts are not in dispute. The plaintiff loaned the defendant 9,000 rubles almost three years earlier.[11] The defendant repaid only 500 rubles. The plaintiff wants the balance. The JP asks whether the parties would be open to a settlement agreement (*mirovoe soglashenie*). Although neither woman is familiar with the phrase, once the JP explains what it entails, both are amenable. The JP declares a recess to allow them to prepare the necessary documents. The plaintiff has to write up a motion to terminate the case. The defendant is charged with preparing the settlement agreement. She is completely at sea. The court secretary provides her with a form. The defendant's first instinct is to fill in the blanks on this form, but this proves futile. The plaintiff tells her that she must rewrite the document, using the form as a guide. The defendant continues to struggle. Eventually, she gives up and simply writes as the plaintiff dictates the terms for repayment to be included in the agreement.

When the hearing resumes, the JP reviews the settlement agreement. She asks what provision the parties have made for payment of the filing fee. The parties tell her that they did not discuss this issue; they did not realize it should be addressed by the agreement. The JP explains that such costs are typically paid by the defendant. The parties add a few

---

10. The defendant is unsettled by my presence in the courtroom. She asks the JP who I am. The judge says that I am an observer and explains that, according to the Constitution, court hearings are open to the public. The defendant was worried that I had come to support the plaintiff.

11. The statute of limitations for civil cases is three years (art. 196, GK RF part 1). The plaintiff is bumping up against it, which helps explain why she resorted to the court after badgering the defendant proved ineffective.

THE VIEW FROM THE TRENCHES

sentences to this effect to the agreement. The JP then uses the text of the agreement to prepare her order (*opredelenie*). She reassures the plaintiff that if the defendant fails to follow through, she would not have to start over, but could return and get an enforcement order (*ispolnitel'nyi list*) immediately.

Petty Theft. A Pskov man who is his forties but looks much older appears to answer administrative charges of stealing goods valued at 300 rubles. He readily admits his culpability. The JP explains that the statute gives him a choice. Either he can spend fifteen days in jail or pay a fine. He opts for the fine. The JP gives the defendant a blank piece of paper and tells him to write a petition to this effect. Confounded by this demand, the defendant keeps asking what he is supposed to say. Though the JP bristles and says that he cannot dictate the content, in the end, that is precisely what he does. The JP clears his office, where the case was heard, to prepare his decision. After about ten minutes, we are invited to return. The JP reads his decision in a rapid monotone. He imposes a fine of 1,000 rubles. If not paid within ten days, then the defendant will go to jail.

Traffic Violation. An Ekaterinburg man in his thirties shows up loaded for bear to protest a traffic ticket. He is carrying a self-help book, *The Rights of Drivers* (*Prava voditel*). Before the hearing starts, he asks the JP whether the policeman who issued the ticket will be appearing. The JP tells him that he isn't sure. The defendant made a video of the aftermath of his incident. He believes that it proves that the behavior for which he was ticketed is commonplace and that he was singled out. The JP tells him that the video is not admissible. After the JP summarizes the traffic report, the defendant gives his version. His refrain is that "I didn't do anything wrong." He is able to respond coherently to the JP's questions, often with references to the appropriate sections of the administrative code. The JP finds that the defendant is guilty of a lesser violation. He imposes a minimal fine, leaving the defendant satisfied.

These scenarios demonstrate the variation in legal literacy among litigants in the JP courts. In my experience, the well-prepared Ekaterinburg defendant is an exception. But his elaborate preparations turn out to be built on a house of cards. Despite the widespread belief that the videos produced by the dashboard cameras that many Russians have installed in their cars will be their saving grace if they land in court,[12] the sad reality is that the admissibility of such tapes is far from certain. They are especially problematic in administrative cases like the third scenario because the relevant procedural code is silent on their admissibility (art. 26.2, KoAP). Once again, the chasm between what Russians believe the law to be and what it is in reality is on view.[13] It is worth noting that the evidence proffered by the Ekaterinburg defendant would be unlikely to be admitted even if the law was more open-ended. He had videoed the traffic police ignoring others who committed the same traffic violation for which they had ticketed him, believing this would be compelling evidence that he had been unfairly singled out. This is not an argument that courts anywhere find convincing.

The participants in the first two vignettes are more typical. They are ready to tell their stories, but have made little effort to educate themselves about the underlying law. One Moscow JP laughed as she told me of a petitioner who disappeared after submitting her complaint. When the JP's secretary finally tracked her down at her summer dacha and told her she was in danger of having her case dismissed if she failed to show up for the next hearing, the petitioner was shocked. She believed that her role was limited to filing the complaint and thought that the judge would take it from there.[14] Though it sounds absurd, this petitioner was not too far off the mark. Even when the parties are physically present, their lack of legal knowledge often leaves JPs in the driver's seat. The first scenario illustrates this point well. If the plaintiff had made an effort to negotiate with the defendant before the hearing, they could easily have come to the same resolution. The JP served as a catalyst. She reasoned that if she could get the parties focused on the absence of any dispute over the facts, then she could avoid a lengthy hearing in which each woman told her sob story. Her driving motivation to get the case off her docket overlapped sufficiently with interests of the parties to allow the settlement.

---

12. On the *Washington Post* website, Khazan (2013) stated definitively: "Dash-cam footage is the only real way to substantiate your claims in the court of law [in Russia]." The legal reality is more complicated. The procedural codes governing civil and criminal cases list videos as permissible evidence, though the language is loose enough to allow judges to exclude it if it proves inconvenient. The administrative procedure code lacks a similar provision. Most traffic cases are handled as administrative, so aggrieved drivers cannot bring in their webcam evidence.

13. In February 2013, several Duma deputies put forward an amendment to the procedural code to make dash-cam videos admissible. By September 2013, passions had dimmed and this amendment died on the vine (Proekt 2013).

14. If this petitioner had included a sentence in her complaint authorizing the court to hear the case in her absence, then she could have retreated to her dacha with no adverse consequences. The JP who presides over the Moscow district where Sberbank (one of the largest Russian banks) has its headquarters tells me that it routinely includes such language. Of course, it has a large team of in-house lawyers who are versed in the intricacies of Russian civil procedure.

By telling the defendant she had to prepare the settlement agreement, the JP threw her into the deep end of the pool. As an experienced judge, she surely realized that someone like the defendant who had struggled to make sense of what was going on in the courtroom was unlikely to be able to handle the task placed before her. The JP stuck to the letter of the law, which required her to wash her hands of the negotiations between the parties.[15] The court secretary gave the defendant a form agreement, which was intended as a life preserver. Like the prototypical drowning victim, the defendant was too busy flailing around to recognize it as such. The plaintiff, who had a strong interest in moving forward with the settlement agreement, had to calm her down and guide her through the process. Though the defendant physically drafted the settlement agreement, her only original contributions were the names of the parties, the amount at issue, and the deadline for repayment. She was the author of the agreement in name only. Had the plaintiff been as legally clueless as the defendant, the court secretary would likely have played a more activist role. In other hearings, court secretaries did not merely supply the forms. Instead, they essentially dictated the terms. As the second scenario shows, occasionally JPs get into this business. Once again, the court's desire to move the proceedings along dovetails with the parties' need for closure.

Not all participants are thrown for a loop when asked to submit an additional written document. The creditor-plaintiff had no trouble drafting a motion to terminate the case. The court's openness to pleadings drafted in plain language (often handwritten) is helpful. Some JPs can be sticklers for details, such as including the address of the court in a motion, but they typically allow litigants to write this information in, even if it results in a rather sloppy looking document, rather than requiring them to start over.

Litigants' lack of knowledge was not limited to the law itself. As the first vignette shows, the language of court hearings can be intimidating for ordinary Russians. The befuddlement of the defendant was replicated by litigants in every court I visited. No doubt JPs could recite the rights and duties of participants in their sleep, but this litany is unfamiliar to most parties. The understandable desire of JPs to get through this procedural nicety quickly only compounds the difficulty for unsophisticated litigants who are actually trying to understand what is being said. Many share the confusion of the Moscow debtor as to precisely what a "motion" is. The word used—*khodataistvo*—is not a standard part of the Russian vocabulary. Even more baffling to litigants was the stock question about recusal.

---

15. The Moscow JP's positivist approach is reminiscent of Kurkchiyan's description of Polish judges handling simple claims (2012, 237).

Typically JPs pose it in two parts: do they trust the court and do they want to recuse the judge.[16] As I watched parties take in these questions, looks of fear and bewilderment often flashed across their faces. Even if parties are distrustful of courts, the start of a hearing is hardly an auspicious moment for that somewhat philosophical debate. Moreover, the concept of recusal is obscure to laymen, as is the verb (*otvodit*). Yet the vocal tone and body language of JPs telegraph the expected answer. I never saw anyone ask for a different judge.[17]

This sort of disconnect between judges and litigants is not unique to Russia. Judges everywhere tend to lapse into legalese out of habit and to expect parties to respond in kind. Often litigants are too cowed to ask for clarification and come away from the process in a bit of a daze, unsure of why the case turned out as it did (Kurkchiyan 2012; Philips 1998; Baldwin 1997; Bezdek 1992). It is an occupational hazard for judges who hear cases in which the parties are mostly unrepresented. The JPs I observed varied in terms of their sensitivity to parties' discombobulation.[18] Their willingness to slow down and explain what was happening tended to be correlated with age. As a rule, they took more care with older people. But I certainly witnessed many cases where JPs studiously ignored the obvious confusion of litigants of all ages in an effort to press forward.

The absence of a verbatim transcript makes it easier for JPs to gloss over the details.[19] A report (*protokol*) summarizing each hearing is prepared and included in the case file. These *protokoly* tend to take a bare-bones approach. The simple notation that the parties had acknowledged being informed of their rights and duties can conceal a multitude of sins. As the first scenario suggests, some JPs are not satisfied by a verbal response to their question of whether litigants understand what they've been told. Instead, these judges have developed a form document that confirms that they have been provided with this information and have understood it. Both approaches—verbal and written—tend to be off-putting for

---

16. The monitoring undertaken by the ILPP Project documented that JPs routinely ask about recusal. They did so in more than 90 percent of hearings observed.

17. The situation is different in the *arbitrazh* courts, which handle disputes between companies. There defendants more often petition for recusal. Typically this is just one of many delaying tactics employed. Such motions are rarely successful, but because they have to be heard by the court chairman, they serve the purpose of delaying the proceedings. By contrast, few litigants in the JP courts are conversant with these sorts of tricks of the trade.

18. I saw nothing as extreme as what Kurkchiyan reports from a Polish court where a judge told a litigant that the word he was using was not part of the Polish language. Because the litigant could not come up with a synonym, he was effectively silenced (Kurkchiyan 2012, 237).

19. Philips (1998) details the various approaches taken by Arizona judges to ensure that defendants who plead guilty appreciate what they are doing. These defendants also struggle to understand the legalese that inevitably comes into the process. Other U.S.-based studies likewise document these difficulties (e.g., MacDowell 2015; Bezdek 1992).

litigants. Given the power differential between judges and litigants, few are comfortable sharing their confusion. When it came to signing the forms, often the court secretary had to show litigants where to sign, a clear indication that they did not grasp the tenor of the document.

The failure of the two Moscow women to discuss a settlement may also be due to their lack of judicial experience. As I have noted earlier, many litigants at the JP courts assume that, by filing their complaint, they have ceded complete control over their dispute to the judge. The parties in the first vignette are a good example of this practice. They are quick to take up the JP's suggestion. Neither noticed that, included with the boilerplate language of the judicial order notifying parties of the time and place of their hearing, had been a paragraph about the right to settle. These women could easily have settled the case on their own. But it took the JP to light a fire under them.

Recognizing that many litigants do not read such documents with sufficient care, JPs are supposed to inform parties of their right to settle and to explain how *mirovye soglasheniia* work as part of their general explanation of litigants' rights and duties. The ILPP Project documented the tendency of JPs to gloss over this requirement. The idea of settlement was raised by judges in less than a third of the monitored hearings.[20] JPs explained the ins and outs of the settlement process in less than 15 percent of hearings (Sidorovich 2011). In all likelihood, JPs skipped over this part of the introductory protocol not because they dislike settlements, but because they had convinced themselves that the parties would not be amenable to it and did not want to waste time. Over time, this assumption becomes a vicious circle.[21]

The extent to which participants picked up on the formal and informal behavioral rules of the JP courts also varied. Litigants frequently failed to observe the Russian custom of removing their coats in public buildings. This is seen as a sign of respect and failing to do so is considered to be rude. Though JP courthouses do not have central cloakrooms, most courtrooms were equipped with coatracks. I was struck by JPs' tolerance. Regardless of whether participants showed up in business suits or hoodies, they took no notice of their clothing. The procedural codes require that parties stand when speaking and address the judge as "your honor." JPs frequently had to remind litigants of these rules. Indeed, some judges

---

20. Even so, when participants in the JP courts were surveyed (who were not necessarily part of the monitored cases), JPs were most often singled out as their main source of information about settlement.

21. Buttressing the findings of the ILPP Project are the results of a 2013 survey of *arbitrazh* judges that revealed that fewer than a quarter of them believed that litigants were prepared to participate actively in their own cases (Hendley 2015, 437).

posted these rules on their doors in an effort to educate those unfamiliar with courtroom procedure. Newcomers coped with their ignorance in different ways. Some were extremely deferential, whereas others openly struggled to understand what was going on by asking endless questions. Some even grew belligerent when they saw things going against them. When hearings became emotional, JPs sometimes struggled to maintain civility. Parties would interrupt one another and raise their voices. Judges would then caution the parties to address their remarks to her and to wait to speak until prompted by her. If a JP felt a hearing slipping from her control, she could call a bailiff to assist her. In some jurisdictions, such as Velikie luki and St. Petersburg, bailiffs routinely attended hearings.[22]

Courtrooms are outfitted in standard fashion. The Russian flag and the national seal are on the wall behind the judge's desk. Sometimes this desk is on a dais, but not always. If the courtroom is used for criminal trials in which the defendant is required to be kept in restraints, then there will be a "cage" (*kletka*) with open bars in which the defendant sits during the proceedings. Because such cases are relatively rare for JP courts, few courtrooms have cages. The presence of the flag and the seal, taken together with the fact that JPs almost always wear their robes,[23] combine to create an atmosphere that conveys seriousness of purpose.

In terms of facilities for litigants, most buildings housing JP courts had benches in the corridors where litigants could wait, if necessary. In her study of Ukrainian courts of first instance, Kurkchiyan (2013) found that parties were routinely kept waiting, which she interpreted as a sign of disrespect for them. I rarely encountered this problem in Russia, perhaps because so many cases were handled through summary proceedings. The courtrooms themselves are uniformly set up with two tables that face one another for the plaintiff and defendant, as well as benches for third parties and spectators. Litigants who are new to the judicial process or are uncertain of themselves tend to sit on the benches. Both parties in the first scenario sat on these benches toward the back of the room. JPs usually let litigants sit wherever they feel most comfortable. The seating arrangements for cases heard in chambers are less formalized. Most often there is a long

---

22. The most senior JP in Velikie luki explained that he had observed the U.S. practice of having law enforcement officials present in all court hearings during his visit to the United States as part of the USAID-funded Open World program. He then instituted this custom when he returned home. In all the locales I visited, I met JPs who had participated in the Open World program (http://www.openworld.gov/).

23. There was surprisingly little regional variation in terms of whether judges wear robes. In several places (Ekaterinburg and Voronezh), I encountered judges who would forego their robes for family law cases. They reasoned that they wanted to be seen as approachable and worried that the robes would send the wrong signal. In Moscow, I spent time observing two newly minted JPs whose robes were being made.

FIGURE 5.2 A courtroom with a cage (Velikie luki)

FIGURE 5.3 A courtroom without a cage (Moscow)

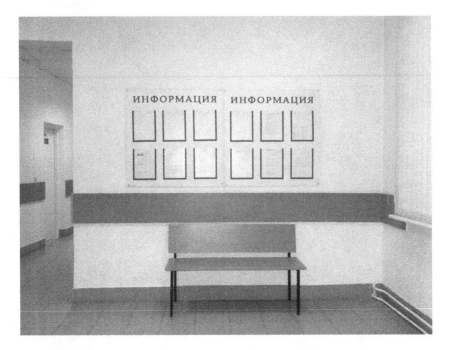

FIGURE 5.4 The corridor of a JP court with an informational bulletin board and benches (Moscow)

rectangular table that juts out from the JP's desk, with room for two people to sit on each side. The court secretary usually sits at this table. Judicial chambers also tend to have several extra chairs positioned along the walls. The man from the third scenario who was protesting his traffic citation walked in confidently and spread out his supporting materials in front of him on the table.

These three scenarios are typical in that the participants were on their own. The willingness of the JPs to lend a hand reinforces the theme raised in the preceding chapter. In all three cases, the JP ended up explaining the substance of the law to the parties. Though they tried to do so in a neutral way, it still represented a form of legal advice. Almost without exception, everyone emerges from these situations frustrated. The parties are openly annoyed by the unwillingness of the judge to tell them what to do. The JPs are more circumspect, but afterward often betray their irritation with the parties' reluctance to seek out qualified legal assistance and their lack of gratitude for the assistance provided by the court. The awkward juxtaposition of the new and the old make it difficult for litigants to understand what they can reasonably expect from JPs. Judges continue to honor the Soviet-era commitment to educating litigants about the process while trying to respect the newer ban on providing substantive legal advice.

Availability and Use of Legal Expertise

In an ideal world, lawyers would be the answer. Lawyers are mandatory for criminal defendants in Russia and are provided by the state at no charge for the indigent.[24] The story is different for civil litigants. They are mostly on their own.[25] Relatively few participants in civil proceedings at the JP courts make use of lawyers. A minority of the cases I observed involved legal counsel. The ABA Survey confirms my findings. Of the 1,200 respondents, less than 30 percent had consulted a lawyer in connection with their case in JP court. The story is the same for the respondents who participated in the ILPP Project. These data show that, in civil cases, plaintiffs are more likely to seek help than defendants.[26]

Understanding Russian litigants' reluctance to appeal to legal professionals for help requires a bit of background on the Russian legal profession. As in many European countries, it is splintered. Traditionally, legal professionals have been divided into *advokaty*, who represented clients in court, *iuristy*, who focused on business law, and *prokurory*, who represented the interests of the state in court. These dividing lines were strictly enforced during the decades of Soviet power (Huskey 1986; Shelley 1984; Barry and Berman 1968). Since the collapse of the Soviet Union and the rise of a competitive market for legal services, the distinction between *advokaty* and *iuristy* has grown increasingly blurry for the public (Mrovchinski 2012). Legal professionals see a stark difference. Becoming an *advokat* is a lengthy process, involving an apprenticeship and successfully passing an exam, whereas anyone who has an undergraduate degree in law can call himself a *iurist*. *Advokaty* retain a monopoly on representing criminal defendants.[27] In

---

24. Lawyers (*advokaty*) receive between 500 and 1,200 rubles ($10–$24) per day, with additional amounts available for working nights or weekends (Postanovlenie 2012). Not surprisingly, this work tends to attract recent law school graduates who often take on many such cases as a way to support themselves. In the ten criminal hearings I observed, the lawyers were passive. The requirement for the defendant to have a qualified representative was formally honored, but no effort was made to mount a vigorous defense.

25. During my fieldwork, a law was passed authorizing free legal services in civil cases for certain at-risk groups such as low-income citizens, minors, invalids, veterans, and the mentally ill (O bezplatnoi 2011; Kirilpovykh 2012; Kruchinin and Arapov 2012). Though I encountered litigants who surely fit into these categories, their right to free legal services was never raised.

26. Of the 478 plaintiffs surveyed, 16.5 percent were represented at the JP courts. Those from Perm were more inclined to seek representation (19.3 percent) than were those from the Leningrad region (13.75 percent). Of the 455 defendants surveyed, 10.8 percent brought representation to the JP court. As with their counterparts, Perm defendants were more likely to have representation (11.9 percent) than were defendants from the Leningrad region (9.7 percent).

27. *Advokaty* attempted to establish a monopoly on representing litigants more generally in a law on the legal profession that went into effect in 2002. The Constitutional Court ruled that this provision violated Russians' constitutional right to have the representative of their choice in court (Jordan 2005, 127; Opredelenie 2003).

civil and administrative cases, litigants are free to seek help from any quarter. They can hire someone with legal training, for example, an *advokat* or *iurist*, or they can rely on a trusted family member or other layperson. Pinning down the extent to which they use legal professionals versus others is difficult because JPs are not entitled to ask representatives about their background.[28] Anyone who shows up with a valid engagement letter (*doverennost*) from a litigant is allowed to represent his or her interests in court.

Not surprisingly, the quality of representation varies widely. As is true throughout Europe, legal training in Russia is an undergraduate enterprise.[29] The post-Soviet period has witnessed a rapid increase in the number of educational institutions offering legal training.[30] The law faculties of major universities now compete with for-profit institutes. In all the locales I visited, JPs complained bitterly about the unevenness of representation. I witnessed this for myself. Legal representatives were frequently unable to respond to judges' questions about the underlying facts or the governing law, betraying their sloppy preparation for court. Yet few seemed embarrassed when their inadequacies were revealed. The data collected by ILPP Project show that most litigants who retained counsel were satisfied with the help they received. Given that plaintiffs tend to prevail, their higher levels of satisfaction with their representatives is not surprising. Whereas 88 percent of plaintiffs expressed satisfaction with their representatives' services, that percent dropped to 79 for defendants. It follows that defendants were more likely to believe that they would have done better had they been represented.[31]

According to the results from the ABA Survey and the ILPP Project, fears of inadequate legal counsel were not the decisive factor for litigants as they decided

28. The ILPP asked respondents who were represented what sort of person they had retained. Among plaintiffs who had lawyers, almost half had hired *advokaty*, whereas another 37 percent had hired *iuristy*. The remainder had retained laymen. Among defendants who were represented, it was a more equal split, with 47 percent opting for *advokaty* and 44 percent for *iuristy*, with the remainder relying on laymen.

29. Russia has embraced the Bologna Process and, in terms of its legal education system, has made the transition from a five-year "specialist" degree to a four-year bachelor's degree (Kapustin 2007). Much as in the United States, legal educators are engaged in an active debate over the proper balance between theoretical and practical education (Shugurov 2014). For an overview of legal education in the USSR, see Hazard (1938).

30. In 2009, Sergei Stepashin, the co-chair of the Association of *Iuristy*, supported a call by then-President Medvedev for improving legal education. He was critical of the explosion of legal educational facilities, particularly in educational institutions that had no background in law. He noted that in the Soviet period there had been 52 institutions that prepared lawyers. Now he counted 1,211 such institutions, most of which had built their reputations in other arenas (e.g., agriculture, aviation, business) (Kulikov 2009).

31. About a third of unrepresented defendants queried agreed that their lack of representation had complicated matters for them, compared with around 20 percent of plaintiffs.

whether or not to consult a lawyer. They did not attribute their failure to retain counsel to difficulties in finding someone reputable. Concerns over the possible cost were brushed aside by respondents in the ABA Survey, but were more troubling for those queried as part of the ILPP Project. Almost a quarter of the participants in the ILPP Project raised cost as a key reason why they did not hire a representative.[32]

Most JP court veterans surveyed as part of these two projects did not see their choice to go it on their own as particularly risky. They felt they could handle the matter without help; they did not see any reason to consult a lawyer.[33] This suggests that litigants go into the process with an undeserved bravado that, according to my observations, quickly crumbles when subjected to questioning from JPs. The availability of codes and form documents on the web may bolster this confidence. Whether this attitude is shared by Russians more generally is doubtful. In both the 2005 and 2012 rounds of the RLMS-HSE, over three-fourths of those surveyed stated that their fear of the high cost to retain counsel had deterred them from going to court.

My more anecdotal findings tell a different story. When I spoke to litigants at the JP courts, the two most common reasons for bypassing legal assistance were the cost and inability to assess the reliability of potential lawyers. These sentiments were echoed in the focus groups. Few were aware that Russia follows the English rule, which requires losers to reimburse winners for fees paid to attorneys (art. 94, GPK RF; Kritzer 1992). Participants lamented the proliferation of fly-by-night lawyers. They worked through friends to find a reputable lawyer. One woman from the focus groups in Shumerlia spoke for many when commenting that, in the wake of an auto accident in which she had not been at fault, her friends told her seeking help from a lawyer would be a waste of time. In her words: "They told me not to bother, not to waste time or energy or money because it would be pointless in the end." There is a kernel of rationality to their thinking, especially when it comes to the JP courts. For many claims, the cost of hiring a lawyer to represent them in court would exceed the amount that could be recovered.

For cases where monetary damages are not at issue, such as divorce, the straightforward nature of the process left little for lawyers to do. As elsewhere,

---

32. Only 1 percent of respondents from the ABA Survey cited financial concerns. For the ILPP Project, 25.7 percent of defendants raised cost concerns, as compared with 22 percent of plaintiffs.

33. Over 80 percent of respondents from the ABA Survey expressed this preference for self-reliance. The participants in the ILPP Project were somewhat less confident. This sentiment was reflected by 56.3 percent of plaintiffs and 55.4 percent of defendants.

parties only hired lawyers when the proceedings turned contentious.[34] The ca-cophony within the Russian legal profession makes it difficult for ordinary Rus-sians to figure out which lawyers are dependable. A reputational market has been slow to develop. Even when lawyers do a poor job, their role in their clients' lack of success in the courtroom is sometimes opaque to the clients. Lawyers are quick to raise the specter of judicial corruption or to point the finger of blame at judicial incompetence.

Sometimes litigants recognized their need for legal assistance midstream. As a general rule, JPs grant requests for continuances when the stated purpose is to find a lawyer. A good example is a case brought by an Ekaterinburg pensioner against an insurance company in the wake of an automobile accident. The insur-ance company did not send a representative to the hearing, but sent an answer in which it alleged that the plaintiff's policy did not cover the accident. The plaintiff was perplexed. He could not understand how a policy bought for the specific purpose of protecting him in case of accident could end up being beside the point. The JP had a conversation with him about where he bought the policy, but stopped short of reviewing its content. She granted a short recess to allow the plaintiff to call his insurance agent to confirm the coverage. When the hearing resumed, he asked for a continuance to consult a lawyer. The JP gave him a week to sort things out. She later told me that in such cases, the petitioners often show up at the next hearing on their own, explaining that they were unable to locate a trustworthy lawyer at a reasonable price. Other JPs shared similar experiences. They insist that they do not hold it against the litigant, even when they suspect it may be part of a strategy to delay the inevitable. Rather, they move forward on the basis of the available information to resolve the case within the statutory deadline.

A halfway option for litigants who are skittish but unwilling to fully sign on is to hire a lawyer to prepare their pleadings. Documenting how often this happens is impossible because there is no obligation to reveal the author of documents submitted to the court. Regardless of who prepares them, they must be signed by the relevant party to the case. But the truth often reveals itself in the course of hearings. The range of judicial response is revealed by contrasting two cases I observed in Velikie luki.

The basic fact pattern of the first is analogous to the insurance case from Ekat-erinburg. As in that case, the defendant insurance company was absent and the unrepresented petitioner struggled to respond to the JP's questions. The Velikie

---

34. The direction of the causal arrow is a matter of controversy. JPs told me that lawyers tended to complicate divorce proceedings. They saw it as a way for these lawyers to ratchet up their fees. Such behavior is, of course, not unique to Russia.

luki JP took a more aggressive stance once he realized that the plaintiff was unfamiliar with the complaint. The plaintiff explained that it had been prepared by a lawyer and that he had not reviewed it in preparation for the hearing. The JP was openly exasperated and declared a five-minute recess, telling the plaintiff to use the time to read it. When the hearing resumed, he engaged in a Socratic dialogue with the plaintiff about the purpose of insurance that seemed more appropriate for a law school classroom than a court. He eventually browbeat the plaintiff into conceding the fallacy of his position that his insurance protected his car. The JP forced him to read aloud from his policy, which clarified that the insurance protected him as the driver. The spectacle was uncomfortable to watch. The plaintiff was clearly embarrassed by his inability to present his claim coherently. Whether the JP's legal point got through to him was unclear. A newcomer to the judicial process, he naïvely assumed that the complaint could speak for him. Given the belligerent stance of the JP, the plaintiff might have fared better had he foregone his personal appearance and, instead, asked the judge to resolve the case on the basis of the complaint.

The next day, I observed a preliminary hearing in which another Velikie luki JP took a different tack. She and the JP from the insurance case were among the most experienced JPs I encountered. Both had been on the bench since the advent of the JP courts. Even so, they reacted differently when confronted with legally inexperienced and incoherent petitioners. In this second case, two men showed up in connection with a complicated land dispute centering on garage ownership. The JP quickly discerned that the claim was improperly framed. When the plaintiffs explained that it had been written by a local *advokat*, the JP advised them to go back to him and detailed the shortcomings of the complaint. As the conversation proceeded, the JP realized that her advice was not getting through to the litigants, neither of whom had any legal training. She picked up the phone and called the lawyer. Failing to reach him on her first attempt, she tried again. When they connected, she laid out the problems with the pleading and set up an appointment for the two litigants to meet with him. The obvious desire of the litigants to get it right and their profound cluelessness triggered some wellspring of compassion within the JP, leading her to go above and beyond to help them. Interestingly, she did not denigrate the *advokat* in earshot of the litigants. Only after they left did she betray her feelings. She revealed that this lawyer had won an important case at the Russian Supreme Court several years ago and had been riding on that reputational high ever since. She was not surprised at the shoddy work.

It goes without saying that these are outlier cases. No doubt the vast majority of complaints prepared by lawyers who take no further part in the case pass without notice. After all, many plaintiffs authorize the courts to hear their cases in their absence, and defendants likewise often opt not to appear. In such cases, the assumption of the Velikie luki plaintiff in the insurance case would be correct. The documents would speak for him. In reflecting on the behavior of these two experienced Velikie luki JPs, I was struck by the very different signals they sent to the participants. Had I been in the shoes of the first petitioner, I would have been reluctant to bring another case to court, whereas the nurturing offered by the JP in the second case would have encouraged me to submit future disputes to the court.

The choice to get help from lawyers with drafting documents, but to forego their services in the courtroom, is primarily motivated on financial grounds. Though prices vary, litigants told me that simply having a complaint prepared cost them around 1,000 rubles (about $20), whereas the minimum charge to have a lawyer appear on their behalf was 5,000 rubles (about $100) per hearing. The cost savings would be "penny wise and pound foolish" if these litigants saw value to having lawyers at their side in court. For the most part, they do not. As I have noted elsewhere, the Russian legal system exists in an amorphous institutional space between adversarial and inquisitorial systems. All too often, lawyers are little more than the proverbial "potted plants," justifying litigants' decision not to rely on them in court.

A closer look at several cases in which lawyers participated provides greater insight.

> *Tax Collection.* A lawyer for the tax collection service in Rostov-na-Donu appears in support of her petition to recover 11,000 rubles in delinquent property taxes, along with penalties of 1,000 rubles, from an individual taxpayer. Though notified, the defendant-taxpayer is a no-show. After dispensing with the procedural rigamarole, the JP turns to the lawyer and asks her to present her substantive argument. The lawyer picks up her copy of the complaint and reads it aloud word-for-word. The JP does not interrupt her with questions. She occupies herself with other tasks, while the court secretary doodles. Even if they wanted to pay attention, the text is read in a monotone at a breakneck speed that makes it almost impossible to follow. After the lawyer finishes, the JP asks several questions about how she calculated the penalties. She then gives the lawyer the last word before leaving to make her decision. She rules in favor of the tax service, awarding it the full amount of the overdue taxes and penalties.

> *Inheritance.* Three women in their fifties show up, along with their *advokat*, for a hearing in a JP's office in Ekaterinburg to establish their

right to a house that their family has long possessed. The nominal defendant is the property registration office of the local government. Though notified of the time and place of the hearing, it has not sent a representative. As always, the JP begins by explaining their rights and duties as litigants. The unfamiliar legalese of the JP leaves them flummoxed when asked about recusal and additional motions. The *advokat* does little to ease their discomfort.

As the case proceeds to the merits, it quickly becomes apparent that the plaintiffs are at sea. One of them emerges as the spokesperson for the group. The JP asks her to present their argument. She is confused by the question. The JP simplifies her request by asking her to explain what she wants from the court. She goes through the familial history of the house, explaining that it was originally owned by their grandfather. Upon his death, ownership rights were divided between his widow and five children. The three plaintiffs are their surviving issue. The group spokesperson says that they want the court to declare that the three of them have equal claim on the property. As she goes through her argument, the JP interrupts to ask for documentary support for various claims. The plaintiffs have a binder full of documents and are constantly leafing through it. Often they give the wrong document to the JP and have to resume searching. The *advokat* does not assist them.

The JP expresses surprise, saying that the claim voiced in court does not match the complaint. The *advokat* pipes up, acknowledging that the family has neglected the legal niceties. He asks the court to formalize the understanding under which these family members have been operating. The women start adding their two cents, talking over one another. The JP attempts to restore order, saying, "There exists a process for how cases are heard. No one can talk unless I say they can." Through a series of pointed questions, the JP discerns that several possible claimants on the property are dead, but that their deaths have not been properly registered.

Poor-Quality Cell Phone. Bothered by a poorly functioning cell phone, an Ekaterinburg man brings a claim against the local store where he bought it. He arrives at the courtroom where the hearing takes place together with his lawyer, who is a *iurist*. The retail store is also represented by a lawyer. At the outset, both lawyers present their authorizing documents. As usual, the JP lays out the rights and duties of the parties, which turn out to be more complicated for cases involving consumer rights than for other cases. The JP details how the burden of proof shifts at various points in the process.

The plaintiff's lawyer jumps in with a motion to "clarify" (*utochnit*) the complaint by including a claim for punitive damages on the grounds that the salesman was rude to the plaintiff. The JP corrects him, saying this is not a clarification, but a supplement (*dopolnenie*). After confirming that the defendant had no objection, she accepts the change to the petition. The defendant's lawyer has her own motion. She wants to have an independent expert weigh in on whether the cell phone is flawed. The plaintiff's lawyer has no objection to seeking an expert opinion, or to the firm recommended by the defendant. The JP works through the questions to which the expert will be asked to respond. She leaves the courtroom to deliberate about whether to order this expertise, but before leaving makes it clear to the parties that this is a formality. She will send the phone to the expert and the hearing will be suspended for the several weeks needed to get the report from the expert.

These three vignettes are reflective of the patterns I observed in cases in which the parties retained counsel. For the most part, judges run the show, regardless of the presence of lawyers. This reflects the civil law legal legacy of Russia, and shows that, despite the embrace of adversarialism in Russian procedural codes, it has yet to become a part of daily life in the JP courts. Parties and their lawyers remain passive, waiting for cues from the bench rather than taking the initiative themselves. JPs do not shrink from the challenge. On both moral and practical grounds, they continue their traditional role as ringmaster. As I argued in the preceding chapter, JPs are determined to ensure a level playing field for all participants. This stems not only from their commitment to ferreting out the truth but also from their pragmatic desire to avoid being reversed.

When prompted for her substantive argument, the in-house lawyer for the tax authority responded by reading the legalese aloud from the complaint filed with the court. This was a common practice. So too was the ho-hum reaction from the other players in the drama. Judges generally busied themselves by reviewing other documents in the case file. Court secretaries stared off into space or checked their phones for messages, as did others in the courtroom. Indeed, the tax lawyer made no effort to connect with her audience. She was not engaged in active advocacy; she was merely going through the motions. When I asked courthouse personnel why they tolerated this sort of behavior by lawyers, they were surprised by the question. They uniformly told me that parties had the right to present their case in any form they saw fit. In other words, JPs' decision not to interrupt lawyers as they read documents available to all was seen as an endorsement of adversarialism. Even more interesting, JPs do not feel empowered to cut these speeches short in the interest of conserving judicial resources. The very idea struck JPs as absurd, even though they privately conceded that such speeches are a waste of time. The lawyer in the first scenario was on her own. In other cases, lawyers' clients witnessed these spectacles. I found none who voiced discontent. For most litigants, the entire judicial process was shrouded in mystery. They felt themselves unqualified to critique any of its elements.

Given that the tax lawyer won her case, my criticism may be overblown. As I discuss in the next section of this chapter, there is a performative aspect to judicial hearings. Perhaps allowing the lawyers the leeway to make their own choices about how to organize and present their cases is a step toward building a more vibrant adversarial process. This argument would be more compelling if the choice to read the complaint aloud contributed to the victory. But my conversations with JPs reveal that these recitations are regarded as little more than white noise. By not signaling this reality to lawyers and their clients, judges enable the continuation of a sort of Kabuki theater. They also fall short in their duty to educate litigants about what they ought to expect from their lawyers.

These chickens come home to roost in the second scenario. Though the tax case may have been an open-and-shut case, the same cannot be said of the inheritance case. It was to the credit of the petitioners that they had finally decided to formalize their ownership rights after decades of legal limbo, but the case was factually complicated and required a nuanced understanding of real estate and inheritance law that was beyond their ken. Recognizing that, they retained an *advokat*. Judging by his performance in the hearing, he was not well versed on the underlying facts or on the governing law. When his clients were floundering, he did not step in to help. In a purer adversarial system, his passivity would have sealed his clients' fate. If neither he nor his clients were able to put forward a convincing argument, the case would be tossed out.[35] But in Russia's mixed system, a JP is loath to dismiss a case without a full airing of the facts, even if this means that she has to enter the fray by taking on the role of investigator that, by all rights, ought to be the responsibility of the *advokat*.[36] His clients were none the wiser. After the hearing, they expressed no dissatisfaction with him, only a vague annoyance with the JP's persistent questioning. Despite their best efforts to prepare for the hearing, they were unable to respond to many of her questions. Though I faulted their *advokat* for not preparing them, they did not.

---

35. Scholars of the U.S. small-claims courts argue that represented parties do better (Weller, Ruhnka, and Martin 1990, 11–12). The same cannot be said for Russian parties.

36. Because small-claims courts are designed to be user-friendly, having judges that take on an investigative role is not unique to Russia or even to countries with civil law traditions (Kurkchiyan 2012, 2013; Rohl 1990, 174). Judges in U.S. small-claims courts and English county courts also see themselves this way (Baldwin 1997; Weller, Ruhnka, and Martin 1990, 14). It is more noteworthy when judges shy away from this role, as in Bulgaria (Kurkchiyan 2012, 244).

The JP did not take their dissatisfaction with her personally. This was part of her daily reality. Afterward we talked about the performance of the *advokat*. She agreed that it had been rather feeble. I asked why such lawyers continue to attract clients. She shrugged and said that she doubts the petitioners realize how bad he was and that his presence may have provided moral support to the women. She noted that it would be inappropriate for her to share with the parties her assessment of the merits of their lawyer. During the hearing, she scrupulously avoided any sign of being troubled by the *advokat*'s behavior (or nonbehavior). Much like the Rostov JP, in talking to me, she pointed out that litigants were free to decide who to hire. It brings to mind Anatole France's well-known saying: "The law, in its majestic equality, forbids the rich as well as the poor to sleep under bridges, to beg in the streets, and to steal bread." It seems that, in the view of Russian judges, adversarialism gives litigants the right to poor lawyering. But in an ironic twist, they do not bear the consequences of hiring unskilled representatives. JPs pick up the slack, thereby undermining any reason for these representatives to change their ways.

Like many JPs, she spoke with nostalgia about the Soviet era. Though she was much too young to have experienced it personally, she said that in those days, a judge could have contacted the head of the law office (*kollegia*) to let him know that his colleague had acquitted himself poorly. This option remains for *advokaty*, the only segment of the Russian legal profession subject to ethical rules (Kodeks 2003), but is almost never exercised. When pressed, many JPs acknowledge that they could be more proactive vis-à-vis poorly prepared representatives of all stripes. The civil procedure code allows judges to fine those who disrupt court hearings or who fail to provide requested evidence (arts. 57 and 159, GPK RF). But judges mostly sidestep these sections of the code, not because they lack cause to use them but because judges regard them as more trouble than they are worth. The amounts authorized are trivial, making it unlikely that they would actually change behavior.[37] Moreover, the court orders imposing such fines can be immediately appealed, which requires suspending the case in chief until the appeal is decided. Likewise, lawyers or others on whom fines are imposed can take their complaints about the JP's behavior to the judicial qualification commissions, which police judicial ethics. JPs are not concerned about the validity of these fines, but do worry that defending themselves will distract them from their main task of resolving cases within the statutory deadline. As a result, they rarely make use of this tool.

---

37. Article 159, part 3, of the Civil Code authorizes judges to impose fines of up to 1,000 rubles for disrupting judicial proceedings. Fines of up to 5,000 rubles are contemplated for failure to present evidence (art. 57, part 3, GPK RF).

It is only in the third scenario that the lawyers seem to be earning their keep. But even here there is less than meets the eye. The plaintiff's *iurist* trumpeted the motion for punitive damages as if it was his contribution. In reality, however, punitive damages are a routine element of consumer claims in Russia. The JP played along, not cluing in the plaintiff. In my discussion of the case with the JP afterward, she said that the decision of the *iurist* to go along with the defendant's choice to seek expertise was a strategic error.[38] She said that he should have verified the impartiality of the institution. But again, she left it to the discretion of the *iurist*. As with the women in the second vignette, the plaintiff himself was likely oblivious to these legal intrigues.

Doubts about the quality of legal assistance being provided in consumer claims was a constant theme as I traveled to different JP courts. These were voiced not by litigants, but by JPs. They saw that such claims had become a lucrative income source for unscrupulous lawyers, who advertised aggressively for clients. These lawyers generally limited themselves to cases in which the consumer had clearly been aggrieved. As a result, they could sit back and let the facts speak for themselves. They jumped into action only when it came time to petition the court for their legal fees (art. 100, GPK RF). JPs would grit their teeth and award the requested amounts. Though they had the discretion to lower the amount, they rarely did so, even though they often privately questioned whether it had truly been earned. They explained that doing so would only punish the litigants, not the lawyers. The litigants had already paid their lawyers' bills; the court award of attorneys' fees simply reimbursed them.

Participating in Judicial Hearings as Performance

As a rule, trials are of interest only to their participants. They rarely have much societal resonance. Exceptions occur when the parties are playing to a larger audience. We are accustomed to this sort of performative element in so-called show trials, which, in the Soviet era, were literally scripted to achieve maximum effect (e.g., Medvedev 1971; Tucker and Cohen 1965). In the early decades after the October Revolution, the Bolsheviks staged plays (some of which were filmed to allow broader distribution) in the form of "agitation trials" with the goal of

---

38. Under Russian law, when expert analysis is required, a single expert is appointed by the court. The judge, together with the parties, develops a list of questions to be answered by the expert (art. 79, GPK RF). In civil cases, the initial cost of seeking expertise is born by the party who requests it. In the final analysis, however, the cost is imposed on the losing side (art. 96, GPK RF). This has given rise to an increase in organizations that provide expert analysis.

shaping the behavior of ordinary Russians (Wood 2005; Cassiday 2000). In later decades, the Kremlin lost its ability to manage political trials, as transcripts of the proceedings leaked out, proving their stage-managed quality (e.g., Litvinov 1972; Siniavskii 1967). The political authorities remained firmly in control of the outcome of such trials. Acquittals were unthinkable (Kaminskaya 1982). In the Putin era, the Kremlin was unable to bar the public from the show trials of Mikhail Khodorkovsky, Alexei Navalny, the members of Pussy Riot, and others. The film about the 2012 Pussy Riot trial, *Pussy Riot: A Punk Prayer*, documented the applause that greeted the final statements of the defendants, as well as the disdain of many Russians for their actions at the Cathedral of Christ the Savior in Moscow. But like their Soviet predecessors, political authorities had the final word by dictating the outcome.

It is not just the state that can hijack a judicial hearing; criminal defendants and/or civil plaintiffs can also use their participation to make larger points. Sometimes the goal is substantive, such as lawsuits brought to publicize environmental degradation or workplace discrimination. In other cases, lawsuits seek to illustrate the patent unfairness of the underlying procedural rules. Of course, such trials assume the presence of a societal spotlight. The audience is a necessary element. The goal is to sway the masses.

For the most part, the litigants I observed in the JP courts had instrumental goals. The petitioners in civil cases were seeking to recover damages allegedly incurred, whereas their opposite numbers were trying to avoid paying. Participants in administrative cases were trying to avoid the wrath of the state, as were criminal defendants. But I occasionally witnessed hearings in which the participants had larger goals. Obtaining damages took a back seat to getting their grievances heard and acknowledged within their families or by society more generally.

Three types of cases stood out. The first is *chastnoe obvinenie*. As discussed in the preceding chapter, these are based on fracases that give rise to physical and psychological injuries that are too minor to interest the police. The victim acts as a private prosecutor in seeking criminal penalties. The cramped living conditions in which multiple generations share small apartments provide fertile ground for the altercations that lead to cases of *chastnoe obvinenie*. The latter two categories are more amorphous. One cluster of cases involved senior citizens. Having time on their hands, they are frequent visitors to the JP courts. Lacking resources to hire lawyers, they try the patience of JPs with their meandering presentations and unclear demands. It often seemed that they were lonely and were using the judicial process as a way of interacting with others. The third type of case involves claims that raise larger issues, such as the persistent problem of how communal charges are allocated by housing management companies.

Family Drama. A pensioner in her seventies has brought a claim against her daughter-in-law in the form of a *chastnoe obvinenie.* Together with the petitioner's son, they share a two-room apartment. The relationship between the two women has long been rocky. The older woman resents being asked to clean up after her daughter-in-law. A few months earlier, their oral contretemps erupted into physical violence when the younger woman struck her elder. The defendant admits to having a short temper and to abusing alcohol, though she insists that this incident was not a product of drunken rage.

The hearing takes place in the spacious office of an Ekaterinburg JP. Owing to the age of the petitioner, a prosecutor has been appointed to help her. With his help, she explained to the court that she was ready to drop her complaint. Both the JP and the prosecutor probe to make sure that her motion is voluntary. We learn that the incident that provoked the claim is only the most recent in a long series of violent outbursts by the younger woman. The older woman insists that she has not been pressured to withdraw the charges, but the prosecutor is doubtful. For her part, the daughter-in-law expresses remorse, saying that she has resolved to tidy up her part of the apartment herself. Both women say they have put the incident behind them and that no residual anger remains. The two generations have decided to separate their household budgets and to work toward exchanging their apartment for two one-room apartments.

Plea for Attention. As the hearing begins in a Moscow courtroom, only an older woman is present. She has brought a consumer complaint against a dental clinic for selling her dentures that, in her opinion, do not fit her properly.[39] Seeing that no representative for the dental clinic has shown up, the JP asks her secretary to phone them to find out where they are. While we are waiting, the JP inquires into the health of the petitioner, and gets an earful about how she spent the morning at the polyclinic and has now been waiting for more than two hours at the courthouse for this hearing to commence.[40] Yet her remarks do not come across as

39. Her choice to bring her grievance as a consumer claim rather than medical malpractice might seem odd. But it did not strike any of the participants this way. The dentures were treated as a good that was sold to her by the dental clinic. As I explain in chapter 3, tort law (including malpractice) is an underdeveloped field. Recovering damages is more straightforward in consumer rights claims than in tort claims.

40. The court had not been keeping the petitioner waiting. The hearing proceeded according to the schedule posted on the court's website. The petitioner had simply arrived early.

kvetching, but as sharing news with interested friends. The JP then asks the petitioner several questions about the case. This exchange reveals the depth of her ignorance of legal procedure. She is initially unable to respond to the JP's question about settlement overtures because she does not know the term for settlement agreement (*mirovoe soglashenie*). When the JP explains it to her, she says that the manager of the dental clinic told her that she should take her claim to court. He was uninterested in settling with her. The JP then asks who prepared her complaint. The plaintiff says that she got help from a lawyer. The JP advises her that if she submits the receipt for payment for these services, she can be reimbursed by the court. She also gives her a minitutorial on the law governing consumer claims, suggesting that she ought to amend the complaint to include a request for punitive damages.

When the representative for the dental clinic arrives, the JP turns her attention to him. He is a young man in his thirties. She is not as solicitous with him as she had been with the pensioner. He has failed to bring a document authorizing him to act as the clinic's agent. He assures the JP that he is the manager of the clinic, but she brushes him off, saying that she needs documentary evidence to support his claim. He rifles through his briefcase and pulls out a document that he believes will do the trick. The JP reads it and gives it back to him, noting that it expired a year earlier. She details what needs to be in the power of attorney. She allows him to continue to speak for the clinic in the hearing, but makes it clear that she will not be so generous in the future if the documents substantiating his authority are found wanting.

Moving forward, she asks the parties if they have any motions that would preclude hearing the case on the merits. The petitioner is stumped by the legalese. The JP explains. The plaintiff takes the opportunity to launch into her story of dental woes. The JP stops her short, saying that it is not yet time for this, but assuring her that she will have a chance to explain what happened.

The JP summarizes the facts. The parties entered into a contract to provide dentures for the plaintiff. The plaintiff alleges that the dentures are of poor quality, that she cannot use them to eat solid foods. She wrote a complaint letter (*pretenziia*) to the clinic, asking them to fix the problem. She received no reply. She returned to the clinic at least eight times to get the dentures adjusted, to no avail. She is seeking compensatory damages of 20,000 rubles (the amount she paid for the dentures) and punitive damages of 20,000 rubles.

The JP asks the plaintiff whether she supports the allegations made in her complaint. Absolutely. She goes on at length about the wrongs done to her. The JP interrupts periodically with questions of clarification designed to keep her on track. She gets the plaintiff to state definitively that she has given up on having the clinic fix the dentures. At this point, she is seeking monetary damages.

Turning to the other side, the JP asks whether he is willing to acknowledge fault on the part of the clinic. She explains that if the case goes forward, then the clinic will have to shoulder the cost of seeking an expert opinion about the dentures because it is their responsibility to prove affirmatively that the goods provided were of good quality. The presentation by the clinic's representative betrays a weariness at dealing with the petitioner. He contends that he has tried repeatedly to settle her claim, but that she is impossible to pin down. He believes that she is simply lonely and has returned to the clinic in search of someone to talk with about her problems. He also worries that if he rewards her for this behavior by paying her claim, then he will be besieged by other pensioners.

His characterization of the plaintiff sets her off. She first grows defensive and insists that she has many friends. Within minutes, however, she is in tears over the recent death of her brother. She explains that she needs to travel to Lipetsk the next week for the forty-day commemoration of his death. The JP is gentle with her, but keeps the hearing moving.

There are some halfhearted negotiations over the amount that each side might be willing to accept. The JP postpones the case for a few days to allow the defendant's representative to obtain the document authorizing him to negotiate on the clinic's behalf. He leaves as soon as the JP declares the hearing closed. The petitioner takes some time to organize her documents. As she is doing this, the JP tells her that she ought to prepare herself to compromise in order to get the clinic to settle the case.

Plea on Behalf of the Larger Community. In a courtroom in Velikie luki, a battle over housing rights plays out. A company that manages several hundred apartment houses has brought a case against an individual resident who has failed to pay the amounts assessed for heating and capital repairs. The plaintiff is represented by a young woman who works as an in-house *iurist* for the management company. The defendant is on his own. He is a sixty-year-old pensioner.

The two parties are fighting different cases. The plaintiff presents it as a straightforward case of a delinquent tenant. The defendant argues that he has been deliberately withholding payment in protest of the poor services provided by the management company. He insists that he is a law-abiding person, but that he has lost patience. He says that his family has endured freezing conditions for the past three years, and asks, "Why am I being asked to pay?" He says that he is speaking for many other families who are likewise suffering. He presents his written response to the plaintiff, along with a packet of documents that provide evidence supporting his claims. The *iurist* tosses them aside dismissively, saying that they have nothing to do with the case at hand. She says that if he is dissatisfied with the services being provided, then he needs to bring his own case. She is annoyed at his effort to piggyback his claims onto her case.

The JP allows the ping-ponging between the parties to continue. The plaintiff asks the defendant whether he participated in the recent Saturday cleanups (*subbotniki*) organized by the management company, bragging that she has taken part in two of these events. The defendant pushed back, saying, "Take off your dark glasses. The city is dirty because management companies like yours are not doing their job." As they grow angrier and begin to talk over each other, the JP tries to restore order, telling them that emotions have no place in court hearings. He repeatedly asks them whether they might be able to settle their differences. The defendant concedes that he is ready to pay for the electricity his family has used, but he draws the line at paying for heat, owing to its inadequacy. He veers off onto a tangent about whether the management company has lived up to its obligation to hold regular meetings among residents, a charge that is hotly disputed by the *iurist*.

Finally the JP loses patience when he cannot get the defendant to recognize his authority. He asks him: "Are you listening to the court or to yourself?" The defendant apologizes. He presents a motion to bring in other residents as witnesses to the poor performance of the management company. Though the JP is open to this idea, the *iurist* strongly opposes it. After about an hour of this sort of bickering, the JP has had enough. He declares a recess until the next day to allow both sides to review the documents in the case file more thoroughly.

What unites these three seemingly disparate scenarios is that the petitioners are seeking something more than monetary damages. They are playing to a larger audience. In the first example, the older woman is trying to draw a line in the sand within her family. The discussion revealed that she had been tolerating emotional and physical abuse from her daughter-in-law for many years. By bringing the claim in court, she has created a formal record and has signaled the younger generation that she has reached the end of her rope. Though she withdrew her complaint, she has succeeded in shaming her daughter-in-law. The younger woman acknowledged her culpability in open court and resolved to change her ways. Stopping short of verdict does not indicate weakness, but a pragmatic recognition of the potentially devastating consequences of a criminal conviction within the family. If the daughter-in-law had been convicted, this would end any hope for the petitioner's son or grandchildren to obtain civil service jobs. Though the older woman clearly had limited power within her home, she seemed to turn the tide by bringing the lawsuit.

Unlike the participants in the second and third scenarios, the petitioner in the first scenario was not garrulous. She had a quiet dignity about her as she responded to the questions of the JP and the prosecutor with one-word answers. She stood her ground, insisting that her decision to withdraw her complaint had not been the result of pressure from her family. She turned the tables on her daughter-in-law, who was on the defensive in the hearing. Her complaint had spurred a serious discussion within her family about how to remedy their situation in the long run, thereby achieving her goals.

This is typical of cases of *chastnoe obvinenie*. As socio-legal theory suggests, claims between those with close personal relationships are not brought lightly, especially when they live on top of each other and have little option for exit (Emerson 2008; Hirschman 1970). Because these lawsuits raise the specter of criminal conviction, they constitute the nuclear option. They inevitably lead to turmoil in familial or other close personal relationships. But that is their purpose. As a rule, they are brought by frustrated family members, former family members, or neighbors as a wake-up call to those near and dear to them. The petitioners have usually tried other strategies for changing the undesirable behavior and are at their wit's end. The fact that most such claims are settled does not indicate a lack of conviction on the part of the petitioners, but rather is a mark of their success. By shining a semipublic light on the behavior, they are able to call the perpetrators to account and improve the situation without ruining their lives.

The petitioner in the second vignette is openly querulous. She is representative of a larger group of cases I observed involving pensioners who were using the JP courts both instrumentally and to reach out for human contact. These petitioners generally had a tenuous hold on their emotions; tears were not uncommon. They were usually legally illiterate and knew little of the norms of courtroom etiquette. Some JPs let this slide, especially when petitioners were physically feeble and had difficulty standing. More problematic was their lack of substantive knowledge of the law governing their case. The court's job was easier when, as in this case of the misfitting dentures, the plaintiff made no pretense of knowing the law. The response of the Moscow JP to explain how the law worked was typical. Grasping the twists and turns of legal logic is difficult for most laymen. Pensioners are no exception. Those who have lost some cognitive capacity struggle more than others. But at least judges do not have to overcome misconceptions of the law. JPs have a tougher time when pensioners show up with a preconceived but mistaken conception of the relevant law. Often their ideas about the law are grounded in common sense. Unfortunately, laws do not always line up perfectly with common sense. A pensioner from St. Petersburg who was convinced that she owed no rent because the manager of her apartment complex had failed to send her a rental contract illustrates the dilemma well. Absent that written document, this woman believed she could not be held liable. Though Russian law has long recognized the principle that an implied contract arises whenever one accepts services from another, this rule was unknown to the pensioner. The efforts of the JP to explain it to her fell on deaf ears. The pensioner saw the court as being in cahoots with the property management company and could not be convinced to pay.

The gaps in legal knowledge are easier for the courts to manage than is the need of these elderly petitioners for emotional sustenance. Their lives are often lonely. They have little opportunity to interact with others. As a result, when they come to court, they are eager to share their stories. The contours of their stories are often quite expansive. Once they get wound up, the twists and turns of their tales can be hard to follow, and can try the patience of the court and the other participants. JPs' efforts to edit them sometimes backfire and can lead to tears as the storyteller feels herself to be misunderstood and belittled. Likewise, intimating that the petitioner is lonely and is in court only to seek human interaction can spark emotional reactions, as the second scenario shows. The challenge for JPs is daunting. They have to manage litigants who are operating at different capacities. Their goal is to validate the legal claims of these emotionally needy petitioners without opening the door to litanies of their lifelong woes. Moreover, they have to do it without unduly annoying the opposing parties, who are eager to get their cases resolved and are uninterested in soothing the feelings of these elderly litigants.

In the case described in the second vignette, the JP managed to strike a good balance. She acted as more of a conciliator than a neutral decision maker. She allowed the clinic manager to speak on behalf of the defendant despite his defective paperwork. Though she never stated her goal openly, she spent much of the hearing working to convince the defendant to settle the claim. She reminded the clinic's representative that if the case were to go forward, the court would need to obtain an expert opinion on the fit of the dentures, and that the clinic would have to cover this expense. She pointed out that it would be cheaper for them to return the pensioner's money. Despite the fears of the dental clinic's office manager that he will be deluged by claims from other *babushki*, the parties are able to reach a settlement at the next hearing.

The pensioner came away from the experience satisfied. Like neophyte litigants everywhere, her goal had been to tell her story. The willingness of the JP to listen was rewarding on its own. For her, the money was somewhat beside the point.

In the third scenario, the defendant is speaking on behalf of his family and his neighbors. He has withheld utility payments to the company managing his apartment complex in protest of its poor performance. Clearly itching for a fight, he pushes aside the questions about his debt from the plaintiff's *iurist* and goes on the offensive. He details his family's suffering in recent winters owing to the inadequate supply of heat. The *iurist* is taken aback by his attacks. She appeals to the JP to shut down his line of inquiry as irrelevant to her complaint. From a technical legal point of view, she is on fairly solid ground. If a tenant is dissatisfied, then his remedy is to initiate an independent lawsuit or to bring a cross-claim in the pending case. But cross-claims are generally limited to the topic of the original lawsuit. Whether the defendant's argument that he should not have to pay for poor service would qualify is not clear. Interestingly, the JP allows him to proceed without jumping through this hoop. This is unusual. Russian judges tend to be sticklers for these sorts of procedural details. In essence, by opening the door to calling witnesses on the extent to which the management company has lived up to its obligations, he is allowing an implicit cross-complaint. Perhaps he tolerates this ham-handed legal strategy because the defendant is not represented and, therefore, is unschooled on the intricacies of the procedural rules. The JP's permissiveness had its limits. The defendant's exuberance in the courtroom, which was evidenced by a failure to acknowledge the judge's authority on several occasions, could likewise be attributed to his lack of legal literacy. Yet the JP showed no tolerance for such shenanigans, requiring a verbal apology before proceeding.

As with the other cases, the defendant in the third scenario had no audience in the courtroom to whom he was playing. At the same time, his defense encompassed his entire neighborhood. His claim that the management company was not using the sums paid by residents for their intended purposes went well beyond his narrow circumstances. It is a claim that is becoming ever more common. Owing to the difficulty of bringing anything akin to a class action in the Russian courts, a variety of creative strategies have been adopted. Like the defendant, some residents have chosen to stop paying for inadequate services. The societal revulsion at evictions has served as an informal protection against being thrown out on the street for nonpayment. Other residents have filed lawsuits against their landlords, alleging that they have violated their legal obligations to hold regular tenants' meetings and to provide annual financial statements to tenants. Such lawsuits are designed as an opening salvo to improve conditions and have met with mixed success.

Litigants' Satisfaction with the JP Courts

Few of the litigants highlighted in my vignettes could be described as satisfied. As I capture them in the midst of their battles, they are mostly frustrated, sometimes with their foes and sometimes with the court. Their inexperience often leaves them mystified by JPs' demands. What seems self-evident to them can turn out to be difficult to prove in court (Kurkchiyan 2012, 2013; Baldwin 1997). The comparative literature on small-claims courts indicates that this is a fairly common reaction. In his study of the county courts of England and Wales, Baldwin (1997, 125) notes that "small claims hearings present . . . a curious paradox: while they appear on the surface to offer an appropriately informal and relaxed setting in which straightforward legal disputes can be resolved, they do not work well when there are unstated legal criteria that must be satisfied." Much like the Russian JPs I observed, the English and Welsh judges intervened actively to try to help parties through the system. Their best efforts may still fall short in the eyes of litigants.

Assessing the views of litigants on the JP courts solely on the basis of my limited observations would result in an incomplete picture. To fill in the gaps, I rely on the data collected in the ILPP Project and the ABA Survey. These research projects benefit from having a larger sample size and from talking to litigants after they have had time to reflect on their experience. In interpreting these data, it is important to remember that the population being surveyed—namely, those who have taken their problems to the JP courts—is not entirely typical. Recall from chapter 1 that only about 13 percent of the respondents from the RLMS-HSE—a more general survey—reported any personal contact with the courts. The percent would shrink further if limited to those who have used the JP courts. On the other hand, as to their basic attitudes toward law, the respondents from the ABA Survey are basically in line with those of the representative sample from the RLMS-HSE. In both the ABA Survey and the RLMS-HSE, about 24 percent of respondents embraced legal nihilism.

The ABA Survey and the ILPP Project are ideally positioned to help us understand how litigants at the JP courts view their experiences. The picture that emerges is remarkably consistent. Litigants are generally satisfied with their experiences at the JP courts. Over one-third of the respondents to the ABA Survey described it as "successful." Another 28 percent said it was successful, but bemoaned the level of bureaucratic red tape involved. Some were more ambivalent. Twenty-two percent said that their problems had been resolved, but the case had not turned out as they had hoped. An additional 5 percent were disappointed because the case could not be resolved for "objective reasons." The remaining 9 percent of respondents were disgruntled for a variety of reasons, including perceived incompetence of the court, overwhelming red tape, and the inadequacy of the underlying law.

In an effort to isolate the characteristics that tended to be associated with those who found their experience at the JP court to be an unqualified success, I used the data from the ABA Survey to create a dummy variable for this group of respondents. Through the use of descriptive statistics and logistic regression analysis, an intriguing picture emerges. The tables with the detailed results of these analyses are set forth in Appendix C. The ABA Survey, which was fielded in 2009, queried 1,200 Russians users of the JP courts about their experiences. Respondents were evenly divided between three regions. Location matters. Court users from Leningrad oblast were much less satisfied than their counterparts in Rostov or Nizhni Novgorod oblast. (See table C.1.) These results are puzzling, given that the ILPP Project, which also focused on Leningrad oblast, did not find their respondents from this region to be down on the courts.

The regression analysis exposed several variables as insignificant that I had assumed would be strong predictors of satisfaction. Comparative experience would suggest that having a lawyer could ease one's path through the judicial system, but whether a respondent had consulted an *advokat* made no difference.[41] It also stands to reason that being well informed about how the JP courts work would be a good predictor of satisfaction, but it is not. The fact that the odds ratio is 1.55 suggests that such knowledge helps, but the lack of statistical significance tells us that the explanatory power is very weak. (See table C.2.) This contradicts the socio-legal literature, which has repeatedly shown that those who have a good understanding of how a judicial system works are more likely to be able to use it to their advantage (Galanter 1974). I tested several other variables that would seem to be relevant, but abandoned them when they turned out to be meaningless. Among these were attitudes toward corruption. Those who admitted to bribing JPs or who were open to the idea of bribing judges were no more or less likely to have had a positive experience than those who were hostile to bribing.[42]

---

41. Not only is the variable statistically insignificant, but the odds ratio is also less than one, which is entirely unexpected, given that it intimates that having a lawyer may decrease one's satisfaction. Unfortunately the survey did not ask about being represented in court, but about whether the respondent had ever felt the need to consult with an *advokat*. The exact phrasing was: "prikhodilos li vam kogda-libo obrashchat'sia k uslugam advokata?"

42. Eleven respondents (0.9 percent) admitted to paying a bribe, while an additional 153 (12.8 percent) equivocated, saying that they had not personally paid a bribe, but that their friends or relatives had done so.

Likewise a belief that felt the courts were unduly influenced by extralegal forces, such as big business or state organs, was not a good predictor of satisfaction levels. Neither was a propensity to rely on oneself (rather than the courts or legal professionals) when problems arose.

When working with the RLMS-HSE, I found education and age to be powerful explanatory variables of legal attitudes and behavior (see tables A.1 and A.2). Following the comparative literature (Tyler 2006), more education generally translates into more support for the integrity of law and the courts. The relationship with age is more complicated. As we saw in chapter 1, it tends to be curvilinear in Russia, with more support for law being expressed by the youngest and oldest cohorts. But these relationships are notably absent in the data from the ABA Survey. Education and age are not significant, either in the descriptive statistics or the regression analysis.

What did matter were gender, class, openness to using the JP courts again, adherence to legal nihilism, belief in the even-handedness of the courts, and plans to appeal. Women, who represent 61 percent of the sample, emerge as more likely to view their experience at the JP courts as successful. Their odds of this were over 30 percent greater than for their male counterparts. Unskilled workers are much less likely to assess their court experience positively than are their more skilled counterparts.

The fact that those who plan to appeal their decision are less likely to view their experience at the JP court as successful might appear to be self-evident. After all, if a respondent plans to appeal, then she is, by definition, unhappy with the decision. The odds of dissatisfaction with their experience are almost 90 percent greater for those who intend to appeal. But as the procedural justice literature reminds us, it is entirely possible to be dissatisfied with the decision in a particular case, yet be satisfied with the process (Gallagher and Wang 2011; Tyler 2006; Benesh and Howell 2001). The fact that more than half of those who plan to appeal responded neutrally by saying simply that their case did not turn out as they had hoped, rather than heaping condemnation onto the courts (as the survey gave them a chance to do), suggests that they can distinguish between their disappointment in losing and an assessment of the overall court system. Well over 85 percent of respondents felt the JP courts were basically fair, at least in terms of even-handedness and outside political influence. Of the variables that captured negative attitudes about the courts, the only one that emerged as significant in the regression analysis isolated respondents who see the JP courts as biased. As would be expected, these litigants were markedly unenthusiastic about their experiences. Their odds of satisfaction are over 60 percent less than respondents who trust in the unbiased nature of the courts.

At the other end of the spectrum, it is hardly surprising that litigants who stand ready to use the JP courts again should the need arise would be more likely to see their recent experience in a positive light. Interestingly, almost half of the respondents (46 percent) put themselves in this category. Holding such an opinion was a highly significant predictor. The odds of having a bullish view were 89 percent greater for this group. Of those who were skeptical of using the courts in the future, most said they would be willing to return to court, but only if they had exhausted all other options. Only a handful said they would never go back.

The weakness of the relationship between attitudes of legal nihilism and satisfaction at court was surprising. It would seem to follow that those who are prepared to go around the law when it proves inconvenient would be generally hostile to the courts. To be sure, those who embrace these views are less likely to have had a good experience in court, but the marginal statistical significance reflects its limited explanatory power.

On the larger question of whether the JP courts are viewed as fair and impartial, the respondents in the ABA Survey generally gave these courts and their judges high marks. Over 80 percent believe that JPs are well trained and competent. Only 10 percent said that their judge had been biased. A plurality of 48 percent said that their judge had been completely independent, while an additional 24 percent said that the judge had mostly, but not always, acted independently.

As to the fairness of the court process, over 70 percent of respondents were convinced that JPs typically rule in favor of the side that is stronger from a legal point of view. A similar majority said that their JPs strictly complied with all procedural norms during their hearing, conducting themselves tactfully, and that they not only gave both sides an equal opportunity to present their arguments but also paid close attention to both. When asked whether their JP had exhibited any preferential treatment toward specific groups, such as members of the middle class, workers, young people, non-Russians, and pensioners, a majority said that they had been even-handed. Some ambivalence was expressed as to the wealthy. Though 57 percent said that rich litigants were treated the same as everyone else, 31 percent said they were treated better, which was the highest score of any group. This same fear reared its head when respondents were asked whether judges responded to various outside influences when making their decisions. Again a majority of respondents felt that judges made their decisions independently. But the data reveal some uncertainty as to big business and state organs. As to each, 26 percent felt that JPs were under their influence, though a solid majority remained confident of their independence.[43]

---

43. The correlation between these two variables is 0.48.

The results from the ILPP Project likewise confirm that litigants at the JP courts felt that the process was basically fair. Over 95 percent of plaintiff-respondents saw judges as unbiased and independent. Defendants were less sanguine; over 10 percent disputed the even-handedness and independence of judges. As a group, however, only a handful of participants in the ILPP Project reported any procedural violations during their hearings. Their complaints centered on matters outside the control of judges. Both plaintiffs and defendants grumbled about the difficulty of assembling evidence. Plaintiffs were annoyed by the propensity of defendants not to show up for hearings.

No doubt the speed at which their cases were resolved contributed to the positive attitudes of these respondents. Over 55 percent were in and out of the court within a month. An additional third of the sample were able to get their case decided within three months. Their experiences line up with the official caseload data, which report that less than 1 percent of civil cases linger on past the statutory deadlines (Otchet–JP Courts 2011).

Images of the JP Courts

The image of the JP courts presented in this chapter is at odds with the usual view of Russian courts as slow, incompetent, and corrupt and deeply distrusted by the public. Yet both my observational research and the data generated by the ABA Survey and the ILPP Project reinforce the generally positive attitude of litigants toward the JP courts. The official caseload data likewise paint a relatively positive picture of these courts, documenting their efficiency and the absence of any bias toward the state. It is worth noting that when I have participated in roundtables in which the results of the ABA Survey or the ILPP Project were presented to audiences of Russian policymakers and scholars, the reaction has been skepticism bordering on hostility (Sidorovich 2011). The reaction has been similar regarding my work. Russians are loathe to believe that any judicial institution could be functional.

As I noted in the Introduction, there is plenty of reliable evidence to support this negativity. Public opinion polling consistently reveals profound public suspicion toward the courts in Russia. But the questions posed tend to ask respondents about the courts without specifying any particular type of court. The steady stream of articles in the Russian press that highlight the shortcomings of the courts fuels misgivings among respondents, as does the emphasis on high-profile cases in which law takes a back seat to political and economic influence. Not surprisingly, trust in courts or judges is invariably shown to be in short supply. When queried in July 2012 by the Levada Center as part of a representative national survey, only 21 percent of respondents expressed full trust in the courts. By contrast, about half of those surveyed had complete trust in the president and in the church (Levada Center 2012).[44]

Because the questions are broadly framed in terms of courts, it is impossible to tease out attitudes toward specific types of courts. A hint of the differentiation in views is provided by a survey focusing on attitudes toward the judiciary fielded by the Levada Center in the spring of 2010 (Gudkov, Dubin, and Zorkaia 2010, 15). Respondents were asked about their trust in different types of courts. An index of trust was created by adding the percentage of people who expressed full trust to half of the percentage of people expressing cautious trust. The same sort of index was created for distrust. The JP courts earned a score of 14.6 for trust and 9 for distrust, compared with 3.4 and 8, respectively, for the courts of general jurisdiction (ibid.).[45] This is supportive of my thesis.[46] It strongly suggests that, when given the chance, Russians are capable of distinguishing between different types of courts and that bulk of their disdain is reserved for the courts of general jurisdiction.

To be fair, these courts have to handle the toughest cases. They hear all serious criminal cases. The reluctance of judges to acquit no doubt contributes to public distrust, as does the sense of the public that verdicts are for sale at these courts. When asked what prevents courts from being effective, the corruptibility of judges and their staff was identified as the most serious problem (ibid., 23). Many (40 percent) saw simple greed as the root cause, though others pointed to legal culture (28 percent), the weakness of institutional oversight (27 percent), and to the desire of litigants to have their cases heard more quickly (27 percent). According to respondents, bribes are the most common extralegal method. Conspiring with the chairman of the court, threatening court representatives, or blackmailing judges are seen to be less frequently used tactics (ibid., 27–28). In addition to corruption, respondents believed that the independence of courts is compromised by pressure exerted by powerful political officials, court chairmen, and wealthy businessmen (ibid., 35). Though these

44. As Putin regained his footing as president, his popularity increased. During 2014 and 2015, his approval ratings were well over 80 percent (Levada Center 2015).

45. In a bizarre twist, it was the elite courts—the Russian Supreme Court and the Russian Constitutional Court—that earned the highest scores. Both had trust scores in excess of 20. By way of explanation, Gudkov and his coauthors (2010, 16) note that these are the most famous courts and point out that one out of five respondents knew nothing about what these courts actually do.

46. In a separate project, I independently reviewed these 2010 Levada data. My analysis confirms that court users generally had positive experiences, but shows that they do not spill over into their overall views. Court users were uniformly less sanguine when it came to courts than were nonusers (Hendley 2016).

results might make it seem as though respondents saw judges as the dregs of society, other questions reveal that other state officials are held in even lower esteem. When asked which group of state officials are the most corrupt, judges came in a distant fifth behind the traffic police, federal officials, local police, and local officials (ibid., 27).

The questions posed by the Levada Center encompass all Russian courts, including JP courts. How can these attitudes be squared with the upbeat responses regarding the JP courts gathered as part of the ABA Survey and the ILPP Project? After all, their respondents reported satisfaction both with the outcome of their cases and with the process more generally. But they were not naïve; they saw the specter of corruption. When asked about its role in the JP courts, 17 percent of those participating in the ABA Survey felt that decisions were generally for sale to the highest bidder, whereas 35 percent thought bribes were a more isolated occurrence. Only 19 percent viewed the JP courts as a corruption-free zone. The remaining 29 percent of respondents found it too difficult to respond. Interestingly, an openness to bribery turned out to be unimportant in predicting satisfaction with the JP courts.

Perhaps the less central role of corruption in the JP courts can be explained by their jurisdictional parameters. Measured in terms of monetary or liberty interests, the stakes are much lower than in other Russian courts. The amounts at issue cannot exceed 50,000 rubles and the maximum criminal sentence is three years in prison. Though Yngvesson and Hennessey (1975, 226) bristle at the description of cases heard by small-claims courts in the United States as simple, arguing that claims brought by the poor are no less complex than those with more resources, it is an appropriate description for the vast majority of cases that come through the Russian JP courts. The very fact that over two-thirds of civil cases are resolved without a hearing speaks to their mundane nature. My observations confirm this. Cases with high emotional stakes were the exception rather than the rule. But even these cases typically involved parties lacking the wherewithal to bribe judges. Thus, the very different incentive structure underlying JP courts explains why corruption is less of an issue.

This structure also helps explain why participants in the ABA Survey and the ILPP Project saw the JPs they had encountered as relatively independent. Unlike judges elsewhere in the Russian judicial system, they had no chairman or other immediate supervisor hovering over them. This may give JPs greater degrees of freedom, though the common goal of being promoted leaves them just as obsessed with maintaining a low reversal rate and avoiding violations of the statutory deadlines for resolving cases as are other judges. As I argued in the previous chapter, this may lead to a desire to avoid rocking the boat that risks undermining the interests of litigants.

On the other hand, JPs' desire to manage their dockets efficiently provides some unexpected benefits to litigants. Judges are slow to toss out cases, even when the cause of action is unclear or the parties are unsure of how to prove their claims. The standard practice of listing the documents to be produced at trial may stymie the transition toward adversarialism, but it provides a much-needed roadmap for litigants. Likewise, the tendency of JPs to provide minitutorials to parties on the substantive law at issue is helpful. These practices, which are often criticized as paternalistic, are a godsend for the fledgling litigants that populate the JP courts.

Such litigants often have difficulty finding their footing. Their way might be eased by engaging a lawyer, but few do so. The JP courts try to reach out to them in several ways. Their websites provide a wealth of information, as do the bulletin boards in courthouses. JPs hold regular open houses for the public and their staff has even greater availability. The unevenness of financial resources available means that JP courts in some regions are less able to serve the community. Not all potential litigants are able to take advantage of these resources, whether because of an inability to understand legal concepts or time constraints. But their availability speaks to a desire on the part of the Russian legal establishment to encourage greater use of the courts.

The positive assessment of the JP courts found in the two Russian studies and my own work may reflect the low expectations of Russians when it comes to the courts and, indeed, to state services more generally. If they buy into the stereotypes put forward by the media, then the reality may benefit by comparison, notwithstanding its flaws. This, in turn, may help explain the stealth demand for law.

RETHINKING THE ROLE OF LAW IN RUSSIA

I began the book by asking whether the existence of telephone law rendered law irrelevant for Russians in their everyday lives. Put more bluntly, does the fish rot from the head when it comes to law in Russia? My research offers an alternative to the common wisdom, as reflected in the media and the mainstream social science literature, which would not hesitate to answer in the affirmative. The window into the lives of ordinary Russians provided by my research shows that the answer to this question is more complicated. Russians are not as nihilistic as usually assumed, but neither are they free of skepticism when it comes to their legal system. Their attitudes and behavior vary depending on the situation. Their primary reservation about using the courts is not concern over telephone law, but dread of the inevitable red tape and emotional turmoil that accompany litigation. Their first reaction to difficulties—whether they arise with a neighbor, a stranger, or a state official—is to work out an informal solution. They contemplate turning to the courts only when such efforts prove unsuccessful.

Thus far, this capsule description of ordinary Russians' thinking about law sounds rather generic. It captures how people in many countries think about law. Few relish going to court; almost everywhere litigation tends to be a last-resort solution. Likewise, the inconsistency reflected in Russians attitudes and behavior toward law—sometimes openly hostile and sometimes welcoming—is not unique to Russia. This universality is worth dwelling on. Russia is often exoticized, both by Russians themselves and by outsiders. The long-standing debate about whether Russia is (or wants to be) part of the West or is sui generis, which began in the seventeenth century under Peter the Great and has never abated, reemerging in the post-Soviet era in the endless back-and-forth over Putin's goals, reflects Russia's schizophrenic identity (e.g., Lukin 2014; Rose and Munro 2008; Massie 1980; Walicki 1975; Riasanovsky 1952). A more interesting line of argument has begun to emerge, contending that Russia ought to be treated as a "normal" country (e.g., Shleifer and Treisman 2004). Although controversial (e.g., Dawisha 2014; Rosefielde 2005), my findings are consistent with this approach.

The focus group discussions show that Russians' willingness to mobilize law in the face of problems is colored by their relationships with disputants. The contrast of their behavior when dealing with friends and acquaintances versus strangers confirms the validity of the relational distance thesis in the Russian context. Few were keen to risk ostracism from their *pod"ezd* communities by suing to recover damages after accidental water leaks in their apartments. To do so would be to violate informal norms built up over generations. Those who opted to litigate tended to be newcomers to the *pod"ezd*. The focus group participants were quicker to invoke their legal rights in the wake of automobile accidents. For the most part, such incidents forced them to interact with strangers. Lacking any basis for trust, they turned to law to protect their interests. This changed only when those involved in the accident had a preexisting relationship that came with its own expectations or when the disputing parties subsequently built a relationship (usually through deliberate campaigns by perpetrators to earn the trust of their victims).

My contention that the Russian courts operate fairly normally when it comes to mundane cases is not the same as saying that they are perfect. Courts everywhere are flawed. Judges do not always live up to their obligations to be even-handed; cases sometimes get bogged down and take longer to come to a resolution than the parties would like. Unequal access to competent counsel and the know-how to put forward a strong defense can contribute to dissatisfaction with the courts, even in the most well-respected legal systems. It is hardly surprising that such shortcomings plague the Russian judicial system, which, as public opinion polls in Russia remind us, does not enjoy popular esteem. I have argued that a potent source for these sorts of problems lies not in the overpoliticization of the courts but in judges' devotion to observing the procedural rules.

This positivism has given rise to two consequences, both of which appear desirable at first glance; their perverse quality is apparent only on closer examination. The first is an obsession with moving cases through the process quickly in order to meet the statutory deadlines. The second is a strong preference for documentary rather than testimonial evidence, which saves judges from having to assess personal credibility. Both contribute to the efficiency of the Russian courts, which would seem to be a positive attribute. But this efficiency sometimes sacrifices justice as it races to resolve cases (Pomorski 2001). It also masks an unwillingness on the part of Russian judges to take risks, which, although fundamental to legal systems with a civil law legal heritage, can result in justice taking a back seat to judges' self-protective career concerns. Judges worry about protecting their track record for on-time resolution and for not being reversed because these are the key criteria of internal success. Less tangible but no less important is not antagonizing their bureaucratic superiors. Not rocking the boat, according to either institutional or interpersonal indicators, enhances a judge's prospects for advancement within the Russian judicial system.

The reactions of Russians to their experiences in the courts buttresses my conclusion that these courts operate fairly normally when it comes to mundane cases. Surveys of those who have used the JP courts to resolve their problems show that, even if dissatisfied with the outcome, they generally believe they were treated fairly (Hendley 2016). The openness to using the courts revealed by the reactions to the hypothetical scenarios laid out in the INDEM survey provide compelling evidence that courts are a viable alternative for those who lack experience in the courts. The inconsistency in the responses—both as to the hypothetical cases and as to real-life experiences—remind us of the existence of a multiplicity of views of law, both within individuals and society more generally. Much like their counterparts elsewhere, Russians' willingness to mobilize law depends on the circumstances.

A potent factor in their calculation is whether the case is, in fact, mundane. When a case involves parties of approximately the same station in life and the outcome is of interest only to those parties, then it can usually be categorized as routine. The parties can reasonably expect the case to be decided according to the written law. As a case edges away from the ordinary to the extraordinary, the risk of telephone law increases. The dividing line between these two categories of cases can be opaque. Many assume that a fear of having their legal rights and interests swept away by telephone law discourages ordinary Russians from going to court (Dawisha 2014, 340). My research reveals that Russians are remarkably savvy. Despite the fuzziness of the dividing line, particularly to outside observers, most Russians believe they can discern what might be subject to telephone law and studiously avoid bring such cases within the formal legal system. Any apprehension about using the courts stems more from a dread of the time and energy required than from a fear that the courts will sidestep the written law in service of the demands of outside puppet masters.

Categorizing Russia: "Rule of Law," "Rule by Law," or Neither?

The inherent dualism of the Russian legal system gives rise to vexing theoretical questions. How should we think about legal systems like Russia's in which law matters most, but not all, of the time? Some commentators dismiss Russia as a country where the mercurial use of law earns it the label of "rule by men" (Browder 2014; Dawisha 2014; Matthews 2010; Hedlund 2005), and others argue that "Putin has done much to restore the ideological mechanisms of the totalitarian system" (Gessen 2015). Yet the reliability of law in most cases makes this charge of fundamental lawlessness misplaced. When seeking to categorize countries where law has some relevance, the existing literature tends to divide them into those that have embraced the "rule of law," and those who have limited themselves to "rule by law" (Rajah 2012; Shapiro 2008; Barros 2003).[1]

Rule of Law

Over the past few decades, the "rule of law" has morphed from a concept of interest to a relatively small group of scholars to a political campaign slogan embraced by world leaders across the spectrum, including Putin. Rachel Kleinfeld (2006, 31) comments that, "like a product sold on late-night television, the rule of law is touted as able to accomplish everything from improving human rights to enabling economic growth to helping to win the war on terror." In the process, its meaning has been muddied. As Randall Peerenboom (2004, 1) concludes, "rule of law is an essentially contested concept."[2]

To oversimplify the state of the field for our purposes, we can distinguish between "thin" and "thick" versions of the rule of law (Chukwumerije 2009; Trebilcock and Daniels 2008; Tamanaha 2004). Proponents of the former focus on procedural protections, such as even-handed treatment, clarity and transparency of written law, and accessible legal institutions (Waldron 2011; Raz 1979; Fuller 1964; Dicey 1939). Advocates for the latter see these procedural guarantees as necessary but not sufficient for the rule of law (Sunstein 2001; Dworkin 1978). They argue that these become meaningful only when anchored by substantive

---

1. A separate category of "wicked legal systems" has emerged to analyze "societies in which law is used to enforce a morally repugnant moral ideology" (Graver 2015, 4). Countries typically placed in this group include Nazi Germany and South Africa under apartheid (Graver 2015; Dyzenhaus 2010). After its abandonment of communism, Russia lacks the sort of coherent ideology that would warrant its inclusion in this group.

2. Others who have bemoaned the fuzziness of the rule of law concept include Tamanaha (2004); Bingham (2010); Shklar (1987); Raz (1979).

political and economic rights. The menu of essential rights varies. Some emphasize the importance of basic human rights, whereas others stress the need to protect property rights.[3] At the heart of both conceptions of the rule of law is the need for law to be the same for all and to serve as a reliably stable foundation on which citizens can order their behavior.

The very existence of telephone law brings the rule of law into question in Russia. After all, cases decided by telephone law hinge on the identity of the parties and their resources, not on the law itself. The use of this extralegal device would seem to undermine the predictability and even-handedness of law. It helps explain why Russia invariably languishes near the bottom of indexes that purport to compare countries' commitment to the rule of law.[4] Not surprisingly, commentators on contemporary Russia, whether memoirists (Browder 2015; Romanova 2011), social scientists (Dawisha 2014; Hale 2015; Hedlund 2005), or journalists (Gessen 2016; Greene 2014; Judah 2013), almost automatically assert that Russia lacks the rule of law. Buttressing this concern with telephone law is a relentless emphasis on the shortcomings of Russia's legislation and regulation. This focus on the "supply" of law, with its inevitable flaws, gives short shrift to the "demand" for law (the day-to-day reality of how law works in practice).[5] In any event, the belief that Russia lacks the rule of law has become a routine part of the explanation for the country's devolution into some sort of authoritarianism.

This simplistic approach—a thumbs up or down on the rule of law—has contributed to the monolithic narrative of law in Russia. Though not disputing the challenge to the rule of law posed by telephone law, I argue that this zero-sum analysis has caused us to neglect the relevance of law to the everyday lives of Russians. Russians' thinking about law is messy. The preceding chapters document the extent to which individuals are capable of holding seemingly contradictory views. Their responses to a particular problem do not necessarily capture the totality of their legal consciousness. As we aggregate the experiences of Russians, damning the entire legal system because a small number of cases are plucked out for special treatment seems unwarranted.

By shifting our analytic approach, the results become immeasurably richer. Instead of treating the rule of law as an all-or-nothing concept, recognizing it as

---

3. Any effort to incorporate substance into the rule of law opens a Pandora's box of questions as to the cultural suitability of the content, giving rise to claims of ethnocentrism (e.g., Bellin 2014; Tay 2007).

4. Rule of law is one of the governance indicators measured by the World Bank (http://info.world bank.org/governance/wgi/index.aspx#home). Between 1996 and 2013, Russia was consistently placed in the second lowest category, along with countries such as Iran, Madagascar, and Bolivia, and below countries whose rule-of-law track record would seem to be worse than Russia's, such as China, Mexico, and Egypt. For a critique of the project, see Rajah (2015, 353–356) and Merry, Davis, and Kingsbury (2015).

5. I have elsewhere laid out the rationale for the importance of demand for law (Hendley 1997). Burlyuk (2015) extends the argument to Ukraine.

the sum of its parts allows us to isolate the elements and assess their relative presence or absence (Hendley 2006). Under this approach, the rule of law or, more accurately, its component parts, are conceptualized as existing along a spectrum. We might conclude that Russia has performed poorly in terms of the impartiality of its courts in politically sensitive cases. But in the same breath, we might find that Russia's efforts to ensure access to its courts have been stellar and conclude that it performs better in that regard.[6] Though the ultimate conclusion might be substantially the same, this more nuanced approach, which requires us to unpack the "rule of law" concept, yields key insights as to the relative functionality of key aspects of the Russian legal system. It also gives voice to the multitude of Russians who have been able to mobilize the law to good effect. Given that the rule of law is an ideal type that exists nowhere in its pure form, it stands to reason that perfect illustrations of the absence of the rule of law are likewise unlikely.

Rule by Law

If the rule of law fails to capture the fullness of Russian reality, then perhaps the Russian legal system is better conceptualized as operating according to "rule by law." This label is applied to polities in which law is valued but is not respected in all settings. Typically, the zones of enforcement and nonenforcement are clearly delineated. Sometimes it is state actors who escape the wrath of the law (Peerenboom 2004, 2). Alternatively, sometimes the differential treatment results from the substance of the case (Shapiro 2008). This brings to mind Singapore under Lee Kuan Yew and Egypt under Mubarak, where the courts religiously protected property rights but turned a blind eye to civil and political rights (Rajah 2012; Moustafa 2007; Jayasuriya 2001). Both regimes had a highly instrumental view of law, treating it as a tool helpful in achieving the goal of stimulating international investment.

Alternatively, if the reliability of judges is uncertain, then sometimes the task of handling potentially problematic cases is taken out of their hands by rewriting jurisdictional boundaries and creating special courts. Examples of this approach include Burma (Cheesman 2011) and Franco-era Spain (Toharia 1975). José Toharia argues that removing the politically sensitive cases from the dockets of the regular Spanish courts preserved their integrity and independence. By contrast, Nick Cheesman documents how the Burmese regime used special courts as a temporary way station while judges were indoctrinated to ensure their reliability,

---

6. The World Justice Project endeavors to break the rule of law down into its component parts. Although Russia's overall score still has it scraping the bottom of the barrel as eighty out of ninety-nine countries studied, it was above the average for the region and for other upper-middle-income countries when it came to resolving civil cases without unreasonable delays (Agrast, Botero, and Ponce 2014).

with the ultimate result being a thorough destruction of any semblance of independence in the courts. The commonality between all these examples of rule by law is that law is treated not as a universal set of rules applied to all equally, but as a cudgel to be used by the powerful to achieve their goals, which may or may not coincide with those of society more generally.

This distinction between rule of law and rule by law resonates in the Russian context. It harkens back to the discussion in chapter 1 of the substantive difference between the two words for law in Russian—*pravo* and *zakon*—that serve as roots for the Russian phrases associated with these broader concepts. When Gorbachev first called for the rule of law in what was then the Soviet Union, the phrase he used was *pravovoe gosudarstvo*, which has its root in the broader rights-based concept of law, *pravo*. Although the precise English translation for *pravovoe gosudarstvo* is debated (Berman 1992), what is not in question is its embrace of a concept of law that is applicable to all. In the words of Gorbachev at the Nineteenth Party Conference in 1988:

> The foremost salient feature of a state committed to the rule of law [*pravovoe gosudarstvo*] is that it effectively ensures the primacy of law. Not a single government body, official, collective, [Communist] Party organization, public association or individual can be exempt from abiding by the law. Just as all citizens have obligations to our state of the whole people, the state has obligations to its citizens. Their rights must be firmly protected against any abuse by the authorities (Gorbachev 1988, 65).

His vision was one of rule of law, not rule by law. And his commitment to respecting human rights suggests a thick version of the rule of law.

Despite spearheading a series of reforms that succeeded in removing the influence of the Communist Party from the judicial system and reinvigorating the legislative process, Gorbachev fell far short of achieving the stated ambition of one law for all (Barry 1992). His post-Soviet successors continued to pursue institutional reforms, such as the introduction of JP courts discussed in the preceding chapters, but tolerated and even took advantage of telephone law (Ledeneva 2013; Politkovskaya 2004; Solomon and Foglesong 2000). On paper, Russia's commitment to human rights was dramatically expanded with the introduction of a Constitutional Court empowered to engage in judicial review and the adoption of a new constitution in 1993. In practice, however, these rights often remained declarative, particularly as Putin's consolidation of power tamped down the willingness of the Constitutional Court to challenge executive and legislative actions (Trochev 2008). A law passed in late 2015 that gave the Constitutional Court the discretion to override decisions of the European Court of Human

Rights serves as potent evidence of the deterioration of Russia's commitment to human rights (O vnesenii 2015).

Reflecting this shift in the political winds, the rhetoric under Putin shifted away from *pravovoe gosudarstvo* to a phrase rooted in positivism, *gospodstvo zakona*. A literal translation of this phrase—supremacy of written law—reveals its qualitative difference from the Gorbachev-era term. It had been featured in some of the scholarly articles explaining Gorbachev's aims, but *gospodstvo zakona* was presented as a necessary but not sufficient condition for *pravovoe gosudarstvo* (Udartsev and Temirbekov 2015; Kudriavtsev and Lukasheva 1988). For Putin, however, the goal is *gospodstvo zakona*. It has been used as a rallying cry in the effort to bring regional legislation in line with federal law, part of Putin's "power vertical" campaign. Belying its literal meaning, it has come to be understood as giving officials a wide berth to decide when and to whom to apply the rules. It is more consistent with rule by law than rule of law.

Yet on closer examination, "rule by law" proves to be a misnomer for Russia. At the heart of this concept is a differential treatment for state institutions, state actors, and other elites at the hands of the legal system. In the classic examples of rule by law, such parties are routinely able to bypass the strictures of the law. This consistency is absent in the Russian case. State agencies are frequent litigants in civil cases, both as plaintiffs and defendants. Both in the JP and other courts, they are more likely to lose these cases than are private actors (Trochev 2012). Their victory in administrative cases involving private citizens, such as traffic violations and fines for noncompliance with various laws, is far from automatic. The same is true in the business setting. Economic actors' challenges to their treatment by tax and other regulatory agencies are frequently successful (Hendley 2002).

The chances of prevailing against the state in the criminal arena are much less. Although that basic fact is not unique to Russia, the deck seems to be particularly stacked against criminal defendants in Russia. The overall acquittal rate has traditionally been represented as less than 1 percent (Barry 2010; Paneyakh et al. 2010).[7] Scholars of the Russian criminal justice system do not attribute this sad reality to telephone law; most agree that politics rears its head in a very small number of criminal cases. Instead, they point to the institutional incentives embedded in the "stick" (*palochnaia*) system for assessing the work of officials

---

7. The validity of this statistic has become a matter of dispute among judicial officials and criminologists. In a January 2015 speech, the chairman of the Russian Supreme Court, Viacheslav Lebedev, argued for a new interpretation of the data that would dramatically increase the acquittal rate. In essence, Lebedev contends that, in calculating this rate, the denominator of the fraction ought to be increased to include everyone who comes in contact with the criminal justice system. Doing so would increase the percentage of those not convicted to over 20. Others strongly disagree with his interpretation (Gutsul and Siverkina 2015). For a comparative analysis of Russia's acquittal rate, see Solomon (2015).

(Paneyakh 2014; Solomon 1987). A case that does not end in a conviction is treated as a mistake and stains the records of those associated with the case, including the arresting officer, the investigator, the prosecutor, and the judge. A former Volgograd judge described acquittals as "a waste of time" and potentially risky.[8] The underlying goal of discouraging baseless prosecutions and encouraging officials to strive to do their best has gotten lost in the obsession with compiling impressive statistical records (McCarthy 2015). The resulting push to convict stands at odds with the stated commitment to uncovering the truth (which the Russian criminal justice system shares with others that evolved out of a civil law tradition) (Merryman and Pérez-Perdomo 2007). On a more practical level, it fuels the suspicions of many Russians that judges are in cahoots with prosecutors to ensure convictions. Although this may help explain the low levels of trust placed in the courts, it is not an indicator of rule by law. The forces at play in guaranteeing convictions have their source in mundane bureaucratic politics, not in a coordinated strategy to bypass the law.

The failure to create a separate hierarchy of courts to deal with categories of cases deemed to be problematic also attests to the ill fit between Russia and rule by law. Although the existence of special courts is not a sine qua non for rule by law, they serve as a powerful indicator of a regime's commitment to ensuring desired outcomes in troublesome cases.

Dualistic Law

If the Russian legal system is neither fish nor fowl—neither a neat fit for "rule of law" nor "rule by law"—then how should we think about it? My first instinct is to advocate for doing away with these categories. But the multibillion-dollar industry that has grown up around the rule of law, which includes doling out aid based on countries' progress toward this elusive goal and the proliferation of indexes that purport to measure it, renders this proposal quixotic at best. Perhaps a more practical first step would be to abandon the fiction that these are discrete categories. Putting any country's legal system under the microscope would reveal some elements that tend more toward "rule of law" and some that veer more to "rule by law." After all, both concepts are ideal types that are best seen as the aggregate of other ideal typical features. For rule of law, these would include due process and access to justice at a minimum, whereas for rule by law, administering justice so as to preference certain insider groups would be a key indicator. Each is

---

8. This former judge reports that in his fifteen years on the bench, he heard thousands of criminal cases, but issued only seven acquittals, five of which were later overturned (Kesby 2012).

best conceived as a set of layered continuums, one for each constituent element. Precisely how each of these elements should be weighted in a final assessment of the relative presence (or absence) of rule of law or rule by law is unclear, complicating the task of building comparative indexes. But maybe the time has come to step back from indexes and to encourage the sorts of thick descriptions that better capture the everyday role of law.

This book represents an effort to do just that with respect to Russia. What emerges is dualistic law: a legal system characterized by two basic realities. On the one hand, ordinary Russians are able to access their legal system with relative ease. Though not perfect, the courts resolve most disputes efficiently and, in doing so, judges are guided by the written law, both procedural and substantive. If assessed in terms of these mundane disputes, the Russian legal system would receive respectable scores on many elements of the rule of law. On the other hand, these routine cases, though representing the vast majority of cases brought to the courts, do not capture the full story of Russian law. Those who bring nonroutine disputes into the legal system (or have such cases brought against them) risk being swept into the shadowy world of telephone law. In such cases, the written law takes a back seat to brute power and any pretense of justice is absent. The more powerful party is able to dictate the outcome of the case. Sometimes this power is rooted in political connections; sometimes in economic resources. The upshot is the same—one side is able to sway the judge to sidestep the dictates of the law in favor of the selfish interests of that party.

In an ironic twist, both routine and nonroutine cases are marked by predictability. It is just that the sources of that much-desired stability are different. For the former category, it stems from the law itself, whereas for the latter category, it is rooted in power. Any instability within the Russian legal system originates in the lack of clarity between these two categories. Law may, but does not always, govern cases in the messy middle.

If Russia did not have a dualistic legal system, if Russia had a legal system that was more fully governed by either rule of law or rule by law, the lines between routine and nonroutine would be clear. If rule of law was more thoroughly embraced, then the need for this distinction would disappear. All cases would be handled according to the written law; the identity of those involved in the case and to whom they are connected would be of no consequence. Telephone law would have no place in such a system. If rule by law was more completely embedded, then the categories of cases to receive special treatment would be known to all, whether as a result of formal rules creating a separate set of courts to handle these cases or through informal norms.

Russians are not naïve; they are aware of the inherent dualism of their legal system and of the resulting lack of predictability. My conversations with the focus group participants indicate that they believe themselves capable of sorting between routine and nonroutine disputes. Certain cases are obviously not routine. Prominent examples include the prosecution of well-known Kremlin antagonists, such as Mikhail Khodorkovsky[9] or Alexei Navalny.[10] Ordinary Russians can become entangled in extraordinary cases when they challenge the Kremlin, as the members of Pussy Riot (Gessen 2014) as well as the defendants in the so-called *Bolotnoe* case (who demonstrated against the alleged electoral fraud in the 2012 May presidential election) were reminded (Lally 2014). Determining which cases might go down an extralegal track becomes more difficult when the measure of power shifts from politics to money.[11] Disputes between business partners over the ownership of their companies, which often involve manufactured evidence designed to hoodwink the criminal justice process, sometimes furthered by side payments to officials, have landed thousands of innocent businessmen in jail (e.g., Browder 2015; Pomerantsev 2014, 77–104; Romanova 2011; Iakovleva 2008).[12]

Not surprisingly, Russians shy away from the formal legal system when embroiled in what they perceive to be nonroutine disputes, preferring to do nothing. The focus group participants, as well as the many other Russians with whom I interacted in the course of researching this book, had no hesitation in delineating between mundane and extraordinary situations. Yet the dividing lines identified were far from identical, suggesting that the confidence with which they differentiated among types of disputes was misplaced. Because these boundaries reflect informal norms, they are constantly shifting. Like most of us, Russians yearn for stability and seek to impose it where it is lacking as a way of

---

9. At the time of his arrest in 2003, Khodorkovsky was one of the richest men in Russia. He was the chief executive officer of Yukos. For a full discussion of his story, see Kahn (2011) and Sakwa (2009) as well as the 2011 documentary *Khodorkovsky*, directed by Cyril Tuschi.

10. Navalny coined the phrase "the Party of Criminals and Thieves" (*Partiia zhulikov i vorov*) for Putin's United Russia Party. He came to public prominence as a blogger and emerged as one of the leaders of the public protests following the elections of 2011 and 2012.

11. Lambert-Mogliansky, Sonin, and Zhuravskaya (2007) document corruption in bankruptcy cases.

12. In an implicit recognition of the unfairness of many of these businessmen's convictions, Putin appointed Boris Titov to be a business ombudsman (Rubchenko 2012). Titov and other activists have worked to amend the criminal laws to lessen the likelihood of such convictions and to encourage presidential amnesties for these unjustly incarcerated businessmen. Several thousand have been released through amnesties, but many remain behind bars (Davies 2013). The hostilities sometimes continue, albeit in a different forum, after the businessmen are released from prison. For example, after Olga Romanova accused her husband's former business partner, Vladimir Sloutsker, of plotting to put him in prison and kill him, he successfully sued her for libel in a London court. The judge reasoned that, although her blog was based in Russia, it reached a substantial audience in the United Kingdom and her unsubstantiated charges had damaged Sloutsker's reputation (Glandin 2016; Cheston 2015).

minimizing uncertainty. Illustrating the inconsistency of responses, some said that they would avoid confrontations with individuals with more power or money, whereas others said they would not want to face off with state institutions. Yet some were entirely open to using the legal system to defend or advance their rights, even when it required them to punch above their weight. To be fair, this group was a distinct minority, often motivated by principle. Stopping to weigh the potential consequences, both formal and informal, of taking on political or economic elites was more typical. Because of the fuzziness of the dividing line between the routine and nonroutine, most Russians tend to overcorrect; they avoid mobilizing the law on their behalf if they perceive the slightest risk of being sucked into the shadowy world of telephone law. As the comments of the focus group participants indicate, this can sometimes be masked by fatalism. Rather than voicing a fear of having their dispute resolved without reference to the written law, they speak of the hopelessness of life in Russia, that trying to get anything accomplished is a fool's errand.

Recent history teaches that Russians have not always been able to read the signals correctly as they work out whether politics will trump law. Several of the most prominent Putin-era examples of politicized justice serve as cautionary tales. Earlier I described the Khodorkovsky case as being an obvious example of telephone law. Although this is apparent in hindsight and, in fact, many commentators assumed his fate was sealed at the moment of his arrest in 2003, Khodorkovsky himself was initially more sanguine about his prospects, saying "certainly I will prove that Russian entrepreneurs are capable of defending their rights but it won't be an easy task" (Mydans and Arvedlund 2003). Yuri Schmidt, one of his Russian lawyers, confirms this upbeat state of mind: "We, old hands at Soviet and Russian justice, knew that judges obeyed orders when the Kremlin took a personal interest in the case. But we were unable to convince our client."[13] Khodorkovsky's closing statement in his second trial for embezzling oil from his own company, by which time he had already served seven years, struck a different chord. He wrote: "Everything's been clear for a long time. Nobody is seriously waiting for an admission of guilt from me.... Neither does anybody believe that an acquittal in the Yukos case is possible in a Moscow court" (Khodorkovsky 2010). When we recall that oligarchs who had previously fallen into disfavor with the Kremlin, such as Vladimir Gusinsky and Boris Berezovsky, had been able to avoid prison (Treisman 2011), Khodorkovsky's optimism at the outset of his ordeal does not seem so Pollyannaish. Of course, the circumstances surrounding these

---

13. Quoted in Mendras (2012, 238). When reflecting on this period, Khodorkovsky recalls that "[a] few weeks after my arrest, I was informed that President Putin had decided I would 'slurp gruel' for eight years. Then it was hard to believe" (Khodorkovsky 2010).

earlier cases were quite different. Both men were willing to emigrate, whereas Khodorkovsky refused to leave Russia. Even so, he likely assumed that his insider status would protect him from the retribution of the Kremlin. Instead, with the shifting political winds, it made him a target. Even Khodorkovsky's release was handled in an extralegal manner, achieved through a presidential pardon on the eve of the Sochi Olympics.

Not everyone agreed on the implications of the Khodorkovsky case. Prominent opponents of Putin recognized that speaking openly put them at risk of a similar fate.[14] Among those whose lives were more anonymous, many saw his story as a lesson for oligarchs, but did not see its relevance to their lives. When authorities began to question the propriety of the business activities of Heritage Capital Management, an investment fund, most of those associated with the fund, including its leader, Bill Browder, an American businessman, as well as several of his Russian colleagues, saw the writing on the wall and left Russia. But Sergei Magnitsky, who worked for a law firm representing the fund, doggedly refused to leave Russia. In his memoir, Browder quotes Magnitsky as saying, "Why would anything happen? I haven't broken any laws. . . . There's no reason for me to leave. . . . The law will protect me. This isn't 1937" (Browder 2015, 253). Events proved Magnitsky wrong as he was arrested and imprisoned on charges of tax fraud. When he stubbornly refused to turn on his client, the conditions of his imprisonment grew increasingly worse. He became ill and died when authorities refused him treatment (Matthews 2010). The Kremlin has never acknowledged its culpability. Indeed, it doubled down on its persecution of Magnitsky and Browder, convicting both of tax evasion in a trial held after Magnitsky's death (and without Browder in attendance) (Browder 2015).

The fuzziness of the distinction between routine and nonroutine cases is facilitated by the persistence of vaguely worded legislation. This tactic was perfected under Stalin when authorities were able to manipulate the equivocal language of the notorious Article 58 of the Soviet Criminal Code to cover any sort of undesirable activity (Zile 1992, 294–296; Solzhenitsyn 1985). High levels of discretion for officials is a hallmark of a legal system lacking in the rule of law (Nonet and Selznick 2001). It undermines predictability. During the 1990s, an effort was made to improve the clarity of law. The introduction of judicial review seemed

---

14. For example, Navalny was not surprised when he was prosecuted for embezzlement in 2013. He described the charges as "absurd" (Krainova 2013). Many saw the case as an effort to discredit him, though it did little to dispel his popularity among his followers (Mackey 2013). What was unexpected about the case was not the conviction, but the suspended sentence. His brother, Oleg, a codefendant, was not so fortunate. He was imprisoned for a three-year term. Though Navalny saw this outcome as a "dirty trick," his brother was not surprised, commenting: "We absolutely knew that sooner or later this all would touch us. It is easy to influence a person through his family" (Herszenhorn 2014).

to provide an institutional guarantee against backsliding. But the emasculation of the Constitutional Court under Putin has left the Putin-controlled legislature free to craft statutes that provide plenty of wiggle room for authorities. The most prominent example is the law on extremism (O protivodeistvii 2002), which has been used against targets as varied as rank-and-file members of Jehovah's Witnesses and Eduard Limonov, the one-time leader of the now-banned National Bolshevik Party. Other examples include laws banning blasphemy and outlawing gay propaganda as well as laws that place limits on the activities of nongovernmental organizations (Flikke 2016). Sometimes those who perceive themselves to be at risk overcorrect. In the days leading up to the celebration of the seventieth anniversary of the victory over Germany in World War II, some Moscow booksellers overreacted to the Kremlin edict against swastikas or other Nazi symbols by removing from their shelves copies of *Maus*, the award-winning graphic novel by Art Spiegelman focused on the Holocaust, because it had a swastika on the cover (Roth 2015).

Only by moving away from the rule-of-law versus rule-by-law debate and conceptualizing Russian law as dualistic can the full range of legal narratives be captured. This framework focuses our attention on the two extremes while leaving room for a wide range of other outcomes. At one end, we find the multitude of ordinary disputes that are resolved by the written law. At the other end, we find the much smaller number but no less important set of cases that touch on sensitive political issues or involve economically powerful actors, for which the outcome is preordained and written law is largely irrelevant. And in between lies the unruly middle. What the future holds for law in Russia remains to be seen. Will the politicized cases swallow up the mundane? Or vice versa? Or will the uneasy truce between the two remain? What is likely to remain unchanged is the highly contextual nature of Russians' thinking about law. Their willingness to mobilize law on their own behalf will undoubtedly continue to depend on the circumstances of the dispute.

EMPIRICAL ANALYSES OF RUSSIAN LEGAL CONSCIOUSNESS

TABLE A.1 OLS regression model for legal compliant attitudes in the 2006 round of the RLMS-HSE

	MODEL 1 DEMOGRAPHIC	MODEL 2 GENERATIONS	MODEL 3 PERSONAL CONTROL	MODEL 4 COURTS	MODEL 5 DEMOCRACY	MODEL 6 ALL-INCLUSIVE
Women	0.475***	0.486***	0.448***	0.432***	0.384***	0.363***
	(0.0526)	(0.0527)	(0.0597)	(0.0514)	(0.0506)	(0.0518)
University graduates	0.460***	0.451***	0.421***	0.441***	0.436***	0.418***
	(0.0813)	(0.0814)	(0.0746)	(0.0793)	(0.0774)	(0.0780)
Age	-0.0819***		-0.0608***	-0.0661***	-0.0476***	
	(0.00935)		(0.00921)	(0.00921)	(0.00889)	
Age 2	0.000986***		0.000759***	0.000809***	0.000616***	
	(0.000103)		(0.000101)	(0.000102)	(9.74e-05)	
Divorced	-0.203**	-0.204**	-0.172**		-0.136	
	(0.0865)	(0.0869)	(0.0855)		(0.0832)	
Urban residents	-0.184**	-0.167**	-0.190***	-0.0984	6.52e-05	0.0276
	(0.0818)	(0.0820)	(0.0647)	(0.0803)	(0.0797)	(0.0803)
Russian	-0.209*	-0.185	-0.189**	-0.153	-0.121	-0.0823
	(0.118)	(0.120)	(0.0920)	(0.116)	(0.111)	(0.110)
Top quintile of income	-0.521**	-0.511**	-0.556***	-0.493**	-0.492**	-0.504**
	(0.209)	(0.211)	(0.161)	(0.202)	(0.196)	(0.202)
Employed	0.267***	0.180**	0.149**	0.277***	0.199***	0.0719
	(0.0732)	(0.0751)	(0.0716)	(0.0720)	(0.0691)	(0.0720)
Reference category:						
Stalin generation						
(born before 1940)						
Khrushchev generation		-0.765***				-0.506***
(born 1941–1950)		(0.129)				(0.123)
Brezhnev generation		-0.756***				-0.409***
(born 1951–1969)		(0.111)				(0.109)
Gorbachev generation		-0.956***				-0.651***
(born 1970–1976)		(0.131)				(0.128)

	(1)	(2)	(3)	(4)	(5)
Yeltsin generation (born 1977–1987)	-0.652***				-0.476***
	(0.114)				(0.110)
Putin generation (born after 1988)	-0.214				-0.435***
	(0.143)				(0.142)
Took on extra work		-0.193***			-0.148***
		(0.0513)			(0.0543)
Believe economic conditions will worsen in the coming year		-0.566***			-0.316***
		(0.112)			(0.115)
Nine point "ladder" of respect (from lowest to highest)		0.0488***			0.0532***
		(0.0178)			(0.0197)
Possible to trust most people		0.591***			0.277***
		(0.0791)			(0.0833)
Completely unsatisfied with current life		-0.131			0.0347
		(0.0995)			(0.109)
Use of courts in prior 5 years			-0.436***		-0.322***
			(0.0900)		(0.0865)
Trust courts			1.281***		0.299***
			(0.0736)		(0.0852)
Belief in democratic principles				0.0329***	0.0287***
				(0.00748)	(0.00752)
Trust in governmental institutions				1.094***	0.964***
				(0.0510)	(0.0597)
Supporter of term limits for elected officials				-0.403***	-0.378***
				(0.0792)	(0.0808)
Nine point "ladder" of rights (from lowest to highest)				0.0302	
				(0.0216)	
Constant	9.997***	10.15***	10.09***	6.456***	6.381***
	(0.159)	(0.224)	(0.204)	(0.314)	(0.299)
Observations	10,928	10,423	10,928	10,928	10,423
R-squared	0.020	0.032	0.057	0.100	0.101

Notes: Robust standard errors in parentheses. *** p<0.01, ** p<0.05, * p<0.1

TABLE A.2 OLS regression model for legal compliant attitudes in the 2012 round of the RLMS-HSE

	MODEL 1	MODEL 2	MODEL 3	MODEL 4	MODEL 5	MODEL 6
	DEMOGRAPHIC	GENERATIONS	PERSONAL CONTROL	COURTS	DEMOCRACY	ALL-INCLUSIVE
Women	0.532***	0.530***	0.500***	0.498***	0.494***	0.478***
	(0.0410)	(0.0410)	(0.0416)	(0.0400)	(0.0455)	(0.0458)
University graduates	0.587***	0.611***	0.579***	0.566***	0.458***	0.458***
	(0.0588)	(0.0596)	(0.0590)	(0.0572)	(0.0624)	(0.0633)
Age	-0.0495***		-0.0380***	-0.0391***	-0.0278***	
	(0.00714)		(0.00728)	(0.00679)	(0.00796)	
Age 2	0.000607***		0.000474***	0.000494***	0.000366***	
	(8.10e-05)		(8.26e-05)	(7.73e-05)	(9.08e-05)	
Divorced	-0.199***	-0.212***	-0.161***		-0.0658	
	(0.0621)	(0.0622)	(0.0621)		(0.0666)	
Urban residents	-0.492***	-0.493***	-0.492***	-0.359***	-0.229***	-0.276***
	(0.0638)	(0.0639)	(0.0645)	(0.0620)	(0.0684)	(0.0691)
Russian	-0.241***	-0.241***	-0.223***	-0.152*	-0.00899	-0.0170
	(0.0811)	(0.0813)	(0.0809)	(0.0785)	(0.0882)	(0.0869)
Top quintile of income	-0.170	-0.182	-0.222*	-0.0804	-0.00404	-0.0295
	(0.122)	(0.123)	(0.123)	(0.120)	(0.124)	(0.124)
Employed	0.0267	0.0485	-0.0631	0.0687	0.151**	0.0471
	(0.0560)	(0.0594)	(0.0573)	(0.0546)	(0.0610)	(0.0663)
Religious believers	0.243***	0.252***	0.204***	0.190***	0.184***	0.160***
	(0.0538)	(0.0538)	(0.0538)	(0.0527)	(0.0587)	(0.0586)
Reference category: Stalin generation (born before 1940)						
Khrushchev generation (born 1941–1950)		-0.424***				-0.274**
		(0.113)				(0.128)
Brezhnev generation (born 1951–1969)		-0.665***				-0.362***
		(0.0984)				(0.113)

	(1)	(2)	(3)	(4)	(5)	(6)
Gorbachev generation (born 1970–1976)	-0.673*** (0.115)					-0.335*** (0.128)
Yeltsin generation (born 1977–1987)	-0.705*** (0.104)					-0.382*** (0.119)
Putin generation (born after 1988)	-0.286*** (0.106)					-0.336*** (0.122)
Took on extra work			-0.367*** (0.0502)			-0.304*** (0.0520)
Believe economic conditions will worsen in the coming year			-0.300*** (0.0901)			0.0431 (0.0963)
Possible to trust most people			0.542*** (0.0671)			0.0765 (0.0745)
Nine point "ladder" of respect (from lowest to highest)			0.0473*** (0.0171)			0.0251 (0.0189)
Completely unsatisfied with current life			-0.614*** (0.116)			-0.247* (0.134)
Use of courts in prior 5 years				-0.676*** (0.0741)		-0.492*** (0.0830)
Trust courts				1.349*** (0.0587)		0.159** (0.0806)
Belief in democratic principles					0.0172*** (0.00661)	0.0182*** (0.00661)
Trust in governmental institutions					1.046*** (0.0363)	0.943*** (0.0449)
Nine point "ladder" of rights (from lowest to highest)					-0.0359* (0.0192)	
Constant	10.65*** (0.152)	10.36*** (0.120)	10.27*** (0.181)	10.01*** (0.149)	6.590*** (0.284)	6.639*** (0.281)
Observations	16,820	16,820	16,280	16,820	12,766	12,612
R-squared	0.031	0.031	0.043	0.072	0.129	0.136

Notes: Robust standard errors in parentheses. *** p<0.01, ** p<0.05, * p<0.1

TABLE A.3 Logistic regression estimated odds ratios for change in attitude about law from legal nihilism to law abiding between the 2006 and 2012 rounds of the RLMS-HSE[1]

	MODEL 1	MODEL 2
	DEMOGRAPHIC	ALL-INCLUSIVE
Stalin generation	1.820*	2.096**
(born before 1940)	(0.599)	(0.782)
Khrushchev generation	2.077**	2.371**
(born 1941–1950)	(0.686)	(0.886)
Brezhnev generation	1.554	1.8[2]
(born 1951–1969)	(0.492)	(0.647)
Gorbachev generation	1.756*	2.019*
(born 1970–1976)	(0.593)	(0.765)
Yeltsin generation	1.585	1.832*
(born 1977–1987)	(0.510)	(0.665)
Reference category:		
Putin generation		
(born after 1988)		
Russian	0.564***	0.605***
	(0.102)	(0.108)
Employed	0.798*	0.841
	(0.0978)	(0.108)
Belief in democratic principles increased		0.911
in 2012 as compared with 2006		(0.160)
Trust in governmental institutions		1.445**
increased in 2012 as compared with		(0.256)
2006		
Went to court between 2007 and 2012		1.095
		(0.217)
Divorced at any time	1.205*	
	(0.135)	
Divorced between 2006 and 2012		1.24
		(0.198)
Trust in courts in 2012 only		1.404**
		(0.205)
Felt more respected in 2012 than in		1.658***
2006		(0.184)
More satisfied with economic conditions		1.441***
in 2012 as compared with 2006		(0.197)
Constant	0.0990***	0.0577***
	(0.0348)	(0.0223)
Observations	5,857	5,504
Pseudo R2	0.0095	0.0226

Notes: Robust standard errors in parentheses. *** p<0.01, ** p<0.05, * p<0.1

[1] Results measuring gender, urban residence, income, education, and religiosity have not been reported in this table because they were not significant.

[2] On the cusp of statistical significance (p=0.102).

TABLE A.4 Logistic regression estimated odds ratios for change in attitude about law from law abiding to legal nihilism between the 2006 and 2012 rounds of the RLMS-HSE[1]

	MODEL 1	MODEL 2	MODEL 3
	DEMOGRAPHIC	COURTS	ALL-INCLUSIVE
Had extra job in 2012 only			1.418*
			(0.262)
Felt less respected in 2012 than in 2006			0.732**
			(0.113)
Religious believers	0.735**	0.743**	0.724**
	(0.0914)	(0.0927)	(0.0937)
Russian	0.659**	0.658**	0.658**
	(0.127)	(0.126)	(0.128)
Went to court between 2007 and 2012		1.408*	1.362
		(0.279)	(0.275)
Trust in courts in 2012 only		0.693**	0.753
		(0.127)	(0.142)
Belief in democratic principles decreased in 2012 as compared with 2006			1.417**
			(0.249)
Trust in governmental institutions decreased in 2012 as compared with 2006			1.674***
			(0.313)
Constant	0.116***	0.119***	0.104***
	(0.0296)	(0.0305)	(0.0286)
Observations	5,857	5,857	5,504
Pseudo R2	0.007	0.0095	0.0179

Notes: Robust standard errors in parentheses. *** $p<0.01$, ** $p<0.05$, * $p<0.1$

[1] Results measuring gender, marital status, age, urban residence, income, and education have been not been reported in the table because they were not significant.

TABLE A.5 Multinomial logit estimated odds ratios for responses to hypothetical 1 in 2008 INDEM survey (illegal workplace reprimand)[1]

	DO NOTHING	SELF HELP	EXIT
Women	0.809	0.809	1.019
	(0.155)	(0.132)	(0.228)
High school graduate	1.309	0.734	0.461
	(0.453)	(0.232)	(0.242)
Employed	1.177	1.109	1.267
	(0.259)	(0.205)	(0.328)
Russian	1.450	0.959	1.215
	(0.368)	(0.196)	(0.362)
Rural resident	1.436	1.229	1.121
	(0.338)	(0.248)	(0.327)
Resident of large city	1.275	1.111	1.611*
	(0.319)	(0.240)	(0.447)

(Continued)

TABLE A.5 (Continued)

	DO NOTHING	SELF HELP	EXIT
Rich	0.652*	0.868	0.632*
	(0.155)	(0.170)	(0.173)
Stalin generation	0.735	0.426**	0.437
(born before 1940)	(0.318)	(0.158)	(0.249)
Khrushchev generation	0.917	0.511**	0.500*
(born 1941–1950)	(0.309)	(0.145)	(0.208)
Brezhnev generation	1.187	0.539***	0.723
(born 1951–1969)	(0.287)	(0.108)	(0.196)
Gorbachev generation	1.153	0.584**	0.703
(born 1970–1976)	(0.357)	(0.152)	(0.247)
Reference group:			
Yeltsin and Putin generations			
(born after 1977)			
Initiated a claim in court	0.796	0.923	0.906
	(0.188)	(0.184)	(0.247)
No plans to go to court in the future	2.795***	1.727	2.151*
	(0.975)	(0.575)	(0.849)
Opted for self-help in 2nd hypothetical	2.779**	3.870***	1.752
	(1.161)	(1.431)	(0.776)
Opted for exit in 2nd hypothetical	2.373**	1.383	2.038*
	(0.840)	(0.434)	(0.752)
Opted for court in 2nd hypothetical	0.183***	0.145***	0.0638***
	(0.0596)	(0.0392)	(0.0245)
Believes that Russian courts are	0.837	0.947	0.448***
independent	(0.176)	(0.166)	(0.124)
Completely trust JP courts	0.788	0.625**	0.383***
	(0.175)	(0.118)	(0.116)
Nihilist	0.918	0.914*	0.935
	(0.0523)	(0.0446)	(0.0623)
No belief in inalienable human rights	0.576**	0.7312	0.560*
	(0.148)	(0.154)	(0.169)
Disagrees that written laws are always fair	1.015	1.103	1.012
	(0.220)	(0.203)	(0.249)
Interested in information about courts	0.923	0.970	0.747
	(0.213)	(0.185)	(0.216)
Constant	1.357	8.946***	2.070
	(0.749)	(4.164)	(1.290)
Pseudo R2	0.1421	0.1421	0.1421
Observations	1,414	1,414	1,414

Notes: Robust standard errors in parentheses. *** p<0.01, ** p<0.05, * p<0.1

[1] Reference category is going to court.
[2] On the cusp of statistical significance (p=0.136).

TABLE A.6 Multinomial logit estimated odds ratios for responses to hypothetical 2 in 2008 INDEM survey (child denied admission to neighborhood school)[1]

	SELF HELP	EXIT
Women	0.951	1.166
	(0.150)	(0.168)
High school graduate	0.659	0.914
	(0.221)	(0.252)

	SELF HELP	EXIT
Employed	1.103	1.177
	(0.201)	(0.195)
Russian	0.501***	0.800
	(0.0986)	(0.153)
Rural resident	0.727	0.663**
	(0.142)	(0.117)
Resident of large city	1.347	1.093
	(0.266)	(0.200)
Rich	1.077	0.976
	(0.205)	(0.173)
Stalin generation	1.335	1.842*
(born before 1940)	(0.488)	(0.583)
Khrushchev generation	1.418	1.925***
(born 1941–1950)	(0.408)	(0.487)
Brezhnev generation	2.064***	2.226***
(born 1951–1969)	(0.400)	(0.397)
Gorbachev generation	1.490	1.689**
(born 1970–1976)	(0.372)	(0.385)
Reference group:		
Yeltsin and Putin generations		
(born after 1977)		
Initiated a claim in court	0.818	0.820
	(0.161)	(0.145)
No plans to go to court in the future	2.939***	1.972***
	(0.775)	(0.501)
Opted for court in 1st hypothetical	0.135***	0.175***
	(0.0436)	(0.0421)
Opted to do nothing in 1st hypothetical	1.853**	2.057***
	(0.509)	(0.474)
Opted for exit in 1st hypothetical	2.834***	4.992***
	(0.963)	(1.423)
Opted for self-help in 1st hypothetical	3.101***	1.626**
	(0.705)	(0.323)
Believes that Russian courts are	0.673**	0.698**
independent	(0.123)	(0.114)
Complete trust in courts of general	1.157	0.668*
jurisdiction	(0.266)	(0.151)
Nihilist	0.927[2]	0.871***
	(0.0443)	(0.0381)
No belief in inalienable human rights	0.956	0.926
	(0.202)	(0.179)
Disagrees that written laws are always	1.665***	1.175
fair	(0.293)	(0.195)
Interested in information about courts	0.816	0.690**
	(0.156)	(0.121)
Constant	0.569	0.649
	(0.242)	(0.252)
Pseudo R2	0.1453	0.1453
Observations	1,571	1,571

Notes: Robust standard errors in parentheses. *** p<0.01, ** p<0.05, * p<0.1

[1] Reference category is going to court.

[2] On the cusp of statistical significance (p=0.112).

TABLE A.7 Logistic regression estimated odds ratios for use of courts by respondents in 2008 INDEM survey

	MODEL 1	MODEL 2	MODEL 3	MODEL 4
	DEMOGRAPHIC	GENERATION	COURTS AND LAW	ALL-INCLUSIVE
Would go to court if rights violated			5.970*** (0.816)	5.964*** (0.818)
Trust in courts based on personal experience			2.160*** (0.326)	2.142*** (0.324)
Distrust of courts based on personal experience			1.892*** (0.253)	1.881*** (0.252)
Believes courts treat rich better			1.648*** (0.242)	1.642*** (0.241)
No plans to go to court in the future			0.919 (0.178)	0.891 (0.173)
Attitude toward law grounded in *pravo* (not *zakon*)			1.103** (0.0530)	1.103** (0.0529)
Women	1.435*** (0.154)	1.436*** (0.155)	1.431*** (0.169)	1.443*** (0.171)
Employed	1.320** (0.166)	1.342** (0.172)	1.359** (0.188)	1.366** (0.192)
Age	1.103*** (0.0237)		1.120*** (0.0268)	
Age 2	0.999*** (0.000236)		0.999*** (0.000263)	
Stalin generation (born before 1940)		1.965*** (0.469)		2.144*** (0.565)
Khrushchev generation (born 1941–1950)		1.963*** (0.381)		2.328*** (0.495)
Brezhnev generation (born 1951–1969)		1.817*** (0.261)		2.108*** (0.332)
Gorbachev generation (born 1970–1976)		1.571** (0.285)		1.810*** (0.361)
Reference group: Yeltsin generation (born 1977–1987)				
Putin generation (born after 1988)		0.235*** (0.123)		0.254** (0.137)
Russian	1.114 (0.159)	1.108 (0.158)	1.119 (0.174)	1.112 (0.173)
High school graduate	1.139 (0.224)	1.044 (0.207)	1.196 (0.261)	1.133 (0.248)
Divorced	3.768*** (0.536)	3.807*** (0.542)	3.751*** (0.600)	3.779*** (0.604)
Rural resident	0.768** (0.0998)	0.781* (0.101)	0.860 (0.123)	0.877 (0.126)
Resident of large city	0.864 (0.121)	0.869 (0.122)	0.930 (0.143)	0.931 (0.143)

	MODEL 1	MODEL 2	MODEL 3	MODEL 4
	DEMOGRAPHIC	GENERATION	COURTS AND LAW	ALL-INCLUSIVE
Rich	1.194	1.202	1.132	1.144
	(0.163)	(0.164)	(0.169)	(0.172)
Opted for court in 1st hypothetical			1.037	1.027
			(0.192)	(0.190)
Opted to do nothing in 1st hypothetical			0.698*	0.702*
			(0.139)	(0.139)
Opted for exit in 1st hypothetical			0.964	0.964
			(0.163)	(0.163)
Opted for self-help in 1st hypothetical			0.765	0.777
			(0.174)	(0.176)
Opted for court in 2nd hypothetical			0.932	0.932
			(0.166)	(0.166)
Opted for self-help in 2nd hypothetical			0.806	0.805
			(0.163)	(0.162)
Opted for exit in 2nd hypothetical			0.822	0.823
			(0.152)	(0.152)
Constant	0.00787***	0.0575***	0.00159***	0.0153***
	(0.00392)	(0.0153)	(0.000952)	(0.00577)
Pseudo R2	0.0716	0.0736	0.1829	0.1841
Observations	2,709	2,709	2,568	2,568

Notes: Robust standard errors in parentheses. *** p<0.01, ** p<0.05, * p<0.1

BACKGROUND INFORMATION ON FOCUS GROUP PARTICIPANTS

NAME	AGE	RESIDENCE	EDUCATION	OCCUPATION	COURT EXPERIENCE?
Aleksandra	51	Tomsk	University degree	Chief specialist	No
Anastasia	44	Saratov	University degree	Professor	No
Anatolii	51	Tomsk	University degree	Manager	No
Angelina	22	Shumerlia	High school degree	Hospital attendant	No
Anna	40	Moscow	University degree	Real estate agent	Yes
Anton	31	Saratov	University degree	Geologist	No
Ariadna	58	Shumerlia	High school degree	Insurance agent	Yes
Arkadii	29	Kushchevskaia	University degree	Psychologist	Yes
Berta	50	Tomsk	University degree	Accountant	No
Boris	24	Saratov	High School degree	Security guard	No
David	25	Kushchevskaia	High School degree	Security guard	Yes
Dmitrii	21	Moscow	University student	Part-time manager	Yes
Elena	35	Moscow	University degree	Office manager	No
Elvira	44	Saratov	University degree	State official	Yes
Emilia	38	Tomsk	High school degree	Senior cashier	Yes
Fatima	25	Moscow	University student	Charitable work	Yes
Feona	52	Shumerlia	High school degree	Chief accountant	Yes
Filipp	22	Saratov	University degree	Salesman	No
Galina	56	Moscow	University degree	College teacher	Yes
Gennadi	61	Tomsk	University degree	Department head in factory	Yes
Gloria	51	Tomsk	High school degree	Tutor	No
Ida	40	Moscow	University degree	Accountant	No
Irina	51	Saratov	University degree	Doctor	Yes
Karina	42	Saratov	University degree	Doctor	Yes
Katia	20	Saratov	Ongoing university	Student	Yes

NAME	AGE	RESIDENCE	EDUCATION	OCCUPATION	COURT EXPERIENCE?
Khristina	21	Tomsk	Incomplete high school	Packer	No
Kira	52	Tomsk	High school degree	Bookkeeper	Yes
Klavdia	35	Shumerlia	High school degree	Inspector	Yes
Liubov	56	Moscow	University degree	Accountant	Yes
Marfa	55	Shumerlia	High school degree	Assembly line worker	Yes
Marina	58	Moscow	University degree	Economist	Yes
Miroslava	40	Shumerlia	High school degree	Seamstress	Yes
Nikolai	42	Saratov	University degree	Manager	No
Oksana	52	Kushchevskaia	8th-grade education	Factory worker	No
Oleg	55	Tomsk	High school degree	Entrepreneur	No
Polina	25	Moscow	University degree	Social worker	No
Regina	55	Shumerlia	High school degree	Cleaning person	No
Rimma	25	Tomsk	University degree	Factory worker	Yes
Sara	45	Saratov	University degree	Manager	No
Simon	35	Shumerlia	High school degree	Unemployed	Yes
Susanna	53	Tomsk	High school degree	Bookkeeper	Yes
Svetlana	38	Saratov	University degree	Doctor	No
Timofei	25	Moscow	University degree	Lawyer	No
Vadim	26	Saratov	University degree	Entrepreneur	Yes
Varvara	27	Saratov	University degree	Graduate student	No
Veronika	58	Shumerlia	High school degree	Railroad station manager	Yes
Viktor	33	Saratov	University degree	Doctor	Yes
Viktoria	44	Tomsk	University degree	Teacher	No
Vladimir	51	Moscow	Incomplete university	Mechanic	No
Vladislava	35	Moscow	University degree	Economist	No
Zina	37	Kushchevskaia	University degree	Doctor	Yes
Zinaida	30	Saratov	University degree	Doctor	Yes

Appendix C

RESULTS FROM THE ANALYSIS
OF THE ABA SURVEY

TABLE C.1 Descriptive statistics from the ABA Survey for demographic and other variables used in the regression analysis of experience with the JP courts (reported as percentages of the total unweighted sample)

	RESPONDENT VIEWED JP COURT EXPERIENCE AS SUCCESSFUL	RESPONDENT VIEWED JP COURT EXPERIENCE AS UNSUCCESSFUL	FULL SAMPLE	CHI VALUE
Full sample	33.5	66.5		
Age:				
Under 34	34.9	65.1	35.8	n.s.
35–44	33.7	66.3	25.5	n.s.
45–54	31.7	68.3	20.5	n.s.
Over 55	32.6	67.4	18.7	n.s.
Gender:				
Men	28.4	71.6	39	
Women	36.7	63.3	61	$p>0.01$
Location:				
Nizhni Novgorod oblast	47	53	33.3	
Leningrad oblast	23.3	76.7	33.3	
Rostov oblast	30.2	69.8	33.3	$p>0.001$
Education:				
No university degree	33.3	68.7	55.9	
University degree	36.2	63.8	44.2	n.s.
Work status:				
Employed as unskilled laborer	22	78	18.2	
Employment other than as unskilled laborer or unemployed	36	64	81.8	$p>0.001$

	RESPONDENT VIEWED JP COURT EXPERIENCE AS SUCCESSFUL	RESPONDENT VIEWED JP COURT EXPERIENCE AS UNSUCCESSFUL	FULL SAMPLE	CHI VALUE
Legal representation:				
Consulted with *advokat*	32.5	67.5	28.2	
Did not consult with *advokat*	33.9	66.1	71.8	n.s.
Legal nihilism:				
Embraces legal nihilism	29.1	70.9	24.3	
Not a legal nihilist	34.9	65.1	77.7	p>0.10
Prepared to go to JP court in the future:				
Yes	41.7	58.3	46	
No	26.5	73.5	54	p>0.001
Knowledgeable about JP courts:				
Well-informed	32.6	39.6	12.8	
Not knowledgeable	67.4	60.4	87.2	n.s.
Plans to appeal case:				
Yes	5.7	94.3	11.7	
No	37.2	62.8	88.3	p>0.001
Views of even-handedness of JP courts:				
See courts as biased	15.6	84.4	11.4	
See courts as unbiased	36.4	63.6	88.6	p>0.001
Views of political independence of JP courts:				
See courts as dependent	34.8	65.2	9.7	
See courts as independent	21.6	78.4	90.3	p>.005
Corruption:				
Has personally bribed JP or friends/family have bribed JP	66.1	68.9	13.7	
Not open to bribery	33.9	31.1	86.3	n.s.

TABLE C.2 Logistic regression estimated odds ratios for respondents' assessment of their experience at the JP courts as successful in the ABA Survey[1]

	VIEW JP COURT EXPERIENCE AS COMPLETELY SUCCESSFUL
	ODDS RATIO (STANDARD DEVIATION)
(Age under 35 is the reference category)	
Age 35–44	0.890
	(0.150)
Age 45–54	0.929
	(0.170)
Age over 55	0.840
	(0.160)
Women	1.468***
	(0.201)

	VIEW JP COURT EXPERIENCE AS COMPLETELY SUCCESSFUL
	ODDS RATIO (STANDARD DEVIATION)
University graduate	0.915
	(0.131)
Employed as unskilled laborer	0.517***
	(0.104)
Consulted *advokat*	0.894
	(0.131)
Legal nihilist	0.768*
	(0.120)
Prepared to go to JP court in future	1.897***
	(0.252)
Knowledgeable about JP courts	1.355
	(0.267)
Plans to appeal case	0.104***
	(0.0392)
Skeptical of even-handedness of courts	0.376***
	(0.0981)
Constant	0.333***
	(0.0915)
Pseudo R2	0.945
Observations	1200

*** p<0.001, ** p<0.01, * p<0.05

[1] Owing to fears of a selection bias, regional variables have been left out of the regression.

Russian Legal Sources

CODES[1]

Grazhdanskii Kodeks RSFSR. 1922. (GK 1922). http://civil-law.narod.ru/wist/gk22/
Grazhdanskii Kodeks RSFSR. 1964. (GK 1964). http://www.tarasei.narod.ru/kodeks/zx4.txt
Grazhdanskii Kodeks Rossiiskoi Federatsii, chast pervaia. 1994. (GK RF part 1). http://
    www.consultant.ru/document/cons_doc_LAW_5142/
Grazhdanskii Kodeks Rossiiskoi Federatsii, chast vtoraia. 1995. (GK RF part 2). http://
    www.consultant.ru/document/cons_doc_LAW_9027/
Grazhdanskii Protsessual'nyi Kodeks Rossiiskoi Federatsii. 2002. (GPK RF). http://www.
    consultant.ru/document/cons_doc_LAW_39570/
Kodeks Rossiiskoi Federatsii ob administrativnykh proavonarusheniiakh. 2001. (KoAP).
    http://www.consultant.ru/document/cons_doc_LAW_34661/
Semeinyi Kodeks Rossiiskoi Federatsii. 1995. (SK RF). http://www.consultant.ru/
    document/cons_doc_LAW_8982/
Ugolovnyi Kodeks Rossiiskoi Federatsii. 1995. (UK RF). http://www.consultant.ru/
    document/cons_doc_LAW_10699/
Ugolovno-Protsessual'nyi Kodeks Rossiiskoi Federatsii. 2001. (UPK RF). http://www.
    consultant.ru/document/cons_doc_LAW_34481/

LAWS AND GOVERNMENTAL DECREES

"O bezplatnoi iuridicheskoi pomoshchi v Rossiiskoi Federatsii." 2011. Federal'nyi zakon
    ot 21 noiabria 2011 g. No. 324-FZ. *Rossiiskaia gazeta*, November 23. http://www.
    rg.ru/2011/11/23/yurpomosh-dok.html
"Ob obespechenii dostupa k informatsii o deiatel'nosti sudov v Rossiiskoi Federatsii."
    2009. Federal'nyi zakon ot 9 fevralia 2009 g. No. 8-FZ. *Rossiiskaia gazeta*.
    February 13. http://www.rg.ru/2009/02/13/dostup-dok.html
"Ob obiazatel'nom strakhovanii grazhdanskoi otvetstvennosti vladel'tsev transportnykh
    stredstv (OSAGO)." 2002. Federal'nyi zakon ot 25 aprelia 2002 g. No. 40-FZ.
    http://www.consultant.ru/document/cons_doc_LAW_36528/
"Ob utverzhdenii pravil obiazatel'nogo strakhovaniia grazhdanskoi otvetstvennosti
    vladeltsev transportnykh sredstv." 2003. Postanovlenie Pravitel'stva Rossiiskoi
    Federatsii ot 7 maia 2003 g., No. 263. *Rossiiskaia gazeta*. May 13. http://www.
    rg.ru/2003/05/13/osago-dok.html.
"O mirovykh sud'iakh v Rossiiskoi Federatsii." 1998. Federal'nyi zakon ot 17 dekabria
    1998 g. No. 188-FZ. http://www.consultant.ru/document/cons_doc_LAW_21335/
"O poriadke i razmere vozmeshcheniia protsessual'nykh isderzhek, sviazannykh
    s proizvodstvom po ugolovnomu delu, izderzhek v sviazi s rassmotreniem
    grazhdanskogo dela, a takzhe raskhodov v sviazi s vypolneniem trebovanii
    Konstitutsionnogo Suda Rossiiskoi Federatsii i o priznanii utrativshimi silu

---

1. The dates provided for these codes reflect when they were originally enacted. Most have subsequently been amended. The website referenced includes all of these amendments.

nekotorykh aktov Soveta Ministrov RSFSR i Pravitel'stva Rossiiskoi Federatsii."
2012. Postanovlenie Pravitel'stva Rossiiskoi Federatsii ot 1 dekabria 2012 g.
No. 1240. *Rossiiskaia gazeta*, December 7. http://www.rg.ru/2012/12/07/izderzhki-
dok.html.

"O protivodeistvii ekstremistckoi deiatel'nosti." 2002. Federal'nyi zakon ot 25 iulia 2002
g. No. 114-FZ. http://base.garant.ru/12127578/.

"O statuse sudei v Rossiiskoi Federatsii." 1992. Zakon ot 26 iunia 1992 g. No. 3132–1.
http://www.consultant.ru/document/cons_doc_LAW_648/.

"O vnesenii izmenenii v Federal'nyi konstitutsionnyi zakon 'O Konstitutsionnom Sude
Rossiiskoi Federatsii.'" 2015. Federal'nyi zakon ot 14 dekabria 2015 g. No. 7-FKZ.
Rossiiskaia gazeta, December 16. http://www.rg.ru/2015/12/15/ks–site–dok.html.

"O vnesenii izmenenii v stat'iu 3 Federal'nogo zakona 'O mirovikh sud'iakh v Rossiiskoi
Federatsii' i stat'iu 23 Grazhdanskogo protsessual'nogo kodeksa Rossiiskoi
Federatsii." 2010. Federal'nyi zakon ot 11 fevralia 2010 g. No. 6-FZ. *Rossiiskaia
gazeta*, February 15. http://www.rg.ru/2010/02/15/miroviye-dok.html.

Proekt federal'nogo zakona No. 216115–6. 2013. "O vnesenii izmenenii v stat'iu 26.2
Kodeksa Rossiiskoi Federatsii ob administrativnykh pravonarusheniiakh,"
February 8. http://base.consultant.ru/cons/cgi/online.cgi?req=doc;base=P
RJ;n=102312;fld=134;from=111441–7;rnd=184768.6264891819239591;;
ts=01847683502102051631419.

JUDICIAL DECISIONS AND DECREES

Iliasov v. Lapin. 2004. Delo No. 2–299. Leninskii raionnyi sud, Saratov, April 15. http://
sud-praktika.narod.ru/12.vred/Lapin-Ilasov.doc.

Opredelenie No. 446-O Konstitutsionnogo Suda Rossiiskoi Federatsii. 2003. http://
lawru.info/base17/part7/d17ru7217.htm.

Postanovlenie No. 1 Plenuma Verkhovnogo Suda Rossiiskoi Federatsii. 2010. "O
premenenii sudami grazhdanskogo zakonodatel'stva, reguliruiushchego
otnosheniia po obiazatel'stvam vsledstvie prichineniia vreda zhizni ili zdorov'iu
grazhdanina." *Rossiiskaia gazeta*, February 5. http://www.rg.ru/2010/02/05/
sud-dok.html.

Postanovlenie No. 3 Plenuma Verkhovnogo Suda Rossiiskoi Federatsii. 2012. "O vnesenii
izmenenii v nekotorye postanovleniia Plenuma Verkhovnogo Suda Rossiiskoi
Federatsii." *Biulleten Verkhovnogo Suda Rossiiskoi Federatsii* (4).

Codes of Professional Ethics

Kodeks professional'noi etiki advokata. 2003. Adopted by the All-Russian Congress of
Advokaty. January 31. http://www.apmo.ru/?show=codex&PHPSESSID=crmf41g
re5qbmrdl2jgct42sj6.

Kodeks sudeiskoi etiki. 2012. Adopted by the All-Russian Congress of Judges.
December 19. http://www.ksrf.ru/ru/Info/LegalBases/Kodeks/Pages/default.aspx.

References

Agrast, Mark David, Juan Carlos Botero, and Alejandro Ponce. 2014. *The World Justice Project: Rule of Law Index: 2014*. Washington, DC: World Justice Project. http://worldjusticeproject.org/sites/default/files/files/wjp_rule_of_law_index_2014_report.pdf.

Aistrup, Joseph A., and Shala Mills Bannister. 1999. "How Previous Court Experience Influences Evaluations of the Kansas State Court System." *Court Review* 36 (3): 32–34.

Albiston, Catherine. 1999. "The Rule of Law and the Litigation Process: The Paradox of Losing by Winning." *Law & Society Review* 33 (4): 869–910.

———. 2005. "Bargaining in the Shadow of Social Institutions: Competing Discourses and Social Change in Workplace Mobilization of Civil Rights." *Law & Society Review* 39 (1): 11–50.

Alexeev, Michael. 2008. "The Effect of Housing Allocation on Social Inequality: A Soviet Perspective." *Journal of Comparative Economics* 12 (2): 228–234.

Alexopoulos, Golfo. 1997. "Exposing Illegality and Oneself: Complaint and Risk in Stalin's Russia." In Solomon, *Reforming Justice in Russia, 1864–1996*, 168–189.

Arakcheev, D. D. 2008. "Dogovory OSAGO: Slozhnye sluchai." *Zakonodatel'stvo* (10): 58–63.

Astakhov, Pavel. 2012. *Zhil'e*. 6th ed. Moscow: EKSMO.

Attwood, Lynne. 2012. "Privatisation of Housing in Post-Soviet Russia: A New Understanding of Home?" *Europe-Asia Studies* 64 (5): 903–928.

Avakian, Elena Georgievna. 2011. "Opyt sozdaniia sistemu elektronnogo pravosudiia v arbitrazhnykh sudakh RF." *Vestnik Vysshego Arbitrazhnogo Suda* (6): 68–74.

Bahry, Donna. 1987. "Politics, Generations and Change in the USSR." In *Politics, Work and Daily Life in the USSR*, edited by James R. Millar, 61–99. New York: Cambridge University Press.

———. 1993. "Society Transformed? Rethinking the Social Roots of Perestroika." *Slavic Review* 52 (3): 512–554.

Baker, Tom. 2009. "Liability Insurance at the Tort-Crime Boundary." In Engel and McCann, *Fault Lines*, 66–79.

Baldwin, John. 1997. *Small Claims in the County Courts in England and Wales: The Bargain Basement of Civil Justice?* Oxford: Clarendon Press.

Baranskaya, Natalya. 1990. *A Week like Any Other: Novellas and Stories*. Translated by Pieta Monks. Seattle, WA: The Seal Press.

Barnes, Andrew Scott. 2006. *Owning Russia: The Struggle over Factories, Farms, and Power*. Ithaca, NY: Cornell University Press.

Barros, Robert. 2003. "Dictatorship and the Rule of Law: Rules and Military Power in Pinochet's Chile." In *Democracy and the Rule of Law*, edited by José María Maravall and Adam Przeworski, 188–222. New York: Cambridge University Press.

Barry, Donald D. 1967. "The Motor-Car in Soviet Criminal and Civil Law." *International and Comparative Law Quarterly* 16 (1): 56–85.

——. 1978. "Soviet Tort Law." In *The Unity of Strict Law: A Comparative Study*, edited by Ralph A. Newman, 319–339. Brussels: Étabtlissements Émile Bruylant.

——. 1979. "Soviet Tort Law and the Development of Public Policy." *Review of Socialist Law* 5 (1): 229–249.

——. 1992. "The Quest for Judicial Independence: Soviet Courts in a *Pravovoe Gosudarstvo*." In Barry, *Toward the "Rule of Law" in Russia?*, 257–275.

——, ed. 1992. *Toward the "Rule of Law" in Russia? Political and Legal Reform in the Transition Period*. Armonk, NY: M. E. Sharpe.

——. 1996. "Tort Law and the State in Russia." In *The Revival of Private Law in Central and Eastern Europe*, edited by George Ginsburgs, Donald D. Barry, and William B. Simons, 179–192. The Hague: Martinus Nijhoff Publishers.

Barry, Donald D., and Carol Barner-Barry. 1974. "The USSR Supreme Court and Guiding Explanations of Civil Law, 1962–1971." In *Contemporary Soviet Law*, edited by Donald D. Barry, William E. Butler, and George Ginsburgs, 69–83. The Hague: Martinus Nijhoff.

Barry, Donald D., and Harold J. Berman. 1968. "The Soviet Legal Profession." *Harvard Law Review* 82 (1): 1–41.

Barry, Ellen. 2010. "In Russia, Jury Is Something to Work Around." *New York Times*, November 16.

Baumgartner, M. P. 1988. *The Moral Order of a Suburb*. New York: Oxford University Press.

Bedford, Sybille. 1961. *The Faces of Justice*. London: Collins.

Bellin, Eva. 2014. *The Road to Rule of Law in the Arab World: Comparative Insights*. Brandeis University, Crown Center for Middle East Studies. http://www.brandeis.edu/crown/publications/meb/MEB84.pdf.

Belova, T. N. 2010. "Statistika dorozhno-transportnykh proisshestvii v kontekste natsional'noi idei." *Voprosy statistiki* (10): 28–33.

Belykh, V. C. 2009. *Strakhovoe pravo*. Moscow: NORMA.

Benesh, Sara C., and Susan E. Howell. 2001. "Confidence in the Courts: A Comparison of Users and Non-users." *Behavioral Sciences and the Law* 19 (2): 199–214.

Ber, Il'ia. 2012. "Korporatsiia neshchastnykh." *Bol'shoi gorod*, February 1. http://bg.ru/society/korporaciya_neschastnyh–9981/.

Berman, Harold J. 1963. *Justice in the U.S.S.R.: An Interpretation of Soviet Law*. Cambridge, MA: Harvard University Press.

——. 1992. "The Rule of Law and the Law-Based State with Special Reference to the Soviet Union." In Barry, *Toward the "Rule of Law" in Russia?*, 43–60.

Berman, Harold J., and James W. Spindler. 1963. "Soviet Comrades' Courts." *Washington Law Review* 38 (4): 842–910.

Best, Arthur, Deborah Zalesne, Kathleen Bridges, with Kathryn Chenoweth, Lisa Fine, Jonathan L. Miller, and Kimberly White. 1994. "Peace, Wealth, Happiness, and Small Claim Courts: A Case Study." *Fordham Urban Law Journal* 21 (2): 343–379.

Bezdek, Barbara. 1992. "Silence in the Court: Participation and Subordination of Poor Tenants' Voices in Legal Process." *Hofstra Law Review* 20 (3): 533–608.

Bingham, Tom. 2010. *The Rule of Law*. London: Penguin Books.

Black, Bernard, and Reinier Kraakman. 1996. "A Self–Enforcing Model of Corporate Law." *Harvard Law Review* 109 (8): 1911–1982.

Black, Donald. 1984. "Social Control as a Dependent Variable." In *Toward a General Theory of Social Control*, edited by Donald Black, 1–36. New York: Academic Press.

Black, Donald, and Margaret P. Baumgartner. 1980. "On Self-Help in Modern Society." In *The Manners and Customs of the Police*, edited by Donald Black, 193–208. New York: Academic Press.

Blankenburg, Erhard. 1998. "Patterns of Legal Culture: The Netherlands Compared to Neighboring Germany." *American Journal of Comparative Law* 46 (1): 1–41.

Bogira, Steve. 2005. *Courtroom 302: A Year Behind the Scenes in an American Criminal Courthouse*. New York: Alfred A. Knopf.

Bol'shova, A. K. 2010. "Sostianie i perspektivy sokrashcheniia nagruzki na sudei." *Zhurnal rossiiskogo prava* (10): 86–92.

Boym, Svetlana. 1995. *Common Places: Mythologies of Everyday Life in Russia*. Cambridge, MA: Harvard University Press.

Browder, Bill. 2015. *Red Notice: A True Story of High Finance, Murder, and One Man's Fight for Justice*. New York: Simon and Schuster.

Burbank, Jane. 1997. "Legal Culture, Citizenship, and Peasant Jurisprudence: Perspectives from the Early Twentieth Century." In Solomon, *Reforming Justice in Russia, 1864–1996*, 82–106.

———. 2004. *Russian Peasants Go to Court: Legal Culture in the Countryside, 1905–1917*. Bloomington: Indiana University Press.

Burlyuk, Olga. 2015. "The Introduction and Consolidation of the Rule of Law in Ukraine: Domestic Hindrances at the Level of the Demand for Law." *Hague Journal of the Rule of Law* 7 (1): 1–25.

Butsevitskii, V. P. 2007. "Mirovye sud'i goroda–kurorta Kislovodska (itogi piatiletnei raboty)." *Mirovoi sud'ia* (2): 26–28.

Calavita, Kitty, and Valarie Jenness. 2013. "Inside the Pyramid of Disputes: Naming Problems and Filing Grievances in California Prisons." *Social Problems* 60 (1): 50–80.

Carnaghan, Ellen. 1996. "Alienation, Apathy, or Ambivalence? 'Don't Knows' and Democracy in Russia." *Slavic Review* 55 (2): 325–363.

Cassiday, Julie A. 2000. *The Enemy on Trial: Early Soviet Courts on Stage and Screen*. DeKalb, IL: Northern Illinois University Press.

Cheesman, Nick. 2011. "How an Authoritarian Regime in Burma Used Special Courts to Defeat Judicial Independence." *Law & Society* Review 45 (4): 801–830.

Chekhov, Anton P. 1991. *The Cherry Orchard*. New York: Dover Publications.

Cheston, Paul. 2015. "Businessman Wins £110,000 Libel Damages at High Court over Hitman Slur on Russian Blog." *Evening Standard*, July 22. http://www.standard.co.uk/news/london/businessman-wins-110000-libel-damages-at-high-court-over-hitman-slur-on-russian-blog-10406742.html.

Chislennost gorodskogo i sel'skogo naseleniia po polu po Krasnodarskomu kraiu. 2010. *Vserossiiskaia perepis naseleniia 2010 goda*. Tom 1, tablitsa 4. http://krsdstat.gks.ru/wps/wcm/connect/rosstat_ts/krsdstat/resources/78c336004176a36791ffdd2d59c15b71/pub-01-04.pdf.

Chukwumerije, Okezie. 2009. "Rhetoric versus Reality: The Link between the Rule of Law and Economic Development." *Emory International Law Review* 23 (2): 383–436.

Clark, William A. 1993. *Crime and Punishment in Soviet Officialdom: Combating Corruption in the Political Elite, 1965–1990*. Armonk, NY: M. E. Sharpe.

Cohen, Jonathan R. 1999. "Advising Clients to Apologize." *Southern California Law Review* 72 (4): 1009–1069.

Colton, Timothy J., and Michael McFaul. 2002. "Are Russians Undemocratic?" *Post–Soviet Affairs* 18 (2): 91–121.

Conley, John M., and William M. O'Barr. 1990. *Rules versus Relationships: The Ethnography of Legal Discourse.* Chicago, IL: University of Chicago Press.

Cormier, Kelley E. 2007. "Grievance Practices in Post–Soviet Kyrgyz Agriculture." *Law & Social Inquiry* 32 (2): 435–466.

Czap, Peter, Jr. 1967. "Peasant-Class Courts and Peasant Customary Justice in Russia, 1861–1912." *Journal of Social History* 1 (2): 149–178.

Davies, Megan. 2013. "Glimmer of Hope for Russia's Jailed Entrepreneurs." *Reuters,* July 9. http://www.reuters.com/article/us-russia-amnesty-idUSBRE9680P420130709.

Dawisha, Karen. 2014. *Putin's Kleptocracy: Who Owns Russia?* New York: Simon & Schuster.

Dicey, A. V. 1939. *Introduction to the Study of the Law of the Constitution.* 9th ed. London: Macmillan.

Dworkin, Ronald. 1978. *Taking Rights Seriously.* Cambridge, MA: Harvard University Press.

Dyzenhaus, David. 2010. *Hard Cases in Wicked Legal Systems: Pathologies of Legality.* New York: Oxford University Press.

Dziadko, Filipp, and Lena Kraevskaia. 2012. "Iuliia Sazonova: Byvshii mirovoi sud'ia." *Bol'shoi gorod,* May 18. http://bg.ru/society/yuliya_sazonova_byvshiy_mirovoy_sudya-10985/.

Ellickson, Robert C. 1991. *Order without Law: How Neighbors Settle Disputes.* Cambridge, MA: Harvard University Press.

Elwell, Suzanne E., and Christopher D. Carlson. 1990. "The Iowa Small Claims Court: An Empirical Analysis." *Iowa Law Review* 75 (2): 433–538.

Emerson, Robert M. 2008. "Responding to Roommate Troubles: Reconsidering Informal Dyadic Control." *Law & Society Review* 42 (3): 483–512.

Engel, David M. 1984. "The Oven Bird's Song: Insiders, Outsiders, and Personal Injuries in an American Community." *Law & Society Review* 18 (4): 551–582.

——. 2001. "Injury and Identity: The Damaged Self in Three Cultures." In *Between Law and Culture,* edited by David Theo Goldberb, Michael Musheno, and Lisa C. Bower, 3–21. Minneapolis: University of Minnesota Press.

——. 2005. "Globalization and the Decline of Legal Consciousness: Torts, Ghosts, and Karma in Thailand." *Law & Social Inquiry* 30 (3): 469–514.

——. 2009. "Discourses of Causation in Injury Cases: Exploring Tai and American Legal Cultures." In Engel and McCann, *Fault Lines,* 251–268.

Engel, David M., and Jaruwan S. Engel. 2010. *Tort, Custom, and Karma: Globalization and Legal Consciousness in Thailand.* Stanford, CA: Stanford Law Books.

Engel, David M., and Michael McCann, eds. 2009. *Fault Lines: Tort Law as Cultural Practice.* Stanford, CA: Stanford University Press.

——. 2009. "Introduction: Tort Law as Cultural Practice." In Engel and McCann, *Fault Lines,* 1–17.

Engel, David M., and Frank W. Munger. 2003. *Rights of Inclusion: Law and Identity in the Life Stories of Americans with Disabilities.* Chicago, IL: University of Chicago Press.

Engelstein, Laura. 1993. "Combined Underdevelopment: Discipline and the Law in Imperial and Soviet Russia." *American Historical Review* 98 (2): 338–353.

——. 2009. *Slavophile Empire: Imperial Russia's Illiberal Path.* Ithaca, NY: Cornell University Press.

Ershov, Valentin V. 2016. "Spetsializirovannoe obuchenie rabotnikov sudebnoi sistemy v Rossiiskoi Federatsii." *Rossiiskoe pravosudie* (1): 5–10.

Ewick, Patricia, and Susan S. Silbey. 1998. *The Common Place of Law: Stories from Everyday Life*. Chicago, IL: University of Chicago Press.

Farnsworth, Beatrice. 1986. "The Litigious Daughter-in-Law: Family Relations in Rural Russia in the Second Half of the Nineteenth Century." *Slavic Review* 45 (1): 49–64.

Feifer, George. 1964. *Justice in Moscow*. New York: Simon and Schuster.

Felstiner, William L. F. 1974. "Influences of Social Organizations on Dispute Processing." *Law & Society Review* 9 (1): 63–94.

———. 1975. "Avoidance as Dispute Processing: An Elaboration." *Law & Society Review* 9 (3): 695–706.

Felstiner, William L. F., Richard L. Abel, and Austin Sarat. 1980–1981. "The Emergence and Transformation of Disputes: Naming, Blaming, Claiming . . ." *Law & Society Review* 15 (3–4): 631–654.

Figes, Orlando. 2007. *The Whisperers: Private Life in Stalin's Russia*. New York: Metropolitan Books.

Flikke, Geir. 2016. "Resurgent Authoritarianism: The Case of Russia's New NGO Legislation." *Post-Soviet Affairs* 32 (2): 103–131.

Finn, Peter. 2008. "A Russian Candidacy in Peril: Authorities Scrutinize Putin Foe's Campaign." *Washington Post*, January 23. http://www.washingtonpost.com/wp-dyn/content/story/2008/01/23/ST2008012300996.html.

Fitzpatrick, Sheila. 1996. "Supplicants and Citizens: Public Letter-Writing in Soviet Russia in the 1930s." *Slavic Review* 55 (1): 78–105.

Floyd, Daisy Hurst. 1994. "Can the Judge Do That? The Need for a Clearer Judicial Role in Settlement." *Arizona State Law Journal* 26 (1): 45–90.

Fond obshchestvennoe mnenie. 2012. *O sudakh i sud'iakh*. http://fom.ru/Bezopasnost-i-pravo/10551.

Fraenkel, Ernst. 1969. *The Dual State: A Contribution to the Theory of Dictatorship*. Translated by E. A. Shils. New York: Octagon Books.

Frank, Stephen P. 1999. *Crime, Cultural Conflict, and Justice in Rural Russia, 1865–1914*. Berkeley: University of California Press.

Friedman, Lawrence, M. 1969a. "Legal Culture and Social Development." *Verfassung und Recht in Ubersee* (2): 261–274.

———. 1969b. "Legal Culture and Social Development." *Law & Society Review* 4 (1): 29–44.

———. 1987. *Total Justice*. Boston, MA: Beacon Press.

Frierson, Cathy A. 1986. "Rural Justice in Public Opinion: The Volost' Court Debate, 1861–1912." *The Slavonic & East European Review* 64 (4): 526–545.

———. 1997a. "'I Must Always Answer to the Law . . .': Rules and Responses in the Reformed *Volost'* Court." *Slavonic & East European Review* 75 (2): 308–334.

———. 1997b. "Of Red Roosters, Revenge, and the Search for Justice: Rural Arson in European Russia in the Late Imperial Era." In Solomon, *Reforming Justice in Russia, 1864–1996*, 107–30.

Fuller, Lon L. 1964. *The Morality of Law*. New Haven, CT: Yale University Press.

Fürst, Juliane. 2006. "Friends in Private, Friends in Public: The Phenomenon of the *Kompaniia* among Soviet Youth in the 1950s and 1960s." In Siegelbaum, *Borders of Socialism*, 229–250.

Galanter, Marc. 1974. "Why the 'Haves' Come Out Ahead: Speculations on the Limits of Legal Change." *Law & Society Review* 9 (1): 95–160.

———. 1985. "Vision and Revision: A Comment on Yngvesson." *Wisconsin Law Review* (3): 647–654.

Gallagher, Mary E., and Yuhu Wang. 2011. "Users and Non-Users: Legal Experience and Its Effect on Legal Consciousness." In *Chinese Justice: Civil Dispute*

Resolution in China, edited by Margaret Y. K. Woo and Mary E. Gallagher, 204–232. New York: Cambridge University Press.

Galligan, Denis J., and Marina Kurkchiyan, eds. *Law and Informal Practices: The Post-Communist Experience*. New York: Oxford University Press.

Gans-Morse, Jordan. 2012. "Threats to Property Rights in Russia: From Private Coercion to State Aggression." *Post-Soviet Affairs* 28 (3): 263–295.

Gerasimova, Katerina. 2002. "Public Privacy in the Soviet Communal Apartment." In *Socialist Spaces: Sites of Everyday Life in the Eastern Bloc*, edited by David Crowley and Susan E. Reid, 207–230. Oxford: Berg.

Gessen, Masha. 2014. *Words Will Break Cement: The Passion of Pussy Riot*. New York: Riverhead Books.

——. 2015. "Is It 1937 Yet?" *New York Times*, May 5. http://www.nytimes.com/2015/05/06/opinion/masha-gessen-putin-russia-is-it-1937-yet.html.

——. 2016. "Putin's Year in Scandals." *New York Times*, January 6. http://www.nytimes.com/2016/01/06/opinion/putins-year-in-scandals.html?_r=0.

Gibson, James L. 1996. "A Mile Wide But an Inch Deep(?): The Structure of Democratic Commitments in the Former USSR." *American Journal of Political Science* 40 (2): 396–420.

——. 2003. "Russian Attitudes towards the Rule of Law: An Analysis of Survey Data." In Galligan and Kurkchiyan, *Law and Informal Practices*, 77–91.

Glaberson, William. 2006. "In Tiny Courts of New York, Abuses of Law and Power: Judges without Legal Degrees of Oversight Rule in Arcane System across State." *New York Times*, September 25.

Glandin, Sergei V. 2016. "Vladimir Slutsker vs Ol'ga Romanova. Anglo-Rossiiskoe diffamatsionnoe pravo." *Zakon* (1): 108–121.

Gorbachev, Mikhail. 1988. *Documents and Materials: 19th All-Union Conference of the CPSU: Report and Speeches by Mikhail Gorbachev, General Secretary of the CPSU Central Committee: Resolutions*. Moscow: Novosti Press Agency Publishing House.

Gorbus, A. K., M. A. Krasnov, E. A. Mishina, and G. A. Satarov. 2010. *Transformatsiia rossiiskoi sudebnoi vlasti: Opyt kompleksnogo analiza*. St. Petersburg: Norma.

Gorlizki, Yoram. 1998. "Delegalization in Russia: Soviet Comrades' Courts in Retrospect." *American Journal of Comparative Law* 46 (3): 403–425.

Graver, Hans Petter. 2015. *Judges against Justice: On Judges When the Rule of Law Is under Attack*. Berlin: Springer.

Grechin, A. S. 1984. "Pravovoe soznanie rabochego klassa (metodologicheskie i metodicheskie problemy sotsiologicheskogo analiza)." PhD diss., Institute of Sociology, the Academy of Sciences of the USSR.

Greene, David. 2014. *Midnight in Siberia: A Train Journey into the Heart of Russia*. New York: W.W. Norton.

Greenspan, Alan S. 1994. "Thoughts about the Transitioning Market Economies of Eastern Europe and the Former Soviet Union." *DePaul Business Law Journal* 6 (1): 1–14.

Greif, Avner, and Eugene Kandel. 1995. "Contract Enforcement Institutions: Historical Perspective and Current Status in Russia." In *Economic Transition in Eastern Europe and Russia*, edited by Edward P. Lazear, 291–321. Stanford, CA: Hoover Institution Press.

Grove, Trevor. 2002. *The Magistrate's Tale*. London: Bloomsbury.

Guarnieri, Carlo, and Patrizia Pederzoli. 2002. *The Power of Judges: A Comparative Study of Courts and Democracy*. New York: Oxford University Press.

Gudkov, Lev. 2012. "'Doveria' v Rossii: Smysl, funktsii, struktura." *Vestnik obshchestvennogo mneniia* (2): 8–47.

Gudkov, Lev, Boris Dubin, and Nataliia Zorkaia. 2010. "Rossiiskaia sudebnaia sistema v mneniiakh obshchestva." *Vestnik obshchestvennogo mneniia* (4): 7–43.

Gutsul, Diana, and Ol'ga Siverkina. 2015. "Eksperty razoshlis' vo mneniiakh, est' li u sodov RF obvinitel'nyi uklon." *RAPSI*, January 29. http://rapsinews.ru/judicial_news/20150129/273057271.html.

Hale, Henry E. 2015. *Patronal Politics: Eurasian Regime Dynamics in Comparative Perspective.* New York: Cambridge University Press.

Haley, John O. 1986. "Comment: The Implications of Apology." *Law & Society Review* 20 (4): 499–507.

Handelman, Stephen. 1995. *Comrade Criminal: Russia's New Mafiya.* New Haven, CT: Yale University Press.

Harris, Steven E. 2005. "'We Too Want to Live in Normal Apartments:' Soviet MA Housing and the Marginalization of the Elderly under Khrushchev and Brezhnev." *Soviet and Post-Soviet Review* 32 (2–3): 143–174.

———. 2006. "'I Know All the Secrets of My Neighbors:' The Quest for Privacy in the Era of the Separate Apartment." In Siegelbaum, *Borders of Socialism,* 171–189.

———. 2013. *Communism on Tomorrow Street: Mass Housing and Everyday Life after Stalin.* Washington, DC: Woodrow Wilson Center Press.

Hay, Jonathan R., and Andrei Shleifer. 1998. "Private Enforcement of Public Laws: A Theory of Legal Reform." *American Economic Review* 88 (2): 398–403.

Hazard, John N. 1938. "Legal Education in the Soviet Union." *Wisconsin Law Review* (4): 562–579.

———. 1952. "Personal Injury and Soviet Socialism." *Harvard Law Review* 65 (4): 545–581.

———. 1962. "Furniture Arrangement as a Symbol of Judicial Roles." *ETC; a Review of General Semantics* 19 (2): 181–188.

Hedlund, Stefan. 2005. *Russian Path Dependence.* New York: Routledge.

Heinzen, James. 2016. *The Art of the Bribe: Corruption under Stalin, 1943–1953.* New Haven, CT: Yale University Press.

Hellbek, Jochem. 2000. "Writing the Self in the Time of Terror: Alexander Afinogenov's Diary of 1937." In *Self and Story in Russian History,* edited by Laura Engelstein and Stephanie Sandler, 69–93. Ithaca, NY: Cornell University Press.

Henderson, Jane. 2015. "Developments in Russia." *European Public Law* 21 (2): 229–238.

Hendley, Kathryn. 1996. *Trying to Make Law Matter: Legal Reform and Labor Law in the Soviet Union.* Ann Arbor: University of Michigan Press, 1996.

———. 1997. "Legal Development in Post-Soviet Russia." *Post-Soviet Affairs* 13 (2): 228–251.

———. 1998. "Remaking an Institution: The Transition in Russia from State Arbitrazh to Arbitrazh Courts." *American Journal of Comparative Law* 46 (1): 93–127.

———. 2001. "Beyond the Tip of the Iceberg: Business Disputes in Russia." In *Assessing the Value of Law in Transition Economies,* edited by Peter Murrell, 20–55. Ann Arbor: University of Michigan Press.

———. 2002. "Suing the State in Russia." *Post-Soviet Affairs* 18 (2): 122–147.

———. 2004. "Business Litigation in the Transition: A Portrait of Debt Collection in Russia." *Law & Society Review* 38 (2): 305–348.

———. 2005. "Accelerated Process in the Russian *Arbitrazh* Courts: A Case Study of Unintended Consequences." *Problems of Post-Communism* 52 (6): 21–31.

———. 2006. "Assessing the Rule of Law in Russia." *Cardozo Journal of International and Comparative Law* 14 (2): 347–391.

———. 2007. "Are Russian Judges Still Soviet?" *Post-Soviet Affairs* 23 (3): 240–274.

———. 2009. "'Telephone Law' and the 'Rule of Law:' The Russian Case." *Hague Journal of the Rule of Law* 1 (2): 241–262.

———. 2010. "Mobilizing Law in Contemporary Russia: The Evolution of Disputes over Home Repair Projects." *American Journal of Comparative Law* 58 (3): 631–678.

———. 2011. "Varieties of Legal Dualism: Making Sense of the Role of Law in Contemporary Russia." *Wisconsin International Law Journal* 29 (2): 233–262.

———. 2012a. "Assessing the Role of Justice-of-the-Peace Courts in the Russian Judicial System." *Review of Central and East European Law* 37 (4): 373–393.

———. 2012b. "Dvadtsatiletie stanovleniia sistemy arbitrazhnykh sudov." *Sud'ia* (1): 73–76.

———. 2012c. "The Puzzling Non-Consequences of Societal Distrust of Courts: Explaining the Use of Russian Courts." *Cornell International Law Journal* 56 (3): 517–567.

———. 2012d. "Who Are the Legal Nihilists in Russia?" *Post-Soviet Affairs* 28 (2): 149–186.

———. 2013. "Too Much of a Good Thing? Assessing Access to Civil Justice in Russia." *Slavic Review* 72 (4): 802–827.

———. 2015. "Judges as Gatekeepers to Mediation: The Russian Case." *Cardozo Journal of Conflict Resolution* 16 (2): 423–455.

———. 2016. "Justice in Moscow?" *Post-Soviet Affairs*. 32 (6): 491–511.

Hendley, Kathryn, Peter Murrell, and Randi Ryterman. 1999. "Do 'Repeat Players' Behave Differently in Russia? An Evaluation of Contractual and Litigation Behavior of Russian Enterprises." *Law & Society Review* 33 (4): 833–867.

———. 2000. "Law, Relationships and Private Enforcement: Transactional Strategies of Russian Enterprises." *Europe-Asia Studies* 52 (4): 627–656.

Herszenhorn, David M. 2014. "Aleksei Navalny, Putin Critic, Is Spared Prison in a Fraud Case, but His Brother Is Jailed." *New York Times*, December 30. http://www.nytimes.com/2014/12/31/world/europe/aleksei-navalny-convicted.html.

Hirschmann, Albert O. 1970. *Exit, Voice, and Loyalty: Responses to Declines in Firms, Organizations, and States.* Cambridge, MA: Harvard University Press.

Hoffman, David E. 2003. *The Oligarchs: Wealth and Power in the New Russia.* New York: Public Affairs.

Huskey, Eugene. 1986. *Russian Lawyers and the Soviet State: The Origins and Development of the Soviet Bar, 1917–1939.* Princeton, NJ: Princeton University Press.

———. 1990. "Government Rulemaking as a Brake on *Perestroika.*" *Law & Social Inquiry* 15 (3): 419–432.

———. 1991. "A Framework for the Analysis of Soviet Law." *Russian Review* 50 (1): 53–70.

Iakovleva, Iana V. 2008. *Neelektronnye pis'ma.* Moscow: Praksis.

Iaroshenko, Klavdia B. 2015 "Zashchita grazhdan, postradavshikh v rezul'tate dorozhno-transportnykh proisshestvii (sostianie zakonodatel'stva i perspektivy ego sovershenstvovaniia)." *Zhurnal rossiiskogo prava* (12): 39–48.

Ivanova, L. O., ed. 2011. *Predlozheniia po povysheniiu dostupnosti pravosudiia dlia maloimushchikh i sotsial'no nezashchishchennykh grazhdan—uchastnikov grazhdanskogo protsessa.* Moscow: OOO "Imformpoligraf."

Jayasuriya, Kanishka. 2001. "The Exception Becomes the Norm: Law and Regimes of Exception in East Asia." *Asian-Pacific Law & Policy Journal* 2 (1): 108–124.

Johnson, Simon, John McMillan, and Christopher Woodruff. 2002. "Courts and Relational Contracts." *Journal of Law, Economics, & Organization* 18 (1): 221–277.

Jordan, Pamela A. 2005. *Defending Rights in Russia: Lawyers, the State, and Legal Reforms in the Post-Soviet Era*. Vancouver: University of British Columbia Press.

Judah, Ben. 2013. *Fragile Empire: How Russia Fell In and Out of Love with Vladimir Putin*. New Haven, CT: Yale University Press.

Kagan, Robert A. 2001. *Adversarial Legalism: The American Way of Law*. Cambridge, MA: Harvard University Press.

Kahn, Jeffrey. 2011. "Report on the Verdict against M. B. Khodorkovsky and P. L. Lebedev." *Journal of Eurasian Law* 4 (3): 321–534.

Kaminskaya, Dina. 1982. *Final Judgment: My Life as a Soviet Defense Attorney*. Translated by Michael Glenny. New York: Simon and Schuster.

Kapitaniuk, V. I. 2010. "Osobennosti proizvodstva po ugolovnym delam chastnogo obvineniia." In *Nastol'naia kniga mirovogo sud'i*, edited by A. L. Alferov, 154–158. Moscow: Americanskaia assotsiatsiia iuristov.

Kapustin, Anatoly. 2007. "The Bologna Process: Practical Steps for Russian Law Schools." *International Journal of Legal Information* 35 (2): 245–261.

Kartushev, A. A. 2011. "Sudebnyi pretsedent v Rossiiskoi Federatsii: Real'nost i perspectiva." *Mirovoi sud'ia* (4): 21–22.

Kazgerieva, E. V. 2006. "Prichiny vozniknoveniia sudebnykh oshibok." *Mirovoi sud'ia* (7): 19–21.

Kesby, Rebecca. 2012. "Why Russia Locks Up So Many Entrepreneurs." *BBC News*, July 5. http://www.bbc.com/news/magazine-18706597.

Khaliullina, L. I. 2005. "Spros na pravonarusheniia i praktika kontrolia za sobliudeniiem pravil dorozhnogo dvizheniia." *Economicheskaia sotsiologiia* 6 (1): 69–77. http://ecsoc.hse.ru/data/2011/12/08/1208204957/ecsoc_t6_n1.pdf.

Khazan, Olga. 2013. "Why Are There So Many Dash-Cam Videos of the Meteor?" *Washington Post*, February 15. http://www.washingtonpost.com/blogs/worldviews/wp/2013/02/15/why-are-there-so-many-dash-cam-videos-of-the-meteor/.

Khodorkovsky, Mikhail. 2010. "The Fate of Every Citizen Is Being Decided." *New York Times*, November 2. http://www.nytimes.com/2010/11/03/opinion/03iht-edkhodorkovsky.html.

Kiewiet, D. Roderick, and Mikhail G. Myagkov. 2002. "Are the Communists Dying Out in Russia?" *Communist and Post-Communist Studies* 35 (1): 39–50.

Kirilpovykh, Andrei A. 2012. "Besplatnaia iuridicheskaia pomoshch' i pravovye osnovy ee okazaniia." *Advokat* (8): 5–20.

Kistyakovsky, Bogdan. 1977. "In the Defense of Law: The Intelligentsia and Legal Consciousness." In *Landmarks: A Collection of Essays on the Russian Intelligentsia*, edited by Boris Shragin and Albert Todd, translated by Marian Schwartz, 112–137. New York: Karz Howard.

Kleinfeld, Rachel. 2006. "Competing Definitions of the Rule of Law." In *Promoting the Rule of Law Abroad: In Search of Knowledge*, edited by Thomas Carothers, 31–73. Washington, DC: Carnegie Endowment for International Peace.

Kolokolov, Nikita Aleksandrovich. 2011. *Mirovaia iustitsiia*. 2nd ed. Moscow: Unity.

Kotkin, Stephen. 1995. *Magnetic Mountain: Stalinism as a Civilization*. Berkeley: University of California Press.

Krainova, Natalya. 2013. "Navalny Defiant in KirovLes Testimony." *Moscow Times*, June 17. http://www.themoscowtimes.com/news/article/navalny-defiant-in-kirovles-testimony/481824.html.

Kritzer, Herbert M. 1992. "The English Rule." *ABA Journal* 78 (11): 54–58.

Kritzer, Herbert M., W. A. Bogart, and Neil Vidmar. 1991. "The Aftermath of Injury: Cultural Factors in Compensation Seeking in Canada and the United States." *Law & Society Review* 25 (3): 499–543.

Kritzer, Herbert M., and John Voelker. 1998. "Familiarity Breeds Respect: How Wisconsin Citizens View Their Courts." *Judicature* 82 (2): 59–64.

Kriuchkov, Sergei. 2010. *Otnoshenie grazhdan k mirovym sudam.* Moscow: Americanskaia assotsiatsiia iuristov.

Kruchinin, Iurii S., and Vladimir V. Arapov. 2012. "Voprosy realizatsii gosudarstvennoi sistemy besplatnoi iuridicheskoi pomoshchi v Rossiiskoi Federatsii." *Advokat* (12): 5–12.

Kryshtanovskaya, Olga, and Stephen White. 2005. "The Rise of the Russian Business Elite." *Communist and Post-Communist Studies* 38 (3): 293–307.

Kucherov, Samuel. 1952. "The Case of Vera Zasulich." *Russian Review* 11 (2): 86–96.

———. 1953. *Courts, Lawyers, and Trials under the Last Three Tsars.* New York: Praeger.

Kudriavtsev, Vladimir N., and Elena A. Lukasheva. 1988. "Sotsialisticheskoe pravovoe gosudarstvo." *Kommunist* (11): 44–55.

Kuhr-Korolev, Corinna. 2011. "Women and Cars in Soviet and Russian Society." In *The Socialist Car: Automobility in the Eastern Bloc,* edited by Lewis H. Siegelbaum, 186–203. Ithaca, NY: Cornell University Press.

Kulikov, Vladislav. 2009. "Diplom—prosvet." *Rossiiskaia gazeta,* May 29. http://www. rg.ru/2009/05/29/uristy-komment.html.

Kurkchiyan, Marina. 2003. "The Illegitimacy of Law in Post-Soviet Societies." In Galligan and Kurkchiyan, *Law and Informal Practices,* 25–47.

———. 2009. "Russian Legal Culture: An Analysis of Adaptive Responses to an Institutional Transplant." *Law & Social Inquiry* 34 (2): 337–364.

———. 2012. "Comparing Legal Cultures: Three Models of Court for Small Civil Cases." In *Using Legal Culture,* edited by David Nelken, 218–250. London: Wildy, Simmonds & Hill Publishing.

———. 2013. "Justice through Bureaucracy: The Ukrainian Model." *Social & Legal Studies* 22 (4): 515–533.

Kushkova, A. 2010. "Female Social Control in the Late Soviet Village: Comrades' Courts as a Nexus of Official and Customary Justice." In *Everyday Life in Russian History,* edited by Gary Marker, Joan Neuberger, Marshall Poe, and Susan Rupp, 283–304. Bloomington, IN: Slavica.

Kuznetsova, I. M. 1996. *Kommentarii k Semeinomu kodeksu Rossiiskoi Federatsii.* Moscow: Izdatel'stovo BEK. http://www.bibliotekar.ru/kodex-semya/.

Lally, Kathy. 2014. "Russia Finds Bolotnaya Protesters Guilty." *Washington Post,* February 21. http://www.washingtonpost.com/world/europe/russia-finds-bolotnaya-protesters-guilty/2014/02/21/07e53342-9afa-11e3-975d-107dfef7b668_story.html.

Lambert-Mogiliansky, Ariane, Konstantin Sonin, and Ekaterina Zhuravskaya. 2007. "Are Russian Commercial Courts Biased? Evidence from a Bankruptcy Law Transplant." *Journal of Comparative Economics* 35 (2): 254–277.

Latynina, Iuliia. 2012a. "Middle Class Fleeing Putin's Russia." *Moscow Times,* August 1. http://www.themoscowtimes.com/opinion/article/middle-class-fleeing-putins-russia/462956.html.

———. 2012b. "Shchedryi prem'er predlozhil gaishnikam vozmozhnost zarabotat do 500 tysiach rublei s odnoi mashiny." *Novaia gazeta,* November 28. http://www.novayagazeta.ru/columns/55627.html.

Ledeneva, Alena V. 1998. *Russia's Economy of Favours: Blat, Networking, and Informal Exchange*. New York: Cambridge University Press.

——. 2006. *How Russia Really Works: The Informal Practices That Shaped Post-Soviet Politics and Business*. Ithaca, NY: Cornell University Press.

——. 2008. "Telephone Justice in Russia." *Post-Soviet Affairs* 24 (4): 324–350.

——. 2013. *Can Russia Modernise? Sistema, Power Networks and Informal Governance*. New York: Cambridge University Press.

Lerner, Mike, and Maxim Pozdorovkin, directors. 2013. *Pussy Riot: A Punk Prayer*. Film. Roast Beef Productions.

Levada Center. 2007. *Doverie institutam vlasti*. http://www.levada.ru/press/2007040901. html.

——. 2008. *Russian Public Opinion 2007*. Moscow: Levada Center. http://www.levada. ru/old/books/obshchestvennoe-mnenie-2007.

——. 2012. *Instituty vlasti teriaiut doverie grazhdan*. http://www.levada.ru/2012/06/26/ instituty-vlasti-teryayut-doverie-grazhdan/.

——. 2013a. *Doverie institutam vlasti*. http://www.levada.ru/07-10-2013/doverie-institutam-vlasti.

——. 2013b. "Ob"edinenie Verkhovnogo i Vysshego arbitrahnogo sudov." November 27. http://www.levada.ru/27-11-2013/obedinenie-verkhovnogo-i-vysshego-arbitrazhnogo-sudov.

——. 2015. *Dekabr'skie reitingi odobreniia i doveriia*. http://www.levada.ru/2015/12/23/ dekabrskie-rejtingi-odobreniya-i-doveriya-5/.

Levy, Clifford J. 2007. "Kasparov Gets 5 Days for Marching." *New York Times*, November 25. http://www.nytimes.com/2007/11/25/world/europe/25russia. html.

Lewin, Moshe. 1985. "Customary Law and Russian Rural Society in the Post-Reform Era." *Russian Review* 44 (1): 1–19.

Lincoln, W. Bruce. 1990. *The Great Reforms: Autocracy, Bureaucracy, and the Politics of Change in Imperial Russia*. DeKalb, IL: Northern Illinois University Press.

Litvinov, Pavel Mikhailovich. 1972. *The Trial of the Four: A Collection of Materials on the Case of Galanskov, Ginzburg, Dobrovolsky, and Lashkova, 1967–1968*. Translated by Janis Sapiets, Hilary Sternberg, and Daniel Weissbort. London: Longman.

Livshits, R. Z. 1989. "Pravo i zakon v sotsialisticheskom pravovom gosudarstve." *Sovetskoe gosudarstvo i pravo* (3): 15–22.

——. 1991. "Jus and Lex: The Evolution of Views." In *Perestroika and the Rule of Law: Anglo-American Perspectives*, edited by William E. Butler, 22–36. New York: St. Martin's Press.

Lukin, Alexander. 2014. "Eurasian Integration and the Clash of Values." *Survival: Global Politics and Strategy* 56 (3): 43–60.

Macaulay, Stewart. 1963. "Non-Contractual Relations in Business: A Preliminary Study." *American Sociological Review* 28 (1): 55–67.

MacDowell, Elizabeth L. 2015. "Reimagining Access to Justice in the Poor People's Courts." *Georgetown Journal on Poverty Law & Policy* 22 (3): 473–543.

Mackey, Robert. 2013. "Cheers for Navalny in Court and Online." *The Lede*, July 19. http://thelede.blogs.nytimes.com/2013/07/19/ cheers-for-navalny-in-court-and-online/.

Maggs, Peter B. 1965. "Soviet Corporation Law: The New Statute on the Socialist State Production Enterprise." *American Journal of Comparative Law* 14 (3): 478–489.

Maggs, Peter B., Olga Schwartz, and William Burnham. 2015. *Law and Legal System of the Russian Federation*. 6th ed. Huntington, NY: Juris Publishing.

Markovits, Inga. 1992. "Last Days." *California Law Review* 80 (1): 55–129.

——. 2010. *Justice in Lüritz: Experiencing Socialist Law in East Germany*. Princeton, NJ: Princeton University Press.

Massie, Robert K. 1980. *Peter the Great, His Life and World*. New York: Knopf.

Matthews, Owen. 2010. "There's Something Rotten in the State of Russia." *The Spectator*, January 6. http://www.spectator.co.uk/features/5686623/theres-something-rotten-in-the-state-of-russia/.

McCarthy, Lauren A. 2015. *Trafficking Justice: How Russian Police Enforce New Laws, from Crime to Courtroom*. Ithaca, NY: Cornell University Press.

McDonald, Tracy. 2011. *Face to the Village: The Riazan Countryside under Soviet Rule, 1921–1930*. Toronto: University of Toronto Press.

McFaul, Michael. 2001. *Russia's Unfinished Revolution: Political Change from Gorbachev to Putin*. Ithaca, NY: Cornell University Press.

McReynolds, Louise. 2012. *Murder Most Russian: True Crime and Punishment in Late Imperial Russia*. Ithaca, NY: Cornell University Press.

Medvedev, Roy Aleksandrovich. 1971. *Let History Judge: The Origins and Consequences of Stalinism*. Translated by Colleen Taylor. New York: Knopf.

Meierhenrich, Jens. 2008. *The Legacies of Law: Long-Run Consequences of Legal Development in South Africa, 1652–2000*. New York: Cambridge University Press.

Melville, Andrei, and Mikhail Mironyuk. 2016. "'Bad Enough Governance': State Capacity and Quality of Institutions in Post-Soviet Autocracies." *Post-Soviet Affairs* 32 (2): 132–151.

Mendras, Marie. 2012. *Russian Politics: The Paradox of a Weak State*. London: Hurst.

Merry, Sally Engle. 1990. *Getting Justice and Getting Even: Legal Consciousness among Working-Class Americans*. Chicago, IL: University of Chicago Press.

Merry, Sally Engle, Kevin E. Davis, and Benedict Kingsbury, eds. 2015. *The Quiet Power of Indicators: Measuring Governance, Corruption, and Rule of Law*. New York: Cambridge University Press.

Merryman, John Henry, and Rogelio Pérez-Perdomo. 2007. *The Civil Law Tradition: An Introduction to the Legal Systems of Europe and Latin America*. 3rd ed. Stanford, CA: Stanford University Press.

Michelson, Ethan. 2007. "Climbing the Dispute Pagoda: Grievances and Appeals to the Official Justice System in Rural China." *American Sociological Review* 72 (3): 459–485.

Mikheev, A. V. 2007. "Institut mirovykh sudei v ugolovnom sudoproizvodstve dorevolutsionnoi Rossii." *Istoriia gosudarstva i prava* (7): 30–31.

Morgan, David L., and Richard A. Krueger. 1993. "When to Use Focus Groups and Why." In *Successful Focus Groups: Advancing the State of the Art*, edited by David L. Morgan, 3–19. Newbury Park, CA: Sage.

Moudrykh, Vladislav. 2002. *Russian Insurance Law*. Moscow: RDL.

Moustafa, Tamir. 2007. *The Struggle for Constitutional Power: Law, Politics, and Economic Development in Egypt*. New York: Cambridge University Press.

Mnookin, Robert H., and Lewis Kornhauser. 1979. "Bargaining in the Shadow of the Law: The Case of Divorce." *Yale Law Journal* 88 (5): 950–997.

Mrovchinski, Rafael'. 2012. "Institutsial'naia professionalizatsiia iuristov v usloviiakh gosudarstvennogo sotsializma i postsotsializma: Sravnitel'nyi analiz organizatsii professional'nogo samoupravleniia v Pol'she i Rossii." In *Antropologiia professii: Granitsy zaniatosti v epokhi nestabil'nosti*, edited by Pavel Romanov and Elena Iurskaia Smirnova, 99–117. Moscow: Variant.

Mydans, Seth, and Erin E. Arvedlund. 2003. "Police in Russia Seize Oil Tycoon." *New York Times*, October 26. http://www.nytimes.com/2003/10/26/world/police-in-russia-seize-oil-tycoon.html.

"Nagruzka mirovykh sudei za. 2009–2010." Unpublished, on file with author.

"Nagruzka mirovykh sudei za. 2010–2011." Unpublished, on file with author.

Natsional'noe agentstvo financovykh issledovanii. 2012a. "Strakhovanie postepenno vozvrashchaetsia." Nasfin.ru, July 11. http://nacfin.ru/straxovanie-postepenno-vozvrashhaetsya/.

———. 2012b. "Pochemu strakhovanie ne rasprostraneno." Nasfin.ru, September 14. http://nacfin.ru/pochemu-straxovanie-ne-rasprostraneno/.

Nelken, David. 2009. "Law, Liability, and Culture." In Engel and McCann, *Fault Lines*, 21–38.

Nemtsov, Boris. 2009. "Don't Abandon Russia's Democrats." *Wall Street Journal*, July 7, A13.

Neuberger, Joan. 1994. "Popular Legal Cultures: The St. Petersburg *Mirovoi Sud*." In *Russia's Great Reforms, 1855–1881*, edited by Ben Eklof, John Bushnell, and Larissa Zakharova, 132–146. Bloomington: Indiana University Press.

Nikoforov, Vladimir. 2009. "Novye uslovie vyplaty kompensatsii po OSAGO." Samru. ru, February 20. http://www.samru.ru/society/gost/44299.html.

Nonet, Philippe, and Philip Selznick. 2001. *Law and Society in Transition: Toward Responsive Law*. 2nd ed. New Brunswick, NJ: Transaction Publishers.

"Nuzhno li OSAGO." n.d. Prosmibank.ru. http://prosmibank.ru/marketinsurance-1.html.

"Obzor sudebnoi statistiki o deiatel'nosti federal'nykh sudov obshchei iurisdiktsii i mirovykh sudei." 2012. Supreme Court of the Russian Federation, Judicial Department. http://www.cdep.ru/index.php?id=80&item=1239.

Osadchuk, Svetlana. 2008. "The Season of Cold Showers." *Moscow Times*, May 13.

"Otchet o rabote raionnykh sudov po rassmotreniiu grazhdanskikh del v apelliatsionnom poriadki za 12 mesiatsev 2011 g." (Otchet–civil appeals). http://www.cdep.ru/index.php?id=5.

"Otchet o rabote sudov obshchei iurisdiktsii po pervoi instantsii o rassmotranii grazhdanskikh del za 12 mesiatsev 2008 g." http://www.cdep.ru/index.php?id=5.

"Otchet o rabote sudov obshchei iurisdiktsii po pervoi instantsii o rassmotranii grazhdanskikh del za 12 mesiatsev 2009 g." http://www.cdep.ru/index.php?id=5.

"Otchet o rabote sudov obshchei iurisdiktsii po pervoi instantsii o rassmotranii grazhdanskikh del za 12 mesiatsev 2010 g." http://www.cdep.ru/index.php?id=5.

"Otchet o rabote sudov obshchei iurisdiktsii po pervoi instantsii o rassmotranii grazhdanskikh del za 12 mesiatsev 2011 g." http://www.cdep.ru/index.php?id=5.

"Otchet o rabote sudov obshchei iurisdiktsii po pervoi instantsii o rassmotranii grazhdanskikh del za 12 mesiatsev 2008 g." Svodnyi otchet po vsem mirovym sud'iam v Rossiiskoi Federatsii (Otchet–JP Courts 2008). Unpublished, on file with author.

"Otchet o rabote sudov obshchei iurisdiktsii po pervoi instantsii o rassmotranii grazhdanskikh del za 12 mesiatsev 2009 g." Svodnyi otchet po vsem mirovym sud'iam v Rossiiskoi Federatsii (Otchet–JP Courts 2009). Unpublished, on file with author.

"Otchet o rabote sudov obshchei iurisdiktsii po pervoi instantsii o rassmotranii grazhdanskikh del za 12 mesiatsev 2010 g." Svodnyi otchet po vsem mirovym sud'iam v Rossiiskoi Federatsii (Otchet–JP Courts 2010). Unpublished, on file with author.

"Otchet o rabote sudov obshchei iurisdiktsii po pervoi instantsii o rassmotranii grazhdanskikh del za 12 mesiatsev 2011 g." Svodnyi otchet po vsem mirovym sud'iam v Rossiiskoi Federatsii (Otchet–JP Courts 2011). Unpublished, on file with author.

Paneyakh, Ella. 2014. "Faking Performance Together: Systems of Performance Evaluation in Russian Enforcement Agencies and Production of Bias and Privilege." *Post-Soviet Affairs* 30 (2–3): 115–136.

Paneyakh, E. L., K. D. Titaev, V. V. Volkov, and D. Ia. Primakov. 2010. *Obvinitel'nyi uklon v ugolovnom protsesse: Factor prokurora*. St. Petersburg: Institut problem pravoprimeneniia. http://www.enforce.spb.ru/images/analit_zapiski/pm_3_prok_final_site.pdf.

Peerenboom, Randall. 2004. "Varieties of Rule of Law: An Introduction and Provisional Conclusion." In *Asian Discourses of Rule of Law: Theories and Implementation of Rule of Law in Twelve Asian Countries, France and the U.S.*, edited by Randall Peerenboom, 1–55. New York: Routledge.

Petrova, Viktoria Vladimirovna. 2012. "Zakonodatel'noe zakreplenie instituta pomoshchnikov sudei." *Zakon* (1): 83–87.

Petrukhin, I. L. 1970. "Prichiny sudebnykh oshibok." *Sovetskoe gosudarstvo i parvo* (5): 100–106.

Philips, Susan Urmston. 1998. *Ideology in the Language of Judges: How Judges Practice Law, Politics, and Courtroom Control*. New York: Oxford University Press.

Pipes, Richard. 1986. *Legalised Lawlessness: Soviet Revolutionary Justice*. London: Alliance Publishers for the Institute for European Defence & Strategic Studies.

Piskunova, Ia. 2011. "Neobkhodimo uzhestochat' otvetstvennost' tekh, kto stoit za kompaniei." *Zakon* (8): 10–19.

Polese, Abel. 2014. "Informal Payments in Ukrainian Hospitals: On the Boundary between Informal Payments, Gifts, and Bribes." *Anthropological Forum: A Journal of Social Anthropology and Comparative Sociology* 24 (4): 381–395.

Politkovskaya, Anna. 2004. *Putin's Russia*. Translated by Arch Tait. London: Harvill Press.

"Polnyi tekst vystupleniia Dmitriia Medvedeva na II Grazhdanskom forume v Moskve 22 ianvariia 2008 goda." 2008. *Rossiiskaia gazeta*, January 28. http://rg.ru/2008/01/24/tekst.html.

Pomerantsev, Peter. 2014. *Nothing Is True and Everything Is Possible: The Surreal Heart of the New Russia*. New York: Public Affairs.

Pomeranz, William, and Max Grutbrod. 2012. "The Push for Precedent in Russia's Judicial System." *Review of Central and East European Law* 37 (1): 1–30.

Pomorski, Stanislaw. 2001. "Justice in Siberia: A Case Study of a Lower Criminal Court in the City of Krasnoyarsk." *Communist and Post-Communist Studies* 34 (4): 447–478.

Popkins, Gareth. 2000. "Code versus Custom? Norms and Tactics in Peasant Volost Court Appeals, 1889–1917." *Russian Review* 59 (3): 408–424.

Popova, Maria. 2012. *Politicized Justice in Emerging Democracies: A Study of Courts in Russia and Ukraine*. New York: Cambridge University Press.

Potapov, S. I. 2007. "Problemy stanovleniia mirovoi iustitsii i puti ikh razresheniia." *Mirovoi sud'ia* (2): 2–6.

Prevost, Dyranda, and Natalia Dushkina. 1999. *Living Places in Russia*. Mulgrave, Victoria, Australia: The Images Publishing Group.

Puzakova, B. K., N. A. Zakharova, and I. C. Sycheva. 2012. *Vrednye sosedy: Kak borit'sia i kuda zhalovat'sia?* Rostov-na-Donu: Feniks.

Rajah, Jothie. 2012. *Authoritarian Rule of Law: Legislation, Discourse and Legitimacy in Singapore*. New York: Cambridge University Press.

———. 2015. "'Rule of Law' as Transnational Legal Order." In *Transnational Legal Orders*, edited by Terence C. Halliday and Gregory Shaffer, 340–373. New York: Cambridge University Press.

Raleigh, Donald J. 2006. *Russia's Sputnik Generation: Soviet Baby Boomers Talk about Their Lives*. Bloomington: Indiana University Press.

"Rassmotrenie del sudami obshchei iurisdiktsii po 1 instantsii za 1996–2007 gg." 2008. http://www.cdep.ru/statistics.asp?search_frm_auto=1&dept_id=8.

Raz, Joseph. 1979. *The Authority of Law: Essays on Law and Morality*. Oxford: Clarendon Press.

Raznikova, M. N. 2004. "Interv'iu s mirovym sudei sudebnogo uchastka No. 7 Sovetskogo raiona g. Voronezha Kudrinoi Galinoi Vasil'evnoi." *Mirovoi sud* (2): 32.

Regiony Rossii: Osnovnye kharakteristiki sub"ektov Rossiiskoi Federatsii 2008. 2008a. Moscow: Goskomstat.

Regiony Rossii: Osnovnye sotsial'no-ekonomicheskie pokazateli gorodov. 2008b. Moscow: Goskomstat.

Regiony Rossii: Sotsial'no-ekonomicheskie pokazateli. 2008c. Moscow: Goskomstat.

Resnik, Judith. 1982. "Managerial Judges." *Harvard Law Review* 96 (2): 374–448.

Rhode, Deborah L. 2004. *Access to Justice*. New York: Oxford University Press.

Riasanovsky, Nicholas V. 1952. *Russia and the West in the Teaching of the Slavophiles: A Study of Romantic Ideology*. Cambridge, MA: Harvard University Press.

Richards, Susan. 1991. *Epics of Everyday Life: Encounters in a Changing Russia*. New York: Viking.

Ries, Nancy. 1997. *Russian Talk: Culture and Conversation during Perestroika*. Ithaca, NY: Cornell University Press.

Rimskii, Vladimir L. 2007. *Obzor sotiologicheskikh issledovanii sudebnoi sistemy SSSR, vypolnennykh v period s serediny 60-x godov XX veka do kontsa 1991 goda*. Moscow: Regional'nyi obshchestvennyi fond "Informatika dlia demokratii," Fond INDEM.

——. 2012. *Rezul'taty sotsiologicheskikh issledovanii ispolneniia gosudarstvom pravookhranitel'noi funktsii: Otsenki grazhdan i neobkhodimye reformy*. Moscow: Komitet grazhdanskikh initsiativ, Fond INDEM.

Rivkin-Fish, Michele. 2005. "Bribes, Gifts and Unofficial Payments: Rethinking Corruption in Post–Soviet Russian Health Care." In *Corruption: Anthropological Perspectives*, edited by Dieter Haller and Cris Shore, 47–64. Ann Arbor, MI: Pluto Press.

Robertson, Annette. 2013. "Police Reform and Building Justice in Russia: Problems and Prospects." In *Building Justice in Post-Transition Europe? Processes of Criminalisation within Central and East European Societies*, edited by Kay Goodall, Margaret Malloch, and Bill Munro, 158–175. New York: Routledge.

Rodina, L. V. 2007. "Istoriia stanovleniia i razvitiia instituta mirovykh sudei v Rossii." *Mirovoi sud'ia* (4): 2–5.

Rohl, Klaus F. 1990. "Small Claims in Civil Court Proceedings in the Federal Republic of Germany." In Whelan, *Small Claims Courts*, 167–182.

Romanova, Ol'ga. 2011. *Butyrka*. Moscow: Astrel'.

Rose, Richard, and Ellen Carnaghan. 1995. "Generational Effects on Attitudes to Communist Regimes: A Comparative Analysis." *Post-Soviet Affairs* 11 (1): 28–56.

Rose, Richard, and Neil Munro. 2008. "Do Russians See Their Future in Europe or the CIS?" *Europe-Asia Studies* 60 (1): 49–66.

Rosefielde, Steven. 2005. "Russia: An Abnormal Country." *European Journal of Comparative Economics* 2 (1): 3–16.

Rosen, Lawrence. 2000. *The Justice of Islam: Comparative Perspectives on Islamic Law and Society*. New York: Oxford University Press. "Rossiiane zhdut ot OSAGO nevozmozhnogo i vozrazhaiut protiv luchshego." 2005. Pravda.ru, July 20. http://www.pravda.ru/economics/rules/lobbyists/20-0-2005/51560-osago-0/.

Rossiiskii statisticheskii ezhegodnik. 2011. Moscow: Goskomstat.

Roth, Andrew. 2015. "'Maus' Book about Holocaust Is Removed in Russia." *New York Times*, April 27. http://www.nytimes.com/2015/04/28/world/europe/maus-book-about-holocaust-is-removed-in-russia.html?_r=0.

Rottman, David B. 1998. "On Public Trust and Confidence: Does Experience with the Courts Promote or Diminish It?" *Court Review* 35 (4): 14–22.

Rubchenko, Maxim. 2012. "Russia's Business Ombudsman 'Will Not Lobby for a Bribe.'" *Russia beyond the Headlines,* July 9. http://rbth.asia/articles/2012/07/09/russias_business_ombudsman_will_not_lobby_for_a_bribe_15715.html.

Rudden, Bernard. 1966. *Soviet Insurance Law.* Leiden: A. W. Sijthoff.

Ruhlin, Charles. 2000. "Credit Card Debt Collection and the Law: Germany and the United States." In *Regulatory Encounters: Multinational Corporations and American Adversarial Legalism,* edited by Robert A. Kagan and Lee Axelrad, 255–274. Berkeley: University of California Press.

"Russia Longitudinal Monitoring Survey, RLMS-HSE." Conducted by the National Research University Higher School of Economics and ZAO "Demoscope," together with Carolina Population Center, University of North Carolina at Chapel Hill, and the Institute of Sociology, RAS. http://www.cpc.unc.edu/projects/rlms-hse.

Sachkov, A. N., and M. B. Titukhov. 2007. "Kandidat po dolzhnost' sud'i: Problemy i regional'nyi opyt professional'noi podgotovki." *Rossiiskii sud'ia* (11): 42–46.

Sakwa, Richard. 2009. *The Quality of Freedom: Khodorkovsky, Putin, and the Yukos Affair.* New York: Oxford University Press.

——. 2010. "The Dual State in Russia." *Post-Soviet Affairs* 26 (3): 185–206.

——. 2013. "Systematic Stalemate: *Reiderstvo* and the Dual State." In *The Political Economy of Russia,* edited by Neil Robinson, 59–96. Lanham, MD: Rowman & Littlefield.

Sandefur, Rebecca. 2007. "The Importance of Doing Nothing: Everyday Problems and Responses of Inaction." In *Transforming Lives: Law and Social Process,* edited by Pascoe Pleasence, Alexy Buck, and Nigel Balmer, 112–132. Ontario: Legal Services Commission.

Sandefur, Rebecca L., and Aaron C. Smyth. 2011. *Access across America: First Report of the Civil Justice Infrastructure Mapping Project.* Chicago, IL: American Bar Association. http://www.americanbarfoundation.org/uploads/cms/documents/access_across_america_first_report_of_the_civil_justice_infrastructure_mapping_project.pdf.

Sarat, Austin, and William L. F. Felstiner. 1986. "Law and Strategy in the Divorce Lawyer's Office." *Law & Society Review* 20 (1): 93–134.

Sarat, Austin, and Thomas R. Kearns. 1993. "Beyond the Great Divide: Forms of Legal Scholarship and Everyday Life." In *Law in Everyday Life,* edited by Austin Sarat and Thomas R. Kearns, 21–61. Ann Arbor: University of Michigan Press.

Satter, David. 2004. *Darkness at Dawn: The Rise of the Russian Criminal State.* New Haven, CT: Yale University Press.

Sem'ia v Rossii 1996. 1996. Moscow: Goskomstat.

Sem'ia v Rossii 2008. 2008. Moscow: Goskomstat.

Shapiro, Martin. 2008. "Courts in Authoritarian Regimes." In *Rule by Law: The Politics of Courts in Authoritarian Regimes,* edited by Tom Ginsburg and Tamir Moustafa, 326–335. New York: Cambridge University Press.

Sharkova, I. G. 1998. "Mirovoi sud'ia v dorevolutsionnoi Rossii." *Gosudarstvo i pravo* (9): 79–85.

Sharlet, Robert S. 1977. "Stalinism and Soviet Legal Culture." In *Stalinism: Essays in Historical Interpretation,* edited by Robert C. Tucker, 155–179. New York: Norton.

——. 1992. *Soviet Constitutional Crisis: From De-Stalinization to Disintegration.* Armonk, NY: M. E. Sharpe.

Shelley, Louise I. 1984. *Lawyers in Soviet Work Life*. New Brunswick, NJ: Rutgers University Press.

———. 1992. "Legal Consciousness and the *Pravovoe Gosudarstvo*." In Barry, *Toward the "Rule of Law" in Russia?*, 63–76.

Shevchenko, Olga. 2009. *Crisis and the Everyday in Postsocialist Moscow*. Bloomington: Indiana University Press.

Shiniaeva, Natal'ia. 2012. "Vstrecha predsedatel'ia Vysshego Arbitrazhnogo Suda s predstaviteliami SMI." Pravo.ru, February 20. http://pravo.ru/review/view/68916/.

Shklar, Judith. 1987. "Political Theory and the Rule of Law." In *The Rule of Law: Ideal or Ideology*, edited by Allan C. Hutchinson and Patrick J. Monahan, 1–16. Toronto: Carswell.

Shlapentokh, Vladimir. 1989. *Public and Private Life of the Soviet People: Changing Values in Post-Soviet Russia*. New York: Oxford University Press.

———. 2006. "Trust in Public Institutions in Russia: The Lowest in the World." *Communist and Post-Communist Studies* 39 (2): 153–174.

Shleifer, Andrei, and Daniel Treisman. 2004. "A Normal Country." *Foreign Affairs* 83 (2): 20–38.

Shmerpina, Irina 2006a. *Rossiiane na rynke uslug strakhovaniia*. Fond obshchestvennoe mnenie. http://bd.fom.ru/report/map/dd062526.

———. 2006b. *Sosedi po domu*. Fond obshchestvennoe mnenie. http://bd.fom.ru/report/map/projects/dominant/dom0619/dd061925.

Shugurov, Mark Vladimirovich. 2014. "Modernizatsiia iuridicheskogo obrazovaniia i globalizatsiia prava: Bolonskii kontekst." *Zakon* (1): 64–77.

Sidorovich, Olga. 2011. "Proekt 'Povyshenie dostupnosti pravosudiia dlia maloimushchikh i sotsial'no nezashchishchennykh grupp naseleniia Rossiiskoi Federatsii.'" Presentation at roundtable held in St. Petersburg, Russia. June 30.

Siegelbaum, Lewis H., ed. 2006. *Borders of Socialism: Private Spheres of Soviet Russia*. Gordonsville, VA: Palgrave Macmillan.

———. 2008. *Cars for Comrades: The Life of the Soviet Automobile*. Ithaca, NY: Cornell University Press.

Simis, Konstantin, M. 1982. *USSR: The Corrupt Society: The Secret World of Soviet Capitalism*. Translated by Jacqueline Edwards and Mitchell Schneider. New York: Simon and Schuster.

Siniavskii, Andrei. 1967. *On Trial: The Soviet State versus "Abram Tertz" and "Nikolai Arzhak."* Translated by Max Hayward. New York: Harper & Row.

Smith, Gordon B. 1996. *Reforming the Russian Legal System*. New York: Cambridge University Press.

Smith, Hedrick. 1976. *The Russians*. New York: Quadrangle/New York Times Book Company.

Solomon, Peter H., Jr. 1987. "The Case of the Vanishing Acquittal: Informal Norms and the Practice of Soviet Criminal Justice." *Soviet Studies* 39 (4): 531–555.

———. 1990–1991. "Gorbachev's Legal Revolution." *Canadian Business Law Journal* 17 (2): 184–194.

———. 1992. "Soviet Politicians and Criminal Prosecutions: The Logic of Party Intervention." In *Cracks in the Monolith: Party Power in the Brezhnev Era*, edited by James R. Millar, 3–32. Armonk, NY: M. E. Sharpe.

———. 1996. *Soviet Criminal Justice under Stalin*. New York: Cambridge University Press.

———. 1997. "The Bureaucratization of Criminal Justice under Stalin." In Solomon, *Reforming Justice in Russia, 1864–1996*, 228–255.

——, ed. 1997. *Reforming Justice in Russia, 1864–1996: Power, Culture, and the Limits of Legal Order*. Armonk, NY: M. E. Sharpe.

——. 2003. "The New Justice of the Peace in the Russian Federation: A Cornerstone of Judicial Reform?" *Demokratizatsiya* 11 (3): 381–396.

——. 2007. "Informal Practices in Russian Justice: Probing the Limits of Post-Soviet Reform." In *Russia, Europe, and the Rule of Law*, edited by Ferdinand J. M. Feldbrugge, 79–91. Leiden: Brill Academic Publishers.

——. 2011. "Sdelka s pravosudiem po-russki: Zhachenie osobogo poriadka sudebnogo razbiratel'stva." *Sudi'ia* (9): 48–52.

——. 2014. "The Unexpected Demise of Russia's High Court and the Politicization of Judicial Reform." *Russian Analytical Digest* (147): 2–4.

——. 2015. "Understanding Russia's Low Rate of Acquittal: Pretrial Screening and the Problem of Accusatorial Bias." *Review of Central and East European Law* (40): 1–30.

Solomon, Peter H., Jr., and Todd Foglesong. 2000. *Courts and Transition in Russia: The Challenge of Judicial Reform*. Boulder, CO: Westview Press.

Solzhenitsyn, Aleksandr Isaevich. 1985. *The Gulag Archipelago, 1918–1956: An Experiment in Literary Investigation*. Translated by Thomas P. Whitney and Harry Willetts. New York: Harper & Row.

Sperlich, Peter W. 2007. *The East German Social Courts: Law and Popular Justice in a Marxist-Leninist Society*. Westport, CT: Praeger Publishers.

Starodubrovskaya, Irina. 2001. "Housing and Utility Services." In *Russia's Post-Communist Economy*, edited by Brigitte Granville and Peter Oppenheimer, 397–418. New York: Oxford University Press.

Statisticheskie svedeniia o rabote sudov obshchei iurisdiktsii za 2011 g. v sravnenii s 2010 g. n.d. http://www.cdep.ru/index.php?id=79&item=836.

Sunstein, Cass, R. 2001. *Designing Democracy: What Constitutions Do*. New York: Oxford University Press.

Tagankina, N. 2011. *Rol predstavitelei obshchestvennosti v povyshenii nezavisimosti i effektivnosti pravosudiia v Rossii*. Moscow: Moskovskaia Khelsinskaia Gruppa. http://www.mhg.ru/files/011/KKC.pdf.

Tamanaha, Brian Z. 2004. *On the Rule of Law: History, Politics, Theory*. New York: Cambridge University Press.

Tanase, Takao. 1990. "The Management of Disputes: Automobile Accident Compensation in Japan." *Law & Society Review* 24 (3): 651–691.

Tay, Alice Erh-Soon. 1969. "The Foundation of Tort Liability in a Socialist Legal System: Fault versus Social Insurance in Soviet Law." *University of Toronto Law Journal* 19 (1): 1–15.

——. 2007. "'Asian Values' and the Rule of Law." In *The Rule of Law History, Theory and Criticism*, edited by Pietro Costa and Danilo Zolo, 565–586. Dordrecht, The Netherlands: Springer.

Toharia, José, J. 1975. "Judicial Independence in an Authoritarian Regime: The Case of Contemporary Spain." *Law & Society Review* 9 (3): 475–496.

Torney-Purta, Judith. 1997. "Links and Missing Links between Education, Political Knowledge, and Citizenship." *American Journal of Education* 105 (4): 446–457.

Transport i sviaz v Rossii. 2012. Moscow: Goskomstat.

Trebilcock, Michael J., and Ronald J. Daniels. 2008. *Rule of Law Reform and Development: Charting the Fragile Path of Progress*. Northampton: Edward Elgar.

Treisman, Daniel. 2011. *The Return: Russia's Journey from Gorbachev to Medvedev*. New York: Free Press.

Trifonov, Yuri. 1983. *Another Life and The House on the Embankment*. Translated by Michael Glenny. New York: Simon and Schuster.

———. 2002. *The Exchange and Other Stories*. Translated by Ellendea Proffer, Helen P. Burlingame, Jim Somers, and Byron Lindsey. Evanston, IL: Northwestern University Press.

Trochev, Alexei. 2008. *Judging Russia: Constitutional Court in Russian Politics, 1990–2006*. New York: Cambridge University Press.

———. 2012. "Suing Russia at Home." *Problems of Post-Communism* 59 (5): 18–34.

Trubek, David, Austin Sarat, William L. F. Felstiner, Herbert M. Kritzer, and Joel B. Grossman. 1983. "The Costs of Ordinary Litigation." *UCLA Law Review* 31 (1): 72–127.

Tucker, Robert C., and Stephen F. Cohen, eds. 1965. *The Great Purge Trial*. New York: Grosset & Dunlap.

Tumanov, Andrey. 2013. "Affordable Housing Sector in Russia: Evolution of Housing Policy through the Period of Transition." *Housing Financial International* 27 (3): 25–31.

Tumanov, V. A. 1989. "O pravovom nigilizme." *Sovetskoe gosudarstvo i pravo* (10): 20–27.

Turner, James C., and Joyce A. McGee. 2000. "Small Claims Reform: A Means of Expanding Access to the American Civil Justice System." *University of the District of Columbia Law Review* (5): 177–188.

Tuschi, Cyril, director. 2011. *Khodorkovsky*. Film. Lala Films!, LE Vision Film- und Fernsehproduktion, and Bayerischer Rundfunk (BR).

Tyler, Tom R. 2006. *Why People Obey the Law*. Princeton, NJ: Princeton University Press.

Uchitelle, Louis. 1992. "The Art of a Russian Deal: Ad-Libbing Contract Law." *New York Times*, January 17. http://www.nytimes.com/1992/01/17/world/the-art-of-a-russian-deal-ad-libbing-contract-law.html.

Udartsev, Sergei Fedorovich, and Zhalas Ramazinovich Temirbekov. 2015. "Kontseptsii 'rule of law' ('verkhovenstvo prava') i 'rechtsstaat' ('pravovoe gosudarstvo'): Sravnitel'nyi analis." *Gosudarstvo i pravo* (5): 5–16.

Varese, Federico. 2001. *The Russian Mafia: Private Protection in a New Market Economy*. New York: Oxford University Press.

Vasil'eva, Elena. 2007. "Otnoshenie k svoemu zhilishchu." *Fom.ru*, November 15. http://bd.fom.ru/report/cat/home_fam/hosehom/d074623.

Vereshchagin, Aleksandr N. 2015. "Mezhdu Stsilloi VAS i Kharabdoi VS." *Vestnik ekonomicheskogo pravosudiia Rossiiskoi Federatsii* (10): 12–15.

Viola, Lynn. 2002. "Introduction." In *Contending with Stalinism: Soviet Power and Popular Resistance in the 1930s*, edited by Lynn Viola, 1–16. Ithaca, NY: Cornell University Press.

Voinovich, Vladimir. 1977. *The Ivankiad: Or, The Tale of the Writer Voinovich's Installation in his New Apartment*. Translated by David Lapeza. New York: Farrar, Straus and Giroux.

Volkov, Vadim. 2002. *Violent Entrepreneurs: The Use of Force in the Making of Russian Capitalism*. Ithaca, NY: Cornell University Press.

Volkov, Vadim, Arina Dmitrieva, Mikhail Pozdniakov, and Kirill Titaev. 2012. *Rossiiskie sud'i kak professional'naia gruppa: Sotsiologicheskoe issledovanie*. St. Petersburg: Institut problem pravoprimeneniia Evropeiskogo universiteta. http://www.enforce.spb.ru/images/analit_zapiski/Jan_2012_NormsValues.pdf.

Voronkov, V. M., and L. V. Ezhova. 2010. *Provedenie monitoringa sudebnykh zasedanii mirovykh sudei i oprosov uchastnikov sudebnykh protsessov: Metologiia, instrumentarii, protsedury realizatsii i kontrolia*. Moscow: OOO "Informpoligraf."

Vserossiiskii tsentr izucheniia obshchestvennogo mneniia. 2007. *Otchet po rezul'tatam obshcherossiiskogo massovogo oprosa grazhdan Rossii po teme: Otsenka deiatel'nosti sudov v Rossiiskoi Federatsii*. http://wciom.ru/courts/.

"VTsIOM: Rossiane ne khotiat pol'zovat'sia OSAGO." 2005. RBC.ru, July 19. http://top.rbc.ru/society/19/07/2005/91417.shtml.

Wagatsuma, Hiroshi, and Arthur Rosett. 1986. "The Implications of Apology: Law and Culture in Japan and the United States." *Law & Society Review* 20 (4): 461–498.

Wagner, William G. 1997. "Civil Law, Individual Rights, and Judicial Activism in Late Imperial Russia." In Solomon, *Reforming Justice in Russia, 1864–1996*, 21–43.

Waldron, Jeremy. 2011. "The Rule of Law and the Importance of Procedure." In *Getting to the Rule of Law*, edited by James E. Fleming, 3–31. New York: New York University Press.

Walicki, Andrzej. 1975. *The Slavophile Controversy: History of a Conservative Utopia in Nineteenth-Century Russian Thought*. Translated by Hilda Andrews–Rusiecka. Oxford: Clarendon Press.

Weller, Steven, John C. Ruhnka, and John A. Martin. 1990. "American Small Claims Courts." In Whelan, *Small Claims Courts*, 5–24.

Whelan, Christopher J., ed. *Small Claims Courts: A Comparative Study*. New York: Oxford University Press.

Wood, Elizabeth A. 2005. *Performing Justice: Agitation Trials in Early Soviet Russia*. Ithaca, NY: Cornell University Press.

Wortman, Richard. 1976. *The Development of a Russian Legal Consciousness*. Chicago, IL: University of Chicago Press.

Yagil, Dana. 1998. "Gender and Age-Related Differences in Attitudes toward Traffic Laws and Traffic Violations." *Transportation Research Part F: Traffic Psychology and Behaviour* 1 (2): 123–135.

Yemtsov, Ruslan. 2008. "Housing Privatization and Household Wealth in Transition." In *Personal Wealth from a Global Perspective*, edited by James B. Davies, 312–333. New York: Oxford University Press.

Yngvesson, Barbara. 1985. "Dispute Processing: Re-Examining Continuing Relations and the Law." *Wisconsin Law Review* (3): 623–646.

———. 1994. "Making Law at the Doorway: The Clerk, the Court, and the Construction of Community in a New England Town." In *Law and Community in Three American Towns*, edited by Carol J. Greenhouse, Barbara Yngvesson, and David M. Engel, 54–90. Ithaca, NY: Cornell University Press.

Yngvesson, Barbara, and Patricia Hennessey. 1975. "Small Claims, Complex Disputes: A Review of the Small Claims Literature." *Law & Society Review* 9 (2): 219–274.

Young, Cathy. 1989. *Growing Up in Moscow: Memoirs of a Soviet Girlhood*. New York: Ticknor & Fields.

Zagainova, S. K. 2009. "O pretsedentno–pravoprimenitel'noi prirode sudebnykh aktov v grazhdanskom i arbitrazhnom protsesse." *Gosudarstvo i pravo* (10): 14–20.

Zaikin, Sergei. 2015a. "Vysshii Arbitrazhnyi Sud: Dannye udaleny. Chast 1: Molchanie i sograsie." *Sravnitel'noe konstitutsionnoe obozrenie* (3): 54–71.

———. 2015b. "Vysshii Arbitrazhnyi Sud: Dannye udaleny. Chast 2: Konstitutsionnye popravki pod mikroskopom obosnovannosti i soravmernosti." *Sravnitel'noe konstitutsionnoe obozrenie* (4): 118–144.

———. 2015c. "Vysshii Arbitrazhnyi Sud: Dannye udaleny. Chast 3: 'Svoi' sud'i—sochtemsia." *Sravnitel'noe konstitutsionnoe obozrenie* (5): 109–129.

———. 2015d. "Vysshii Arbitrazhnyi Sud: Dannye udaleny. Chast 4: *Obiter dictum*, ili Nemnogo ob istorii, iridicheskoi tekhnike i zakonodatel'noi taktike." *Sravnitel'noe konstitutsionnoe obozrenie* (6): 110–122.

Zavisca, Jane, R. 2008. "Property without Markets: Housing Policy and Politics in Post-Soviet Russia, 1992–2007." *Comparative European Politics* 6 (3): 365–386.

———. 2012. *Housing the New Russia*. Ithaca, NY: Cornell University Press.

Zernova, Margarita. 2012. "The Public Image of the Contemporary Russian Police: Impact of Personal Experiences of Policing, Wider Social Implications and the Potential for Change." *Policing: An International Journal of Police Strategies & Management* 35 (2): 216–230.

Ziabkin, V. M., and I. A. Antonov. 2008. "Organizatsionnye, pravovye i nravstvennye voprosy otbora kandidatov na dolzhnost sudei." *Rossiiskii sud'ia* (10): 46–47.

Zile, Zigurds L., ed. 1992. *Ideas and Forces in Soviet Legal History: A Reader on the Soviet State and Law*. New York: Oxford University Press.

Zinenko, Il'ia. 2009. "Novye pravila OSAGO budut rasprostraniat'sia ne po vse." RB.ru, February 25. http://www.rb.ru/article/novye-pravila-osago-budut-rasprostranyatsya-ne-na-vseh/5694787.html.

Zorkaia, N. 2012. *Obshchestvennoe mnenie—2012*. Moscow: Levada Center.

Index

Note: Page numbers followed by f, n, and t indicate figures, notes, and tables.

Abel, Richard L., 97–98, 104, 110, 117–18, 122
Advokaty. *See* Lawyers
Age
  attitudes toward law and, 56–57
  legal consciousness and, 29, 35, 36, 54–55, 242t, 246–47t
  strategies of neighbors during water leak disputes and, 74–76, 85–86
  use and nonuse of courts, 46–47, 243–44t, 244–45t
Alcoholism, water leak disputes and, 74, 75, 84, 87
Alexopoulos, Golfo, 11
American Bar Association (ABA) survey, 180, 195, 196–97, 214–17, 218, 220, 251–52t, 252–53t
Apologies, automobile accidents and courts, 129–30
Arbitrazh courts, 12–13, 15, 15n8, 152
  justice of the peace courts contrasted, 135, 141n14
  technology and, 158
Attention, performance aspects of trials and pleas for, 207–9, 211–13
Automobile accidents, dealing with consequences of, 90–133
  apologies and, 129–30
  avoidance strategy, 94, 99–103, 117, 132–33
  bilateral negotiation, 94, 103–9
  bribery and, 108–9, 91–93, 92n5, 111, 114, 117, 121, 126, 127, 129
  courts and litigation, 94, 96–98, 97t, 111–17, 125–26
  institutional environment and, 92–98, 97t
  institutional infrastructure and, 122–30
  insurance companies and, 92–98, 101–2, 105–6, 108, 110–11, 114–15, 119, 121–22, 125, 128–29, 132–33
  in Japan, 127, 129
  legal culture and, 130–33
  methodology of study of, 91–92
  post-Soviet increases in car ownership and accidents, 90–91

  relationships and, 118–21, 223
  third-party intervention and, 94, 110–17
  tort law and, 95–96, 123–24
  traffic police corruption and, 92–93, 92n5, 100–102, 105–7, 109–10, 121–22, 127–29
Avoidance strategy
  automobile accidents and, 94, 99–103, 117, 132–33
  water leak disputes and, 58, 65, 70–73, 86, 89

Babushki (older women). *See* Age
Barry, Donald D., 123
Berezovsky, Boris, 233
Black, Donald, 88
Blat, 42–43, 49. *See also* Bribery
Bogart, W.A., 98n18
Bologna Process, 196n29
Bolotnoe case, 232
Boym, Svetlana, 14
Bribery, 43, 49, 215, 219–20
  after automobile accidents, 108–9, 91–93, 92n5, 111, 114, 117, 121, 126, 127, 129
Browder, Bill, 234
Burbank, Jane, 6, 7, 8, 19–20
Burma, 227–28

"Cage" (*kletka*), in courtroom, 192, 193f
Canada, 98
Cars. *See* Automobile accidents, dealing with consequences of
Caseloads, of JPs, 136–38, 147–55, 149t, 150t, 160–64, 174, 175, 176–78
Ceiling leaks. *See* Water leaks, problem solving among neighbors and
Cell phone quality litigation, lawyer participation in, 201–2, 205
Chastnoe obvinenie (criminal cases brought by individuals), 161–64, 174, 206–7, 211
Cheesman, Nick, 227–28
Chernomyrdin, Viktor, 73
Child support payments, Russian courts and, 53, 140, 151–53, 166, 169, 182, 185

China, 98

Civil cases, 142, 170, 180, 181t, 182, 188n12, 218, 220

  caseloads of JPs, 137, 149t, 150t, 151–54

  legal representation and, 195–96, 202–6, 205n38

  rule by law and, 229

  see also Automobile accidents, dealing with consequences of; Water leaks, problem solving among neighbors and

Clerks, in justice of the peace courts, 116, 138, 138n11, 140–41, 144

Comparative negligence theory, 100, 123

Constitutional Court, 15, 135, 142n17, 195n27, 219n45, 228–29, 235

Corruption

  automobile accidents and, 92–93, 92n5, 129

  medical system and, 109, 113–14, 119, 121–22, 126

  see also Bribery

Courts

  automobile accidents and, 94, 96, 97t, 98–99, 111–17, 125–26, 133

  legal consciousness and prior exposure to, 32–33, 238–39t, 240–41t

  strategies of neighbors in disputes and, 79, 81–83, 87–88, 89

  see also Justice-of-the-peace courts (mirovye sudy) *entries*

Courts, hypotheticals and use and nonuse of, 38–40

  child's denial of school admission responses, 39t, 41–43

  hypothetical responses versus actual behavior, 51–55, 243–44t, 244–45t, 246–47t

  illegal workplace reprimand responses, 39t, 40–41

  patterns of responses, explained, 45–51, 243–44t, 244–45t

  variation in responses, 43–45, 43t

Criminal cases, 3, 6–8, 188n12, 192, 206–7, 211, 219–20

  caseloads of JPs, 137, 154–55, 160–64, 174, 176–77

  legal representation and, 171–72, 195–96

  routine and non-routine cases and, 234

  rule by law and, 229–30, 232

  see also Automobile accidents, dealing with consequences of

Czap, Peter, 7

Debt, Russians courts and, 147, 151–53, 182–83, 213

courtroom experience without lawyer and, 185–91

Democracy

  legal consciousness and amenability to, 33–35, 54, 56, 238–39t, 240–41t

  legal nihilism and changes in attitudes toward law, 37

Dental claim litigation, performance aspects of trials and, 207–9, 211–13

Disputing pyramid framework, 97–98, 98n18

Divorce, Russian courts and, 33n15, 35, 37, 53, 55, 124, 137, 155–59, 162n48, 166, 181, 197–98

Documentary evidence, required by courts, 54, 97, 114, 125–26, 138, 170, 208, 223–24.

  See also Positivism, courts and

"Doing nothing." *See* Avoidance strategy

Drunk driving

  auto accidents and, 91, 104, 110, 112–13, 119, 121

  Russian courts and, 165, 167–68, 171

Dualism, in Russian legal system

  in contemporary Russia, 3–4, 12–15

  routine and non-routine cases and, 231–35

  rule by law and, 227–31

  rule of law and, 225–27, 230–31

  in Soviet Russia, 9–12, 14

  in Tsarist Russia, 5–9

Economic security, legal consciousness and, 31, 56, 238–39t, 240–41t

Education levels, use and nonuse of courts, 45

Egypt, 227

Emerson, Robert M., 62, 71, 72–73, 89

Employment status

  legal consciousness and, 54, 246–47t

  use and nonuse of courts, 45–46

Engel, David M., 59, 61, 62, 88, 96, 120, 130–32

European Court of Human Rights, 228–29

Family litigation, performance aspects of trials and, 207, 210–11

Farnsworth, Beatrice, 7, 9

Feifer, George, 10, 21

Felstiner, William L. F., 70–71, 97–98, 104, 110, 117–18, 122

Fitzpatrick, Sheila, 11

Foundation for Public Opinion survey, 63

Fraenkel, Ernst, 4

France, Anatole, 204

Frank, Stephen, 7

Friedman, Lawrence, 19, 123, 130–32, 179
Frierson, Cathy, 6, 7–8
Fuller, Lon L., 20

Galanter, Marc, 79, 125, 128
Garant, 183
Gender, legal consciousness and, 29, 54, 242t, 246–47t
Generational effects. *See* Age
Gibson, James, 25, 33
Gorbachev, Mikhail, *pravovoe gosudarstvo* and, 20, 228–29
Gospodstvo zakona, Putin and, 20, 229
Grechin, A. S., 21
Greenspan, Alan, 12
Gross negligence (*grubaia neostorozhnost*), automobile accidents and, 123
Gusinsky, Vladimir, 233

Hazard, John, 21
Hellbeck, Jochem, 14
Hennessey, Patricia, 220
Heritage Capital Management, 234
Herzen, Alexander, 5, 8, 13
Hirshman, Albert O., 60, 86
Housing authority. *See* ZhKU (*Zhilishchno-Kommunal'nye Uslugi*)
Housing rights litigation, performance aspects of trials and, 209–10, 213–14
Human rights (*prava cheloveka*), 20, 50–51, 225–26, 228–29

INDEM (Information Science for Democracy) survey, 23, 33, 39–40, 39t, 43t, 45–46, 48–49, 51, 54–57, 224, 243–44t, 244–45t, 246–47t
Inheritance litigation, lawyer participation in, 200–201, 203–4
Institute of Law and Public Policy (IPPP) project, 150t, 180, 191, 195, 196–97, 214–15, 218, 220
Institutional infrastructure
    automobile accidents and, 122–30
    water leak disputes and, 84–85
Insurance
    automobile accidents and, 92–98, 101–2, 105–6, 108, 110–11, 114–15, 119, 121–22, 125, 128–29, 132–33
    home ownership and, 65n19
Iuristy, 195–96

Japan, 127, 129
Jehovah's Witnesses, 235

Judicial orders (*sudebnye prikazy*), 96, 151–55, 175
Justice-of-the-peace courts (*mirovye sudy*), 6, 13, 138–39
    child's denial of school admission hypothetical and, 48
    fixtures and atmosphere of, 192, 193f, 194, 194f
    illegal workplace reprimand hypothetical and, 40–41, 48
    legal consciousness and, 33n15
    locations of, 136–37, 139, 178
    methodology of study of, 134–35
    post-Soviet evolution of, 135–36
    role of lawyers in, 171–72
    staffing of, 136, 138, 140–41, 144
    technology and websites, 141–42, 158–60, 221
Justice-of-the-peace courts (*mirovye sudy*), litigants' experience and, 179–221
    access to justice and, 179, 181–85, 183f
    civil cases by type of litigant, 181t
    images of courts and, 218–21
    methodology of study of, 180
    participation as performance for larger audience, 203, 205–14
    plaintiffs' success rates and, 180–81
    satisfaction with courts and, 214–18
    with legal representation, 195–205
    without legal representation, 185–94
Justices of the peace (JPs), 155–60
    appeals and, 169–71
    availability to public, 184–85
    caseloads and, 136–38, 147–55, 149t, 150t, 174, 175, 178
    conciliating of litigants and, 160–64
    empathy and common sense used by, 168–69
    justice and efficiency and, 174–75
    notifying of parties and, 155–60
    paternalism and, 175–76, 221
    plea bargaining (*osobyi poriadok*) and, 147, 155, 177
    politics and, 176–78
    procedural codes and, 138, 166–68
    qualifications, 141–43
    rarity of challenges to orders of, 152–54
    relationships with other courts, 145–46
    reversals avoided by, 142, 146, 170–71, 172, 175, 176, 224
    self-image of, 173–74
    terms of, 144

Justices of the peace *(continued)*
  websites and, 221
  women and, 144–45, 173–74

Kasparov, Gary, 177
Khodorkovsky, Mikhail, 206, 232–34
Kistiakovsky, Bogdan, 5, 8, 13
Kleinfeld, Rachel, 225
Konsul'tant plus, 183
Korovinskikh, S. P., 136n3
Kosolapov, Mikhail, 66
Kotkin, Stephen, 14
Kozyreva, Polina, 66
Kritzer, Herbert M., 98n18
Krylenko, N. V., 9
Kurkchiyan, Marina, 13–14, 171, 173, 192

Latynina, Iuliia, 121
Law
  myth of Russia as lawless state, 1–2
  RLMS-HSE survey question and living
    within, 24, 26–27, 27f, 27t
  volume of cases heard by Russian courts, 2
  see also Dualism, in Russian legal system;
    Rule by law; Rule of law
Lawyers
  automobile accidents and, 109, 112, 115–17,
    124–25
  income, 195n24
  professional divisions and training, 195–96
  roles in justice-of-the-peace courts, 171–72
Lawyers, negotiation of courts with, 195–205
  litigants' reluctance to use, 196–98
  scenarios, 200–205
  self-representation with pleading written by
    lawyer, 198–200
Lawyers, negotiation of courts without, 185–94
  appropriate courtroom behavior and,
    191–92
  courtroom atmosphere and, 192–94
  scenarios, 185–89
  unfamiliar courtroom language and, 189–91
Lebedev, V. M., 136, 229n7
Lee Kuan Yew, 227
Legal consciousness
  amenability to democracy factor, 33–35,
    238–39t, 240–41t
  attitudes toward law, assessed, 24–25,
    239–40t, 241–42t
  attitudes toward law, changes in, 25f, 26f,
    27f, 35–38, 242t, 243t
  automobile accidents and, 130–33

demographic factors, 29–31, 35–38,
    238–39t, 240–41t, 242t
  insight from home water leaks study, 59, 89
  media's reporting on, 18–19
  methodology of study of, 22–23, 27–29,
    39–40
  personal control factors, 31–32, 238–39t,
    240–41t
  post-Soviet socio-legal scholarship, 21–22
  prior court exposure factor, 32–33, 238–39t,
    240–41t
  Soviet period socio-legal scholarship, 20–21
  universal nature of Russian, 222–23
  Western socio-legal scholarship, 19, 21
  see also Courts, use and nonuse of
Legal culture, Friedman's definition of, 179.
    See also Legal consciousness
Legality (*zakonnost*), dual legal system and, 4
Legal nihilism
  changes in attitudes toward law, 26f, 27f,
    35–36, 35f, 37, 38, 243t
  in contemporary Russia, 12–14, 222
  court experiences and, 49–51
  hypothetical survey responses versus actual
    behavior, 54
  lack of personal control and, 34–35
  legal consciousness and, 56–57
  litigants' satisfaction with courts, 216
  move away from, 18–19
  RLMS-HSE survey question and,
    24–25, 25f
Levada Center, 26–27, 218–20
Limonov, Eduard, 235

Magnitsky, Sergei, 234
Markovits, Inga, 175, 176, 177, 178
Maus, 235
McDonald, Tracy, 10–11
Medical system, corruption and, 109, 113–14,
    119, 121–22, 126
Medvedev, Dmitrii, 13
Merry, Sally Engle, 19, 60, 62, 63, 84, 88
Methodology, of current study
  automobile accidents, 91–92
  justice-of -the -peace courts, 134–35, 180
  legal consciousness, 22–23, 27–29, 39–40
  water leaks, 65, 66–70, 67t, 249–250
  see also INDEM; RLMS-HSE
Mirovoi sud'ia (journal), 135, 148
Moral damages, and automobile accidents,
    96, 112
Mubarak, Hosni, 227

Naming/blaming/claiming pyramid, 97–98, 100, 104
National Agency for Financial Research, 93, 94
Navalny, Alexei, 206, 232, 234n14
Navalny, Oleg, 234n14
Need, litigation and, 57
Negotiation, after automobile accidents, 94, 103–5
  successful efforts, 105–8
  unsuccessful efforts, 107, 108–9
Neighbors. *See* Water leaks, problem solving among neighbors and
Nelkin, David, 121

Opredelenie (decree/judicial order), 158, 185, 187
Osobyi poriadok (plea bargaining), justice-of-the-peace courts and, 147, 155, 177

Party orientation (*partiinost*), dual legal system and, 4
Peasants
  in Soviet Russia, 9–12
  in Tsarist Russia, 6–9
Peerenboom, Randall, 225
Personal beliefs, strategies of neighbors in disputes and, 86
Personal control factors, legal consciousness and, 31–32, 238–39t, 240–41t
Petty theft. *See* Theft, Russians courts and
Pipes, Richard, 9
Plea bargaining (*osobyi poriadok*), justice-of-the-peace courts and, 147, 155, 177
Po-chelovecheski (civilized) behavior
  automobile accidents and, 103, 108, 118
  reactions to water leaks and, 59, 65, 66, 70, 72, 74, 76, 81, 83, 86, 89
Pod"ezd (entryway), defined, 58n1. *See also* Water leaks, problem solving among neighbors and
Police. *See* Traffic police
Pomerantsev, Peter, 14
Pomorski, Stanislaw, 148
Pomoshchnik. See Clerks, in justice of the peace courts
Popkins, Gareth, 7
Poriadochnyi (upstanding) behavior, 59
Po-sosedski (neighborly) behavior, 59, 69, 76–77
Positivism, courts and, 10, 54, 97, 126, 131–32, 168, 223–24, 229
  consequences of, 223–24

see also Documentary evidence, required by courts
Post-Soviet era Russia, socio-legal scholarship during, 21–22
Prava cheloveka (human rights), 20, 50–51, 225–26, 228–29
Pravo
  attitudes toward law and, 50–51, 56, 228–29
  defined, 20
Pravovoe gosudarstvo, 228–29
Procedural codes, 13, 97, 125, 132
  admissibility of evidence and, 188
  courtroom behavior and, 191–92
  justices of the peace and, 138, 148, 151, 157–58, 173, 175–76
Prokurory, 154, 195
Protokol, traffic police and courts, 125–28
Public opinion about law. *See* Courts, hypotheticals and use and nonuse of; Legal consciousness
Pussy Riot trial, 206, 232
Putin, Vladimir, 219n44, 223, 225, 232n12, 233–35
  gospodstvo zakona and, 20, 228–29
  legal consciousness and democracy, 31, 33, 34
Putin era, 5, 7, 14, 57, 206

Relationships, among disputants
  automobile accidents and, 118–21, 223
  water leaks problems, 63–64, 70–72, 74–75, 78–79, 83–84, 86–89, 223
Religion
  automobile accidents and, 108, 119–20, 131
  legal consciousness and, 30–31
  water leaks and, 86
RLMS-HSE (Russian Longitudinal Monitoring Survey-Higher School of Economics), 16, 16n9, 22–23, 66, 88, 197, 214, 216
  legal consciousness and, 28–40, 54–57, 238–39t, 240–41t, 242–43t, 243–44t
  questions of, 24–27, 26f, 27f, 27t
Romanova, Olga, 232n12
Rosett, Arthur, 129
Rossiiskaia gazeta, 183
Rule by law, 227–30
Rule of law
  RLMS-HSE survey question and, 24, 25–26, 26f
  "thick" and "thin" versions of, 225–27, 228, 231

Samosud, 7–9, 11n7
Sandefur, Rebecca, 99, 101, 103
Sarat, Austin, 97–98, 104, 110, 117–18, 122
Sazanova, Iuliia, 177–78
Scams, after automobile accidents, 108–9
Schmidt, Yuri, 233
School admission denial. *See under* Courts, hypotheticals and use and nonuse of
Self-help strategy, of neighbors in water leak disputes, 58, 65, 69–70, 73–78, 84–89. *See also* Negotiation, after automobile accidents
Settlement agreement (*mirovoe soglashenie*), 115, 164n50, 186–89, 208
Sharlet, Robert, 4, 10
Shevchenko, Olga, 32
Show trials, in Soviet era, 205–6
Sicily, 121
Singapore, 227
Sloutsker, Vladimir, 232n12
Solomon, Peter, 9–10
Socio-legal research and theory, 29, 43, 48
    Russian, 20–22, 32, 211, 215
    Western, 16, 19–20, 98, 130
    see also Dualism, in Russian legal system; Methodology, of current study
Soviet Russia
    dualism of legal system in, 9–12, 14
    socio-legal scholarship during, 20–21
Spain, 227
Spiegelman, Art, 235
Stalin, Josef, 10, 234
Stalinist era, 4, 14, 29–30, 46, 57, 64, 123
Statutory law, freely available to Russian citizens, 183–84
Stepashin, Sergei, 196n30
Sudebnye prikazy (judicial orders), 96, 151–55, 175

Tanase, Takao, 127, 129
Tax disputes, Russian courts and, 151–54, 200, 202–3, 234
Tay, Alice Erh-Soon, 93
Telephone law and justice, 1, 10, 42
    citizens' attitudes toward courts and, 16, 87, 112, 222, 224
    dualistic legal system and, 3, 4, 231, 233
    in post-Soviet era, 34, 228
    rule of law and, 226
Thailand, 98, 120, 130–32
Theft, Russians courts and, 147–48, 155, 165–66, 168, 187
Third-party intervention
    after automobile accidents, 94, 110–17

    courts and litigation, 79, 82–83, 89
    strategies of neighbors in water leak disputes and, 58, 65–66, 70, 78–83, 87, 89
    ZhKU housing authorities and, 70, 79–81, 82, 87, 89
Titov, Boris, 232n12
Toharia, José, 227
Tort law, automobile accidents and, 95–96, 123–24
Traffic police, 91, 92, 111–12, 114–15, 122, 128, 132–33, 165, 168, 220
    corruption and biases of, 92–93, 92n5, 100–102, 105–7, 109–10, 121–22, 127–28
Traffic violations
    courtroom experience without lawyer and, 187–88
    judicial discretion and, 165, 167–68
Tsarist Russia, dualism of legal system in, 5–9

Urban courts. *See* Justice-of-the-peace courts (*mirovye sudy*)

Videos, traffic violations and, 187–88
Vidmar, Neil, 98n18
Voice mechanism, relationships with neighbors and, 60, 86
Volost courts, in Tsarist Russia, 6–9

Wagatsuma, Hiroshi, 129
Wagner, William, 7
Water leaks, problem solving among neighbors and, 58–89
    age and, 74–76, 85–86
    attitudes toward courts and, 87–88
    avoidance strategy, 58, 65, 70–73, 86, 89
    generally, 62–64
    institutional infrastructure and, 84–85
    legal consciousness and, 59, 89
    methodology of study of, 65, 66–70, 67t, 249–50
    nature of damages and, 86–87
    personal beliefs and religion and, 86
    relationships and, 63–64, 70–72, 74–75, 78–79, 83–84, 86–89, 223
    self-help strategy, 58, 65, 69–70, 73–78, 84–89
    third-party intervention, 58, 65–66, 70, 78–83, 87, 89
    U.S. research, 59, 60–63, 71, 72–73, 83–85, 88–89
Western socio-legal scholarship, 19, 21
"Wicked legal systems," 225n1
Witnesses, automobile accidents and, 91, 101, 102n21, 107, 114, 122, 125–26, 132

Witte, Sergei, 6, 8, 13
Women, as justices of the peace, 144–45, 173–74
Workplace reprimands. *See under* Courts, hypotheticals and use and nonuse of
Wortman, Richard, 6

Yngvesson, Barbara, 60–61, 62, 63, 83–84, 88–89, 220

Zakon
    attitudes toward law and, 50–51, 56, 228–29
    defined, 20
    see also Gospodstvo zakona
Zasulich, Vera, 6
ZhKU (Zhilishchno-Kommunal'nye Uslugi)
    defined, 65n18
    strategies of neighbors in disputes and, 70, 79–81, 82, 87, 89